# Bankruptcy Restructuring Strategies

*Leading Lawyers on Evaluating Bankruptcy Alternatives, Protecting the Client, and Developing Negotiation Strategies*

D1823179

## ASPATORE

Mat #40762765

ISBN 978-0-314-19553-1

For corrections, updates, comments or any other inquiries please e-mail TLR.AspatoreEditorial@thomson.com.

First Printing, 2008
10 9 8 7 6 5 4 3 2 1

# Praise for *Inside the Minds*

"Need-to-read inside information and analysis that will improve your bottom line - the best source in the business." – Daniel J. Moore, Member, Harris Beach LLP

"The Inside the Minds series is a valuable probe into the thought, perspectives, and techniques of accomplished professionals..." – Chuck Birenbaum, Partner, Thelen Reid & Priest

"Aspatore has tapped into a gold mine of knowledge and expertise ignored by other publishing houses." – Jack Barsky, Managing Director, Information Technology & Chief Information Officer, ConEdison *Solutions*

"Unlike any other publisher – actual authors that are on the front-lines of what is happening in industry." – Paul A. Sellers, Executive Director, National Sales, Fleet and Remarketing, Hyundai Motor America

"A snapshot of everything you need..." – Charles Koob, Co-Head of Litigation Department, Simpson Thacher & Bartlet

"Everything good books should be - honest, informative, inspiring, and incredibly well-written." – Patti D. Hill, President, BlabberMouth PR

"Great information for both novices and experts." – Patrick Ennis, Partner, ARCH Venture Partners

"A rare peek behind the curtains and into the minds of the industry's best." – Brandon Baum, Partner, Cooley Godward

"Intensely personal, practical advice from seasoned dealmakers." – Mary Ann Jorgenson, Coordinator of Business Practice Area, Squire, Sanders & Dempsey

"Great practical advice and thoughtful insights." – Mark Gruhin, Partner, Schmeltzer, Aptaker & Shepard, PC

"Reading about real-world strategies from real working people beats the typical business book hands down." - Andrew Ceccon, Chief Marketing Officer, OnlineBenefits Inc.

"Books of this publisher are syntheses of actual experiences of real-life, hands-on, front-line leaders--no academic or theoretical nonsense here. Comprehensive, tightly organized, yet nonetheless motivational!" - Lac V. Tran, Sr. Vice President, CIO and Associate Dean Rush University Medical Center

"Aspatore is unlike other publishers...books feature cutting-edge information provided by top executives working on the front-line of an industry." - Debra Reisenthel, President and CEO, Novasys Medical Inc

## www.Aspatore.com

Aspatore Books, a Thomson Reuters business, is the largest and most exclusive publisher of C-level executives (CEO, CFO, CTO, CMO, partner) from the world's most respected companies and law firms. Aspatore annually publishes a select group of C-level executives from the Global 1,000, top 250 law firms (partners and chairs), and other leading companies of all sizes. C-Level Business Intelligence™, as conceptualized and developed by Aspatore Books, provides professionals of all levels with proven business intelligence from industry insiders—direct and unfiltered insight from those who know it best— as opposed to third-party accounts offered by unknown authors and analysts. Aspatore Books is committed to publishing an innovative line of business and legal books, those which lay forth principles and offer insights that, when employed, can have a direct financial impact on the reader's business objectives, whatever they may be. In essence, Aspatore publishes critical tools—need-to-read as opposed to nice-to-read books—for all business professionals.

# Inside the Minds

The critically acclaimed *Inside the Minds* series provides readers of all levels with proven business intelligence from C-level executives (CEO, CFO, CTO, CMO, partner) from the world's most respected companies. Each chapter is comparable to a white paper or essay and is a future-oriented look at where an industry/profession/topic is heading and the most important issues for future success. Each author has been selected based upon their experience and C-level standing within the professional community. *Inside the Minds* was conceived in order to give readers actual insights into the leading minds of business executives worldwide. Because so few books or other publications are actually written by executives in industry, *Inside the Minds* presents an unprecedented look at various industries and professions never before available.

# Contents

# Representing Clients in Commercial Restructurings

### Todd C. Meyers

*Partner and Head of Bankruptcy & Financial
Restructuring Team*
Kilpatrick Stockton LLP

ASPATORE

I am the head of the fifteen-lawyer Bankruptcy and Financial Restructuring Team of a 500-lawyer firm that represents debtors, trustees, examiners, creditors' committees, individual creditors (secured and unsecured), and buyers of assets in the area of insolvency or bankruptcy—we do not handle any consumer bankruptcy cases. We also provide advice to clients that allows them to structure business deals in anticipation of the possibility that one party might end up in bankruptcy, but most of what we do entails representing parties in connection with an actual bankruptcy proceeding. Our primary emphasis is on creditors' committee representations, and we do significant work in the areas of debtor representations and examiner/trustee representations in connection with major fraud investigations.

## The Value of the Attorney

I believe that we add value for our clients because we are experts at looking at the big picture in these matters, and solving problems within the framework of the bankruptcy laws so that all parties can end up with a reasonable solution, rather than spending too much in attorney's fees fighting over a limited pot of money. Unfortunately, many companies do not seek bankruptcy advice before entering into transactions, and when these companies finally consult us after the other party to the transaction files for bankruptcy, they often find that there are things that they could have done to prevent that situation had they consulted with us first.

For instance, paying money up front to the other party instead of putting it into trust or escrow is a common mistake. If the client puts up a large deposit without requiring that it be escrowed or held in trust, and the other party then files for bankruptcy, those funds become general funds of the bankruptcy, and the client becomes a general creditor. Had the client put that money in escrow or trust, they could have potentially gotten it back, instead of standing in line with everyone else. Indeed, up-front payment for goods or services is usually a recipe for disaster.

## Basic Restructuring Strategies

Many companies file bankruptcy in order to sell their business as a going concern. Absent bankruptcy protection, their lender may foreclose on their assets, or a potential buyer of their assets will not want to go through with the purchase because of successor liability issues. An insolvent company can correct either or both of these problems by filing bankruptcy (thereby staying the lender from foreclosure) and then getting a court order allowing the sale of their assets free and clear of liens, so that the buyer has comfort that they will not get sued as a successor. There is usually value in a company that is still a going concern, and an insolvent company can preserve that value by filing a bankruptcy and giving the buyer sufficient comfort that it will not be stuck with successor liability.

If a client tells me that they want to buy an insolvent company for $10 million and that is not enough to pay all of the insolvent company's debts, we often will recommend that they have the target company first file bankruptcy so the client can get a clean title. Some companies do not want to go into bankruptcy and liquidate because the business still works, but if they are layered with too much debt, bankruptcy can allow for a balance sheet restructuring; such a business needs to turn some debt into equity so that it does not have to make interest payments. For example, a retailer may have several stores that are profitable, but at some point, it borrowed $50 million to buy another line of business that did not work out, and it still has that $50 million of debt on its balance sheet. At an interest rate of 10 percent a year, the yearly interest payments on that debt total $5 million; therefore, even though the retailer's core business may be making $2 to 3 million year after year, it is still losing money because it is paying $5 million on its debt. Therefore, it may make sense for that retailer to file bankruptcy in order to convert that debt to equity in a balance sheet restructuring.

For retailers with failing stores, bankruptcy can also provide relief against massive claims by landlords. For example, a retailer may want to shut down fifty stores with five-year leases, but if it breaches those leases it could get claims for five years' worth of rent for each of those stores (particularly where the market is such that the landlords will be unable to find new tenants for a significant period of time or in states where landlords are not required to mitigate damages). However, filing bankruptcy can allow you to cap that rent claim at one year's rent. Consequently, retailers often find it necessary to file bankruptcy in order to close unprofitable locations.

### Bankruptcy Trends

Due to current economic conditions, any industry that is related to the homebuilding and mortgage areas is being hard hit at the present time. A number of large national mortgage lenders are filing for bankruptcy these days, as are homebuilders, construction companies, and suppliers to the residential home industry.

Health care is also experiencing many difficulties currently; Medicare and Medicaid reimbursements are causing many problems in the health care industry because of limits on what can be paid for particular procedures. In addition, airlines have been hard hit in recent years, and three or four of the smaller carriers have filed for bankruptcy this year alone.

Fortunately, I believe that law firms that handle bankruptcy matters are prepared for the onslaught of filings to come. There are always fluctuations in filings as the economy changes, and bankruptcy groups will shrink or rise accordingly. The size of our group has been steady, but we are ramping up for this particular wave of filings, and trying to grow the group by a few lawyers. In addition, because our core emphasis on creditors' committee representations causes us to handle substantial litigation arising out of bankruptcy cases (particularly director and officer liability litigation), we now have several non-team members in the litigation department who spend a significant amount of their time handling this type of bankruptcy litigation.

### Best Practices for Handling Clients' Restructuring Needs

The best practice for firms that specialize in bankruptcy law is to have a capable bench of quality lawyers that can advise clients properly. In today's bankruptcy market, a group with one lead partner and a bunch of young associates will not be able to fully handle all of the work that is out there—you need to have a strong bench of quality lawyers with Chapter 11 experience.

Another best practice is to make sure your clients know there are things you can do to help them anticipate the bankruptcy of vendors and customers. Indeed, since many of their customers are probably in trouble, clients ought to be tightening credit and taking other measures (such as obtaining collateral, letters of credit, or personal guarantees) to anticipate the bankruptcy of those customers. They may also want to diversify among their vendors so production doesn't come to a halt due to the bankruptcy of one of their key vendors. We send bulletins to our clients and other helpful information in order to let them know they are more likely to get hung up in a bankruptcy proceeding these days and possibly sued for preferences (i.e., for the return of monies they received within ninety days of the customer's bankruptcy), and therefore they need to be properly prepared.

## Representing Creditors' Committees

The restructuring strategy chosen largely depends on the type of client for whom we are working. For instance, we do a lot of creditors' committee work, and our strategy in those cases is usually to be very aggressive and to move quickly as counsel for the committee. We also have the committee take an extremely active role in the case in order to try to control the outcome—especially if the outcome is going to primarily affect creditors rather than shareholders. In other words, if the shareholders are already out of money and will not be getting anything as a result of the bankruptcy filing, whereas the unsecured creditors (the constituency represented by the creditors' committee) stands to get very little or very much depending on the outcome, then I believe that since the creditors' committee has the most to lose they should have significant control over what occurs in the bankruptcy proceedings.

In that effort, we often meet resistance from debtor's management who is concerned about being sued for the errors of the past, and therefore they may try to control things as much as possible by obtaining releases that essentially get them off the hook (i.e., released under a plan of reorganization so they cannot later be sued). In such cases, the challenge lies in trying to get control from debtors' legacy management, who should no longer be controlling the case. This can be done in certain cases (i.e., where there is evidence of fraud or mismanagement or the current management putting their own personal interests ahead of the interests of the debtor's creditors and other stakeholders) by seeking the appointment of a trustee, but usually by convincing the debtor that they cannot confirm a plan without creditors' committee support, and only giving that support in connection with a joint plan that places a creditor representative in charge of the ultimate liquidation of the bankruptcy estate.

## Obtaining Information from Creditors and Debtors

In large Chapter 11 cases, the U.S. Trustee's office (a division of the Department of Justice that oversees the proper functioning of the bankruptcy process within the framework of the judicial proceedings) will appoint an official creditors' committee from those among the debtor's largest creditors who are willing to serve on such a committee. These people are often trade creditors who are unsophisticated with respect to bankruptcies; therefore, they will immediately hire counsel in this area who can guide them with respect to how the process works, and make recommendations. Since these creditors know a lot about the company that has filed for bankruptcy, they can typically help counsel to understand key information in relation to the case, including why the company is not profitable; what their bad practices were; and if there are any competitors that might be interested in buying the company—information that can help us to understand how to fix the company.

When representing debtors, on the other hand, I ask them to fill out a questionnaire that covers the key information I need to obtain in order to commence a Chapter 11 case—the names of all their creditors, their largest creditors, the names of management, all of their subsidiary information, copies of their corporate governance documents, key contracts, asset and liability information, bank accounts, etc. Indeed, the basic bankruptcy filing process (i.e., the act of actually commencing a bankruptcy proceeding) is largely form and data driven; therefore, we have templates to get the information that we need from our debtor clients before we can file bankruptcy for them.

## Key Elements of a Turnaround Strategy

A client that is facing insolvency may have a turnaround strategy as to how to become profitable, which they will often implement outside of bankruptcy; and it is only when it is not working that they will finally file for bankruptcy. Once we understand their turnaround strategy, we can advise them as to whether bankruptcy would likely allow them to implement that strategy. In some cases, we may look at the situation and determine that bankruptcy will not allow them to implement their turnaround strategy because they need more money to implement it—and nobody is going to lend it to them.

For example, in a typical relationship with an asset-based lender, the debtor sells its product and collects its accounts receivable, but its collections go into a lockbox that is controlled by the lender who uses it to pay down the loan, and the debtor can submit a request to borrow more money when needed. However, if the lender calls a default it can "lock down the lockbox," which can only be "reopened" if the debtor files for bankruptcy—with limitations. The debtor will have to take some steps with the court to show that the lender is adequately protected, i.e., that in the event the company's restructuring fails, the lender will be no worse off for having been forced to let the debtor use its cash collateral to fund operations, and if the debtor's turnaround strategy is based on borrowing extra money to increase its inventory, bankruptcy will not force its lender to lend it more money.

## Restructuring Negotiations

In a bankruptcy restructuring, the debtor has to comply with the legal requirement to use cash collateral; therefore, an important component of any restructuring strategy is to be able to use cash by adequately protecting the interests of those with security interests in that cash (as described above). A second component is to be able to keep other creditors enjoined from pursuing collection activities, and a third component would be to understand the requirements for getting rid of other unprofitable contracts. In addition, it is important to have some kind of exit strategy that could be implemented in a bankruptcy. For example, the exit strategy is often to sell all of the assets free and clear of liens, thereby creating a pot of money that can be distributed to creditors in order of their bankruptcy priorities (secured, priority unsecured, general unsecured, equity). Another exit strategy would be to eliminate unprofitable operations, than obtain new financing based on a revised business plan, and convert all or a portion of old debt to equity (or some combination of these).

Any restructuring strategy largely depends on what assets the client has, and what assets are pledged as security. Consequently, achieving a successful restructuring requires negotiations with the client's lenders; with the creditors' committee on behalf of the client's unsecured creditors; with landlords; with contracting parties and utilities; and with the U.S. Trustee's office. It is important to note that there are certain things that debtors may try to accomplish that require the permission of the U.S. Trustee. The bankruptcy statutes say that in order to file for bankruptcy, the debtor must close every bank account it has and open new ones; however, that is a totally unworkable solution for companies with sophisticated cash management systems. Standard motions are often filed seeking a waiver of this requirement, but the debtor should first negotiate that waiver with the U.S. Trustee's office so that it is satisfied that the debtor is not allowing creditors to get paid on pre-petition debt.

The restructuring process may also entail negotiations with the SEC, the IRS, and the state taxing authorities, because many debtors are public companies or have significant tax issues, and all of these constituencies are going to mandate some form of negotiation. Sometimes we go into the filing process right before the lender forecloses and everybody trenches for warfare, but if all the parties are able to outline their position before the filing a negotiation can usually take place that will benefit everybody.

In the recent past, there have been several large bankruptcies for companies that were in good financial shape, but they had mass torts involving asbestos issues. Since our judicial system has not figured out a good way to resolve mass torts, bankruptcy has been viewed as the best way to do so, as it allows the company to pool its assets in one place and put some money aside for people who have been injured by a product. Bankruptcy is a great way to pull everyone together into a negotiation, as in these large asbestos cases, while letting the company move on with its business.

## Meeting the Client's Goals

Sometimes our clients have unrealistic goals in terms of what they can accomplish through a bankruptcy filing. Therefore, knowing the law with respect to what they can and cannot do in this area is critical. For example, I have had clients say to me, "Our whole business centers around this contract, and the other party terminated it because we were in default; and we want to file bankruptcy so that we can continue under the contract." However, if the contract was properly terminated, then it will not be reinstated if the client files for bankruptcy; consequently, understanding such issues is critical.

If a client calls to ask us if bankruptcy can help them to get out of a certain problem and achieve their goals, we always play a mental "chess game" that involves trying to determine who will do what if we file. Based on previous experience, we typically know what everyone else is going to do in this strategic game, and we have to be able to anticipate those actions and figure out an exit strategy (obtain replacement financing to get rid of a difficult lender, sell off all or part of the assets to raise capital, etc.) Indeed, no company should file for bankruptcy unless they first have an exit strategy.

The client's ability to work something out with its lender is most often the key element to whether its bankruptcy exit strategy is going to work or not. Money is king, and if they cannot work out an acceptable resolution with their lender to fund what they need to do to implement their restructuring strategy, it is very difficult to move forward in an adversarial posture. When you file for bankruptcy you start out in an adversarial posture, and you might convince the court that you can use a lender's cash collateral, but in the long run it is difficult to implement a strategy without some resolution from your lender, because the lender has so many cards to play—it can seek stay relief to foreclose if its position is deteriorating, and it can seek termination of use of cash collateral if there are any defaults in the conditions placed by the court on that use, it can object to any plan that doesn't provide for certain bankruptcy code mandated treatment of its claim, etc.

## Helpful Resources

There are several resources I believe are instrumental in developing an effective restructuring strategy on behalf of a client. For example, I read several publications that keep me up to date on the latest decisions in this area and what is going on in other bankruptcy cases. Even if I am not directly involved in a case, I like to read the pleadings that were filed, and see what other professionals are doing. Sometimes if I get involved in a case, I will look to see what other lawyers in another similar case did in order to deal with certain issues. For example, in trying to obtain court-approval of an employee incentive plan, I will study what has been approved and disapproved in other recent cases.

It is also important to keep abreast of recent changes in the law. For example, there were some sweeping changes to the bankruptcy code in late 2005 that are just being interpreted now, and reading those interpretations helps me to understand what my clients can and cannot do. My favorite source for updated information is the American Bankruptcy Institute, of which I am a member. They have a monthly journal as well as a Web site to keep abreast of recent decisions affecting our practice.

## Final Thoughts

When advising other bankruptcy lawyers regarding restructuring strategies, I always emphasize that you should try not to get too bogged down in all the different constituencies, because there is usually a deal to be had that is palatable for everyone, and that deal is usually the most efficient and effective solution for your client. Sometimes litigation is unavoidable, but reasonable minds should be able to come to a resolution based on the probabilities in that litigation, so that everyone saves money and time, and gets moving forward as quickly as possible.

In addition, you should never advise clients to file bankruptcy just because they are facing some financial trouble. The client should always make sure that they have explored other alternatives (sale, refinancing, reduced operations, etc.) and that they have an exit strategy before they jump into bankruptcy, because it is an expensive and time-consuming process. While bankruptcy solves many problems, it can create others as well (loss of control, elimination of vendor credit, devaluation of the business due to market stigma, loss of key employees).

*Todd C. Meyers is chair of Kilpatrick Stockton's nationally recognized Financial Restructuring Team and practices in the firm's Atlanta office. Mr. Meyers' practice focuses on bankruptcy and insolvency matters. He represents committees, creditors, and debtors in both workouts and bankruptcy proceedings. Mr. Meyers can be reached at tmeyers@kilpatrickstockton.com .*

*While in law school, he served as executive articles editor of the* Bankruptcy Developments Journal. *He was the 1991 Emory Tax Scholar and recipient of the Sutherland, Asbill & Brennan Tax Award. Mr. Meyers is a member of Order of the Coif. Mr. Meyers co-authored the chapter on secured transactions under Article 9 of the Georgia Uniform Commercial Code for the treatise Georgia Jurisprudence, published in 1995 by Lawyers Cooperative Publishing. He is listed in the 2006-2007 edition of* Chambers USA: America's Leading Business Lawyers for Bankruptcy Law.

# The New Variables for the Coming Recession: Credit Default Swaps

Gary S. Lee

*Partner*


G. Larry Engel

*Partner*


Morrison & Foerster LLP

ASPATORE

## Prelude to the Coming Crises and Opportunities

Buyers of credit default swaps (CDSs) have powerful incentives to block out-of-court restructurings by "reference party" debtors whose debt is "insured" in the CDS instruments. If and when such over-leveraged debtors cannot refinance their debt in the continuing credit crunch, Chapter 11 bankruptcy is the debtor's most likely alternative to a failed restructuring effort. Such bankruptcies are "credit events" that require the CDS seller-insurer to pay the buyer-insured the CDS obligation.

Considering the comparatively modest cost of the CDS protection in the past, analogous to an insurance premium, a large profit is available upon the bankruptcy trigger event for the CDS buyer. However, that profit for the buyer corresponds to an equally large loss for the CDS seller-insurer, whose reserves for that contingent liability typically are substantially less than the CDS purchase price/"insurance premium."

While many CDS sellers themselves may be forced into bankruptcy or liquidation, those bankruptcy cases often will not discourage or delay the CDS buyers. The special derivatives carve-outs in the Bankruptcy Code generally allow the CDS buyer to enforce its remedies with few of the usual bankruptcy protections available to the CDS seller debtor. Many such buyers are eager for the opportunity to acquire the CDS sellers' assets at distress prices. As a consequence, almost all constituencies in the bankruptcy cases of CDS reference party debtors, except the CDS buyers, will be materially worse off due to the CDS dynamics.

As illustrated in the citations at the end of this article, the market is awakening to the risks and benefits inherent in CDS trading, particularly as the recession deepens. For example, there is growing attention to the lessons from the CDS risks at Bear Stearns that inspired the Federal Reserve's unprecedented rescue. Counterparty risk concerns already have caused working groups of regulators and market players to begin work on a CDS exchange that would reduce systemic exposures for exchange-traded CDSs. Unfortunately, many existing CDS trades greatly exceed the risk tolerance for such exchange trading.

## Understanding a CDS Deal

A CDS functions as private debt default insurance, in which the CDS seller acts like an unregulated insurer, paying the CDS buyer in the event of a "credit event," such as bankruptcy or other specified default, of the reference-party issuer of the referenced debt obligations.

Some analogize a CDS deal to "selling short" the referenced debt. Others analogize the CDS deal to the sale of cheap term life insurance on a referenced party with respect to the referenced debt, with bankruptcy or other default the analogous equivalent of death. Still others are reminded of the regulated insurers' equivalent product, a "financial guaranty bond," although "monoline" bond insurers also have suffered from market and regulators' concerns about their CDS exposures.

The documentation for a CDS is often arranged under an International Swaps and Derivatives Association (ISDA) master netting agreement between two parties that are eligible under the Commodity Futures Trading Commission (CFTC) rules for such derivative trading. The contingent liability of the seller is often secured in whole or in part by collateral, often consisting of assets held under those master netting agreements.

While CDS deals initially were intermediated by investment banks that bought and then resold the "insurance," eventually many hedge funds began to deal with each other directly and cut out the middleman. Additionally, while these CDS deals began as hedges to cushion the consequences of bond defaults, CDS transactions soon expanded to include many types of reference-party debt. Many CDSs then became "naked" bets. Thus, while a CDS buyer may acquire some CDSs to hedge a strategic block of actual debt referenced in its CDS, that buyer also may have much larger naked bets with other CDS purchases. Such positions enable the CDS buyer to profit more from a reference-party bankruptcy than from any feasible restructuring that does not trigger the CDS payouts. As the market value of reference-party collateral continues to decline and tolerable refinancing options vanish, it will become easier for CDS buyers to block such restructurings.

Distressed debt experts, like NYU Professor Edward Altman, have charted the high levels of maturing debt from the reference-party debtors with high leverage and impaired liquidity beginning in the third quarter of 2008 and continuing throughout 2009. Even without the burden of CDS buyer debt holders resisting such reference-party restructurings, such debtors will suffer many challenges in avoiding bankruptcy. The existence of large CDS buyer bets on bankruptcy can make that fate seem inevitable to the constituents on whom such reference-party debtors must depend for credible alternatives, including lenders, suppliers, and customers whose defensive planning for bankruptcy of such debtors could doom other alternatives.

There now exists at least $62.2 trillion in "notional" amount of CDS exposure "insuring" against bankruptcy, payment, or some other defaults on at most $5.7 trillion of actual debt. (Some now believe that this notional amount has increased to $65 trillion, despite the increased anxiety about the future of the economy.) Because of the dramatic size of these notional CDS exposures, market players and regulators are beginning to arrange for netting solutions to more closely model the actual net exposures. As with other reforms, however, forward solutions generally do not eliminate existing concerns as to the size of the potential problems and opportunities.

## Predictions of Coming Attractions

Warren Buffet has called CDSs "financial weapons of mass destruction" for several good reasons. As we go to press, there is evidence that, in the coming months, a substantial number of net CDS sellers could collapse, like insurers whose policy liabilities mature in amounts far exceeding their reserves and other assets. A significant number of CDS buyers who acquired CDSs as backup reinsurance for their own CDS sales, also will collapse, on account of the collapse of their reinsurer-CDS sellers. Conversely, many net CDS buyers will profit by the reference-party bankruptcies and other defaults, entitling them to collect from CDS sellers very large amounts in excess of the buyers' costs, sometimes liquidating the CDS sellers.

CDS sellers typically have charged low "insurance premiums" and established low reserves, allowing them to report huge, but contingent, profits. These CDS sellers historically have relied upon rating agency data, reflecting the low default rates during the boom, as every problem could be refinanced with ample and easy loans in the prior period of extraordinary liquidity. Now, sellers are confronting the resurgence of economic fundamentals, whose gravity (as in all past cycles) would eventually prevent the hot air balloons from flying high indefinitely.

Such CDS sellers may have sometimes "reinsured" their CDS exposure by buying more CDS hedges for that risk, but in many cases, there are extraordinary counterparty risks for such "reinsurance" CDS deals. For example, many at-risk, net CDS sellers are smaller hedge funds (e.g., $1 billion or less from investors with short lockups). When their theoretical CDS profits are replaced by real losses, such net seller funds confront the likelihood of a "run on the bank" by investors and consequent liquidation.

Many net CDS buyers are aggressive hedge funds with distressed debt opportunity strategies. Some are pitching themselves to the net CDS seller counterparty investors as a hedge, when the buyers "clean out" the sellers, and when the over-leveraged reference-party debtors cannot refinance their maturing debts in the credit crunch. These CDS buyers typically engage in many transactions with the CDS sellers serving as collateral under ISDA master netting agreements, entitling the CDS buyers to acquire such CDS seller assets, as well as the large CDS payout, upon the reference-party bankruptcy or other default. Relative to the generally low cost of the CDS "insurance premiums" collected by the CDS sellers, the CDS buyer's recovery is very large, especially on the many naked CDSs.

Net CDS sellers' attempts to delay CDS payout obligations have not yet yielded much success. *See, e.g., XL Capital Assurance Inc. v. Merrill Lynch Int'l,* No. 08 CV 2893, --- F.Supp.2d ----, 2008 WL 2738075 (S.D.N.Y. 2008). (granting the CDS buyer summary judgment, overcoming the seller's theory of repudiation by impairment of voting rights). In any event, the CDS buyer also typically has some collateral and the right under the ISDA master netting agreement to trigger closeout netting as to all of the subject transactions thereunder. As demonstrated below, the CDS seller has few effective defenses against such buyer remedies, even if the CDS seller files a Chapter 11 case, since these master netting agreement and CDS transactions are generally excepted from the usual bankruptcy protections.

Unhappy CDS sellers who believe that they have been wronged by excessive collateral or other demands have begun to sue, but with little resulting relief thus far. *See VCG Special Opportunities Master Fund Ltd. v. Citibank, N.A.*, No. 08 CV 01563 (S.D.N.Y. 2008); *CDO Plus Master Fund Ltd. v. Wachovia Bank*, No. 07 CV 11078 (S.D.N.Y. 2007).

## Blocking Restructuring: The Benefits of Bankruptcy to CDS Net Buyers

In past down cycles, debtors were more often than not able to restructure their debts outside of bankruptcy, even when the over-leveraged debtors needed the creditors to discount their debt claims. Now, however, the CDS dynamics will make those restructurings outside of bankruptcy more difficult, especially where declining asset values and creditworthiness of the reference party debtor require large discounts and concessions from creditors.

In the past, most or all of the creditors could see the benefit of compromising and keeping the reference-party debtor viable without a formal bankruptcy. Now, however, the CDS net buyer creditors can often profit and benefit more from a bankruptcy of the reference party debtor, even if that bankruptcy harms the debtor's ability to pay its creditors. The risk-benefit analysis of the CDS net buyer is especially high in favor of bankruptcies when dealing with naked CDSs, where the buyer is paid the insured amount without suffering any risk of harm.

Having paid a premium to collect because of both losses on bonds they hold, and on naked bets, the net CDS buyers have every incentive to encourage a reference party bankruptcy or other CDS triggering default. Not only do these CDS buyers recover large profits on their bets, but they also may be in a position to acquire the CDS sellers' collateral on attractive terms by enforcing the ISDA master netting agreement when the CDS sellers have insufficient cash to pay off their liabilities. Indeed, when there is an investment bank or commercial bank financial intermediary between the ultimate CDS seller and buyer, that intermediary may be eager to swap its rights against the ultimate CDS seller for relief on that intermediary's own exposure on the CDS that it sold to the ultimate buyer. Often an ultimate hedge fund CDS buyer may find the ultimate CDS seller fund's collateral or other master net agreement assets more attractive than would the intermediary.

If the CDS buyers and their allies decline to support a cooperative restructuring outside of bankruptcy, the reference party debtor will often be forced to restructure in a bankruptcy case. (That will trigger the CDS payment by the CDS seller-insurer.) This "power of no" is hard for supporters of the reference-party debtor to overcome. Stated another way, it is easier to push a reference-party debtor into bankruptcy than to save it from bankruptcy. Among the reasons for that self-fulfilling prophecy is that a successful restructuring often requires that the debtor's ability to avoid bankruptcy be credible. Absent that needed credibility, too few essential parties want to gamble on their concessions or accommodations being counterproductive in the expected bankruptcy. Since the interests of key creditors are not often obscured from other parties to a restructuring effort, credibility is an increasing challenge for debtors, who may not even know about the extent of the CDS exposures that determine the debtors' fates.

Many restructurings at a discount require a unanimous vote of debt holders, which can be easy for CDS buyers to block. Even as to majority vote issues as to debt held by several or many holders, it is often difficult to achieve that vote over opposition from CDS buyers or their allies.

For example, in many debt indentures, even 25 percent of one tranche of debt can direct the indenture trustee, absent a majority override vote. That direction early in the restructuring process for the trustee to be aggressive can obstruct the process and prevent the necessary parties from ever achieving a consensus, especially as among different classes, priorities, and types of debt.

In addition, CDS buyers holding even a small, strategic block of debt may be able to obstruct a consensual restructuring and force a reference party debtor's bankruptcy. For instance, when the senior and junior priority lenders need to divide their respective shares of restructured debt or to compromise as to the amount of any concessions proposed by the reference party debtor, a negative position by CDS buyers (who have little to lose and much to gain in a bankruptcy filing) can often obstruct any timely compromise. In a situation where the realistic value of the junior lien position is $0 and the senior lenders offer the usual, token recovery of 5 to 10 percent, CDS buyers of junior debt can insist on a deal that the senior lenders would not find acceptable, especially if the CDS buyers or their allies also are holders of senior debt resisting their own junior debt demands.

The going-concern value and prospects of a reference party debtor can be debated within a huge range of value variation, even with reputable financial advisors on each side. If each side produces a contrary value making a consensual compromise appear unfair to its side, it can become hard to achieve such a compromise outside of bankruptcy. A distressed debtor's self-valuation, whether internal or from its chosen advisors, typically is far larger than the lower ranges deemed appropriate by senior creditors. A junior lienholder's valuation is also more likely to exceed the senior lienholders' more conservative valuation. Thus, valuation has often become a political variable for which third-party support is obtainable anywhere along a large continuum of possible values. In this environment, it is often easy for consensus or compromise to be obstructed.

Furthermore, if the CDS buyers believe that their best recovery comes from acquiring the equity in a reorganized reference party or its assets, it may be hard to reconcile that ambition with a consensual, out-of-bankruptcy restructuring. The reason that consensus was more often achieved in the past can be explained by the fact that in prior cycles the dominant bank creditors did not want to convert their debt to controlling equity. Now, however, the hedge funds or PE funds, which often have replaced the banks as the dominant, relevant creditors, may prefer that acquisition strategy. Obviously, a CDS buyer receiving a large recovery upon the bankruptcy of the reference party has a cash advantage in the liquidation or reorganization bidding to come. Indeed, some CDS buyers foresee using their profits as sufficient to fund their acquisitions.

Cram-downs in bankruptcy (11 U.S.C. § 1129(b)) can force compromises that elude any consensus outside of bankruptcy. Moreover, the reference party debtor often needs financing, which can be achieved as Chapter 11 DIP financing, but may not be otherwise available in time, where a consensual deal is delayed or obstructed. Therefore, the reference party whose restructuring efforts are obstructed or delayed, often will be advised that Chapter 11 is the only strategic alternative. While historically such bankruptcy filings also had negative effects on the creditors resisting the out-of-court restructuring, the bankruptcy has no impact on a naked CDS buyer. Such naked CDS profits can also be sufficiently large as to make the actual debt held by the CDS buyer a non-decisive factor in its strategy.

## Bluffing Debtors and Creditors

The problem for many debtors and their other creditors is that the motivations of CDS buyers may not be obvious to anyone else who matters in the restructuring process. If debtors or other creditors rely on the restructuring and financing dynamics from past down-cycles, they may be disappointed. Worse, they may fail to prepare for the inevitable bankruptcy in time. History shows that "free fall" Chapter 11 filings cause much worse results for all parties-in-interest than do properly planned bankruptcies, but as noted those impacts do not harm CDS buyers.

Some CDS buyers separate their naked versus hedged CDS positions, so that one affiliate can appear as a debt holder with CDS insurance, while the other affiliate with the naked CDS position never appears, because it holds no debt to be paid by the debtor. Indeed, those two affiliates may do a CDS deal between them to allocate the greater profits from the naked CDS position that may benefit from the CDS position involving actual debt hedging.

When the debtor and other negotiating parties lose visibility as to such motivations, it becomes even easier for the CDS buyers to "bluff" debtors (or their creditors) into a bankruptcy filing. If a reference party debtor's bankruptcy is believed to be inevitable, because of real or imagined opposition from CDS players, the other parties may quickly lose interest in an out-of-court restructuring compromise. Typically, if the only choice is perceived to be bankruptcy sooner or bankruptcy later, most sophisticated parties would rather invest in an organized bankruptcy sooner, especially in a falling market with continuing credit crunch and other structural problems. Creditors who make a series of concessions preceding the bankruptcy usually have a lower aggregate recovery than those who suffer only once.

When the other parties who depend on the debtor begin to understand this new CDS game, it will be more difficult for the debtor to charm them into providing their traditional accommodations, credit, and forbearance in reliance on the feasibility of a restructuring based on historical practices that may no longer apply. For example, if partly invisible CDS problems appear likely to prevent a win/win restructuring outside of bankruptcy, then one can expect earlier defensive play from vendors, customers, licensors/licensees, lessors/lessees, and other key collaborators with the debtor. Where these key constituents move in more defensive directions, either because of the fear of a CDS-inspired bankruptcy or in reaction to how other creditors appear to be reacting defensively, the resulting pressures on the reference party debtor may often force a bankruptcy, rewarding the CDS buyers.

## Negotiating Concessions: Key Challenges

When a vendor or other ally makes a concession in a pre-bankruptcy workout process, they often end up worse off in the bankruptcy than if they had made no concession until the bankruptcy. Thus, to negotiate concessions the debtor typically has to assure the vendors, customers, licensors/licensees, lessors/lessees or other collaborators that their concessions will make a bankruptcy unnecessary. If that assurance is not credible, then the workout option will be either nonexistent or less meaningful for the debtor.

The other challenge is that, as workout efforts are increasingly met with demands for "everyone" to come to the negotiating table to match up benefits and burdens in a fair and transparent way, there likely will be some missing parties. After a few unpleasant surprises in deals where creditors and other key parties suffer from making concessions only to regret them in the bankruptcy that was supposed to have been avoided, the burden of proof will shift to the debtor to prove that it can actually accomplish the restructuring goal without bankruptcy. Under the foreseeable circumstances, it will become progressively harder for debtors to satisfy that burden of proof, and CDS-related fears will become more difficult to overcome.

Ultimately, there will be a clash in these bankruptcies, similar to what was widely debated in the *Northwest Airlines* Chapter 11 case under Rule 2019, regarding disclosure of CDS positions and motivations. *In re Northwest Airlines*, 363 B.R. 704 (Bankr. S.D.N.Y. 2007). Those insisting on disclosure from CDS buyers under Bankruptcy Rule 2004 will likely be met with counter-arguments about trade secret and proprietary-trading strategies. However, bankruptcy judges likely will develop concerns about the obstacles that undisclosed CDSs could create to consensual, creative solutions. Among the possible, indirect responses to the CDS difficulties could be:

- Evasion of blocking positions by the CDS debt holders, if the court approved a separate classification for the CDS-insured debt in plans of reorganization. While this arguably would be unprecedented, some perceive the logic to be compelling by analogy to subordinated debt being separately classified.
- Other limitations on, or arrangements of, the voting or exercise of creditor rights by CDS debt holders that prevent blockages by CDS debt holders.
- Attempts to disqualify CDS debt holders from creditors' committees or other fiduciary roles as not being generally representative of the creditors.

## Disallowing and Recovering Claims

A question that is often raised is whether CDS buyers are immune from avoidance power exposures and related defenses of debtors seeking to disallow claims under 11 U.S.C. § 502(d) or to debtors' claims to equitably subordinate such CDS buyers under § 510(c). In fact, buyers of naked CDSs can recover from CDS sellers entirely outside of the reference party's bankruptcy case, because they do not hold debt that must be allowed in the bankruptcy case.

CDS buyers who hold both naked and hedged positions can arguably cover any losses on hedged CDS debt in the bankruptcy case with recoveries on their naked CDS positions outside the bankruptcy case. However, CDS buyers often separate their naked and hedged CDS positions between affiliates, as described above.

If CDS buyers holding debt in the reference party's bankruptcy case suffer an equitable subordination of that debt claim under 11 U.S.C. § 510(c), the CDS buyer may claim entitlement to a full recovery without deduction, because there would not have been any equitable subordination without a bankruptcy filing to trigger the CDS. On the other hand, the CDS sellers argue that this equitable subordination creates a defense by impairing their subordination rights. At present, there is little direct precedent for resolving such disputes.

Similarly, if a CDS buyer's claim is disallowed under § 502(d) because of a failure to pay a preference or fraudulent-transfer liability, the CDS buyer may still seek a full recovery from the CDS seller, again on the theory that the problem arises in bankruptcy that was the subject of the insurance. However, the CDS seller may resist on the argument that its subrogation rights have been impaired, but with naked CDS positions, there is no debt to which there would be subrogation. Again, there is little direct precedent for resolving these disputes at present.

Nevertheless, especially with the naked CDS positions to protect them, CDS recoveries appear to cushion CDS buyers from the normal bankruptcy litigation threats. If reference party debtors attempt to leverage out-of-court restructurings with litigation threats of such bankruptcy claims and defenses by the debtor, those threats now may have less impact on CDS buyers.

## CDS Seller Bankruptcies and Their Effects on Reference-Party Debtors

Even CDS *seller* bankruptcies seem unlikely to obstruct the CDS buyers from aggressive tactics against the reference party debtors. If a CDS seller bankruptcy were to impede the CDS buyers' strategies, that might create alliance opportunities for reference-party debtors, who fear being forced into bankruptcy by the buyers. Clearly, many CDS sellers are vulnerable to bankruptcy and liquidation risks when their CDS buyers "cash in" upon the reference party bankruptcy filings. Unfortunately for such reference-party debtors, however, the strategic carve-outs in the Bankruptcy Code for CDSs, for "settlement payments," and for other "derivative" rights, combine to protect the CDS buyers from much harm or delay in the CDS seller bankruptcy cases.

Consider, for example:

- § 546(e) excludes from preference, fraudulent transfer, and other avoidance power claims what are defined as "settlement payments" under § 101, except as to *actual* fraudulent transfers under § 548(a)(1)(A). If one qualifies as a "financial participant," "settlement payment" recoveries from the CDS seller debtor are protected from disgorgement.
- § 362(b)(27) excludes from the automatic stay the rights of CDS buyers under master netting agreements with the CDS seller to close out their positions in accordance with such terms for netting on termination and setoff. *See also* §§ 555, 560, and 561. *Cf.* § 562 (timing of damages measurements).

## Concluding Comments

Among the coming problems associated with the CDS exposures is that they may be invisible to everyone besides the CDS buyer and seller. Indeed, because of the frequent chain of CDS exposures, involving intermediaries between the ultimate CDS seller and buyer, even the buyer and seller may not be clear to each other. However, the CDS dynamics will typically affect the reference party debtors and, through those debtors, all other creditors and equity holders of those debtors. In the early phases of the coming recession, these often may result in unpleasant surprises, especially when debtors rely on out-of-court restructurings or refinancings that are blocked by CDS buyers, who profit on reference party debtor bankruptcies. Later in the cycle, more informed debtors and their other creditors and equity holders will assume the worst, unless someone can convince them that CDS buyers will not become a problem in that deal. Given the size of the CDS exposures ($62.5 trillion in notional amount of CDS liability on at most $5.7 trillion of debt), the challenges will be broader and deeper than most now expect.

The tactics of CDS buyer-creditors will often be new, because the CDS opportunities and challenges are also comparatively new, since the last down-cycle. Because CDS buyers can achieve huge profits on the CDS reference party debtors' bankruptcies, especially on naked positions, many CDS buyers may perceive that they have little to lose by recovery/acquisition strategies. After collecting from the CDS sellers, the

CDS buyers will be well funded and strategically positioned for acquisitions of the debtors in their bankruptcy cases.

The disputes early in the bankruptcy cases will likely begin as fights for strategic information about the CDS buyers' positions. Thereafter, the other creditors will use other strategies to attempt to gain balancing counter-leverage. Nevertheless, in many cases the CDS buyers will have advantages, including surprise and ample cash from the CDS sellers.

**Related Resources**

Demonstrations of the Core Thesis of this Chapter:

Larry Engel, "Hedge Fund Failures Prediction and Strategies: How to Catch a Falling Knife and Not Get Cut," *Derivatives* (Dec. 2007).

"Credit Default Swap Market Value Hits $2 Trillion Last Year," *Daily Bankruptcy Review* 6/10/08, reporting that, besides ISDA's $62.2 trillion in national CDS amounts outstanding at the end of 2007, the Bank of International Settlements calculated these CDS market values at $2 trillion, of which more than half were for a single reference party debt issuer.

"Swap Shop," *The Economist* 4/25/08, generally explaining the rise of CDSs as an ability to "short" debt issues even where the buyers could not (or chose not to) acquire the actual debt, but noting the counterparty risk issues in a $62.2 trillion notional value CDS market; illustrated by the Bear Stearns CDS problems, and the risk of a sudden freeze in existing CDS trading, if the market becomes illiquid, as illustrated by the auction rate debt market and other markets impacted by "contagion" from subprime mortgage and similar risks.

"Credit Default Swaps: The Next Crisis?" *Time* 3/17/08, reporting on the CDS role in the Bear Stearns crisis, the $11 billion CDS write-down by AIG, the impact of the CDS exposures on the monocline bond insurers (e.g., MBIA, Ambac), and the dynamics, including how "an original CDS can go through 15 or 20 trades" to create a counterparty risk mystery.

"CDS Market Enters New Territory as Defaults begin to Rise," *Daily Bankruptcy Review*, p. 9, 7/2/08, reporting on the lack of standardization across a $62 trillion market of privately negotiated contracts and ISDA's continuing effort to develop a "big bang" protocol for standard auction settlements and dispute resolutions, extrapolating from the ad hoc salvage efforts.

"The Credit Default Swap Litigation Threat," *The D&O Diary* (6/5/08), reporting beyond the prior story in "First Came the Swap. Then It's the Knives," *N.Y. Times* 6/1/08, illustrating the litigation expected between bank and hedge fund counterparties in failed CDS deals, and exposing the following risk issues:

- ". . . UBS considered a special purpose entity with only $4.6 million in capital to be an appropriate source of default insurance for instruments with a face value of $1.31 billion [AAA rated notes that "reflected performance of subprime mortgages in a collateralized debt obligation underwritten by UBS"]. UBS's contractual right to demand additional collateral from the hedge fund, which itself had capital of only $200 million . . ."
- The CDS seller received a fee of 0.155 percent of the $1.31 billion risk ($2 million) and posted an aggregate total of $33 million in collateral before refusing to provide more, triggering the CDS buyer's lawsuit.
- The author then speculates about follow-on investor litigation when the default "insurance" on which they depended failed because of such counterparty CDS seller's inability to perform.

*Credit Default Swap Trading*

*See* Bloomberg (extensive databases for CDS trading, as well as for the distressed debt "insured" by the CDSs, including the Altman "Z-Score" that is more predictive of defaults than the traditional rating agency models).

"Credit Default Swaps: What You Need to Know Now," *Secured Lender* Sept./Oct. 2007, a general overview that describes how the CDS market has expanded from bonds to commercial loans (so-called Loan-Only Credit Default Swaps or LCDS).

*XL Capital Assurance Inc. v. Merrill Lynch International*, S.D.N.Y. No. 08 CV 2893 (JSR) (6/11/08).

*CDS Exchange and Systemic Ris:*

Federal Reserve Bank of New York Press Release 6/9/08, reporting on its efforts to promote an over-the-counter derivatives market, including standardization of forms and use of a central counterparty for CDS risk management.

"Fed Turns Focus to Derivatives Market, Wants Improved Infrastructure Soon," *Wall St. J.* 6/10/08, reporting on the Federal regulators' CDS related anxieties and desires for a CDS exchange (e.g., The Clearing Corp. in Chicago) to reduce counterparty risks, and noting:

- Bear Stearns had 750,000 derivative contracts outstanding when it collapsed.
- Hedge funds were invited because they are parties to more than 90 percent of the transactions directly between individual firms.

"ISDA Looks to Slice Outstandings," *Derivatives Week* 6/23/08, reporting how ISDA, in coordination with the Federal Reserve Bank of New York, is working to reduce the growth of the $62.2 trillion notional amount of CDS by increased netting.

- Although different, the long-continuing liquidity crisis in "auction rate debt" (ARD) shows how difficult it is to fashion solutions that can become implemented. *See* the Clearing-Bid solution, which, while workable, still has not been able to overcome inertia in the system or achieve critical mass from participants. This example shows how challenging will be the ISDA solutions to implement when resolved in theory. In the case of ARD solutions, there are state attorneys general and customers suing broker dealers to inspire action, but in the case of the bond insurers, the state insurance regulators may prefer insurance insolvency practices that conflict with implementing such solutions.

*Special Bankruptcy Exceptions For CDS Risks*

"CDS Market May Boost Bankruptcies," *Bank Loan Report* 6/30/08, reporting on a June 2008 Credit Sights analysis by Dot Matthews and Brian Yelvington, consistent with this chapter and these authors' prior work published as Larry Engel, "Hedge Fund Failure Predictions and Strategies: How to Catch a Falling Knife and Not Get Cut. *Derivatives* (Dec. 2007).

ISDA CDS Index Protocol for Delphi Corporation dated 10/28/05, creating an auction settlement arrangement for swap participants whose CDS rights to payment far exceeded the actual, available Delphi debt corresponding to those CDSs ($28 billion of CDS on $2 billion of senior debt outstanding auctioned per the ISDA protocol for a settlement price of 63.3 percent).

"Not Your Ordinary Swap Meet," *N.Y. Times* dated 2/22/08, reporting, in the context of AIG's $3.6 billion CDS value miscalculation, how a dozen CDS auctions established values under ISDA protocols for bankrupt debt issuers, such as Delphi Corp., Calpine Corp., Dana Corp., Dura, Delta Airlines and Northwest Airlines.

*In re American Home Mortgage Holdings Inc.*, No. 07-11047, 2008 WL 2156323 (Bankr. D. Del. 2008), holding that the transaction for the purchase and sale of notes secured by mortgage loans was a "repurchase contract" entitled to the safe harbor protections from bankruptcy under 11 U.S.C. §§ 555 and 559 as well as from the "commercial reasonableness" standards of UCC Article 9. But see *In re American Home Mortgage Holdings Inc.*, Chap. 11 Case No. 07-11047 (Bankr. D. Del. 2007), allowing the sale of servicing agreements by severing those rights from the other obligations under master mortgage loan purchase agreements.

*Illustrations of CDS Risks*

"MBIA Debt Is Setting Up a Quandary," *N.Y. Times* 6/18/08, reporting on the problems associated with $137 billion of CDS to insure buyers against an insolvency proceeding against its at-risk bond insurance subsidiary, as a kind of "poison pill" to restrain the NY Insurance Commissioner.

"Credit Default Swaps Pose Threat to Bond Insurance Firms," *Daily Bankruptcy Review* 6/25/08, reporting what could happen to counterparty risk as to $500 billion in CDS exposure of the seven major bond insurers, if insurance regulators took control, since CDS buyers would have to stand in line "for years" with "other claimants in a runoff portfolio" before CDS resolutions occurred.

"Monoline Madness," *Financial Times* 6/23/08, reporting on $125 billion in CDS contracts sold by bond insurers to insure CDS exposures that could affect those insurers' futures.

"Bond Downgrades May Sour After BNIA, Ambac Are Cut," *Bloomberg* 6/23/08, reporting on the bond insurers' long-expected initial downgrades that "may only 'scratch the surface' of rating cuts" for monoline insurers who ISDA calculates cover as much as $1.28 trillion of debt.

"Moody's Cuts MBIA, Ambac Top Insurance Ratings," CNBC.com 6/20/08, reporting on such downgrades and "negative outlooks" for additional downgrades, as well as the MBIA protest that: "This is an issue of ratings not solvency," alluding to its argument that it can cover "policyholders" which may not include creditors, such as CDS buyers.

*M&T Bank Corp. v. Gemstone CDO VII, LTD, et. al.*, New York Supreme Court, Erie County, Index No. 0070641/2008 filed 6/16/08, illustrating the facts and theories plaintiffs use against failed CDO originators and their prime broker-lenders, including the CDS component of those leveraged structures.

"Fed Releases Details of Bear Stearns Rescue," *Wash. Post* 6/28/08, reporting among others on the "contagion" risks requiring an emergency response that included large CDS exposures and counterparty risks.

"CDS Market Enters New Territory as Defaults Begin to Rise," *Daily Bankruptcy Review* p. 9, 7/2/08, reporting on the unsolved problem of how best to deal with monoline bond insurers' failures when the CDS exposures were attached to thousands of <u>insured</u> bonds and other obligations with no easy means to develop a standard recovery rate, adding to the market anxieties that, for example, have already raised MBIA protection costs to bankruptcy risk pricing (e.g., to insure $10 million of bonds for five years one must now pay $4 million down plus annual fees).

"Athilon, Credit Derivative Company, Faces Rating Cut," Bloomberg.com 7/2/08, reporting how this CDS seller to banks that are worried about their CDO exposures is now on negative-ratings watch as the "insured" CDO ratings continue to sink.

*Illustrations of Exotica*

At least until mid-2007, the appetite for structured financial products was insatiable and creative derivatives were perceived as a means of satisfying that hunger. In the mix of instruments within the broad category of "credit default swaps" are many exotics or hybrids. One illustration moved beyond the often intertwined use of a CDS to insure a CDO in a combined transaction. Because there were fewer corporate bonds than needed to meet CDO demand, underwriter investment bankers created "synthetic" CDO's composed of a portfolio of CDSs. "Swap shop," *The Economist* 4/25/08.

*Gary S. Lee is a partner in and co-chair of the Bankruptcy and Restructuring Group in the New York office of Morrison & Foerster LLP. For the past seventeen years, he has been involved in domestic and international restructuring and insolvency matters in the United States, arising particularly out of corporate and insurance company insolvencies.*

*Mr. Lee represents financial institutions in domestic and cross-border workouts and insolvencies. He is currently involved in several hedge fund and insurance company cases. Mr. Lee has been heavily involved in the implementation of foreign liquidations and schemes of arrangement in the U.S. and has been closely involved with issues arising under Chapter 15 of the U.S. Bankruptcy Code.*

*Mr. Lee is a member of the Association of the Bar of the City of New York and the New York State Bar Association. He is a member of the City Bar's Insurance Law*

*Committee and the former co-chair of its Insolvency Subcommittee. He is currently co-chair of the Transnational Bankruptcy Committee of the International Insolvency Institute. He is also a member of the American Bar Association, where he previously served as vice chairman of the Litigation Committee of the Young Lawyers Division. He is Fellow of the American Bar Association and is cited in* Euromoney's Guide to the World's Leading Lawyers. *He also served on the American Bankruptcy Institute's International Insolvency Committee.*

*He received his law degree with honors from Manchester University, England. Mr. Lee is admitted to practice before the courts of New York and U.S. federal courts, and as a solicitor in the U.K.*

**G. Larry Engel** *is a partner at Morrison & Foerster LLP. His practice focuses on bankruptcy, restructurings, hedge fund and insurance insolvency, and risky leveraged buyouts, DIP, exit, and complex financings, including for private equity funds, hedge funds, for real estate and other industries, as well as "commercial tech," outsourcing and intellectual property transactions, including "bankruptcy proofing" licenses, technology ventures and collaborations. Mr. Engel's experience covers a broad range of legal disciplines applicable in transactions involving financially distressed businesses and real estate, including salvage and/or recovery services and the purchase of assets, both in and out of bankruptcy.*

*Mr. Engel has been honored by numerous legal and business organizations and publications, including, among others:*

- *American College of Bankruptcy*
- *International Insolvency Institute*
- *American College of Commercial Finance Lawyers*
- *Corporate Counsel's* The Best Lawyers in America
- *PLC/Global Counsel 3000* "Highly Recommended" *lawyer for Restructuring/Insolvency*
- Chambers USA: America's Leading Lawyers for Business
- *World's Leading Insolvency and Restructuring Lawyers (*Euromoney *Guide)*
- *United States Lawyers Rankings 2008 List of the Nation's Top 10 Bankruptcy Lawyers*
- *Northern California "Super Lawyer,"* Law & Politics *and* SF Magazine

*Mr. Engel received his B.A., magna cum laude, Phi Beta Kappa, from Northwestern University in 1969 and his J.D., cum laude, Order of the Coif, from Northwestern University School of Law in 1972, where he was executive editor of the* Northwestern University Law Review.

*Mr. Engel is a frequent lecturer and author for numerous business and legal organizations, including the ABI, the III, the PLI, the ABA, and the State Bar of California.*

# The Business of Bankruptcy: Realizing Restructuring Objectives through Strategic Ingenuity

Harley J. Goldstein

*Partner and Chair of Bankruptcy and Restructuring Group*

Bell, Boyd & Lloyd LLP

ASPATORE

## The Curious Regime of Bankruptcy Law

Bankruptcy may well be the final frontier of corporate law. Although bankruptcy has been a component of Western jurisprudence for hundreds of years, it has evolved into a strategic tool which would not be recognized in its roots of divvying up a debtor's assets ratably and debtor's prison. To the contrary, bankruptcy law in the United States today is a means and not an end, and one of the most remarkably powerful tools of accomplishing certain business objectives that is available.

Non-bankruptcy attorneys are generally shocked upon entry into the world of bankruptcy. Bankruptcy law is like the Wild West. We speak our own language. Authority is sparse and malleable. Things move fast in our world: cases that would take years to conclude in the ordinary world of litigation may be resolved in mere days, and a deal which is not cut until the courtroom stairs may indeed be an early resolution, compared to many.

Similarly, a successful bankruptcy practitioner is a different breed. Many successful bankruptcy attorneys lack pedigree compared to colleagues in other practice areas (a law school professor went so far as to advise my classmates that if we did not possess the credentials to procure jobs in corporate law, we should look to corporate restructuring). My Juris Doctor was not obtained at an Ivy League institution. Yet, at the age of thirty-five, I head one of the largest bankruptcy and restructuring groups in the city, at both one of the oldest and largest law firms in Chicago, and a national firm with offices on both coasts of the country.

Indeed, study skills do not breed a successful bankruptcy attorney. Ingenuity does. My practice is half law and half business. The half that is law is neither transactional nor litigation alone, but a balance of the two. Most importantly, I use the Bankruptcy Code as a tool to accomplish my clients' goals, not as a rigid road map dictating a prescribed path. While attorneys are generally trained to counsel clients as to what they cannot do under the law, the dearth of rigid and developed rules in many areas of bankruptcy permit a good practitioner to use the Bankruptcy Code creatively to accomplish a client's goal within the confines of the law. A good bankruptcy attorney is a deal maker rather than a deal breaker.

The lack of extensive authority in bankruptcy practice is distinct from many other areas of the law. Although the predecessor of the Bankruptcy Code, the "Bankruptcy Act," was promulgated in 1898, it was superseded by today's Bankruptcy Code in 1978, and has subsequently undergone major revisions in 1984, 1988, 1994, and 2005. Perhaps the dearth of authority exists as a result of the speed at with which bankruptcy matters traverse the courts (compared to traditional litigation) and concomitant lack of published judicial opinions, perhaps as a result of the youth of much of the statutory law or its constantly evolving nature, perhaps because of the interstices between the elements of the statutory framework, or perhaps as a result of the small quantity of bankruptcy judges compared to judges who hear other matters. Whatever its source, bankruptcy practitioners are permitted wide latitude in creative lawyering.

**Framework for Assessing Purpose**

I mentioned the importance of using restructuring as a tool accomplishing a client's goals. An implicit predicate for achieving a goal is identification of that goal. The key to the restructuring strategy in bankruptcy is to have an aim—be result-oriented. Absent understanding the goal to be achieved, bankruptcy is a ship without a destination; without a port for which to aim, there is no tack. And without direction, bankruptcy is simply a waste of energy and resources—you are likely to wind up either nowhere or somewhere you do not want to be. Nor can clients always assess their own goals; rather, very frequently, a client is focused on quelling the latest fire, or is unable to identify the existence of the true malady and instead believes an additional equity infusion will provide a panacea for resolution of the company's woes (as we say in the practice, "Denial ain't just a river in Egypt!").

Setting the framework with some basic assumptions is necessary for purposes of this discussion. For a variety of reasons stemming around transaction costs, bankruptcy should be treated as a last resort, and non-bankruptcy turnaround alternatives should be exhausted first. Since this discussion focuses on bankruptcy, I assume that a workout or other remedy outside bankruptcy either failed, is not possible, or will not achieve the purpose sought.

Second, since this guide addresses restructuring, any discussion germane to liquidation is omitted. Likewise, I assume that Chapter 11 (rather than Chapter 7) of the Bankruptcy Code provides the vehicle to be employed, as while Chapter 11 may also be used for a liquidation in a somewhat more controlled environment than Chapter 7 (which is a liquidation mechanism involving the immediate appointment of a trustee), Chapter 11 is the primary vehicle for a business reorganization in bankruptcy.

Finally, as parties other than those on the side of the table of the borrower (or the "debtor," as commonly referred to in bankruptcy parlance) have interests other than restructuring, this discussion focuses on the point of the view of the debtor, rather than that of the secured lender, unsecured creditors, or other parties to the bankruptcy.

Narrowed within these parameters, the mechanics of the restructuring may be approached. A restructuring (within or without bankruptcy) generally has one or both of two components: an operational or a financial restructuring. An operational restructuring fixes the "business" itself—in simplest terms, efficiency—how much it costs to produce each widget versus how much revenue is derived from widget sales. A financial restructuring, on the other hand, rearranges the balance sheet, modifying the debt and equity (i.e., capital) structure. A variety of other elements obviously have an impact on performance—today, we hear much about the prices of commodities such as oil, or the ostensible state of the economy. Certainly, these factors can make a particular business or industry more challenging. But the crux to determining whether a particular business model works hinges on first determining whether a business can be operationally optimized or its balance sheet can be further rationalized.

Of course, a restructuring may not address all issues or remedy a flawed business model. Thus, the success of a business may be driven by factors that are not rectifiable through a typical restructuring. For example, some industries witness endemic and recurrent restructurings or liquidations. Many airlines are plagued with repeated forays into the world of bankruptcy. While many factors are cited, it appears that the airline industry suffers a pervasive menace—a successful business cannot, in the long term, sell the product produced at a loss. Instead, goods or services must be sold for a price in excess of the cost of production.

## Accounting for Equity Redistribution

An important factor to consider in assessing the goal to be achieved in a bankruptcy restructuring is one of its fundamental tenets: bankruptcy generally results in the redistribution of equity ownership. To fully understand this principle requires grasping a pivotal element of Chapter 11 of the Bankruptcy Code: the absolute priority rule.

By way of background, the culmination of a restructuring in Chapter 11 is "confirmation" of a "plan" of reorganization. While this is, to a degree, oversimplification as, for example, parties other than debtor may be permitted to propose a plan under certain circumstances (notably where the debtor does not propose its own plan with the passage of time or where the debtor's principals lose control of their right to manage the debtor's business and affairs), a plan is essentially a contract (albeit frequently a non-consensual contract) between the debtor and its creditors dictating the exit from bankruptcy and going-forward relationship between the debtor and creditors. Confirmation occurs when the bankruptcy court presiding over the Chapter 11 case approves a proposed plan as complying with the requirements of the Bankruptcy Code (in particular, Section 1129 of the Bankruptcy Code). Upon confirmation of a plan (and fulfillment of conditions prescribed by the plan), "effectiveness" of the plan is achieved. While confirmation (and attaining effectiveness) of a plan often does not spell the end of a restructuring, it does end much of the bankruptcy court's involvement in approval of ongoing operational aspects of the debtor (although the bankruptcy court typically continues to preside over many other matters, such as litigation involving the bankruptcy estate).

Within a plan, claims against (i.e., debt) and interests in (i.e., equity) a debtor are categorized into different "classes" based on any number of attributes. Each class is then assigned a "treatment," which governs what a claimant or interest holder in such class will receive in exchange for its claim or interest under the plan.

In this regard, it is important to understand that under bankruptcy and non-bankruptcy law, a certain "priority scheme" exists which determines the order in which various non-debtor parties are to be paid by the debtor. For purposes of this priority scheme, claims and interests are separated into a number of categories, generally including secured claims, unsecured claims (including varieties of priority and general unsecured claims), and equity interests; in addition, each of these categories may be subordinated to other claims or interests.

Each of these broad categories merits additional explanation. Starting with secured claims, in the context of bankruptcy, because a security interest is a property interest protected by the due process clause of the United States Constitution, claimants are entitled to value to the extent they maintain a valid and properly-perfected security interest in the debtor's property (that is, the creditor's collateral). To the extent the collateral is insufficient to cover the secured claim, or where senior secured claims consume the value of the collateral prior to junior unsecured claims being paid, the "undersecured" portion of a secured claim is rendered an unsecured claim (also known as a "deficiency claim") pursuant to Section 506(a) of the Bankruptcy Code.

Unsecured claims stand behind secured claims (or to be technically accurate, are paid from unencumbered assets after secured creditors receive payment from their collateral as described above). Unsecured claims have certain priorities of payment among themselves—in bankruptcy, "priority" unsecured claims are paid (to the extent of their priority) before "general" unsecured claims, and priority claims have their own pecking order, with "administrative expenses" (the expenses of administering the bankruptcy estate, such as the professional fees of the debtor and official committees, and post-petition trade debt) being entitled to first payment, and certain other categories of claims (such as certain wages and taxes) being entitled to payment in the order dictated by Section 507 of the Bankruptcy Code.

Holders of equity and equity-type interests fall below all claims in the priority scheme.

One other concept is important in understanding the priority scheme— subordination. Any level of claim or interest may by contract (contractual subordination is generally enforced in bankruptcy) or by law. With regard to the latter, for example, are the rules of perfection of liens, as well as equitable subordination (generally subordination resulting from bad acts of the claimant), or, where authority permits, recharacterization of debt as equity (where equity is, in essence, disguised as debt).

With the understanding of how the various claims and interests are treated vis-à-vis each other under this priority scheme, the absolute priority rule itself must be defined. In essence, the absolute priority rule states that unless agreed otherwise or a claim is "disallowed" (i.e., not permitted by the bankruptcy court or operation of law based on procedural or substantive infirmities), no claimant or interest holder may receive or retain any property under a plan on behalf of its claim or interest unless all parties senior to it in the priority scheme are satisfied (the treatment required for such satisfaction depends on the type of claim in question).

Thus, after secured claims have been satisfied and unencumbered assets are identified, each respective category of priority claims must be paid prior to paying each subsequent category of priority, and all priority claims must be paid in full prior to paying general unsecured claims. And importantly (as it regards this discussion), equity interests are not entitled to retain or receive any consideration on behalf of such interests unless all debt claims are paid in full (typically, with interest). Thus, unless the debtor is solvent (assets exceed liabilities), equity and equity-type interests cannot receive any property, distribution, or opportunity on behalf of their existing interests.

There is a significant exception to the absolute priority rule, known as the "new value" exception. The new value exception provides that a holder of a junior claim or interest may receive rights or property (such as equity of the reorganized debtor) under a plan on account of a post-bankruptcy contribution of new value. However, such new value must be, among other things, in money or money's worth, and the distribution received in exchange must be on account of the new value contributed (rather than the prior claims or interests). Because the distribution (i.e., the new equity) received must be on account of the new value contributed rather than the old interests, this is a somewhat idiosyncratic principle, as the old equity is essentially worthless for purposes of the new value analysis. This exception is very difficult to satisfy and has been the subject of much litigation (particularly in single-asset real estate cases), including the decision in the case of *Bank of America, NT & SA v. 203 North LaSalle Street Partnership*, in which the United States Supreme Court, without passing on the validity of the new value exception (although such exception is widely accepted in the courts), essentially mandated market exposure as a condition of assessing the value of the consideration provided in exchange for new equity. As a result, retaining equity under a reorganization plan in Chapter 11 may require some form of market exposure of such interests (such as an auction), permitting other parties to the bankruptcy (or non-parties, for that matter) to bid. Of course, as a practical matter, existing equity holders will likely have more perfect information more efficiently than third parties; however, this does present a significant hurdle to retaining equity through a bankruptcy reorganization.

As a result, equity ownership subsequent to effecting of a reorganization plan of an insolvent company through a Chapter 11 bankruptcy case is based on variations on two basic scenarios: (1) equity interests are redistributed to parties other than their pre-bankruptcy owners; and/or (2) pre-bankruptcy owners of equity retain some or all of their equity interests based on a contribution of new value. It is important to understand this concept because the pre-bankruptcy owners of the company will no longer own the company subsequent to a restructuring via bankruptcy, absent the successful confirmation of a new value plan (over any challenges by other parties to the bankruptcy).

## Recognizing the "Client"

There is another important consideration in understanding the goal of the client—and that is, who exactly is the client? It is important to realize a fundamental tension in this regard—to represent a corporate debtor in bankruptcy (and pre-bankruptcy planning) is, in many ways, to represent a placeholder. The reason underlying this principle is that once a company enters the "zone of insolvency," the company (and, therefore, its officers and directors) owe a fiduciary duty to maximize the value of the company and its assets for creditors. Thus, while officers and directors of a healthy company generally owe a fiduciary duty to shareholders, once the company enters the zone of insolvency, this fiduciary duty expands or shifts to include the company's creditors. Accordingly, while there are many economic parties in interest to a restructuring, the debtor is bound by its fiduciary duties to creditors. As the corporate debtor is a fictitious entity borne of the law outside of bankruptcy (and controls a "bankruptcy estate" of the property, rights, and interests of the debtor within bankruptcy), this tension results in the individuals controlling the debtor, such as officer, directors, and (ultimately) equity holders, frequently having interests misaligned or contrary to the interests of the debtor itself. Each have their own self-interest directed at any numbers of factors (such as keeping the company in business, maintaining their positions or employment, protecting themselves as targets, or retaining their equity), and their exercise of direction is frequently shaded by these views. Thus, while outside a restructuring, fiduciary duty requires loyalty to constituencies, conflicts of interest tend to be exacerbated within a restructuring.

The role of retained professionals is also affected by this tension. Since the same principals control retention (and termination) of professionals, attorneys and other restructuring advisors are often placed in an uncomfortable position, with their duty to their client (the debtor) causing uneasiness in the advisors' relationship with the debtors' principals. Thus, retained professionals are somewhat habitually placed in the unenviable position of delivering unpalatable information and advice to those they take direction from. It can indeed be a tricky situation to educate those at whose behest one may be hired and fired of how they must sacrifice their own interests in order to fulfill their fiduciary duties to creditors. While somewhat pervasive in bankruptcy, this situation is particularly prevalent in companies where the management and ownership are common. I do not make any attempt in this essay to square the conflicting goals of equity owners in achieving a new value scenario; I simply reiterate the law with regard to fiduciary duties in the zone of insolvency, and note that this duty must be reconciled with any new value proposal. Very typically, the plight of the debtor's professionals is aided (though not eliminated) by the principal's retaining individual counsel (separate from company counsel).

## Thought Leadership

With the explanation of the fundamental tenets of the absolute priority rule and identification of the "client," I return to my point regarding properly assessing the goal to be achieved in a bankruptcy restructuring. One other point in this regard bears mentioning: earlier, I explained how transaction costs compel treating bankruptcy as a last resort in many situations. In addition to the hefty professional fees which are incurred in bankruptcy (not only does a debtor support its own array of professionals, but also is responsible for the fees of professionals retained by one or more official committees appointed in the bankruptcy case), non-ordinary course actions of the debtor (including, ultimately, all the elements of the plan of reorganization) require bankruptcy court approval, and hence, permit parties in interest an opportunity to object—causing additional hurdles in bankruptcy. Furthermore, parties have the ability to scrutinize transactions both prior to and during the bankruptcy, leaving the debtor's principals exposed as targets, even for "nuisance value." Thus, bankruptcy can be both cost-prohibitive and counterproductive to the client's goals.

For these reasons (among others), a foray into bankruptcy must be well thought out and alternate options exhausted. In fact, I believe that one common mistake of bankruptcy attorneys in assessing both restructuring strategy and their clients' goals is determining to precipitously file their clients into bankruptcy—a decision that may, in itself, be complicated by a bankruptcy attorney's own self-interest. This is not only due to the legal fees that a bankruptcy representation will generate, but is also because many restructuring attorneys measure their success by how many companies they have filed into bankruptcy. However, generally speaking, a good practitioner should count the "notches on their belt" by how many companies they have kept out of, rather than put in, bankruptcy. Of course, the general rule that a client's goals are best met by keeping the company out of bankruptcy is simply a general rule which may not be valid upon assessment of the client's goals, as certain operational or balance sheet restructurings require implementation through bankruptcy.

For example, there are legitimate strategic goals to be accomplished through bankruptcy, and it is in this regard that the full potency of the Bankruptcy Code as a restructuring tool may be measured. While succinctly detailing an appropriate resolution for every situation would be a formidable task (if even possible), one series of examples of using bankruptcy to achieve an assessed goal is the bankruptcy cases of asbestos manufacturers. In those cases, because the afflictions of those who suffered as a result of illness caused by asbestos exposure had not yet been discovered at the time of the bankruptcy filing, the pool of potential claimants could not be identified. However, it became apparent that companies that manufactured asbestos would be financially strangled by the existence of these claims. To free the companies of liability for claims asserted in the future, Chapter 11 plans were confirmed establishing trusts from which future claims would be ratably paid. It is in this manner that a company may be freed from the bonds of existing claims based on a past product defect.

Another example of creative application of the Bankruptcy Code to accomplish a client's goal is Zenith Electronics Corporation's "pre-packaged" bankruptcy. By way of explanation, a pre-packaged bankruptcy, or "pre-pack" as it is commonly referred to, is a bankruptcy in which acceptance of a plan is solicited prior to the bankruptcy filing. This differs significantly from other types of voluntary bankruptcy proceedings, such as "pre-arranged" bankruptcies (in which the terms of a proposed plan are negotiated with certain classes of constituents prior to the bankruptcy filing, but the actual solicitation is not conducted until after the bankruptcy filing) and "free fall" bankruptcies (in which the debtor has not determined its proposed exit from bankruptcy upon filing the bankruptcy). As an important side note, because solicitation of acceptances in pre-packaged bankruptcies are not protected by the safe-harbor provisions of Section 1125(e) of the Bankruptcy Code, the company thus has to comply with non-bankruptcy (i.e., securities) law, pre-packaged bankruptcies can be extremely expensive and are usually not cost-effective for all but sizeable companies. In addition, while a pre-packaged bankruptcy can greatly accelerate the bankruptcy process, if the bankruptcy court is not satisfied with the solicitation process, it may disapprove the solicitation and force it to be repeated.

In the Zenith case, the debtor was, at the time of the bankruptcy filing, a publicly-held company. However, the majority of Zenith's equity interests was owned by a single shareholder, LG Electronics. Furthermore, in addition to its majority equity share, LG also held substantial debt claims against Zenith.

A substantial dispute in the case involved valuation of a particular asset belonging to Zenith—as described in the disclosure statement accompanying Zenith's proposed reorganization plan:

> The Company has developed the vestigial sideband ("*VSB*") digital transmission system adopted by the

Federal Communications Commission as part of the Advanced Television Systems Committee ("*ATSC*") digital television broadcast standard for terrestrial broadcasting. Any consumer product that receives an ATSC digital television signal will require the use of the Company's technology.

As a result, the official equity holders' committee appointed in the case argued that due to the future income stream payable on behalf of royalties for a component which would become essential in manufacturing all products receiving a digital television signal, the value of the Zenith's assets far exceeded its liabilities. The bankruptcy court, however, declined to adopt the valuation offered the equity committee (which I and a number of colleagues represented at a former firm), and accordingly confirmed Zenith's pre-packaged reorganization plan providing that all equity interests would be eliminated, including both LG's majority interests and the publicly-held minority interests. However, even though its old equity interests were eliminated, Zenith's new equity, under the plan, was distributed to LG on behalf of its debt claims. Thus, in essence, Zenith's single majority shareholder "squeezed out" Zenith's public minority shareholders and brought the company private through a bankruptcy vehicle. While this could not be accomplished under the Bankruptcy Code by exchanging LG's pre-bankruptcy equity interests for equity in the reorganized debtor, it was nevertheless accomplished within the confines of the priority scheme, by exchanging LG's debt for new equity.

Significantly, Zenith's lead bankruptcy counsel was James (Jamie) Sprayregen, who at the time chaired Kirkland & Ellis's restructuring practice. While I have been pitted against Mr. Sprayregen on behalf of clients, I believe he provides an excellent model of the successful bankruptcy attorney I described above. While he is no more perceived an academic than many other successful bankruptcy attorneys (and is fond of articulating that Kirkland rejected his initial application for an associate position), he is admired for his skill as a strategist, and is widely respected for bringing a great deal of credibility to Chicago bankruptcy practice. Perhaps indicative of his business acumen, Mr. Sprayregen later joined Goldman Sachs, trading his legal practice for one of business, and following a path that has become increasing popular for successful bankruptcy attorneys.

Without passing judgment on the fairness or propriety of the results obtained in either the asbestos or Zenith cases, a lawyer is by nature an advocate, and both of these situations are innovative examples of how practitioners used the Bankruptcy Code as a creative tool to accomplish their clients' objectives (whether such objectives are appropriate or not). Indeed, these examples evidence that bankruptcy may be one of the best kept secrets for attaining corporate objectives.

*Harley J. Goldstein is an equity partner at Bell, Boyd & Lloyd LLP, where he chairs the Bankruptcy and Restructuring Department. He represents secured creditors, unsecured creditors, debtors, committees, trustees, and equity security holders in all transactional and litigation aspects of bankruptcy cases. He also represents lenders and borrowers in out-of-court operational and financial restructuring matters and has represented various clients with respect to debtor-in-possession financing and cash collateral agreements, sales of assets in bankruptcy, reorganization plan structuring and confirmations, multinational insolvency proceedings, motions for relief from the automatic stay, dischargeability litigation, and fraudulent conveyance and preference litigation, as well as other issues. Prior to practicing, Mr. Goldstein served as law clerk to the Honorable Erwin I. Katz, U.S. Bankruptcy Judge for the Northern District of Illinois. Mr. Goldstein, who has been noted for his skill as counsel in some of the nation's highest profile corporate insolvency proceedings, was profiled at the age of thirty-two as one of 40 Illinois Attorneys Under 40 to Watch by the Law Bulletin Publishing Company (publisher of* Chicago Daily Law Bulletin *and* Chicago Lawyer*), in which he was praised for his creative application of the Bankruptcy Code to accomplish his clients' goals. In addition, he has been named as a Rising Star in the* Illinois Super Lawyers *magazine, from the publishers of* Law & Politics *and* Chicago *magazine.*

***Dedication:*** *I dedicate this chapter to my first mentor in bankruptcy, The Honorable Erwin I. Katz, U.S. Bankruptcy Judge (retired), who, at the commencement of my term as his law clerk, inquired whether I knew the difference between two chapters of the Bankruptcy Code—which, at the time, I did not.*

# Factors in Seeking Bankruptcy Relief

## Robert Kugler

*Shareholder*

Leonard, Street and Deinard

ASPATORE

## Introduction: Insolvency and Distress

It comes as no surprise that the recent economic downturn correlates with an increasing number of companies experiencing distress and insolvency. Just as it does for individuals facing insurmountable debt, bankruptcy relief provides a "safety valve" for businesses that have overextended themselves. Bankruptcy relief should never be sought lightly, and good counsel, no matter their point of view, will advise distressed clients that relief under the Bankruptcy Code is never an "easy out." Nevertheless, bankruptcy is a powerful feature of the commercial landscape in this country. Article I, § 8 of the U.S. Constitution gives Congress the power to make bankruptcy laws and the prevailing policy rationale for bankruptcy is optimistic—by allowing for the possibility of bankruptcy, the Bankruptcy Code both encourages business and (usually) provides creditors the right to some partial recovery which, while unpopular, is better than nothing at all.

Most business bankruptcies are governed by Chapters 7 and 11 of the Bankruptcy Code; these chapters govern liquidation and reorganization, respectively. *See* 11 U.S.C. § 701 *et seq.*; 11 U.S.C. § 1101 *et seq.* Not all distressed businesses seek relief under the Code, however. In some instances, a business considering bankruptcy may stop short of actually filing a petition for relief and embrace an out-of-court restructuring option, often termed a "workout." This chapter will discuss these strategies, as they affect both debtors and creditors, and will highlight important factors to be considered by decision makers in their dealings with businesses facing insolvency. This chapter, however, is by no means exhaustive and creditors and debtors alike should seek the advice of counsel to determine the best course of action in the face of insolvency or an insolvent business partner.

## Restructuring Strategies

Before filing for bankruptcy relief, or undertaking a private workout plan, a distressed company should carefully assess its position to determine whether its situation is truly dire or can be remedied by strategic repositioning and/or reduction of expenses, and, if the latter, which restructuring strategy is most appropriate.

It goes without saying that a company should pinpoint, to the extent it is able, the source of its distress. Have revenues fallen? Have expenses increased unexpectedly? Is cash flow insufficient? Is one particular business unit hemorrhaging capital? Is the company carrying too much debt? Is the company's market position not what it was forecasted to be? Is there suspicion of fraud, embezzlement, or other internal malfeasance? Depending on the size of the company, this analysis may be performed by its own internal finance and accounting teams or the company may want to bring in a turnaround professional to conduct these analyses. Particularly where malfeasance is suspected, however, it may be worthwhile for a distressed company to hire forensic accountants or other experts to find the leak. There is no "one-size-fits-all" analysis and the questions above are meant merely as examples. The appropriate scope of any given company's self-audit can only be determined on a case-by-case basis, but to the extent that such an analysis may help a company identify its own weakness, it is almost always worthwhile.

Once a company has determined that some sort of restructuring is necessary, the question becomes to file or not to file? If, for example, a distressed company has strong, long-standing relationships with its creditors and believes that it can satisfy its debts with only minor renegotiations of its terms of credit, a private workout between the parties is feasible and may well be the best and cheapest strategy for all involved. If, on the other hand, the company does not anticipate being able to pay its creditors in full and the creditors are anonymous vendors to whom the debtor's ongoing viability is unimportant, the creditors may be less amenable to the workout route and relief under the Bankruptcy Code may be the appropriate route for the distressed company. Here again, while there are no hard-and-fast guidelines, a distressed company is well advised to determine, for each creditor, the strength of the relationship, the likelihood that the creditor will continue to do business with the company during and after the restructuring process, the relative importance of the company's account to the creditor, and the likelihood that the creditor will be willing to negotiate terms more favorable to the debtor. Here, as throughout the bankruptcy process, the advice of experienced counsel is critical.

## Bankruptcy Relief

Once a distressed company has determined that relief under the Bankruptcy Code is its best option, it should consult counsel to determine whether it is positioned to be able to emerge from a Chapter 11 reorganization as a going concern, or whether a liquidation under Chapter 7 is the most appropriate way to wind down its business and address creditors' claims.

All bankruptcy cases under the Code are brought in United States Bankruptcy Courts, in the U.S. Bankruptcy Court for the judicial district in which the debtor (1) is incorporated/domiciled; (2) in the case of an individual, resides; (3) has its principal place of business (in the United States); or (4) maintains its principal assets in the United States. Bankruptcy cases are presided over by bankruptcy judges, but debtors and creditors also need to understand the important role trustees play. There are several types of trustees, but most relevant for our purposes are the U.S Trustee and "case" trustees. The U.S. Trustee, along with the Court, oversees the administration of bankruptcy cases, and supervises the private case trustees that are appointed to administer the bankruptcy estate in Chapter 7, and in some situations Chapter 11 cases.

The concept of "discharge" is central to bankruptcy court actions—indeed, discharge is the defining characteristic of a bankruptcy case. The discharge is the court order that releases the debtor from liability for certain debts. In a Chapter 7 case, the discharge is usually granted upon expiration of certain deadlines. It is typically interrupted only if a party timely files a complaint objecting to the discharge or a motion to dismiss the case for abuse of the bankruptcy process. Unlike an individual Chapter 7 debtor, however, a business Chapter 7 debtor does not receive a discharge. This makes sense— once all of a business debtor's assets are liquidated, the business ceases to exist and is judgment proof. In a Chapter 11 reorganization, the discharge occurs upon confirmation of the Chapter 11 plan, discussed in more detail below. The discharge is a permanent order directed at creditors and informing them that they may no longer take collection action on discharged debts.

## Chapter 7 – Liquidation

Chapter 7, as noted above, provides for the liquidation of the debtor's non-exempt assets. Most Chapter 7 petitions are filed by individuals seeking a discharge of their debts and a "clean slate." Although the Bankruptcy Abuse Prevention and Consumer Protection Act of 2005 (BAPCPA) made it significantly harder for individual debtors to obtain a discharge, Chapter 7 offers business debtors a relatively convenient mechanism by which to liquidate assets and wind up their business.

While the majority of business bankruptcies are Chapter 11 reorganizations, there are situations in which a debtor may find liquidation under Chapter 7 to be the more attractive option, even where the company has some assets. For example, if a distressed company has assets and significant tax debt, a Chapter 7 liquidation ensures that the IRS is paid before other creditors. Alternately, a debtor's relationships with its creditors, whether strong or acrimonious, may dictate that it is preferable for a third-party trustee to administer the liquidation and distribution of assets. Finally, a debtor may determine that the odds against its future success upon emergence from a Chapter 11 reorganization are simply too great, and that the relative expediency of liquidation is its best option. Retail businesses with inventory and unsecured assets are often candidates for Chapter 7 liquidations. Debtors should be careful, however, where the company's principals have personally guaranteed debt as, in such cases, the business debtor's Chapter 7 filing may result in the principal's own individual Chapter 7 filing.

*Process and Procedure*

As compared to Chapter 11, Chapter 7 is relatively quick and inexpensive for the debtor. The debtor must file a petition, schedules, and a statement of financial affairs. All of the debtor's non-exempt assets become property of the bankruptcy estate. (Again, because the corporate Chapter 7 debtor will cease to exist, there are no exempt assets (e.g., a homestead) comparable to those in an individual Chapter 7 case.)

The bankruptcy action commences with the filing of the petition for relief. Fed. R. Bankr. P. 1002. In addition to the petition, the debtor must file (1) a schedule of assets and liabilities; (2) a schedule of the debtor's current income and expenditures; (2) a schedule of executory contracts (contracts under which neither party has fully performed) and unexpired leases; and (4) a statement of financial affairs. Fed. R. Bankr. P. 1007(b). Debtors must also provide the case trustee with copies of its recent tax returns. If the debtor is a corporation, it must also file a corporate ownership statement. Fed. R. Bankr. P. 1007(a). Ideally, these documents should be filed with the petition, but under the Rules of Bankruptcy Procedure, the debtor must file them within fifteen days. Contemporaneously with the petition, the debtor must file a list of the names and addresses of all creditors, holders of executory contracts and unexpired leases, and co-debtors. (This ensures that the court can give proper notice to all interested parties of events and filings in the bankruptcy proceeding.) The petition and schedules must be prepared as prescribed by the Official Forms, available online at http://www.uscourts.gov/bkforms/bankruptcy_forms.html. Finally, the debtor must also pay the requisite filing fees to the Court, in accordance with 28 U.S.C. Section 1930.

*The Automatic Stay*

In both Chapter 7 and Chapter 11, the filing of the petition for relief operates as the order for relief. This has several consequences, one of which is the attachment of the automatic stay. 11 U.S.C. § 362 (2006). The stay requires all creditors to immediately cease collection efforts. As a practical matter, in a Chapter 7 the stay gives debtors and case trustees "breathing room" to organize the assets and prepare for an orderly liquidation. Although, at first blush, the stay seems detrimental to creditors, in actuality the stay preserves the estate for the benefit of all creditors. The somewhat extraordinary scope of the automatic stay renders the bankruptcy process subject to abuse. Faced with imminent foreclosure, a debtor may seek bankruptcy relief just to buy time. In passing BAPCPA, Congress attempted to address such abuses and limited the circumstances under which the automatic stay would attach to debtors with a history of seeking bankruptcy relief.

Because the automatic stay attaches immediately upon filing, creditors need to be particularly careful in their dealings with business partners who they know or believe to on the brink of bankruptcy. Whether a creditor knows about the bankruptcy or not, any acts in violation of the stay are void. The

Bankruptcy Code, moreover, provides that a debtor injured by a willful violation of the stay *shall* recover damages incurred by the violation, including costs and attorneys' fees and, in some instances, punitive damages. 11 U.S.C. §362(k). Creditors should be especially conscious of any automated communications that it may send to defaulting debtors. Creditors should also be aware of the scope of the stay; they are barred not only from foreclosing and repossessing, but also from obtaining, perfecting, and enforcing liens, and from setting off debts owed the debtor. That is, once the automatic stay is in place, the creditor cannot subtract the debtor's debt from monies the creditor may owe the debtor. (In some instances, however, the creditor may be able to place a "hold" on such monies. Counsel can advise parties of the applicability of the stay in a given situation.) Generally, the stay is terminated when the bankruptcy case is closed. As to particular property, the stay remains in place until the property ceases to be property of the estate, i.e., until it is sold or abandoned. 11 U.S.C. §362(c).

Creditors are not completely helpless in the face of the automatic stay. Upon request of a "party in interest," the court may grant relief from the automatic stay. 11 U.S.C. §362(d). The court will grant relief "for cause," and the relief granted can be termination, annulment, modification, or conditioning of the stay. Secured creditors often move for relief from the stay on grounds of it is not "adequately protected." For example, if the debtor owes the creditor $100,000 but the property securing the debt is worth only $50,000, the creditor is not adequately protected and the court may lift or modify the stay as to that creditor. A creditor can also obtain relief from the stay if it can show that it has an interest in certain property of the debtor, that the debtor has no equity in the property, and that the property is not necessary to an effective reorganization of the debtor.

### The Section 341 Meeting and Trustees

The Rules of Bankruptcy Procedure order that a meeting of the debtors' creditors be convened between twenty and forty days after the order for relief (the filing date of the Petition). Dubbed the "341 Meeting" (after the Code section that requires it), this meeting is usually the first official event of the bankruptcy. During this meeting, the creditors will have the opportunity to elect a case trustee. Trustees are often lawyers or accountants. The trustee, in turn, is the major actor in a Chapter 7 liquidation, and is charged with the duties of collecting the property of the estate and reducing it to cash for distribution to the creditors, subject to certain priorities. Under the Bankruptcy Code, different classes of creditors are accorded different "priorities" and receive distributions from the estate according to that order. Generally, secured creditors (creditors that have a security interest in property of the debtor) receive distributions first, then administrative creditors, followed by unsecured creditors, and finally, equity holders. Under the Code, the trustee has many tools available to maximize the value of the estate; she can, for example, use, sell, or lease property of the estate (11 U.S.C. § 363), obtain credit (§ 364), and assume or reject executory (incomplete on both sides) contracts and unexpired leases (§ 365).

The trustee is also responsible for investigating the financial affairs of the debtor and, where proper, can oppose the discharge of the debtor. The trustee must act to protect the rights and interests of creditors, and therefore has the power to bring actions the debtor could have brought outside the bankruptcy context. Once the trustee has maximized the cash value of the estate and distributed it to the creditors, the matter is closed.

*Property of the Estate*

Obviously, because a primary role of the trustee is to gather and distribute the property of the estate, debtors and interested creditors must understand what exactly is considered property of the estate. Section 541 of the Bankruptcy Code provides that the property of the estate includes "all legal or equitable interests of the debtor in property as of the commencement of the [bankruptcy] case." 11 U.S.C. § 541(a)(1) (2007). This includes intangible assets, as well, such as account receivables, legal causes of action, intellectual property, a company's goodwill. Section 541 also contemplates the inclusion of "proceeds, profits, offspring, rents, or profits of or from property of the estate." 11 U.S.C. § 541(a)(6). Whole chapters could be devoted to the myriad complexities surrounding what is and what is not considered property of the estate for § 541 purposes, e.g., tax liabilities and deductions, assignment of rents and property held in trusts. Here again, assistance of skilled counsel is crucial.

*Administration, Liquidation and Distribution*

Section 363 of the Bankruptcy Code provides that the trustee, after notice and a hearing, "may use, sell, or lease" property of the estate. It is rare in Chapter 7 business bankruptcies for a trustee to "use" the property of the estate to maintain the business as a going concern but, in some instances where limited continuation of the business (through the holiday shopping season, for example) will benefit creditors, the trustee may do so. As will be discussed further, use of the property of the bankruptcy estate is far more common in Chapter 11 reorganization because (1) the debtor's goal is to emerge from Chapter 11 as a going concern, and (2) the debtor itself is often allowed to act as trustee in Chapter 11 reorganizations and is therefore often able to carry on the business with minimal disruption during the bankruptcy.

In Chapter 7 bankruptcies, the sale of estate assets pursuant to § 363 is often the single major event in the bankruptcy proceeding. Under the Bankruptcy Rules, twenty days' notice of a § 363 sale must be given to creditors and certain other parties. *See* Fed. R. Bankr. P. 2002. The sale may be public or conducted as a private auction. Because the trustee's aim is to maximize the value of the estate, there is incentive for the trustee to invest some effort into ensuring that the sale or auction attracts buyers or bidders and that there is enough interest generated that the buyers will have to bid competitively for the assets. Often, a trustee will bring in an investment banker or similar professional with expertise in identifying interested buyers. Depending on the scope of the sale and the value of the assets, the trustee may seek to have the court establish bidding procedures. Upon completion of the sale, the trustee, or auctioneer in the case of an auction, must file with the Bankruptcy Court an itemized statement listing each item sold, the sale price, and the purchaser. Fed. R. Bankr. P. 6004. Once the court has confirmed that the sale was valid, the trustee distributes the cash to creditors, in accordance with the scheme of priorities discussed above, and closes the case.

## Chapter 11 – Reorganization

The burst housing bubble, escalating fuel prices, and the general downturn in the economy have all contributed to Chapter 11 filings across a variety of industries. Industries that depend on discretionary consumer spending have seen a number of recent filings, e.g., Linens 'n' Things, The Sharper Image, Steve and Barry's. Similarly, homebuilders and home construction companies have struggled as have several airlines, e.g., ATA and Frontier. Finally, the subprime mortgage crisis has threatened the viability of some financial service providers.

Most corporate debtors opt to seek bankruptcy relief under Chapter 11 of the Code because it allows them a chance to "come out the other side" as a going concern. Still, as compared to Chapter 7, Chapter 11 is a complicated and involved process for both debtors and creditors. As in Chapter 7, the automatic stay attaches immediately upon filing.

Again, the primary advantage of Chapter 11 reorganization is that it allows a struggling debtor a bit of breathing room although the focus here is to use that breathing room to negotiate its obligations to creditors and to assess its best strategies going forward. For creditors too, Chapter 11 can be preferable to Chapter 7, as creditors have some incentive to negotiate with the debtor in order to preserve a future profitable relationship with the debtor.

Up through the Section 341 meeting, a Chapter 11 case is very similar to a Chapter 7 case. The debtor commences the case by filing the Petition and required schedules, just as in Chapter 7. (As will be discussed in a moment, however, there are a number of additional "first-day" issues facing a Chapter 11 debtor.) Again, the automatic stay attaches immediately upon filing, and the property set forth in Section 541 becomes the property of the bankruptcy estate. And, just as in Chapter 7, a Section 341 meeting is called. This section will explore some of the main differences between liquidations and reorganizations, namely the use and extent of first-day orders, the formation and role of the creditors' committee and, most importantly, the proposal, confirmation, and execution of the Chapter 11 plan.

*First-Day Orders*

Because the point of a reorganization is that it allows the debtor business to continue operations, there are a number of "first-day orders" that need to be entered to ensure the effective administration of the bankruptcy proceeding and the interrupted flow of the debtor's business operations. These orders can be administrative or substantive in nature. For example, the debtor will want to ensure that an order is in place authorizing it to employ and pay its counsel. In a complex or very large case, a debtor may seek an extension of time to file the required schedules of debts and lists of creditors. If two or more cases are related, the debtors may seek joint administration of their cases (under one case number, presided over by one Bankruptcy Court judge). Still other first-day orders may establish procedures for giving notice to creditors of events in the bankruptcy, and paying for essential employees, suppliers, and utilities. In some instances, debtors bring motions for the use of "cash collateral"[1] (discussed below) right away. Here again, the number and types of first-day orders will depend on the nature and needs of the debtor's business(es) and the particular facts of the case. Experienced debtor's counsel will work with a debtor to grasp what order needs to be in place when the bankruptcy petition is filed and will, in many instances, provide draft "first-day" motions to the U.S. Trustee prior to the filing so as to iron out any potential issues in advance of the first-day motions hearing.

## Chapter 11 First Meeting of Creditors

Again, up through the 341 meeting, the Chapter 11 process is similar to the Chapter 7 process. However, unlike in Chapter 7 cases, in Chapter 11s, the debtor itself—called a "Debtor-in-Possession," or DIP—usually acts as the trustee does in a Chapter 7.

---

[1] "Cash collateral," mentioned above, is an important term in bankruptcy. The Bankruptcy Code defines that term to mean "cash, negotiable instruments, documents of title, securities, deposit accounts, or other cash equivalents." 11 U.S.C. § 363(a). Section 363(c)(2) governs the use, sale, or lease of "cash collateral." Cash collateral can also include rents on real estate that is part of the bankruptcy estate. Because these assets are part of the bankruptcy estate, the trustee must get consent from any entity that has an interest in the cash collateral, i.e. a lender or mortgagee. After notice, an interested entity can object to the debtor's use of cash collateral and if, after a hearing on the matter, the Court "shall prohibit or condition such use, sale, or lease as is necessary to provide adequate protection of such interest." 11 U.S.C. §363(e).

*Creditors' Committee*

The creditors also decide whether to form a creditors' committee to monitor the case and, where necessary, challenge actions of the DIP. This may be done at or before the 341 meeting. The Creditors' Committee is appointed by the U.S. Trustee with oversight of the case, and usually comprises the creditors with the seven largest unsecured claims against the estate. *See* 11 U.S.C. § 1102 (2008). The powers and duties of creditors' committees are set forth by § 1103, and include the power to employ counsel, investigate the "acts, conduct, assets, liabilities, and financial condition of the debtor," as well as the ongoing viability of the debtor's business. The creditors' committee is also charged with sharing information with creditors who are not represented on the committee and soliciting comments from those members in relation to the committee's participation in formulation of the Chapter 11 plan, discussed in more detail below.

*Trustee/DIP Duties in a Chapter 11 Case*

Like a Chapter 7 trustee, a Chapter 11 DIP is charged with certain duties. Because the business operations are ongoing, the DIP is often the debtor, cloaked with the additional duties and powers of a trustee. In very large or very complex cases, however, or where creditors have managed to force out the management that let the company become insolvent, the DIP may be an appointed "turnaround" professional—a specialist who has expertise in managing and reorganizing Chapter 11 debtors.

There are several important differences between the duties and powers of a Chapter 7 trustee, and a Chapter 11 DIP, however. For example, a DIP is not required to investigate itself, but it is also not empowered to compensate itself. *See* 11 U.S.C. § 1107 (2008). Finally, a trustee may be appointed in a Chapter 11 case if, after a motion and hearing, the court determines that there is cause to do so. 11 U.S.C. § 1104 (2008). "Cause" is defined to include "fraud, dishonesty, incompetence, or gross mismanagement" by the DIP. Under BAPCPA, furthermore, the U.S. Trustee is required to move for the appointment of a trustee if there are indications that any of the debtor's directors or managers have participated in actual fraud, dishonesty, or criminal conduct in the course of the debtor's financial reporting activities.

## The Chapter 11 Plan

Perhaps the most important element of the Chapter 11 reorganization process is the formulation, confirmation, and ultimate execution of the debtor's plan for reorganization (the Plan). In that the Plan ultimately controls the creditors' recovery (remember that, in a Chapter 11, the discharge attaches upon confirmation of the Plan), the Plan is in some ways a corollary to the Section 363 liquidation sale in a Chapter 7 case. The filing, contents, acceptance, and confirmation of Plans are governed by 11 U.S.C. §§ 1121-1129. Plans themselves can be hundreds of pages long. This section will highlight some of the most important rules and procedures related to the Plan.

### *Proposal*

In a Chapter 11 case, during the first 120 days after the debtor files its petition, the DIP has the exclusive right to propose a plan of reorganization, subject to certain requirements set forth in the Code. *See* 11 U.S.C. § 1121(b) (2008). The court may extend this period up to eighteen months, but after the period of exclusivity expires, any party with an interest may submit a plan.

### *Contents of Plan; Classification of Claims; Disclosure Statement*

The Plan will define different classes of creditors and, usually, different levels of treatment for each class. 11 U.S.C. § 1122 (2008). After filing the Plan, the DIP must prepare a disclosure statement that explains the implications of the Plan to the various classes that will have to vote on it. Fed. R. Bankr. P. 3016. The court must then approve the disclosure statement.

### *Acceptance by Creditors; Confirmation by Court*

Once the disclosure statement is approved by the court, the Plan must be accepted by the various classes of creditors. 11 U.S.C. § 1126 (2008). Acceptance can be by majority vote (majority of shares, not shareholders), or constructive if the particular class is "unimpaired," meaning that, under the proposed Plan, the claims of that class are not discounted or restructured. If, for example, a class of creditors will have their loans reinstated on the original terms with all defaults cured, that class will be considered "unimpaired." *See* 11 U.S.C. § 1124 (2008). If the creditors representing a significant majority of the value of the claims vote for the plan, the DIP then asks the Court to approve, or "confirm" the plan, which the Court will do only after satisfying itself that the Plan meets the requirements of 11 U.S.C. Section 1129(a). This Code section sets forth sixteen requirements a Plan must meet in order to be confirmed, including, for example:

- That the plan was proposed in good faith
- That each impaired class has accepted the plan or that the members of that class will recover under the Plan an amount not less than they would have received in a Chapter 7 liquidation
- That the Plan provides for the cash payment of administrative expense claims and other specified pre-bankruptcy claims
- That confirmation of the Plan is not likely to be followed by the liquidation or further reorganization of the debtor, unless set forth in the Plan
- That all transfers of property made pursuant to the Plan are made in accordance with any applicable non-bankruptcy law

*Discharge*

If the Plan meets with creditor acceptance and Court approval, the Court will confirm the plan and the discharge will occur. Again, in a Chapter 11, the discharge operates as an order that the creditors can no longer pursue collection actions against the debtor. Intuitively, this makes sense; the creditors have, by this point, voted to accept the plan.[2]

Once confirmed, the plan is executed according to its terms. Where appropriate, the DIP can also act to maximize the value of the estate by

---

[2] Certainly, in some instances, creditors or classes of creditors may be dissatisfied with their treatment as proposed by the Plan and vote against it. Where the DIP seeks to obtain confirmation of its plan over the objection of a class of creditors, it is called a "cramdown." Generally, a plan will not be crammed down unless it is deemed by the court to be "fair and equitable."

assuming or rejecting unexpired leases and executory contracts, and can bring actions to recover payments made to creditors during the ninety-day "preference period" prior to the bankruptcy filing.

*Preference Actions*

Creditors should be particularly attuned to their preference exposure. Under 11 U.S.C. § 547(b), the trustee/DIP can "avoid" (that is, recover from the creditor for inclusion in the bankruptcy estate) any transfer of a interest of the debtor in property that meets five criteria: that the payment (1) was made to or for the benefit of a creditor; (2) was made on account of a prior debt owed by the debtor before the transfer was made; (3) was made while the debtor was insolvent; (4) was made on or within ninety days before the date the debtor filed its petition for bankruptcy relief (or even up to a year earlier, if the creditor had a close, "insider" relationship with the debtor); and (5) enabled the creditor to receive more than it would have under a Chapter 7 liquidation. Creditors have several available defenses, however, that will in, some instances, allow them to retain payments made during the preference period. For example, payments that were made "in the ordinary course of business" are not avoidable by the trustee/DIP. The term "ordinary course of business" has a particular meaning under the code and counsel can determine whether a given payment is likely to fall into that category. Similarly, if the creditor shipped new goods to the debtor because of the payment, the payment may not be avoidable by the trustee/DIP. Here again, counsel will determine if any of these or other affirmative defenses are applicable to preference actions brought against a creditor.

## Out-of-Court Restructuring Options

It should not be forgotten that bankruptcy relief, whether under Chapter 7 or 11, is meant to be an avenue of last resort for a struggling business—a "safety valve." Prior to filing a petition, debtors should seek pre-filing counsel and determine if formal bankruptcy relief is their only option, or whether a non-bankruptcy alternative is feasible. Where, for example, the debtor has been driven to its current state by identifiable mismanagement and waste, a temporary receivership (where a third party takes over the entity, for a fee, in an attempt to "turn it around") may placate creditors and allow the debtor to avoid bankruptcy.

Similarly, where the debtor and its creditor are able to agree on a reduction of the debtor's debt or different terms more favorable to the debtor, such a private out-of-court workout may prove advantageous to all involved. Obviously, the relationship(s) between the parties, the magnitude of the debt, the nature of the business, and the future prospects of the particular debtor make the feasibility of an out-of-court workout case-specific.

## Best Practices for Law Firms Handling Restructuring Strategies

The law firms best equipped to handle bankruptcy strategies and restructuring are those that have a comprehensive understanding of their clients' businesses, be they creditors or debtors. Of course, in-depth understanding and experience in bankruptcy litigation and workouts is also critical, but clients are best served by counsel who understands the "big picture" insofar as the bankruptcy or workout in question will affect its employees, partners, profits, reputation, and viability going forward.

It goes without saying that professionalism and pragmatism are imperative in reaching the best and most cost-effective solutions for our clients. As to the handling of each particular case, most are staffed with a shareholder with significant experience in the bankruptcy and restructuring arena, and with one or more associates from a law firm's bankruptcy, creditors' remedies, and/or banking practice groups.

With respect to creditor representation, it is very helpful to often counsel clients whose business counsel knows well. It is important that counsel understands the history of the relationship between the client and the debtor; the nature of that relationship, and whether there have been any prior problems getting paid by the debtor; the existence (or lack thereof) of documents memorializing the parties' relationship; and the appetite of the client for extensive litigation versus prompt resolution.

At our firm, our most valuable resources are our fellow attorneys, both within our bankruptcy practice and throughout the other practice areas in the firm. That is, our colleagues in other practice areas lend their expertise to help us more fully comprehend our clients' businesses and interests and therefore inform our advice, analysis, and strategy. Colleagues in our employment and labor law, tax, and products liability groups, to name just a few examples, can often provide valuable counsel in connection with ongoing bankruptcy proceedings.

In addition, we often work with individuals in a client company's finance, accounting, and operations groups to get an understanding of the company's business practices, especially as they relate to the shipment of goods and the processing of payments. Of course, in-house counsel is usually involved to some degree as well. Finally, whether they are C-level executives or not, the individuals who personally deal with the debtor's representatives can provide critical insight into the matter.

## Meeting Challenges

As explained above, each of the primary strategies—liquidation, reorganization, and out-of-court workout—have advantages and disadvantages for each party. Chapter 7 liquidations are the least "challenging" in a traditional sense because they rarely involve extensive attorney involvement. A complicated Chapter 11 case, conversely, is challenging in that there are a number of moving parts that often seem to work at cross-purposes—that is, the debtor and creditor often have conflicting goals: the debtor's chief concern is the maintenance of the business as a going concern, whereas that concern, to the creditors, is secondary to the recovery of their claims against the estate. A debtor's ability to negotiate with creditors will depend heavily upon its capacity for turnaround and the likelihood that it will be able to satisfy its debts going forward.

As in any litigation or transaction, it is critical that counsel have as comprehensive an understanding as possible of the client's position and interests. As often as not, there is a human element to the bankruptcy story, and to the extent that the client has not kept its word or has been (or feels it has been) personally betrayed, reconciling such animosities with a sound legal analysis can be challenging from both a strategic and client-relations perspective. One secondary role of bankruptcy attorneys is that, in some instances, counsel can act as a buffer between the debtor and creditor, allowing the parties to reach equitable and fair results without undue personal attacks or animosity.

## Key Documents

The legal documents produced in a restructuring, on both the debtor and creditor side, are voluminous. Some of the documents—the Petition, Schedules, and Proofs of Claim—are prepared using standardized forms. Beyond these, a bankruptcy case proceeds in large part by notice and motion. Plans and disclosure statements, as mentioned above, can be very involved and are, obviously, tailored to the creditors and classes of creditors in a particular case.

On the debtor side, the debtor has significant involvement in preparing the initial petition and the schedules of assets and liabilities, lists of creditors, and the statement of financial affairs and, with the creditors' committee, the Plan. These documents are generally prepared by counsel, with factual input from the client. Similarly, on the creditor side, the creditor will have significant involvement in the preparation of a proof of claim documenting its claim against the estate, but here again, counsel will then prepare the necessary pleadings and correspondence. Both creditors and debtors can expect that their counsel will require access to their accounting and financial records. Debtors' counsel will likely be interested in the debtors' historical financial reporting records; creditor's counsel, obviously, will inquire into its clients' documentation and records of transactions with the debtor.

## Restructuring Negotiation

Restructuring is, by definition, a series of negotiations between the debtor and its creditors. Generally, in a Chapter 11 or sizable workout, the negotiations will take place between counsel for the parties.

The major obstacles and pitfalls in any restructuring negotiation are that the bankruptcy estate is finite, and the secured and unsecured creditors and administrative and priority lien holders are owed, in aggregate, an amount that is larger than the estate. Otherwise, there would be no bankruptcy.

## Achieving Post-Bankruptcy Success

For our creditor clients, it is important that they feel secure in their relationship with the debtor post-bankruptcy. To the extent they have likely suffered some loss and had to pay attorneys' fees, they do not want to "get burned" again. In the context of a reorganization where the creditor will have an ongoing relationship with the ex-debtor, it is important that they feel they can protect themselves—be it by payment on delivery, or taking a security interest in goods sold to the debtor.

Restructuring, in or out of court, does not lend itself to quantitative analysis or benchmarking. The best measure of a strategy is whether the parties walked away from the process with an equitable result—i.e., that the creditors were not irreparably damaged by the debtor's insolvency or near-insolvency, and that the debtor is able to emerge from the process as a going concern with a profitable future.

*Robert Kugler is an experienced business and commercial litigator, with an emphasis on bankruptcy litigation. Mr. Kugler provides counsel to creditors, shareholders, trustees and committees in all matters relating to bankruptcy protection and litigation. He also serves as the principal litigator in complex commercial litigation disputes representing lessors, lendors, financial services providers, manufacturers and retailers. These matters range from SEC investigations to intellectual property disputes to the defense of class actions.*

*Among his notable cases, Mr. Kugler represents the liquidating trustee of Delaware-based Fruehauf Trailer Corporation in a variety of matters including fiduciary, intellectual property, and bankruptcy litigation and has acted as litigation counsel to the Equity Committee in the Cone Mills bankruptcy case. He also serves as litigation counsel for Alliant Techsystems in numerous commercial matters and serves as lease enforcement counsel for U.S. Bancorp Equipment Finance.*

*Mr. Kugler has served as an adjunct bankruptcy professor at Hamline University and has regularly provided pro bono legal services through the Volunteer Lawyers Network and the Children's Law Center of Minnesota. He began his legal career as a law clerk to the Honorable Dennis O'Brien of the U.S. Bankruptcy Court for the District of Minnesota. Prior to joining Leonard, Street and Deinard, he was a partner at the firm of Robins, Kaplan, Miller & Ciresi in Minneapolis.*

*Mr. Kugler was former chair of the Minnesota Supreme Court Board of Legal Certification. He is a member of the Minnesota State Bar Association, Bankruptcy Section, the American Bar Association, the American Bankruptcy Institute, the Federal*

Bar Association, the Commercial Law League of America, the Equipment Leasing Association, the Turnaround Management Association, the National Association of Bankruptcy Trustees, the London Courts of International Arbitration, and the State of Pennsylvania and District of Columbia Bar Associations.

Mr. Kugler received his J.D. from William Mitchell College of Law and his B.A. from Gustavus Adolphus College. He is admitted to practice before the U.S. District Court for the District of Minnesota, the U.S. District Court for the Northern District of California, the U.S. District Court for the Western District of Wisconsin, and the U.S. Courts of Appeals for the Eighth Circuit.

# The Development and Implementation of Restructuring Strategies for Secured Creditors

Raniero D'Aversa Jr.

*Partner and Co-Chair, Restructuring, Bankruptcy and Insolvency Group*

Mayer Brown LLP

ASPATORE

## Things Secured Creditors Should Consider When Developing a Strategy

Secured creditors face difficult decisions and challenges when a borrower becomes distressed and cannot perform under its loan agreement. Unlike the company's general unsecured creditors, the secured creditor's liens on the company's property give it legal vested interest in that property. Careful consideration should be given to the collateral—this interest must be safeguarded and protected through this period of distress in order for the lender to reap the benefit of being secured. Thus, much like the mother whose baby's fate was laid in the hands of King Solomon, an "all-or-nothing" strategy can do a secured creditor more harm than good—a secured creditor typically should not put all of its collateral at risk in executing such an approach.

Clearly, a creditor's legal position and relative leverage vis-à-vis the borrower and other creditors is a major consideration that will influence strategy. Secured creditors often approach a restructuring scenario from a relatively strong position. The secured creditor's liens will give it a front seat at the negotiating table. The secured creditor has a higher legal priority than general unsecured creditors, and thus will typically exert more control over the borrower and the restructuring process.

Another factor that will affect a lender's strategy is the borrower's behavior. Does the borrower acknowledge the situation and the need for a workout, or is the borrower inflicted with a case of "distress denial?" Companies face the prospect of having to go through a restructuring for many diverse reasons and the common factor is always distress. A company that may be suffering through some pains and misfortunes cannot begin to enter into a workout with its lender and to formulate a restructuring strategy until the cause of this distress can be identified and acknowledged.

Another item that must be considered before formulating the strategy is that although restructuring strategies are often ground in the law (i.e., bankruptcy law), the strategies are usually a combination of legal and commercial strategies. In that regard, a successful restructuring practitioner has to essentially be part general practitioner, and part businessperson. For example, a company may be in distress because of competitive pressure, labor problems, regulatory issues and so forth, and bankruptcy will not be a solution to any of those problems. The company will continue to have those problems in bankruptcy. So in essence, what bankruptcy does is allow you to deal with those problems in certain ways that you otherwise could not have done outside of bankruptcy. Whether you can heal an ailing company is often not an exercise in legal analysis, as the answer often requires some creative big picture thinking to incorporate micro and macro economic and commercial issues together with legal issues.

One last thing the lender should keep in mind when developing the strategy is that rarely can a single creditor (even a secured creditor) effectuate a restructuring without dealing with the borrower and/or other creditor classes. These interactions are often, by their nature, adversarial. Nevertheless, it is important to remember that the borrower and other creditors may actually be on your side of the table in some respects. By this, I mean that despite the adverse nature of a restructuring, debtors and creditors often share some common goals and thus may have common strategies. For example, a common goal shared by all parties in a restructuring is the desire to maximize value, albeit parties may differ greatly as to the methods to maximize the value. To the extent that goals overlap among the different parties, common ground can be found to reach a consensual restructuring among the parties.

### Five Essential Steps to Developing a Restructuring Strategy

**(i). Identify the Warning Signs.** The first basic step used to developing the restructuring strategy requires that one initially take a step back, as you first need to identify the warning signals that a restructuring is imminent. It is a best practice for lenders to monitor their loans for signs of distress and the warning signs arise from numerous sources. One source in particular is macroeconomic indicators. Historically, we have seen industry-wide distress caused by macroeconomic factors beyond the control of an individual borrower. These factors include technological advances/obsolescence of markets, political instability in regions where business operates, negative interest and exchange rate fluctuations, changing commodity pricing, and finally labor and employment issues.

Micro-level indicators of a restructuring phase, on the other hand, include enduring the loss of market share, having poor quality controls, a quickening concentration of customers and vendors, lawsuits for product liability, and disrepair of facilities.

Financial or managerial indicators of a restructuring are also plentiful, and include cash flow shortfalls, defaults on covenants or payment provisions; failure to timely deliver reports; an increases in payables, receivables or inventory levels; decreased profit margins; and finally changes in management or auditors. When these indicators are present, a secured creditor should be concerned that poor performance may lead to dissipation of cash and other assets of the company. While there may be valid reasons that these financial indicators have been tripped, it is important to identify these items and to see if they expose larger issues.

**(ii). Diligence the File.** The second major step in evaluating a restructuring strategy requires due diligence of the file. Conducting a thorough diligence of the loan file is extremely important to lenders for several reasons. First, it gives a workout loan officer and counsels an overview of the history of the relationship, including whether there is a history of prior distress. Second, it allows you to identify any weaknesses in the loan documentation and/or collateral perfection. Third, it allows you to determine what your leverage is.

The typical loan diligence includes that one follow the cash, so to speak, and be certain that they understand the debtor's cash collection and management system. Diligence also entails that one has installed proper safeguards to avoid "leakage."

The diligence process must include a review of the loan file, including all reports delivered to the lender or prepared by the lender's loan officers. In addition, it is necessary for a discussion with the loan officers to occur, so as to obtain information on the loan administration history and determine if there have been any oral discussions or agreements between the parties. The discussion will also determine if the lender's actions may have created a possible "waiver" argument (i.e., the lender de facto waived a default as a result of certain actions).

A thorough review of the loan documentation requires that one analyze whether the borrower is in default and what remedies may the lender take. This may also be an opportune time to educate loan officers on the risks of lender liability. Lender liability generally occurs when a lender commits an egregious act in connection with its administration of the loan, and harmed the borrower as a result of its conduct. The typical lender liability allegation involves a lender that improperly refuses to advance money or takes substantive remedial enforcement actions in the absence of a properly noticed material default by the borrower. Because of the contractual rights afforded to secured creditors under standard loan and collateral documentation, restructurings tend to be fertile breeding grounds for lender liability accusations.

The diligence process is also the time to determine whether you have signed originals of all of the documents, and whether there are any errors or omissions in the documents, or unfavorably negotiations positions. By this, I refer to both (i) unintentional gaps or mistakes in the loan and collateral documentation and perfection, and (ii) material concessions given to the borrower in the loan and collateral documentation during the negotiation of the loan. For example, a borrower may have negotiated to exclude some assets from the collateral granted for the loan. These are items that may be amended as part of the restructuring.

A review of the collateral is one of the most important diligence elements for a secured creditor. It is extremely important to determine whether the security interests have been properly perfected. This will typically require an analysis of the accuracy of the perfection instruments as well as a search of the debtor's filings. It should also be determined whether the debtor has other secured creditors with interests in your collateral or whether the borrower has any assets that are outside the scope of the security interest granted under the loan documents. If there are any considerations with respect to foreclosing on the collateral, one must ask what the level of difficulty is to foreclose. Some assets (such as accounts receivables and pledged bank accounts) are more amendable to foreclosure because it can be conducted without court intervention. Other "hard" collateral poses additional challenges because access may be blocked. A lender cannot "disturb the peace" when repossessing collateral, and so court intervention may be required. You must also question whether there is a market for this collateral. Is the collateral valuable on a stand-alone basis, or is it more valuable as part of a going-concern? The answers to these questions will ultimately impact any remarketing efforts. Lastly, you should consider the quality and condition of the collateral. It is important to get an inspection of the collateral and any recent appraisal of the collateral as well.

It is important to review any third party guarantees or sureties and to prepare appropriate notices. If the borrower is in default, the lender should send a notice of default and Reservation of Rights. Care should be given to make sure that all procedures are followed, as provisions specifying method of service and parties entitled to notice must be strictly followed.

**(iii). Set Your Objectives.** The third major step maintains that you set clear objectives. A lender's objectives in the workout will depend on several factors, and the degree of leverage a lender has over the borrower will help craft these objectives. Leverage can be affected by several factors, including the issue of the lender in default. Obviously, a lender has more leverage over a borrower that is in default because the default usually opens the door to remedial action. Not all defaults are the same, as generally, lenders are advised that they can take more aggressive remedies only where defaults are material, rather than technical. For example, a lender is less likely to be scrutinized (or accused of lender liability) for accelerating a loan after a payment default rather than because a report was not timely delivered.

Does the borrower need something from the lender, such as a waiver of a default, consent to do an act that is prohibited under the agreement, additional loans or other financial accommodations? These are examples of significant questions that must be asked in order to assess the relative leverage of the parties.

The relationship between lender and borrower will also be an essential consideration in setting objectives. This process can be categorized by another series of hypothetical questions. Do you value this customer and are inclined to rehabilitate the customer? Are you willing to lend this company additional money in order to keep it as a going concern if this is the case? Do you want to exit the relationship and move on, and what are realistic options for maximizing collateral value?

It should also be determined if the lender can use this opportunity to enhance its position, or find out if there are holes in the documents or lien perfection that can be fixed. If the lender can obtain additional collateral or third party guarantees, can they also determine if the lender can increase control over the business, perhaps by compelling business plan changes, managerial changes, divestitures or asset sales.

**(iv). Develop the Restructuring Strategy.**  Once the file is diligenced and the objectives are set, the next step is for the lender to determine its goals and implement a restructuring strategy to achieve those objectives. Although restructurings tend to be unique and often unpredictable situations, and often require novel approaches and strategies, there are tried and tested restructuring strategies that lenders avail themselves of. Furthermore, a lender may employ a dual-track approach if, for example, it pursues enforcement remedies to effectuate a liquidation while negotiating a restructuring of an agreement. It may also choose to apply a multi-strategy approach. For example, the strategy may be to continue certain profitable operations as going concerns while liquidating undesirables operations. In almost every case, these strategies can be achieved through an out-of-court restructuring (whether by enforcement action or through some arrangement among the company and its major creditor constituencies), through a bankruptcy, or through a combination of both. The following is a non-exhaustive list of typical lender strategies:

**1. Reorganization or Rehabilitation.** This is where a lender wants to continue the relationship with the borrower because it has continued faith in the company or there is no better alternative. Here, the strategy decision may be to "fix" the cause of distress and keep the company as a going concern through a reorganization or rehabilitation. Oftentimes, a lender may be able to enhance its position in the context of reorganization, such as to obtain additional collateral or third-party guaranties. Likewise, fixing the distress may require additional commitments from the lender in the form of additional loans to the borrower. Implicit in the reorganization/rehabilitation process is the lender's comfort with management. An essential element of a reorganization or rehabilitation is assuring that the company has the support of all of its creditor classes. The company will need to focus on its business and attempts by unhappy creditors to collect against the company will disrupt those efforts. If there is no way to effectively quiet those creditors in an out-of-court scenario, the company can obtain a breathing spell by filing bankruptcy and obtaining the benefits of the automatic stay.

**2. Recapitalization/Debt for Equity Exchange.** This is where a lender forgives debt in exchange for an equity stake in the company. This is often a good fix for a company that is fundamentally sound but has too much debt. The secured creditor's goal under this strategy is to trim the fat off the balance sheet by reducing the debt to a level that the company can timely service given its current and projected financial condition. The result is that the lender will have a performing (albeit smaller) loan plus stock in the company. This strategy is not a favorite of all secured creditors. Traditional bank lenders do not often favor this strategy because (i) it requires that debt be written off as uncollectible, and (ii) they are generally not in the business of owning all or part of their borrowers. This strategy is thus more attractive where the secured lenders are non-typical lenders, i.e., hedge funds or private equity funds that are more accustomed to taking equity positions and, in fact, rely on equity-like returns on their investments. This strategy is also effective where there are multiple layers of debt. For example, if a company has secured debt held by bank lenders and unsecured bonds, a recapitalization can result in a conversion of only the unsecured bonds to equity while preserving the secured debt for the bank lenders. This is a win-win result for the secured lenders because the company has a healthier de-leveraged balance sheet and the full amount of the secured debt is preserved.

**3. Refinance/Debt Sale.** This is where the company raises new debt to take the existing lenders out. Beauty is in the eye of the beholder—and what looks like an "exit" scenario for one group of lenders, can often be an attractive deal to a different set of lenders. This was especially true several years ago when the refinance market was extremely hot and many troubled companies were able to refinance rather than restructure their defaulted debt. But a refinance requires the willingness of the company to find a new lender. If the company is unwilling, lenders have the option of selling their loans to a secondary buyer of debt (typically a hedge or private equity fund). This is commonly referred to as loan trading. The loan trading market has expanded exponentially over the last fifteen years, particularly with respect to underperforming or "distressed" debt. In fact, it is now common for bank lenders to sell their loans to secondary buyers upon learning of a borrower's distress. This strategy is often employed where the secured lender values a quick exit, perhaps because the lender believes that the company's value will continue to decrease and that the current trading price for the debt exceeds the likely ultimate recovery in a restructuring.

**4. Going Concern Sale.** This occurs where the maximum value for the lenders is to keep the business alive as a going concern, but there is no appetite for the existing lenders to continue the relationship. Likewise, there are no refinance alternatives available to the company. There are many reasons why a company is worth more in the hands of another operator. Often, third parties have better strategic, financial or managerial platforms and resources that will enhance the value of the going concern. Ideally, the amount this strategic or financial buyer will pay for the company as a going concern is greater than any value that can be achieved through implementation of an alternative restructuring strategy. It is important to point out that a secured creditor cannot, by itself, sell a company as a going concern. The sale requires approval by the company's board of directors, and often requires retaining an investment banker to market the company. The sale of the company is often initially resisted by a borrower—especially in situations where it is obvious that management will be replaced. A company will pursue many alternative strategies before pursuing a going concern sale. In my experience, the company will proceed to a going concern sale only after a combination of persistent leverage by secured creditors and the failure of the company to propose a feasible alternative strategy. The sale itself can be structured as either an asset sale or a sale of stock in the company. The asset sale is the most prevalent form of going concern sale because, if structured properly, only the assets and none of the liabilities will be transferred to the buyer. While these transactions can be consummated outside of bankruptcy court, the bankruptcy setting has clear benefits (such as the ability to transfer assets free and clear of liens, and the ability to assign contracts without consent) not available outside of bankruptcy.

**5. Liquidation/Asset Sale.** A liquidation sale is where the borrower's assets are sold piece meal, typically at an auction on an "as-is" basis. This is usually the last resort because it yields the lowest prices because of the perceived leverage—the seller often places a premium on speed and is not likely to spend a great amount of time negotiating price. Furthermore, from a buyer's perspective, because these assets are typically sold "as-is" with no warranties, a buyer will often apply a discount to offset this increased risk of defect. Lastly, unlike in a going concern sale where an investment banker is retained to market the assets, liquidation sales are usually done with minimal notice and advertising, there is minimal opportunity to inspect or diligence the assets, and the seller or sales agent often does not have significant additional information (such as product manuals, inspection or maintenance reports) that buyers typically request. These sales are often done through secured lender foreclosure sale or through a Chapter 7 bankruptcy liquidation. As one would suspect, this strategy is employed where the ultimate goal is to terminate the lending relationship at any cost.

**(v) Set a Timetable.** The fifth and final step is to commit to a timetable. A borrower that is in default will typically ask the lender for a standstill or forbearance agreement, during which time the lender agrees not to take remedial enforcement action while the parties are negotiating or implementing a strategy. It is important for lenders to establish the agenda for this standstill period. In doing so, they must create a timetable with achievable deadlines and adhere to it. If they are not met, the lenders must be prepared to act. It is important to remain vigilant to be certain that the company's financial condition and collateral values do not deteriorate during this period. Any standstill agreement should contain milestones to track progress, should keep the lender abreast of progress by requiring adequate reporting from the company, and should provide for reasonable access and inspection to the company's operation's and the lender's collateral.

## The Importance of Building Creditor Consensus

The biggest challenge for a company trying to implement a restructuring strategy is obtaining support from creditor constituencies. Creditor support is essential because virtually every exit strategy, whether in court or out of court, requires the support of some (and sometimes all) of the company's credit constituencies. For example, loan agreements often contain restrictions on a company's ability to undertake certain acts, such as asset sales and mergers. A company will need to obtain requisite lender approval to modify those loan covenants if, for example, an asset sale or merger is part of the restructuring strategy. Likewise, in bankruptcy, a debtor needs at least half in number and two-thirds in dollar amount of a class of creditors to support a plan of reorganization in order for it to be approved.

It is also important to start the dialogue among the different creditor classes. The restructuring process is a forced collaboration among parties whose only common element is an interest in a financially distressed company. The company, secured lenders, bond holders, and trade creditors are compelled to sit at the negotiating table to undertake a process that they hope will result in a successful restructuring from their perspective. From a company's perspective, it is very important to gain a consensus among creditor constituencies early in the process. The line of communications must be open so that one can identify the creditor constituencies. For loan facilities that are syndicated to multiple lenders, it is typically the administrative agent that is entitled to receive notices under the loan documents. This administrative agent will typically coordinate all communications to and from the lender group. Bondholders are not as easy to identify. Although an indenture trustee acts on behalf of all bondholders, it is typical for lenders to form ad hoc groups to coordinate among the larger bondholders. For trade creditors, it may be a trade association or one or more of your bigger vendors that will act as a representative.

The most difficult restructuring negotiations are those that are commenced hastily after an adverse event. Creditors should be notified well in advance of any default, negative prospect or other adverse situation, as they do not want to be surprised. At a minimum, it looks poorly upon the relationship manager that is responsible for monitoring the loan with this borrower. Note that securities laws may restrict the dissemination of material non-public information and that any disclosure must obviously be made in compliance with those provisions.

## A Few Tips for Effective Creditor Communication

A distressed borrower should designate an officer or retain a chief restructuring officer to be the liaison for the creditor group. Companies should expect creditors to want substantially more information and require additional reports, meetings and other materials once a company becomes distressed. Typically, existing management is not capable of handling these increased burdens, so it is important for the company to demonstrate that it has a handle on the situation and that creditors will not suffer any continued erosion in position while negotiating. Some companies make the mistake of underestimating the effect that distress (no matter how small) may have on a debtor/creditor relationship. You cannot be in denial about the reality. It is equally important to retain experienced restructuring professionals, such as attorneys, restructuring consultants, and turnaround managers, maybe even investment bankers. Show that you have a plan, or are working towards a realistic plan and have up-to-date financial information available to creditors. Finally, you will want to prepare business plans and cash flow projection to give creditors comfort that value will not dissipate while negotiating a restructuring. Ideally, news of an impending default or other adverse condition should be accompanied with a business plan, supported by financials, that addresses and remedies the situation.

## Essential Secured Creditor Documents During the Restructuring

There are six major legal documents generated during the negotiation and implementation of the strategy. Listed below are these six documents, with consideration given to their preparers and their overall significant to executing the strategy.

1. *The Notice of Default and Reservation of Rights/Acceleration of Debt.* It is important to give a borrower notice of any default or potential default under a borrowing facility because defaults will give rise to various enforcement rights. If the lender does not intend to immediately exercise rights, the notice will typically include a reservation of all rights relating to the default. If the lender is looking to exercise rights, the notice should include an acceleration of debt and demand for repayment. Careful scrutiny must be given to the terms of the credit agreement. Often certain events become a default only after notice is given and the borrower has had an opportunity to cure the condition. Other events of default happen automatically and do not require any notice. In the context of a loan that is syndicated to a group of lenders, it is important to determine if an agent may declare a default unilaterally or requires direction from some consortium of lenders.

2. *The Pre-Workout letter.* At the outset of any negotiations, a pre-workout letter is an inducement to the lender to enter into negotiations. The main purposes are for the borrower to (i) acknowledge that defaults have occurred, (ii) agree in advance that any discussions with the lender are non-binding and will not constitute a waiver or amendment unless in writing, and (iii) acknowledge all of lender's rights are reserved. Lenders often seek additional acknowledgments, such as (i) that the borrower is indebted to the lender with no counterclaim or offset and (ii) all of lender's legal fees will be paid.

3. *Forbearance or Standstill Agreement.* This agreement allows parties a standstill from enforcement by the lender while the parties negotiate. Often, the lender will negotiate for certain benefits in exchange for the standstill. These may include: mandatory principal payments and increased fees and interest during the standstill period; enhanced reporting and auditing rights. It is often possible to negotiate milestones to "incentivize" the borrower. For example, standstill periods can be extended if certain financial milestones are achieved during the period. Conversely, the standstill can be terminated if certain milestones are not met or other bad acts occur, such as additional defaults or actions by third parties that have a material adverse impact on the company.

4. *Waivers and Consents.* If a deal is struck, or as part of a bigger strategy, it may make sense for a lender to waiver a default or consent to an action that is prohibited under the credit documents. This should be approached cautiously because lenders may be irrevocably giving up legal rights to take action based on defaults.

5. *Amendments.* The objective of the amendment is to embody the restructure with the result being a performing loan. In that regard, the amendment will include, for example, (i) changes to the economics (pricing, term, amount); (ii) cures of any deficiencies in the original documents, (iii) credit enhancements, (iv) documentary enhancements, such as increased covenants and protection of collateral; and (v) acknowledgments of amounts due to lender and waiver and release of any claims against lender. The release of claims is especially important to lenders because of the risk of lender liability (previously discussed).

6. *Lockup Agreement.* Loans that are syndicated to multiple lenders raise additional issues with respect to amendment approvals. While amendments to most credit agreement terms require approval by holders of a majority of the loans, there are certain so-called "sacred rights" that can only be amended with the approval by all of the lenders. These terms include any reductions in the amount of debt, changes in interest rates or fees, releases of material portions of collateral, and release of any guarantors. It is very important to consider the objectives and strategies of each lender if a restructuring contemplates an amendment of any sacred right. With increased levels of debt trading, it is becoming increasingly more difficult to find complete consensus within a lender group and to effectuate a restructuring in light of the ever-changing composition of lender groups. If unanimity within the lender group cannot be achieved, it is possible to effect such an amendment in a bankruptcy process where the approval levels are lower. A whole class of creditors accepts a reorganization plan if accepted by the holders of at least two-thirds in amount and a majority in number of creditors that voted on the plan. Thus, it is typical to file a bankruptcy to consummate a restructuring plan that has less than full lender approval. Of course, before filing bankruptcy, the company will want adequate assurances that the lenders will in fact vote to accept the plan. Parties will often enter into voting and lockup agreements where the requisite number of lenders agrees in advance to support the negotiated plan. Furthermore, to avoid the negative impact brought about by a change in lender composition as a result of debt trading, this agreement will be binding on any subsequent assignees of the lenders.

## Key Questions to Ask when Preserving Collateral

The preservation of collateral value is of paramount importance to lenders in discussing security and asset issues for bankruptcy restructuring strategies, as the value of that collateral will be a determining factor in implementing a strategy. Top issues with respect to collateral include the following questions and considerations:

- Is the collateral package complete? Does the security interest cover all of the collateral? You need to make sure that the debtor has no other assets that can pledge (except, perhaps, certain undesirable assets, such as environmentally toxic land). It is best practice to periodically demand a "perfection certificate" that identifies all assets of the borrower and confirm that the lender has a perfected security interest in that collateral.

- Does you collateral cover all access and ancillary parts? For example, a lien on a single piece of equipment that comprises a larger mechanism or system is not likely to be very valuable on a stand-alone basis. Likewise, manufacturing equipment that can only operate with parts that are outside the scope of your security interest will lose value once disconnected from the system.

- Has the security been properly perfected? Not all assets are covered by a general UCC or mortgage. For example, certain items require physical possession (e.g., stock certificates) or control agreements (e.g., bank accounts). Furthermore, certain intangibles, such as commercial tort claims, must be explicitly pledged and will not fall under a blanket UCC.

- What is the practical affect of having a pledge of collateral? An important tool in the lender's arsenal is the threat of enforcement action. A lender must understand the full implications of commencing an action before even making the threat. For example, if collateral is not susceptible to non-judicial remedies, a borrower need not fear of a precipitous act by the lender to collect its collateral.

- What are the legal steps for an enforcement action? The first step is usually to repossess the collateral. This will depend on the type of collateral. Some collateral requires judicial action to repossess (e.g., equipment), while other can be "possessed' through notice (e.g., receivables). The actual foreclosure process will also depend on the type of collateral. While most collateral can be sold in a public or private foreclosure sale, certain collateral (such as real estate) requires court intervention. In determining the commercial implications of a foreclosure, it is important to remember that the ultimate goal in a foreclosure is to maximize value.

- Can the lender take possession of the assets if there are buyers for the assets? The public foreclosure process is typically an open auction. Often, a lender becomes the owner of the collateral by credit bidding its lien—in other words, if no third party bids as much as the amount of debt owed to the lender, the lender can become the winning bidder by bidding the debt owed to it. There are various regulatory limits on the type of assets that regulated banks may own. Although most statutes have exceptions for assets acquired in exchange for forgiveness of debt, care must be given to the regulatory implications.

- Do you have sufficient information and control over your collateral? Do you have inspection and audit rights; can you inspect the quality of inventory, or verify the validity of receivables? Is the collateral properly insured and is lender named as additional insured or loss beneficiary? These questions are great value in this process.

Ultimately, it's the value that matters most in developing a strategy. Often it is the value of the company that will determine which creditors are "in the money" or out, and will form the basis for distributions under a Chapter 11 plan. It is thus important to get an accurate appraisal of the collateral. Value should be scrutinized as a going concern as well as a liquidation to determine the proper strategy. The appraisal must be tailored to the purpose. For example, an "in-use-in-place" appraisal of a piece of equipment that is integrated into a larger system does not make sense if that equipment will not be sold as part of a going concern.

Collateral value plays an especially important role in bankruptcy. In bankruptcy, a secured lender is prohibited by the automatic stay from pursuing remedies against collateral. The doctrine of adequate protection, however, mandates status quo by entitling a secured lender to receive compensation for any erosion of the value of its collateral during the course of the case as a result of the stay, or as a result of the use of its collateral (including cash collateral). The right to obtain adequate protection in bankruptcy is an important secured creditor tool because a secured creditor is entitled to cash or replacement collateral (or both) if the collateral values decrease during the bankruptcy. A lender may be entitled to relief from the stay if, among other things, the debtor has no equity in the collateral (i.e., the lender is under-collateralized) and the collateral is not necessary for an effective reorganization. A lender is also entitled to post-petition interest and contractual fees and expenses to the extent the lender is over-collateralized.

## Closing Thoughts

While the early years of this century were characterized by dramatic changes in the underwriting standards for debt instruments and an unprecedented increase in the amount of asset-backed structured vehicles in the capital markets, we are currently in the midst of a substantial credit crunch and near illiquidity in many sectors of the capital markets. As a result, it is safe to assume that there will be a significant increase in restructurings and bankruptcies in the coming years. While we will see many of the same participants in this next wave of restructurings and employ many of the same strategies, we must realize that the nature of the relations among the various parties at the table will differ substantially from prior restructuring cycles. Financing structures are increasingly more complex, involve significant intercreditor issues, and often limit a lender's ability to act unilaterally. This will directly impact a lender's leverage over a borrower and other creditors. Likewise, the nature of collateral will have an increasingly bigger impact on restructuring strategies. Strategies for restructuring operating companies will not necessarily work for distressed portfolios of mortgage backed securities. With this in mind, I want to reemphasize that restructurings are unique and strategies must be developed based on the particular facts and circumstances of the scenario.

*Raniero D'Aversa Jr. is co-chair of the Restructuring, Bankruptcy and Insolvency group at Mayer Brown LLP, a leading global law firm with 1,800 attorneys in offices in key business centers across the Americas, Asia, and Europe. He resides in the New York office.*

*Mr. D'Aversa's practice is primarily a creditor and investor side practice. The majority of his clients are lenders to companies that are in distress. The typical engagement is the representation of an agent or arranger of a credit facility. For the most part, the loans were performing at the time made, but they've since encountered some turbulence. He also represents secondary buyers of distressed debt that are purchasing the debt after the company becomes distressed, and often at a discount. In either situation, the typical engagement involves a review and analysis of the documents, advice regarding potential solutions and the implementation of an exit strategy—either in court, out of court, and sometimes both.*

*Mr. D'Aversa's practice also includes the representation of distressed investors, or "white knights." These are buyers of distressed companies in a court-approved proceeding or out-of-court process. And in some circumstances, the lender (or some sub-group of lenders in a syndicated deal), is in fact the white knight.*

# Chapter 11 Bankruptcy Restructuring Strategies and Issues

Paul Kizel

*Director*

Kenneth A. Rosen

*Member*

Lowenstein Sandler PC

ASPATORE

## Filing a Chapter 11 Bankruptcy Case

The decision to file a Chapter 11 bankruptcy case typically occurs after the client and its restructuring counsel and other professional advisors have thoroughly explored non-bankruptcy restructuring alternatives and determined that a Chapter 11 proceeding is the best vehicle for maximizing the value of the client's business for all constituencies.[3] By filing a chapter 11 petition, all creditors (with certain limited exceptions) are automatically "stayed," by virtue of Section 362 (a) of the United States Bankruptcy Code (the Bankruptcy Code), from taking any actions to enforce claims against the company or assets of the company. *See Midlantic Nat'l Bank v. New Jersey Dep't of Environmental Protection, 474 U.S. 494, 503 (1986).* Similarly, upon the commencement of the Chapter 11 case, the company is precluded from making any payments to creditors because of claims that arose prior to the commencement date. The automatic stay is a fundamental feature of Chapter 11 because it, along with other provisions of the Bankruptcy Code, affords a troubled company the necessary time and protections to analyze its operations, develop a business plan, and execute a strategy to either restructure its debt or maximize its value through an orderly sale process. *See House Report No. 95-595*, 95th Cong., 1st Sess. 340-2 (1977); *Senate Report No. 95-989*, 95th Cong., 2d Sess. 49-51 (1978).

## Basic Restructuring Strategies

Although each Chapter 11 proceeding faces its own issues and challenges, there are three basic Chapter 11 restructuring strategies. The first is a classic "stand-alone" strategy where the company files its own plan of reorganization that provides for distributions to some or all of its creditor groups and shareholders. In a typical case, when a company files a Chapter 11 petition its capital structure consists of (1) secured debt owed to an institutional lender or group of lenders which debt is

---

[3] The board of directors of a financially healthy company owes a fiduciary duty of care and loyalty solely to shareholders. However, once a company becomes insolvent, the board owes a fiduciary duty to the corporation as a whole. *See Credit Lyonnaise Bank Nederland v. Pathe Communications Corp.*, 1991 Del. Ch. LEXIS 215 (Del. Ch. 1991). Therefore, during restructuring negotiations, directors of a troubled company should not take extraordinary operational or other risks that are designed to enhance value for the benefit of the company's shareholders if there is a reasonable likelihood that those risks can jeopardize the ability to maximize value for the benefit of creditors.

secured by a lien on all or substantially all of the company's assets; (2) unsecured bond debt owed to institutional lenders under one or more indentures; (3) unsecured trade debt; and (4) common stock of shareholders. Under the classic "stand-alone" plan, a company first utilizes the various tools made available by the Bankruptcy Code to identify and fix its operational problems. Perhaps the most powerful of these tools is the company's ability, pursuant to Section 365(a) of the Bankruptcy Code, to "assume" favorable contracts and leases and to "reject" unfavorable contracts and leases, including, but not limited to, real estate and equipment leases, employment agreements, and, under certain conditions, collective bargaining agreements. Through this process, the company can downsize its operations, exit unprofitable business lines, and otherwise reduce expenses. After addressing its operational issues the company then develops a business plan, including projections to demonstrate to its various creditor and shareholder constituencies what the restructured company will look like and how much income it expects to generate during the years immediately following the restructuring.

Because of the operational adjustments and the preparation of reliable and credible projections, the company will be in a position to determine its "enterprise" value and formulate its stand-alone plan of reorganization that provides for the restructuring and payment of its debt without the need for a cash infusion from new investors. Theoretically, the aggregate value of consideration to be distributed to creditors and equity holders under the stand-alone plan will equal the enterprise value of the company. In most cases, however, the company does not have sufficient funds on hand to pay the enterprise value in cash upon emergence from Chapter 11. Instead, assuming the enterprise value exceeds the amount of secured debt, the company's plan will typically provide for the payment in full of its secured debt in cash over a period of a few years, or payment in full in cash upon emergence from Chapter 11 through a refinancing with a new lender. The refinancing may also provide additional funds for the company's projected working capital needs and for the payment of cash to unsecured creditors. The balance of the enterprise value would typically be distributed to unsecured creditors in the form of a combination of cash, debt securities, and equity securities.[4]

The form of consideration to be allocated to creditors depends upon the ability of the company to generate cash and the desire of creditors to accept equity in the reorganized company in lieu of cash or notes. The more confident creditors are that the company will meet or exceed its projections, the more likely they will be to accept a larger piece of equity, in the hope that it will appreciate in value. Ultimately, the exact amount and form of consideration to be allocated will be the product of negotiations among the company and its major creditor constituencies.

A second common type of restructuring strategy is similar to the stand-alone plan in that it involves the company filing a plan that provides for the continuation of the business and the distribution of various forms of consideration (cash, debt securities, and equity securities) to stakeholders. However, under this modified stand-alone strategy, the company is forced to raise capital from investors in order to satisfy claims of certain pre-petition creditors (often those already involved in the company's capital structure). In exchange for their investment, the investors will receive a portion of the equity of the reorganized company and the company uses the proceeds of the investment to repay their pre-petition creditors. This strategy is most often utilized when the company's pre-petition creditors are reluctant to accept debt or equity securities and demand a large portion of their plan distribution in the form of cash.

The third basic type of Chapter 11 restructuring involves the sale of all or substantially all of the assets of the company pursuant to a "363 Sale." The term "363 Sale" refers to Section 363 (b) of the Bankruptcy Code. This section authorizes a company in Chapter 11 to sell assets, outside the

---

[4]   In most chapter 11 cases, the interests of common stockholders and other equity holders are cancelled and they do not receive any distributions because of their equity interests. The reason for this result is that under the Bankruptcy Code, ,equity holders are last in the payment priority scheme, and they are not entitled to eceive any distributions unless all creditor claims are paid in full (including interest). *See* 11 U.S.C. § 1129(b). Since in most cases the enterprise value of the distressed company is less than the aggregate amount of all creditor claims, creditors do not get paid in full and equity holders are left with worthless securities that are cancelled upon the company's emergence from Chapter 11.

ordinary course of business, subject to approval by the Bankruptcy Court, and after notice to creditors and other parties in interest. Although at one time there was a debate as to whether all or substantially all of the assets of a Chapter 11 debtor could be sold pursuant to Section 363(b) absent exigent circumstances (i.e., the value of the company's assets are rapidly deteriorating), courts have uniformly adopted a more flexible approach and have approved 363 Sales when the debtor is able to articulate a good business reason for allowing the sale, full disclosure has been made, and the assets have been appropriately marketed. *See In re Abbotts Dairies of Pennsylvania Inc.*, 788 F. 2d 143 (3rd Cir. 1986); *In re Continental Airlines Inc.*, 780 F. 2d 1223 (5th Cir. 1986); *Stephens Indus. Inc., v. McClung*, 789 F. 2d 386 (6th Cir. 1986); *In re Lionel Corp.*, 722 F. 2d 1063 (2d Cir. 1983).

After the sale is consummated, the company proposes a plan of liquidation that provides for the distribution of the sale proceeds to its creditors in accordance with the priority scheme embodied in the Bankruptcy Code. Although not technically a "restructuring," in recent years there has been a growing use of Chapter 11 to implement a sale strategy. Sometimes the sale strategy is in place at the time the company files its Chapter 11 case, and other times it is a strategy that develops during the Chapter 11 case after efforts to develop "pure" restructuring alternatives are not successful.

## The Restructuring Team

Regardless of which strategy is ultimately adopted, at the outset of a Chapter 11 restructuring and during the course of the case, bankruptcy counsel for a distressed company is likely to draw upon a wide range of legal resources to assist in the analysis, development, and implementation of a bankruptcy plan. Although the bankruptcy process is governed by the Bankruptcy Code, modern Chapter 11 cases more often that not involve a variety of environmental, labor, tax, corporate, real estate, securities, litigation, and other "non-bankruptcy" issues that are intertwined with, and may impact upon, the bankruptcy restructuring process.

For instance, in almost every Chapter 11 case, bankruptcy counsel will require the assistance of corporate counsel to provide advice regarding corporate governance issues and to draft appropriate corporate resolutions authorizing the Chapter 11 filing. Moreover, in public company cases, securities counsel will be required to assist with disclosure and reporting requirements.[5] Moreover, in the event a company employs a large unionized workforce, it is crucial that bankruptcy counsel and the client consult with labor counsel prior to the commencement of a Chapter 11 case to consider the interplay of labor and bankruptcy laws and obtain an understanding of how the company can utilize the provisions of the Bankruptcy Code to most effectively deal with short- and long-term wage and employee benefit costs that may place the company at a competitive disadvantage with others in its industry.[6]

Similarly, if a company owns or otherwise is responsible for liabilities associated with contaminated real estate, consultation with experienced environmental counsel is critical, at the earliest possible time, to ascertain the nature and extent of potential environmental claims. Bankruptcy counsel can then attempt to determine whether those environmental claims can be compromised and discharged through a Chapter 11 case or whether those claims must be satisfied in full. The treatment of environmental obligations in bankruptcy is a complex and unsettled area of the law. For example, in *U.S. v. Kovacs*, the Supreme Court ruled that a debtor's cleanup obligations were discharged in bankruptcy because the state had dispossessed the debtor of the contaminated land, thereby preventing him from performing the cleanup, and then sought money damages for his non-compliance. *See U.S. v. Kovacs*, 469 U.S. 274 (1985). Courts since have used *Kovacs* to justify decisions on both sides of the discharge issue. Compare *In re Torwico Elec. Inc.*, 8 F. 3d 146 (3rd Cir. 1993), where the United States Court of Appeals for the Third Circuit ruled that environmental obligations cannot be discharged in bankruptcy with *U.S. v. Whizco Inc.*, 841 F. 2d 147 (6th Cir. 1988), where the United States Court of Appeals for the Sixth Circuit held that such obligations are discharged to the extent that a debtor would have to spend money to satisfy the obligation. In light of such uncertainty, the assessment of environmental liabilities is an important issue that should be analyzed in the early stages of a Chapter 11 case.

---

[5] The filing of a chapter 11 case does not exempt a public company from complying with its disclosure and reporting requirement under the federal securities laws.

[6] Pursuant to sections 1113 and 1114 of the Bankruptcy Code, a Debtor has the ability, subject to Bankruptcy Court approval, to reject collective bargaining agreements, provided that certain stringent procedural and substantive requirements are satisfied.

During the Chapter 11 case, a company may decide to sell a portion of its assets. In order to effectively and efficiently handle the disposition of assets, bankruptcy counsel will work closely with his or her corporate colleagues to negotiate, structure, document, and close the transaction. Then, at the conclusion of the restructuring process, corporate and securities counsel may be necessary to guide the company through the process of issuing new debt and equity security instruments. These are but a few examples of the myriad issues that may need to be addressed both before and during a Chapter 11 case, and why it is important for a company in distress to retain a law firm that has both experienced bankruptcy counsel and other diversified practice area groups.

In addition to the legal team, the distressed company and its counsel typically interact and work closely with a host of other professional advisors during the period leading up to the bankruptcy filing through the emergence from the Chapter 11 process. In a typical case, the company will retain a financial advisor with expertise in working with troubled companies in bankruptcy. The role of the financial advisor is to assist the company in reviewing its operations, offer advice regarding potential operational improvements, assist in the preparation of financial projections, and interface with professionals retained by the major creditor constituencies in connection with the formulation of a Chapter 11 plan of reorganization.

In addition, in larger cases, a company in Chapter 11 often retains an investment banker. The investment banker's primary role is to explore strategic alternatives, including merger, financing, and sale opportunities. The investment banker also plays a key role in determining the enterprise value of the company and is instrumental in the company's efforts to allocate the enterprise value to the various creditor and equity constituencies.

Depending on the size and nature of the case, a company may also retain a crisis management firm that has experience in running the day-to-day operations of a Chapter 11 case. This most frequently occurs when the company's senior management team is perceived as weak by the key creditor constituencies. Indeed, as a condition of providing financing to a company in Chapter 11, secured lenders may condition the extension of credit upon the company's retention of a crisis manager acceptable to the lender.

Furthermore, a large publicly held company may also choose to retain a public relations firm to advise them about public relations concerns, including the preparation of appropriate press releases and establishing procedures to handle inquiries. The public relations firm would also be available to assist the company's human resources department in communicating with its employees regarding the bankruptcy process. In almost every case, effective communications with employees about the impact of the Chapter 11 process is crucial to preserve and enhance employee morale. Although a large company may have an in-house public relations department, the retention of a firm specializing in providing services to financially distressed businesses may be worthwhile.

## The Chapter 11 Process and the Role of the Bankruptcy Court

Unlike out of court workouts, the restructuring of a distressed company through a Chapter 11 proceeding involves extensive procedural requirements with virtually any major decision subject to approval by the Bankruptcy Court upon notice to the key constituency groups. The Chapter 11 process is commenced by the filing of a bankruptcy petition with the Bankruptcy Court. At that point, without any further action, the automatic stay is triggered and creditors, with limited exceptions, are precluded from taking any enforcement actions against the company or its assets. *See* 11 U.S.C. § 362 (2006).

Once the company files its Chapter 11 petition, it is authorized to engage in transactions in the "ordinary course of business." However, transactions that are not in the ordinary course of business require the approval of the Bankruptcy Court. *See* 11 U.S.C. § 363(b)(1) (2008). A transaction is in the "ordinary course of business" if it is consistent with the internal workings of the company, i.e., creditors would expect the company to enter into the transaction (vertical dimension), and is consistent with the company's industry standards (horizontal dimension). For instance, while the retention of a public relations firm may be in the ordinary course of business for one company, it may not be in the ordinary course for another. *See In re Johns Mansville Corp.*, 60 B.R. 612 (S.D.N.Y. 1986). When in doubt as to whether a transaction is in the ordinary course of business, the company should seek court approval.

Immediately upon the filing of the Chapter 11 petition, the company usually files a host of pleadings seeking various forms of emergent relief from the Bankruptcy Court. These pleadings are known as "first-day motions," and they are intended to provide a smooth transition into the Chapter 11 process and to allow for the uninterrupted continuation of the company's business operations.

Perhaps the most important first-day motion is the company's request to permit it to use "cash collateral" and to enter into a secured lending facility, frequently called "DIP financing," which will provide it with financing to operate its business during the Chapter 11 process.[7] The need to use cash collateral and to obtain DIP financing is obviously crucial because the company can only continue to operate if it has funds to pay for post-petition goods and services. Any interruption in its business at the outset of the case could have a material negative impact on operations and could permanently impair the company's ability to reorganize. The Bankruptcy Court usually conducts a hearing to consider the cash collateral and financing motion within one day after the Chapter 11 petition is filed and, provided that the company makes the appropriate factual showing, will approve the use of cash collateral and financing only in the amount as is necessary to avoid immediate and irreparable harm to the estate pending a final hearing. The final hearing is usually conducted within thirty to forty-five days after the initial hearing, although it is not unusual for several interim hearings to be conducted prior to the final hearing in order to allow the various parties in interest to analyze the proposed financing arrangements and to attempt to negotiate and settle any disputed issues.

Other typical first-day motions include motions by the company seeking court approval to retain professionals. As noted earlier, in addition to counsel, a company entering Chapter 11 often requires a host of

---

[7] "Cash collateral" is the cash generated from assets, such as accounts receivable, that are subject to a security interest of a pre-petition lender. The Bankruptcy Code prohibits the company from using cash generated from pre-petition collateral unless the secured creditor consents or the Bankruptcy Court approves its use after finding that certain requirements are satisfied. *See* 11 U.S.C. § 363.

professionals, including financial advisors, investment bankers, crisis managers, accountants, and a public relations firm. Under the Bankruptcy Code, all "professionals" retained by the company during the Chapter 11 case must be approved by an order of the Bankruptcy Court. *See generally* 11 U.S.C. § 327 (2008). This process requires the company's counsel to prepare numerous pleadings for each proposed professional. These pleadings outline the services to be performed, the proposed compensation, and any connections or relationships that each professional may have with the company's major creditors, equity holders, and other parties in interest. In addition to requiring Bankruptcy Court approval prior to retaining professionals, all fees and expenses paid to professionals retained by the company are subject to court approval. *See generally* 11 U.S.C. § 330 (2008). Moreover, creditors and other parties in interest have the opportunity to review and object to the fees and expenses.

It is also customary for a Chapter 11 company to file a First-Day Motion seeking authority to pay certain pre-petition obligations. As previously noted, upon the filing of a Chapter 11 petition, the company is precluded from paying obligations that accrued prior to the petition date. This includes payments to employees and all vendors. While a company may attempt to pay all employee wages prior to filing, this is not always possible given payroll cycles, and it is likely that many employees will not have cashed or deposited their checks prior to the filing of the Chapter 11 petition. Because the company has a strong interest in maintaining, as best as possible, the morale and dedication of its rank and file workforce, Bankruptcy Courts typically allow a company to satisfy pre-petition wages and related employee obligations up to certain limits. In addition to payroll obligations, a company in Chapter 11 sometimes attempts to obtain a first-day order to approve the payment of pre-petition obligations to certain "critical" vendors. Although the use of this practice has been reduced significantly in the last few years as a result of certain judicial decisions, such relief can still be obtained in certain jurisdictions if the company can provide sufficient proof that the goods or services supplied by a specific vendor are critical for the company's operations, cannot be obtained from another source, and the value to be obtained by the company exceeds the cost of making the payment. *See, e.g., In re Kmart Corp.*, 359 F. 3d 866 (7th Cir. 2004).

Having filed and obtained relief under its First-Day Motions, the company begins or continues the process of analyzing and adjusting its business operations. As discussed above, this often involves decisions to assume or reject executory contracts and leases. In order to effectively assume or reject a lease, the company must file a motion pursuant to Section 365(a) of the Bankruptcy Code and obtain the approval of the Bankruptcy Court. Similarly, if the company decides to exit a business it will require court approval because it is a transaction outside the ordinary course of business. Likewise, if the company wants to dispose of a significant amount of equipment and/or real estate which is no longer utilized by the company and which does not fit within the company's business plan, a motion to approve the sale must be filed and court approval must be obtained.

The final stage of a Chapter 11 proceeding also involves the preparation and filing of significant documents that require Bankruptcy Court approval. In particular, after the company develops its business plan and financial restructuring plan, it is required to prepare and file a plan of reorganization (or plan of liquidation) together with an accompanying disclosure statement. For the 120-day period following the filing of a petition, the debtor has the exclusive right to file a plan of reorganization. *See* 11 U.S.C. § 1121(b) (2008). The Bankruptcy Court is authorized to grant requests for extensions of this exclusive period for cause, but the extension may not extend beyond a date that is eighteen months after the Chapter 11 petition is filed. *See* 11 U.S.C. § 1121(d)(2)(A). An interested party may file a plan of reorganization if a trustee is appointed in the case, or if the debtor did not file a plan within the exclusivity period, or if the debtor did file a plan within the exclusivity period but the plan was not accepted by creditors and equity holders within 180 days of the petition filing. *See* 11 U.S.C. § 1121(c).

In general, the plan outlines in detail (often with numerous exhibits) how the claims and interests of creditors and equity holders will be treated and describes how the company will implement its business and restructuring plans. *See* 11 U.S.C. § 1123 (2008). Among other things, the disclosure statement summarizes the plan, and provides detailed information to creditors and equity holders concerning the history of the company; why the company filed for Chapter 11; what the company accomplished during the Chapter 11 process; and what it expects to achieve after emerging from Chapter 11. The disclosure statement will typically contain historical financial statements, projections of future financial performance, a valuation of the company, and a liquidation analysis that reflects the company's estimate of what creditors would receive in the event the assets of the company were liquidated and the net proceeds distributed to creditors. The fundamental purpose of the disclosure statement is to provide creditors with adequate information upon which they can rely when they are asked to vote in favor of the plan. *See* 11 U.S.C. § 1125 (2008). As noted below, the voting process occurs after the Bankruptcy Court approves the disclosure statement.

Once the plan and disclosure statement are filed, they are mailed to creditors and other parties in interest, and the Bankruptcy Court schedules a hearing to approve the adequacy of the disclosure statement. This hearing usually is scheduled thirty to forty-five days after it is filed (but no earlier than twenty-five days), and creditors have an opportunity to object to the adequacy of the disclosures. Shortly after the disclosure statement is approved, both the plan and disclosure statement are mailed, together with a form of ballot, to creditors and equity holders who are entitled to vote to accept or reject the plan. After the ballots are tabulated and creditors and other parties have an opportunity to object to the plan, the court conducts a "confirmation hearing" to determine whether the conditions for confirming the plan have been satisfied. *See* 11 U.S.C. § 1128 (2008). In most cases, the time between the approval of the disclosure statement and the scheduling of the confirmation hearing is approximately forty-five days, although the period could be as short as twenty-five days. Assuming the Bankruptcy Court confirms the plan (and no party files a timely appeal and obtains a stay pending appeal), the plan may become effective immediately upon the satisfaction of any conditions that may be contained in the plan.

## Bankruptcy Restructuring Negotiations

The primary parties to bankruptcy restructuring negotiations are the company's pre-petition and post-petition secured lenders and a creditors committee comprised of a group of the company's largest unsecured creditors that is selected by the Office of the United States Trustee. In addition, depending upon the size, nature, and financial condition of the company, unions and an equity committee (comprised of the largest equity holders as selected by the Office of the United States Trustee) may also be key participants in restructuring negotiations. All of these constituents are generally represented by professional advisers and the company is responsible for paying the fees and expenses of professionals retained by a creditors committee and equity committee. Moreover, it is not unusual for the company to pay the fees and expenses of the professionals retained by the secured lenders.

The negotiations generally revolve around two key areas. First, at the outset of the case, the creditors committee and, if one has been appointed, the equity committee attempt to negotiate more favorable terms with respect to the post-petition financing that the company has arranged with its secured lenders. These negotiations are often contentious but more often than not result in consensual orders approving the financing although on slightly revised terms. The next critical round of negotiations centers on the plan negotiations process. In particular, negotiations deal with the enterprise value of the company and the extent, form, and allocation of distribution to stakeholders. In cases where the company cannot fully repay the secured lenders in cash, the secured lenders will generally argue for a lower enterprise valuation (although high enough to allow it to receive payment in full) in an effort to persuade the company that it is entitled to receive the bulk of the debt or equity securities that are being issued under the reorganization plan. On the other hand, unsecured creditors and equity holders, relying on valuations prepared by their own financial advisers and/or investment bankers, will argue for a higher valuation thereby allowing them to receive a greater slice of the financial pie. As noted earlier, it is the rare case where equity is "in the money" but at times creditors will offer equity holders a de minimis recovery to avoid the expense and delay that accompany a contested confirmation process.

*Kenneth A. Rosen leads Lowenstein Sandler PC's Bankruptcy, Financial Reorganization & Creditors' Rights Group. Mr. Rosen is listed among* The Best Lawyers in America *in the bankruptcy and creditor-debtor rights section, the 2008* Chambers USA Guide to America's Leading Lawyers for Business, *and was featured in the 2005, 2006, and 2007 issues of* New Jersey Super Lawyers *in the Bankruptcy and Workout section of the publication. In addition, Mr. Rosen is ranked among the top unsecured creditor attorneys in the country by* The Deal's Bankruptcy Insider.

*He has extensive experience helping companies develop viable solutions to financial crises, including Chapter 11 reorganization, out-of-court workouts, financial reorganization, and litigation. Mr. Rosen is a regular contributor to New York metro area real estate publications, and has written extensively about bankruptcy in real estate and the general business press.*

**Paul Kizel** *concentrates his practice in Chapter 11 reorganizations. Mr. Kizel has more than twenty years of experience representing debtors, creditors committees, liquidating trustees, secured lenders, asset purchasers, and other parties in interest in reorganization proceedings. Mr. Kizel has been recognized in the Bankruptcy and Creditor/Debtor Rights section of the 2007 and 2008 editions of* New Jersey Super Lawyers.

*Mr. Kizel has appeared in bankruptcy courts in various jurisdictions throughout the country, including Delaware, New York, New Jersey, Texas, California, Illinois, Missouri and Maine. Among others, Mr. Kizel has represented significant parties in interest in the following recent Chapter 11 cases: Tower Automotive Inc. (New York) — represented purchaser of assets in $1 billion transaction; Foamex International Inc. (Delaware) — represented creditors committee; Interstate Bakeries Inc. (Missouri) — represents creditors committee; Pegasus Communications, Inc. (Maine) — represents liquidating trustee; Calpine Corp. (New York and Canada) — represented bondholder, Kara Homes (New Jersey) — represented post petition secured lender; and Able Laboratories Inc. (New Jersey) — represented debtor.*

# Financial Restructurings: A Lawyer's View of the Process, Challenges, and Opportunities

Peter C. Blain

*Attorney*

Reinhart Boerner Van Deuren s.c.

ASPATORE

## Meeting Key Challenges in the Restructuring Process

We are entering into some very interesting economic times. Certainly, the real estate sector is challenged by the tightening credit markets. Commercial real estate projects, especially condominium developments in many parts of the country, are in serious jeopardy. There is oversupply, and the slowdown in sales has caused many projects to go into default. Lenders are faced with difficult choices—do they foreclose and hold the projects burdened by the taint of foreclosure; sell them at a substantial loss; or do they try to reach a forbearance agreement with the borrowers and hope things will turn around?

I also believe that increasing energy costs will start to ripple through most business sectors, and the effects will start to be felt widely. The low cost airlines have already become victims. However, almost every industry with delivery networks will be similarly affected. Marginal companies which are unable to pass along those costs to customers may find it very difficult to survive.

While there is no direct strategy to directly deal with tightening credit markets and spiraling energy costs, I would advise clients to avoid debt and conserve cash. Those ventures which can weather this period will emerge stronger and as market leaders. Additionally, those clients with strong balance sheets may find the opportunity to make strategic acquisitions at very attractive prices.

## The Role of the Law Firm in Handling Restructuring Needs

Many law firms have experienced bankruptcy practitioners. Those firms with strong business, finance, tax, and real estate practice groups will be best equipped to address the complex problems (or opportunities) their clients may face. The best and most creative solutions will likely be developed on a team approach basis. Because of the cost of the bankruptcy alternative, creative out-of-court resolutions may actually lead to a better result for the client.

Distressed clients are best served when their advisor team approaches the workout as a business problem to be solved, rather than as a litigation matter to be won or lost. The most successful restructurings are the result of creative business and financial solutions, with as few resources as possible devoted to the formal process, such as the requisite costs of a Chapter 11 proceeding. Sometimes it is necessary to incur these costs, but every effort should be made to find an alternative solution. The transaction costs of Chapter 11 proceedings do nothing to solve the fundamental business issues, and in many cases approximate or exceed the financial savings achieved by the restructuring. In addition, in most cases the Chapter 11 proceedings are a fairly traumatic experience for an enterprise, its customers, suppliers, and employees.

## Evaluating Alternative Restructuring Strategies for Bankruptcy Clients

There are six steps that I use to evaluate a client's financial problem:

*1. Define the problem.*

It is crucial that the problem be clearly identified and understood. Without clearly knowing the objective, it is impossible to fully solve the problem. For example, is the problem poor management, inefficient operations, improper pricing, or competition? The appropriate and complete solution to a problem cannot be crafted unless the problem is properly identified.

Often clients are either not sure what the problem is, or have focused on the wrong problem. For example, in closely held corporations, it is not uncommon for the owners to fail to recognize or refuse to accept management failings.

Careful analysis is often required to correctly identify the real issues involved. This sometimes requires extensive due diligence investigation of the client's operations, financial history, market conditions, and management team before the scope of the problem can be understood. Often a thorough conclusion cannot be reached solely by discussions with company management.

*2. Identify the alternatives.*

This step involves creativity and is often best done on a team approach basis by brainstorming. All ideas should be considered; and after discussion and debate, a list of plausible, achievable solutions should be identified.

It is important that all solutions be considered, even those which at first blush do not seem to be workable. Often the best solutions are derived by combining two or more possible but unlikely solutions. For example, draining litigation with a strong competitor might be solved by a merger with that party. It is important not to fall into the trap of only considering the most obvious solutions and to "think outside of the box."

*3. Assess the risks.*

In order to properly determine which alternative solutions should be considered, a thorough risk analysis must be undertaken. Some strategic solutions may be optimal, but the risks of the strategy are so great that other alternatives should be considered first. For example, while a Chapter 11 proceeding might be the solution that would best resolve the client's overall financial issues, if the potential adverse impact of a Chapter 11 on customers, suppliers, or employees is too severe, perhaps another solution should be selected. While the alternative solution may not address the financial issues as well a Chapter 11, it may be less risky and therefore more desirable.

*4. Develop a plan.*

Once the solution is identified, an appropriate plan must be developed. Issues to be considered include identifying the resources needed (financing, equity investment, management enhancement or change, etc); the steps which must be taken; and the sequence in which they should be taken in order to achieve the objective. Stated differently, what is the critical path which must be followed to achieve the selected solution, and what milestones need to be met to proceed further? The plan must be detailed and consider factors such as timing and the appropriate negotiation strategy or strategies to be employed.

*5. Check the details.*

This step is crucial. The plan developed must be thoroughly analyzed to ensure that all potential obstacles are considered in advance and planned for. For example, what if the desired response is not given by the lender, how do you proceed if a class fails to vote for a plan or what response is made if a competing bid is made for the business? The ideal plan is vetted sufficiently so that no response by any party is a surprise to the implementing team. While it is impossible to predict with absolute certainty what reactions the plan might cause, as many reactions as can be thought of should be considered, and a strategy devised to deal with each of them. This ensures the greatest chance for success.

*6. Implement boldly.*

Once the details of the plan are checked, it is important to implement the plan quickly and decisively. Oftentimes delay prevents smooth execution and might allow other parties additional time to mount opposition to the selected strategy. While undue haste which prevents proper planning is to be avoided, delay, once the plan is developed, is also undesirable.

One aspect of the restructuring process which is always challenging is the lack of sufficient time to follow the steps described above. Often, severe time constraints are placed on a client because of a financial crisis, or by third parties such as lenders. A primary goal for a restructuring attorney who has become involved in a client's financial problems should be to try to find ways to afford the restructuring team sufficient time to develop the optimal strategy. Insufficient time precludes the thoughtful and careful analysis described above, which consequently narrows available options. Conversely, additional time often permits the creation of additional options.

## Understanding the Client's Goals

The primary question that I ask my clients when I am first brought in to handle a restructuring process is simply this: What is their most desirable objective? Their answer helps me understand their goals and manage their expectations. By understanding how they would like their financial situation to be resolved, I am better able to try to address the situation in terms of finding realistic solutions that are also able to meet the client's goals. For example, if the client's objective is to retain control of their enterprise, it becomes important to identify solutions that meet that objective but still address the primary financial issues, such as seeking investment capital, selling a division, closing a business unit, etc.

Reaching agreement with the client about the objectives to be achieved is essential to the success of most restructurings. Hopefully, the client's stated objectives are attainable. If they are not, assisting the client in understanding that they are not and getting buy-in on the next best alternative is important. Unless this consensual agreement on the objective to be achieved is reached, the likelihood of achieving success, or at least having the client agree that the result achieved is successful, may be very difficult.

Because of the complexity of many businesses, it is very important to have expertise in many areas of law in order to fully address a restructuring effort. Labor, tax, real estate, finance, environmental, intellectual property, and litigation are only a few of the disciplines that may be implicated during the course of an engagement. A firm that can quickly address most if not all questions that arise is best able to implement a successful restructuring strategy.

## Key Players

The corporate individuals who are most involved in the restructuring process will depend on the particular situation. If the business is closely held, the interaction may be with the ownership team and the financial team. If the business is larger, there may be corporate counsel and additional levels of the management team included in the process. In either case, it is important to try and assess the political atmosphere and determine how decisions are made and who really makes them. It is important to do this early on so that valuable time is not spent dealing with the wrong parties. At the same time, it is imperative that the lawyer start to build a relationship of trust and confidence with both the decision maker and the supporting management team.

It is sometimes useful to suggest that the client engage a financial advisor to assist in the restructuring process. The advisor may be able to suggest alternative solutions in a non-political way and thus create quicker buy-in. In addition, it is sometimes helpful to have an expert with substantial experience assess the client's goals and help manage expectations.

## Challenges of the Restructuring Process

One of the most challenging developments during a restructuring is the occurrence of an unexpected development. This could be an extrinsic event that was not foreseen such as the loss of a key, long-standing customer, or a position taken by a party in interest that was not expected, such as the unwillingness of a borrower to agree to a lender's reasonable forbearance terms.

As previously stated, the best way to manage these events is to engage in the proper planning during the course of the planning phase. While it is not possible to predict all future events with certainty, proper planning permits the attorney to have a well thought-out action plan to deal with most occurrences. This permits the restructuring team to respond promptly and effectively, and continue the progress toward reaching the overall objective.

Having unencumbered assets available to the client, whether in the enterprise or owned by the owners personally, permits the restructuring team to have more flexibility in creating a workable plan. The assets may be available to be pledged in order to buy additional time, or be used to induce additional loans to an investment in the enterprise in order to create liquidity and working capital. Conversely, the absence of unencumbered assets constrains the process by reducing the potential options available.

## Primary Legal Components of the Restructuring Strategy

Developing a successful restructuring strategy entails achieving a result as close to the client's stated objective as possible; achieving that objective as quickly and efficiently as possible; and doing so with as little disruption to the enterprise, its customers, employees, and suppliers as possible. Of course, in some cases it is not possible to achieve the client's stated objective. Therefore, as previously stated, the strategy must include obtaining the client's buy-in and agreement to achieve the next best alternative. For example, if restructuring a business in a way that permits the owners to continue in control is not achievable, selling the business with a return of value to equity may be the next best alternative. The challenge is to persuade the owners to accept and agree to the alternative.

The above is a description of the strategy. How the strategy is achieved entails tactics. The use of the bankruptcy process can be an effective tactic in the right circumstances. However, because of the cost, the delay, and the possible impact on the business (including customers, employees, and suppliers), it is a tactic that may not be a first choice. Where a prepackaged Chapter 11 can be used to implement a restructuring over the objections of dissenting lenders, or a pre-negotiated plan can be filed with the petition and quickly confirmed, Chapter 11 may be the ideal tactic to use. *See* Blain, Peter C., *The Growth of the Prepackaged Chapter 11's and the Alternatives*, Aspatore Books (to be published in Summer 2008). However, because of the above factors, Chapter 11 may not be the ideal tactic to use while the restructuring plan is being developed. In that case, out of court resolutions or even federal or state court receiverships, where applicable, may be better tactics to consider. In some states, a statutory receivership is a much faster and a much less costly tactic to use to sell a business as a going concern than Chapter 11. While the sale is court supervised and authorized by court order, there is usually not a creditors committee or the equivalent of the US Trustee to raise objections and cause delay.

## Documentation in a Restructuring Process

In many situations, the initial document that is prepared in a restructuring process is a forbearance agreement, running between the borrower and its lenders. This document often sets the ground rules for the restructuring process. In it, the borrower is often required to acknowledge its obligations are in default, and waive claims against the lenders. In exchange, the borrower is given a period of time to develop a restructuring plan. As stated above, because having the time necessary to follow the steps discussed may make all the difference in achieving a more successful restructuring, the concessions made by the borrower in the forbearance agreement may be a worthwhile trade-off. The agreement may also set milestones to be achieved by the borrower in order for the forbearance period to continue. These may include meeting certain financial performance milestones or divesting product lines or business segments by a specific date. An advantage of the forbearance agreement is that it is generally able to be kept confidential unless it is required to be disclosed in financial statements prepared in accordance with generally accepted accounting principles, or in securities law filings by publicly-traded companies. This may permit the borrower to avoid having to deal with suppliers or customers while a plan is being developed. A sample Forbearance Agreement is attached in the Appendices.

If the workout proceeds out of court, the loan is often re-documented. If the plan entails seeking accommodations for unsecured creditors, the negotiated agreements may be contained in a composition or intercreditor agreement among the borrower and its key unsecured creditors.

If the workout proceeds in a federal or state court receivership, the documents required will be determined by the applicable state law and practice, or by federal law and Section 66 of the Federal Rules of Civil Procedure. These proceedings often involve a complaint, motion, and order appointing the state court receiver, or motion and order appointing the federal receiver. In state court proceedings, there may be additional motions, orders, and agreements, such as financing agreements and orders; and sale and bid procedures, motions, and orders, if appropriate.

If the workout proceeds as a bankruptcy case, the full panoply of bankruptcy pleadings may be involved, including financing motions and orders; sale and bid procedure motions and orders, if appropriate; a disclosure statement; and a plan of reorganization.

At each stage, the workout attorney, with the assistance of the restructuring team, must make sure that the various documents are reconciled with ancillary documents negotiated with other constituents in the case.

## Negotiating the Restructuring Strategy

Negotiations are essential to utilizing the tactics to achieve the selected strategic objective. During the course of the restructuring process, the legal team negotiates with almost every player involved. There are usually negotiations with lenders to make sufficient time available to develop and implement the restructuring plan. There are often simultaneous negotiations with unsecured creditors, customers, suppliers, and employees. Finally, there are often negotiations that occur between the client and restructuring team. There is often a need to persuade the client to agree to strive for what is achievable, and to accept what is not. Unless the client and the team agree upon the ultimate objective, it will be very difficult to achieve a result that is considered a success. Failure to achieve this common agreement can lead to discord and mid-course changes of direction which could inhibit the restructuring effort.

The objectives of each negotiation should be consistent with the achievement of the overall plan. Each separate negotiation event should advance the process either by gaining required time or reaching key agreements. The negotiations should be targeted and not become ends in and of themselves. *See* Blain, Peter C. (Co-Author), *Inside the Minds: Bankruptcy and Financial Restructuring Settlements and Negotiations*, Aspatore (2006).

In some cases, the ultimate objective of restructurings utilizing the bankruptcy process is the confirmation of a plan of reorganization. Today, the Chapter 11 process is increasingly used as a vehicle to sell a debtor enterprise as a going concern. In either event, it is essential that an agreement be worked out with the debtor's lenders to finance the debtor's operations during the case. As stated above, it is also important to have the ultimate objective clearly in mind before the filing occurs in order to avoid unnecessary costs and delay during the Chapter 11 process. If a plan is the objective, preparation and approval of the disclosure statement and confirmation of the plan by the Bankruptcy Court are the major milestones. If the objective is a sale, the sale motion, bid procedures motion, and sale order are important benchmarks. A sample Bid Procedures Motion and Bid Procedures are attached in the Appendices.

Stated generally, the primary benchmark of a successful restructuring negotiation process is negotiating sufficient time to formulate and implement an appropriate restructuring strategy which is as close to the client's objectives as possible. A corollary benchmark is implementing the strategy efficiently and quickly in order to permit the client's enterprise to move forward with the appropriate financial base.

## The Post-Bankruptcy Period

One of the key factors that I focus on immediately after the confirmation of a restructuring plan is using the successful conclusion as a public relations opportunity. Widely publicizing the confirmation can be used as a way to reassure customers and suppliers. It is a way for the client to say in effect, "We addressed and solved our problems, and are now ready to continue our success." This is of such importance that I encourage clients to consider hiring a public relations firm with experience to make the most of this public relations opportunity.

During the post-reorganization period, I look for ways to add value for the client. For example, if the plan provides for the payment of creditors over time and if the client's operations permit, there may be an opportunity to offer to pay classes of creditors ahead of schedule but at a discount.

As a restructuring attorney, I do not have the opportunity to follow clients for extended periods of time post-restructuring. The client's corporate counsel, outside financial advisors, or the management team are usually best positioned to monitor the success of the restructuring effort by comparing performance to projections.

## Creative Strategies

One creative strategy that I have successfully employed on a number of occasions in client restructurings is what I call the "Hobson's Choice." I have structured plans that provide that unsecured creditors can choose among various options, one of which may be to receive payment of their claims in full over an extended period of time. Another choice is to receive payment of a portion of the claims over a shorter period of time, and a third choice would be to pay the creditor a much smaller amount at confirmation in full satisfaction of the claim. I have also provided that the third option would be available to the first group of creditors who accept it whose claims aggregate to a limited dollar amount, in order to create an "auction" atmosphere.

This strategy has several benefits. First, the client can truthfully say that it has offered to pay all claims in full. Second, with the second and third options, the client may generate substantial discounts from the face amount of the claims. However, the discounts are elected by the creditors based upon their own circumstances or assessment of the client's prospects, and are not forced upon them. This permits the client to obtain substantial benefits without the fractured relationships which sometimes accompany reorganizations.

## Recent Landmark Cases in Bankruptcy Restructuring

The recent landmark cases in bankruptcy restructuring are largely jurisdiction specific. For example, the 7th Circuit decision in *In re Kmart Corp.*, 359 F.3d. 866 (7th Cir. 2004) significantly limits the ability of the debtor to seek authority to pay critical pre-petition vendors. This decision will influence the strategy of the restructuring in that jurisdiction. Decisions on this or other key issues in other jurisdictions will similarly shape the restructuring strategy in those jurisdictions.

The recent amendments to the Bankruptcy Code are universally applicable and make it more difficult to successfully reorganize enterprises, especially large companies. The time limitations on making decisions to assume or reject executory contracts in section 365 would make it difficult for a case like *Kmart*, which was in many respects a real estate case, to succeed. Other revisions such as limiting the length of the debtor's exclusive period to file a plan under section 1121 or limiting the ability to use key employee retention programs to retain essential managers under section 503, place additional hurdles in front of a business trying to reorganize.

## Final Thoughts

The most important aspect of the restructuring process is the intrinsic strength of the subject enterprise. Many businesses are fundamentally sound and can be rehabilitated by a financial restructuring. Some enterprises, however, are flawed or wounded to the point where there is not sufficient time or resources available to implement a successful restructuring strategy. Although these are difficult cases, the attorney's challenge is to help his client accept the situation; conserve resources rather than waste them on an effort which will likely fail; and make the best out of the situation by selling or liquidating the enterprise for maximize value in order to avoid personal exposure for the owners.

Experience is the best teacher in these matters. It is important to try to analyze each engagement after conclusion to determine which efforts were successful and which were less so. Study your opponents' strategies and tactics critically, and incorporate practices used by the other side that were effective. By a careful, critical review of past engagements, the attorney's current "best practices" can be continually improved, and the attorney can enhance his or her abilities for the benefit of their clients in future engagements.

*Peter C. Blain is a shareholder and chair of Reinhart Boerner Van Deuren s.c.'s Bankruptcy and Creditor's Rights Department. Mr. Blain also served as a vice president and director of the firm from 1992 to 2005.*

*Mr. Blain regularly represents financial institutions, creditors, debtors, creditors' committees, trustees and others in bankruptcy proceedings, receiverships, and workouts. He uses the skills and expertise acquired in almost thirty years of practice to achieve uniquely successful results for his clients in complex business and commercial matters.*

*Mr. Blain's professional achievements include being elected a Fellow in the American College of Bankruptcy, an honor granted to only a handful of Wisconsin attorneys. In addition to being listed in* Who's Who Legal USA: Insolvency and Restructuring 2006, *Mr. Blain is also included in* Woodward and White's Best Lawyers In America *since 1987 and is listed in* Who's Who In American Law, Who's Who in America, *and* Who's Who in the World. *Since 2005, Law & Politics has consistently named Mr. Blain as one of Wisconsin's Super Lawyers, ranking him in the top 5 percent of Wisconsin attorneys, and has also recognized him as one of the top fifty lawyers in the state. He is a member of the American Bar Association, Turnaround Management Association and the American Bankruptcy Institute.*

*In 2007, at the request of the U.S. Ambassador and the American Chamber of Commerce, Mr. Blain led a team including a U.S. Bankruptcy Judge and a crisis manager to Prague, Czech Republic to instruct Czech Bankruptcy Judges and lawyers about the dynamics of reorganization proceedings prior to the effective date of that country's newly enacted bankruptcy statute.*

*In addition to having served as chair of the State Bar of Wisconsin's Bankruptcy, Insolvency & Creditors' Right Section, chair of the Milwaukee Bar Association's Bankruptcy Section, co-chair of the MBA Bankruptcy Bench/Bar Committee, and co-chair of the MBA Pro Bono Project Committee, Mr. Blain currently serves as co-chair of the Bankruptcy Section of the Eastern District of Wisconsin Bar Association.*

*Mr. Blain is also a member of the Eastern District of Wisconsin Local Bankruptcy Rules Committee. Mr. Blain is a noted author and speaker on bankruptcy topics and is a lecturer at the University of Wisconsin-Milwaukee School of Business at the undergraduate and graduate level.*

*Mr. Blain received his undergraduate degree with honors from the Wisconsin State University-Stevens Point and his law degree from Georgetown University Law Center where he served as an editor of the* American Criminal Law Review. *Prior to law school, Mr. Blain served as a U.S. Army Lieutenant for two years. While attending law school, he also worked for the Office of the Controller at the Veterans Administration in Washington, D.C.*

*Mr. Blain is active in his community, serving as a member of the City of Mequon's Open Space Planning Commission and as a former member of the City's Ethics Committee.*

# The Basic Restructuring Strategies Used Today By Companies Pursuing Bankruptcy Protection

Joseph J. Wielebinski

*Shareholder*

Munsch Hardt Kopf & Harr PC

ASPATORE

**Historical Perspective**

Historically, there was only one strategy when it came to bankruptcy—run like the wind and avoid it all costs. The word bankruptcy is an amalgamation of two Latin words meaning, "bench" and "break." The literal translation is "broken bench." During Roman times, when a merchant could no longer pay his debts, his workbench was broken and his assets divided up and distributed to his creditors. This was meant both as a punishment to the debtor and a warning to other tradesmen.

Over time, conditions did not radically improve for bankrupt debtors. Before the Bankruptcy Act of 1869 did away with debtor prisons, men and women in England were typically imprisoned for debt at the discretion of their creditors. Sometimes, this imprisonment would last for decades. Lucinda Cory. *A History Perspective on Bankruptcy*, On the Docket, Volume II, Issue 2, April/May/June 2000. Bankruptcy debtors would frequently take their families with them because the only other option for women and children of these debtors was the shame of uncertain charity that existed outside the debtors' prison. This resulted in whole communities rising up inside debtors' prisons, with children being born and raised there. Although other European countries enacted legislation that limited imprisonment for debtors to one year, debtors in England were imprisoned until their creditors were satisfied, no matter how long that lasted. For example, when the Fleet Prison closed in 1842, some debtors were found to have been there for upwards of thirty years. *Id.* These debtors' prisons were privately administered with the prison charging for rent; bailiffs charging for food and clothing; attorneys charging legal fees for futile attempts to get the debtors released; and creditors (frequently trades people) increasing the debt because the debtor was in jail. This resulted in the prisoners' families, including the children, being sent to work simply to pay the costs of keeping the debtor in prison, the debts growing to a point where there was no practical chance of release. Id.

By 1641, approximately 10,000 people in England and Wales were imprisoned for debt. Beginning with King George III, legislation prevented debts of under 40 shillings from leading to jail, but even the smallest debts could quickly exceed that amount once a lawyer's fee was tacked on. Under the Insolvent Debtors Act of 1813, debtors could declare themselves insolvent and request release after fourteen days in jail by taking an oath that their assets did not exceed 20 pounds. But if any of their creditors objected, they had to stay inside. Even after a lifetime in prison, debts very often remained unpaid.

Fast-forward to today, and it is easily seen that bankruptcy has come a long way. No longer stigmatizing the debtor with the proverbial Scarlet A, bankruptcy is now seen as an acceptable alternative in a corporation's financial arsenal. This is borne out by the litany of well-known corporations that have filed for bankruptcy including, without limitation, Continental Airlines, Converse, Delphi Corporation, Delta Airlines, Dow Corning, Eastern Airlines, Enron, Fredericks of Hollywood, Fruit of the Loom, KB Toys, K-Mart, Lionel Corporation, Maidenform, Montgomery Ward, Northwest Airlines, Owens Corning, PanAm, Polaroid, Purina Mills, Schlotzsky's, Sizzler International, Smith Corona, Texaco, TransWorld Airlines, Vlassic Foods International, Western Union, Winn Dixie Stores, and Zenith Electronics.

With the current Bankruptcy Code, there are essentially three main bankruptcy strategies: liquidation under Chapter 7, reorganization under Chapter 11, and a hybrid of the two, the sale of assets under a Chapter 11 reorganization that results in a later liquidation under either a Chapter 11 plan of liquidation or through a conversion to Chapter 7.

## Critical Legal Features of a Chapter 11 Reorganization

Reorganization, under Chapter 11, enables a corporate debtor to continue with the possession and control of its assets and property and the continuation and operation of its business and management of its affairs. If the goal of the debtor is to emerge in order to reenter the marketplace, then reorganization facilitates that purpose. Within Chapter 11 itself, there are a number of alternatives (that could also be pursued pre-petition as well): resurrection (the internal rehabilitation of a company without outside assistance); refinancing (borrowing money from a new post-petition lender or getting a new influx of capital from the pre-petition lender); re-equitizing (obtaining new capital from investors); and re-amortizing (rescheduling loan payments). Bobby Guy, *Six Ways Out: Distress as the Art of Exit Strategies*,

Turnaround Management Association Journal, April 10, 2008. There are a number of key critical legal features to this bankruptcy alternative.

## 1. Operational Issues

Whenever a corporate bankruptcy case is filed, there a number of operational issues that must be addressed immediately:

*Joint Administration*

If, for example, there is more than one corporate debtor filing a bankruptcy petition, it will make sense to seek the joint administration of the Chapter 11 cases. The authority for this relief is Bankruptcy Rule 1015(b), which provides, in relevant part, that "If . . . two or more petitions are pending in the same court by or against . . . a debtor and an affiliate, the court may order joint administration of the estates." When there are numerous corporate Chapter 11 debtors that are affiliates, joint administration will negate the need for duplicative notices, applications, and orders, thereby saving the debtors the time and expense that could be far too burdensome on their estates. The rights of creditors will not be adversely affected because the requested relief is only administrative, not a substantive consolidation of the estates. In fact, the rights of creditors will be enhanced by the reduced costs that would result from joint administration. Each creditor will still be allowed to file its respective proofs of claim against any particular estate. The court will also be relieved of the burden of entering into duplicative orders and maintaining redundant files. Joint administration will also simplify the supervision of the administrative facets of a reorganization case. Another impact of joint administration is the filing of monthly operating reports required by the United States Trustee's Operating Guidelines on a consolidated basis, if the debtors determine, after consultation with the United States Trustee, that consolidated reports will advance administrative autonomy and efficiency without prejudice to any party in interest, and that the reports accurately reflect the debtors' consolidated business operations and financial affairs.

*Notice Procedures*

Debtors often request an order limiting notice on various matters only to affected parties. Due to the large number of debtors in certain filings, the parties in interest to receive notice include in excess of thousands of creditors. Giving notice of all pleadings and papers filed in such cases to each party in interest would be unnecessary, labor intensive, and expensive due to the photocopying and postage expenses associated with extensive mail outs, and also extremely burdensome and costly to the debtors' estates. Therefore, consistent with an approach taken in large Chapter 11 cases, courts often establish a master service list which includes: (1) the Office of the United States Trustee in the district where the bankruptcy cases are filed; (2) the debtors; (3) the attorneys for the debtors; (4) the attorneys for the agent of the debtors' pre-petition lenders; (5) the attorneys for the agent of the debtors' post-petition lenders; (6) the attorneys for the statutory committee for unsecured creditors; (7) the attorneys for any other committee appointed by the bankruptcy court; (8) any party whose interest is directly impacted by the specific pleading; (9) those persons who formally appear and request service in the bankruptcy cases; and (10) the U.S. Securities and Exchange Commission, the Internal Revenue Service, and any other governmental agencies, to the extent required by the Bankruptcy Rules or the local Bankruptcy Rules.

Before the unsecured creditors' committee is appointed, each debtor will include on the initial master service list the debtor's twenty largest unsecured creditors (on a consolidated basis). Once that committee is formed, the debtor will add the attorneys for the committee to the master service list and remove from that list the twenty largest unsecured creditors, unless any of those creditors formally appear and request service of process. Often in these large cases, the debtor updates the master service list on a periodic basis, perhaps monthly, to include the names and addresses of any party in interest that has formally appeared and requested service. These parties receive notice from the time of appearance, but are not added to the master service list until the end of each period, when the master service list is updated and refiled with the court. Upon the completion of noticing any certain matter, the debtor will then submit to the court either an Affidavit of Service or a Certificate of Service attaching the list of those parties to whom notice was given. Administrations of bankruptcy cases are more efficient and cost effective when such notice procedures are implemented.

*Extension of Time to File Schedules and Statement of Financial Affairs*

Under § 521 and Bankruptcy Rule 1007, debtors are required to file (1) schedules of assets and liabilities, (2) schedules of executory contracts and unexpired leases, and (3) statements of financial affairs within fifteen days after the petition date. In addition, debtors are required to file a list of equity security holders during that time period as well. Very often, with the filing of large bankruptcy cases, this fifteen-day deadline is inadequate for debtors to comply with these requirements, and debtors often file a motion requesting an extension of this deadline. The justification for this request is the complexity and diversity of a debtor's operations. In order to prepare these filings, the debtors must compile information from a wide array of sources including books, records and documents related to a plethora of transactions, claims, assets, and contracts all dealing with potentially numerous entities. This information can be extraordinarily voluminous and, in many situations, located in separate and disparate places not only throughout the debtor's organization but, perhaps, throughout the country as well. Culling this information necessitates a tremendous amount of time and effort on the part of the debtor's employees. In many instances, resources to accomplish this are limited; and this situation is made even direr because of the necessity to file this information at the beginning of a bankruptcy case when a debtor's employees are focusing on keeping the debtor up and running.

*Cash Management Systems*

It is often extremely helpful to debtors to maintain, post-petition, the same cash management systems that were used pre-petition. In many cases, debtors use a centralized cash management system that collects, concentrates, and distributes the money generated by their operations. This is done to maximize the value of their business. Under a cash management system, a debtor collects and transfers cash to satisfy its financial obligations and fund its investments. A cash management system also assists a debtor in cash forecasting and reporting, monitoring the collection and disbursement of funds, and maintaining control over the administration of bank accounts located at numerous banks. Debtors will often request from the bankruptcy court authority to (1) continue to operate an existing cash management system, (2) maintain existing bank accounts, and (3) maintain existing business forms.

*Pre-Petition Sales, Use, and Other Excise Taxes*

In connection with their normal day-to-day business operations, debtors collect and remit a variety of taxes, fees, and other charges constituting sales/use taxes, and other excise taxes. Debtors remit them to the various federal, state, and local government and quasi-government authorities. The debtors pay to the taxing authorities the sales/use and other excise taxes on a periodic basis with funds by checks or by means of electronic funds transfers that are processed through the debtors' banks and/or other financial institutions.

Debtors often seek authority pursuant to §§ 105(a) and 363(b) to pay, in their sole discretion, any of the sales/use and other excise taxes that arose pre-petition, including all sales/use and other excise taxes that are later determined based upon audits, or otherwise to be owed for periods prior to the petition date. To the extent that any checks or electronic transfers have not cleared a bank as of the petition date, debtors request that the bankruptcy court authorize and direct the bank, when asked by the debtors in their sole discretion, to receive, process, honor, and pay such checks or electronic transfers. To the extent that the taxing authorities have not received payment for pre-petition sales/use and other excise taxes, debtors seek authorization to issue replacement checks, or provide for other means of payment to the taxing authorities to the extent necessary to pay all outstanding sales/use and other excise taxes owing for pre-petition time periods.

Debtors seek to pay pre-petition sales/use and other excise taxes in order to, among other things, discourage taxing authorities from taking actions that might interfere with the debtors' reorganization, including bringing personal liability actions against directors, officers, and other employees in connection with this non-payment. Actions against a debtor's directors, officers, and other employees would probably distract key personnel and result in delays of services to the debtor's customers. Any type of delay of this type would deteriorate the debtor's customer base and negatively affect the Chapter 11 reorganization.

Authority for this relief is often § 363(b)(1) which provides that: "[t]he trustee, after notice and a hearing, may use, sale, or lease, other than in the ordinary course of business property of the estate, . . . " and § 105(a) which states that: "[t]he court may issue any order, process, or judgment that is necessary or appropriate to carry out the provisions of this title . . . " In addition, sales/use and other excise taxes are given priority status under § 507(a). As priority claims, these taxes must be paid in full before general unsecured claims of a debtor may be satisfied. In addition, many of these taxes are collected or withheld by the debtors on behalf of applicable taxing authorities, and are held in trust by the debtors for the benefit of those taxing authorities. Therefore, these taxes are not considered to be property of the estate under § 541. *Begier v. Internal Revenue Service*, 496 U.S. 53 (1990). *In re Shank*, 792 F.2d 829, 830 (9th Cir. 1986) (sales taxes required by state law to be collected by sellers from their customers are "trust fund" taxes). *DeChiaro v. New York State Tax Commission*, 760 F.2d 432, 433-434 (2nd Cir. 1985) (same). *In re American International Airways Inc.*, 70 B.R. 102, 103 (Bankr. E.D.Pa. 1987) (excise and withholding taxes). *In re Tap Inc.*, 52 B.R. 271, 272 (Bankr. D.Mass. 1985) (withholding taxes). Since these taxes are not property of the estate, they are not available for the payment of creditors' claims in a bankruptcy case.

Payment of these taxes will make the continuation of uninterrupted operations by debtors. Non-payment might trigger a taxing authority to take severe action including, without limitation, conducting audits; filing liens; pursuing payment of those taxes from a debtor's directors, officers, and other employees; and seeking to lift the automatic stay, all of which will be detrimental to the continuation of the debtor's normal daily operations and might result in tremendous costs on the bankruptcy estate. Prompt payment of these taxes to the taxing authorities will negate such detrimental actions.

A number of federal and state laws hold officers and directors of collecting entities personally liable or criminally liable for certain taxes that remain unpaid to those entities. If those taxes remain unpaid by a debtor, the debtor's officers and directors can be the target of lawsuits or criminal prosecution during the term of a Chapter 11 case. This would distract the debtor and the implicated officers and directors from continuing and successfully following through with the debtor's reorganization, all to the detriment of the debtor's creditors and other parties in interest.

*Pre-Petition Obligations to Employees*

By virtue of simply operating in business, debtors incur payroll and other obligations to their employees that are unpaid as of the petition date because they accrued, either in whole or in part, prior to that time. Even though they arose before the petition date, they become due after the petition date in the ordinary course of the debtor's business. Debtors often file a motion requesting authority to pay these obligations during the early stages of a bankruptcy case.

The obligations that a debtor might owe its employees include wages, salaries, incentive plans, retirement saving plans, health and welfare benefit plans, tuition reimbursement obligations, expense reimbursement obligations, workman's compensation programs, liability and property programs, vacation time, and vacation pay. Debtors often request the authority, but not the requirement to, pay, at their discretion, these obligations and continue to honor these practices, programs, and policies, and to authorize and direct the applicable banks and other financial institutions to receive, process, and pay on all checks drawn on the debtor's payroll and general disbursement accounts to the extent that those checks relate to these programs. Under § 507(a)(4) and (5), the claims of a debtor's employees for "wages, salaries or commissions, including vacation, severance and sick leave pay" earned within ninety days before the petition date, and claims against debtors for contributions to employee benefit plans arising from services rendered within 180 days before the petition date, are afforded priority status to the extent of $10,950 per employee.

Debtor corporations cannot continue without the presence and full participation of their employees. In addition, an employee's morale affects its effectiveness and productivity. Therefore, it is extremely important that debtors continue, in the ordinary and normal course of their business affairs, their personnel policies, programs, and procedures that existed pre-petition. Disaffected employees "vote with their feet" and look for employment elsewhere, thereby depriving the debtor of knowledgeable and productive employees. Hiring replacements is costly if, for no other reason, than educating these employees in how the debtor operates and what their responsibilities are. If pre-petition checks to employees are dishonored, and/or not timely paid post-petition, employees will, typically, leave the debtor and seek other employment. In addition, many employees will suffer personal financial distress and may be unable to make ends meet on a daily basis. This potential state of affairs negatively affects debtors and their ability to perform under Chapter 11. Furthermore, it is unfair to have a debtor's employees shoulder the burden of the debtor's bankruptcy case by withholding from them business expenses while they were under the impression that they would be reimbursed. Maintaining employee morale is paramount to a debtor, especially in the introductory stages of a bankruptcy case. Any considerable erosion in this area will have a considerably negative impact on debtors, their customers and vendors, and the ability of the debtor to continue in business.

*Administrative Expense Status*

In the normal and ordinary course of their business affairs, debtors often purchase a variety of goods and services from vendors, suppliers, and creditors. Shipment of goods is accomplished through the employment of common carriers, custom brokers, third party logistics providers, freight forwarders providers, and third parties that own and operate storage facilities. Debtors often request that the bankruptcy court (1) grant these vendors administrative expense priority status under § 503(b) for undisputed obligations arising out of outstanding pre-petition transactions relating to goods delivered post-petition, and authorize the debtors to pay those obligations in the ordinary course of business; (2) authorize the debtors to pay pre-petition amounts due on account of customs duties and pre-petition customs broker charges; and (3) authorize the debtors to pay pre-petition amounts owed to common carriers, logistics providers, freight forwarders, and storage facility providers.

Under § 503(b)(1)(A), all obligations that arise in connection with the post-petition delivery of goods, including those goods that were ordered pre-petition, are administrative expense claims. Therefore, granting administrative expense status to those vendors for the post-petition delivery of goods that are ordered pre-petition will not give those vendors greater priority than they would have gotten in any event. Without that relief, debtors may be required to divert a considerable amount of time and expense in reordering goods and providing vendors with the assurance that they will, in fact, obtain administrative expense priority status. This distraction and disruption can well result in insufficient supplies that will negatively affect a debtor's business. The result can lead to dissatisfied customers and other negative fallout detrimentally impacting the bankruptcy case.

Pre-petition customs duties are accorded priority status in accordance with § 507(a)(8)(F) and are paid in their entirety in any event. Therefore, creditors are not prejudiced by those payments made by debtors. Making those payments actually benefits creditors and parties in interest because they allow a debtor's business operations to continue without any negative effect.

Debtors rely on § 105(a) in requesting this relief. A bankruptcy court's reliance on this section of the Bankruptcy Code to authorize the payment of a pre-petition debt when such payment is needed to facilitate the reorganization of the debtor is well recognized. *In re Ionosphere Clubs Inc.*, 98 B.R. 174, 175 (Bankr. S.D.N.Y. 1989). This section of the Bankruptcy Code has been used to allow a debtor to make a pre-plan of reorganization payment on a pre-petition obligation when needed to continue its business. *In re NVR L.P.*, 147 B.R. 126, 127 (Bankr. E.D.Va. 1992). It is not uncommon for bankruptcy courts to allow the post-petition payment of pre-petition obligations to critical vendors when it is necessary to preserve or enhance the value of a debtor's estate for the benefit of all of the debtor's creditors. This has been termed the "doctrine of necessity."

Debtors believe that the uninterrupted supply of goods and services on customary trade terms and the continuing support of their customers are essential to their ongoing business operations and chances for reorganization and economic survival. Debtors will seek to only pay critical vendors where non-payment of those claims would lead to the interruption of the delivery of goods and services and, of course, seriously disrupt the debtor's operations.

This sort of relief has been granted in a number of large Chapter 11 cases. *In re A-One Realty Marketing of New York Inc.*, Case Nos. 01-40252-40190 (AJG) (Bankr. S.D.N.Y. 2001). *In re R.H. Macy & Co.*, Case No. 92-B-40477 (BRL) (Bankr. S.D.N.Y. 1992). *In re LTV Steel Company Inc.*, Case No. 00-43866 (Bankr. N.D.Ohio 2000). *In re Pillowtex Inc.*, Case No. 00-4211 (SLR) (D. Del. 2000). *In re Purina Mills Inc.*, Case No. 99-3938 (SLR) (D. Del. 1999). *In re Loewen Group International Inc.*, Case No. 99-1244 (BJW) (D. Del. 1999) (Judge Farnan). *In re The Imperial Home Decor, Group, Inc.*, Case No. 92-115 (HSB) (Bankr. D. Del. 1992). *In re Enron Corp., et al.*, Case No. 01-16034 (AJG) (Bankr. S.D.N.Y. 2001).

*Adequate Assurance to Utility Companies*

By operating a business and the properties incidental thereto, debtors make use of utilities in the form of electricity, telephone, garbage removal, natural gas, and other services from utility companies. In some cases, the debtors will pay the utility companies directly, and in other cases, the debtor's landlord will pay the utility company. Debtors often seek an order from the bankruptcy court (1) prohibiting utility companies from altering, refusing, or discontinuing service on account of pre-petition invoices; (2) providing that the utility companies have adequate assurance of payment under § 366, without the need for payment of additional deposits or security; and (3) establishing procedures for determining requests for additional adequate assurance of payment beyond those established in the motion and consistent with other procedures from Chapter 11 cases.

Obviously, it is common sense that uninterrupted utility service is necessary for a debtor to continue in business and for the debtor's reorganization to reach its intended conclusion. Debtors cannot go forward with their businesses without utility service. Interruption of utility service could well spell the demise of a debtor.

Debtors often propose to provide adequate assurance of payment to utility companies in the form of existing security deposits, if there have not been any previous defaults, and in the form of an administrative expense priority claim pursuant to §§ 503(b) and 507(a)(1) for utility services provided to the debtor by the utility companies post-petition. Utility companies are still within their rights to request additional adequate assurance throughout the remainder of a bankruptcy case.

Under § 366, within twenty days after a petition date, utility companies are not entitled to alter, refuse or discontinue service to or discriminate against a debtor solely because of the filing of a bankruptcy case. This provision of the Bankruptcy Code applies to entities providing electricity, natural gas, water, garbage removal and/or telephone services, as well as any other entity that provides services that cannot be readily obtained or replaced anywhere else, or which constitutes a monopoly in respect of those services. *One Stop Realtour Place Inc. v. Allegiance Telecom of Pa. Inc., (In re One Stop Realtour Place Inc.)*, 268 B.R. 430, 436-437 (Bankr. E.D.Pa. 2001) (provider of telephone service is a utility regardless of whether telephone service maybe available from another provider). *In re Coastal Dry Dock & Repair Corp.*, 62 B.R. 879, 883 (Bankr. E.D.N.Y. 1986) (landlord of the Brooklyn Navy Yard occupies a special position with respect to the debtor in its role as the debtor's utilities supplier). After this twenty-day period, utility companies may discontinue service to the debtor if the debtor does not provide adequate assurance of payment of its post-petition obligations. Adequate assurance under § 366 is not the same thing as adequate protection. In calculating adequate assurance, the court does not have to bestow upon the utility companies a guarantee of payment, but must only conclude that the utility company is not subject to an unreasonable risk of non-payment for the provision of post-petition utility services. *In re Adelphia Business Solutions Inc.*, 280 B.R. 63, 80 (Bankr. S.D.N.Y. 2002) (*Adelphia*). *In re Caldor Inc.*, - N.Y., 199 B.R. 1, 3 (S.D.N.Y. 1996); *In re Santa Clara Circuits West Inc.*, 27 B.R. 680, 685 (Bankr. D.Utah 1982). *In re George C. Frye Co.*, 7 B.R. 856, 858 (Bankr. D.Me. 1980). When deciding on whether there is a need for any further post-petition deposit, the court should make certain the utility company is treating the debtor the same as a non-bankruptcy entity in similar circumstances. *In re Whitaker*, 84 B.R. 934, 943 (Bankr. E.D.Pa. 1988), affirmed, 882 F.2d 791 (3rd Cir. 1989).

The question of whether a utility company is exposed to an unreasonable risk of non-payment must be answered on a case-by-case basis by looking at the facts and circumstances. *Adelphia*, 280 B.R. at 80. *Massachusetts Electric Co. v. Keydata Corp. (In re Keydata Corp.)*, 12 B.R. 156 (1st Cir. BAP 1981). Bankruptcy courts are endowed with the responsibility for deciding what constitutes adequate assurance for payment of post-petition utility company services and are not bound by local or state regulation. *In re Begley*, 41 B.R. 402, 405-406 (Bankr. E.D.Pa. 1984), affirmed, 760 F.2d 46 (3rd Cir. 1985).

There is a long list of cases that have approved of this method of furnishing adequate assurance of payment of post-petition utility services. *In re UAL Corp., et al.*, Case No. 02-B-48191 (ERW) (Bankr. N.D. Ill. December 9, 2002). *In re U.S. Airways Group Inc.*, Case No. 02-83984-SSM (Bankr. E.D.Va. August 12, 2002). *In re Global Crossing Ltd., et al.*, Case No. 02-40188 (REG) (Bankr. S.D.N.Y. January 28, 2002). *In re Ames Department Stores Inc.*, Case No. 01-42217 (REG) (Bankr. S.D.N.Y. August 20, 2001).

## 2.    Employment Issues

*Retention of Professionals*

In any reorganization case, the debtor is going to have to employ any number of different professionals, which include, without limitation, primary bankruptcy counsel; conflicts counsel; financial advisers; accountants; and official claims and noticing agents. Each of the professional entities will file an affidavit of disinterestedness to show the court that there are no conflicts of interest and that the professionals employed are, in fact, disinterested.

If the bankruptcy cases are large enough, the debtors may file a motion to employ professionals that are utilized in the ordinary course of business without the submission of separate employment applications and the issuance of separate retention orders for each individual professional. Debtors in this situation request permission from the court to continue to employ these "ordinary course professionals" so that there can be rendered the wide variety of services to the estates in the same way and for the same purpose as that which occurred pre-petition. These services can be legal, financial, accounting, and tax related. In addition, debtors may employ other sorts of professionals such as real estate appraisers, brokers, and leasing agents.

These ordinary course professionals, for the most part, are already familiar with the debtor's business and operations, which makes their employment important, because any discontinuation or disruption of their employment can negatively affect the debtor's business operations. Hiring ordinary course professionals in this way has the potential to save the bankruptcy estates a considerable amount of money, since each individual professional will not have to apply for employment before the bankruptcy court and there will not be the necessity for the filing and hearing of separate interim fee applications.

*Compensation of Professionals*

Under a typical compensation procedure for ordinary course professionals, a debtor would propose, without a prior application to the court, to pay 100 percent of the fees and disbursements incurred, upon submission to, and approval by, the debtors of an appropriate invoice that sets forth in reasonable detail the nature of the services rendered and the disbursements actually made, up to the lesser of (1) a certain specified amount, such as $40,000 per month per ordinary course professional; or (2) $500,000 per month in the aggregate, for all ordinary course professionals. In the event that an ordinary course professional seeks more than the $40,000 in a single month or $500,000 in the aggregate in the Chapter 11 case, the professional will be required to file a fee application for the full amount of the fees in accordance with §§ 330 and 331.

The ordinary course professional will be required to serve upon the debtor's attorney (1) an affidavit certifying that the professional does not represent or hold any interest adverse to the debtor or its estate with respect to the matter on which the professional is to be employed, and (2) a completed retention questionnaire. The debtor's attorney will then file the ordinary course professional's affidavit and retention questionnaire with the court and serve them upon the United States Trustee. The United States Trustee will then have fifteen days following service to notify the debtor, in writing, of any objection to the retention originating from the contents of the ordinary course professional's affidavit or retention questionnaire. If, after fifteen days, no objection is filed, then the retention of such ordinary course professional will be deemed approved and the ordinary course professional can be paid 100 percent of its fees and 100 percent of its expenses without the need to file fee applications, based upon the submission of the appropriate invoice setting forth in reasonable detail the nature of the services rendered and disbursement outlay actually incurred.

The debtor will, of course, reserve the right to supplement the list of ordinary course professionals as the bankruptcy case moves forward; and depending upon the nature of a debtor's business, ordinary course professionals might be periodically hired in the future.

In large and complicated Chapter 11 cases, debtors will seek the entry of an order establishing an orderly, regular process for the allowance and payment of compensation and reimbursement for attorneys and other professionals whose services are authorized by the bankruptcy court, and who will be required to file applications for the allowance of compensation and the reimbursement of expenses. In these sorts of cases, the debtors have employed a number of different professionals, including attorneys, financial advisers, balloting agents, etc. It is not uncommon for any committees to also have the same complement of professionals.

Within the framework of the Bankruptcy Code, all professionals are entitled to submit fee applications for interim compensation and reimbursement of expenses every 120 days, or more often if the court permits, pursuant to § 331. Debtors will seek the entry of an order establishing a procedure for the monthly compensation and reimbursement of expenses of their professionals. Such procedures have been instituted and approved in a number of large Chapter 11 bankruptcy cases. *In re Loral Space & Communications Ltd., et al.*, Case No. 03-41710 (RDD) (Bankr. S.D.N.Y. July 15, 2003). *In re WestPoint Stevens Inc., et al.*, Case No. 03-13532 (RDD) (Bankr. S.D.N.Y. June 1, 2003). *In re Bethlehem Steel Corp.*, Case Nos. 01-15288-01 - 15302, 01-15308-01 - 01-15315 (BRL) (Bankr. S.D.N.Y. 2001). *In re Magellan Health Services Inc., et al.*, Case No. 03-40515 (PCB) (Bankr. S.D.N.Y. March 11, 2003).

**Practice Pointer.** A typical compensation procedure of this variety would have the elements set forth in the order which is attached as Appendix .

*Key Employees*

A debtor's key employees are critical to the success of a debtor's attempts to reorganize. Without their continuing and future services, the estate would suffer, as would all creditors and parties in interest. Despite their loyalty to the debtors, key employees have, of all of the debtor's employees, the greatest potential to suffer and lose the most, and will continue to be paid substantially less than they could get in the open market. Under these circumstances, debtors often attempt to retain the services of what they deem to be key employees by proposing and seeking court approval for a key employee retention plan. An example of such a plan would include bonuses for the sales of assets if the sales reach a certain level.

**Practice Pointer.** An example of a key employee retention plan is found in the order that is attached as Appendix .

### 3. Financial Issues

*Cash Collateral*

Cash collateral is money that is encumbered by a lien held by a secured creditor. It includes cash, negotiable instruments, documents of title, securities, deposit accounts, cash equivalents, proceeds, products, offspring, rents, profits, and hotel/motel room charges. Under § 363(c)(2), a debtor is not entitled to use, sell or lease cash collateral unless one of two alternatives is met. First, each entity that has an interest in cash collateral must consent; or second, the court, after notice and a hearing, authorizes the usage in accordance with the provisions of the Bankruptcy Code.

**Practice Pointer.** It is not uncommon for a debtor and its secured creditor with a lien on cash collateral to reach an agreement and enter into a cash collateral order. There are a number of provisions that any cash collateral order should include, and an example of this is found in the order that is attached as Appendix .

*Post-Petition Financing*

Restructuring bankruptcy cases almost always have motions seeking post-petition financing. These motions are typically filed at the beginning of the bankruptcy case. Usually, they are emergency motions which request interim orders authorizing the debtor to obtain post-petition secured financing pursuant to §§105, 361, 362, 364(c)(1),(2), and (3), and 364(e); utilizing cash collateral pursuant to §363; and providing adequate protection to certain pre-petition lenders pursuant to §§361, 362 and 363 (if those pre-petition lenders are going to be lending the debtor money post-petition). This motion will also request a final hearing and final orders authorizing the relief sought.

Section 364 provides that bankruptcy courts have the power to authorize post-petition financing for a Chapter 11 debtor-in-possession. *In re Defender Drug Stores Inc.*, 126 B.R. 76, 81 (Bankr. D.Ariz. 1991). "Having recognized the natural reluctance of lenders to extend credit to a company in bankruptcy, Congress designed [Section] 364 to provide 'incentives to the creditor to extend post-petition credit.'" *Id.* Section 364(c) sets forth the conditions under which a debtor can obtain certain types of secured credit.

Typically, courts apply a three-part test to determine whether a debtor may obtain secured credit pursuant to §364(c). Specifically, the debtor must demonstrate that (1) it cannot obtain credit on an unencumbered basis or without super-priority status; (2) the credit transaction is necessary to preserve the assets of the debtor's estates; and (3) the terms of the credit transaction are fair, reasonable, and adequate given the particular circumstances of the debtor and the proposed lender. *In re Crouse Group Inc.*, 71 B.R. 544, 549 (Bankr. E.D.Pa. 1987), aff'd., 75 B.R. 553(E.D. Pa.1987) (debtor must show that it has made a reasonable effort to seek other sources of financing under §§364(a) and (b).

Courts will review the facts and circumstances of a debtor's case and give significant weight to the necessity for obtaining the financing. *In re Ames Department Stores Inc.*, 115 B.R. 34, 40 (Bankr. S.D.N.Y. 1990). Debtors are given the chance to exercise their fundamental business judgment consistent with their fiduciary duties when evaluating the necessity of proposed protections for a party extending credit under §364. *In re Trans*

*World Airlines Inc.*, 163 B.R. 964, 974 (Bankr. D.Del. 1994) (noting that an interim loan, receivables facility and asset based facility were approved because they "reflected sound and prudent business judgment . . . reasonable under the circumstances and in the best interest of [the debtor] and its creditors").

To show that the loan required is not obtainable on an unsecured basis, a creditor is only supposed to demonstrate "by a good faith effort that credit was not available" without the protections afforded by potential lenders by §364(c). *In re Snowshoe Co.*, 789 F.2d 1085, 1088 (4th Cir. 1986). A debtor's unsuccessful efforts to obtaining post-petition financing from a large group of sophisticated lending institutions meets the statutory requirements of §364(c). *In re Ames Department Stores*, 115 B.R. at 40 (approving §364(c) financing facility and holding that the debtor made reasonable efforts to obtain less onerous terms where it approached four lending institutions, was rejected by two, and selected the least onerous financing option from the remaining two lenders). *In re 495 Central Park Ave. Corp.*, 136 B.R. 626, 630 (Bankr. S.D.N.Y. 1992) (the debtor "must make an effort to obtain credit without priming a senior lien"). *In re Reading Tube Industries*, 72 B.R. 329, 332 (Bankr. E.D.Pa. 1987) (requiring demonstration that less onerous financing was unavailable). *In re Phoenix Steel Corp.*, 39 B.R. 218, 222 n.9 (D. Del. 1984) (same).

## 4.    Contract Issues

Section 365(a) assists debtors in their efforts to reorganize by allowing them to assume favorable pre-petition executory contracts and reject unfavorable ones. This enables the debtor to maximize the value of its estate. *Pharr-Mor Inc. vs. Strouss Building Associates*, 204 B.R. 948, 951(N.D. Ohio 1997) ("Pharr-Mor"). *Cinicola vs. Scharffenberger*, 248 F.3d 110, 119 (3rd Cir. 2001) ("Cinicola"). Usually, if the debtor assumes a pre-petition executory contract, the contract is effectively converted into a post-petition contract, so that both the debtor and the contracting party can still compel each other to perform. On the other hand, if the debtor rejects the pre-petition executory contract, the contract is treated as having been terminated before the debtor's filing of bankruptcy, so that the contracting party's claim for damages, if any, has the same status as all other pre-petition claims. *Pharr-Mor*, 204 B.R. 951.

Although this provision of the Bankruptcy Code speaks in terms of what the trustee can do, a Chapter 11 debtor in possession enjoys the same powers with respect to executory contracts, as a trustee. *See* § 1107(a). This means that a debtor may assume or reject and executory contract at any time before the confirmation of a plan of reorganization. *See* §365(d)(2). *Stevens vs. CSA Inc.*, 271 B.R. 410, 412 (D. Mass. 2001) (*Stevens*).

Whether an executory contract is favorable or unfavorable to an estate is left to the sound business judgment of the debtor. *Pharr-Mor*, 204 B.R. at 952. *Lubrizol Enterprises Inc. vs. Richmond Metal Fasteners, Inc.*, 756 F.2d 1043, 1046-1047 (4th Cir. 1985), cert. den'd., 475 U.S. 1057 (1985) ("Lubrizol"). Courts usually defer to the debtor's decision on the assumption or rejection of an executory contract. *Pharr-Mor*, 204 B.R. at 952. *Lubrizol*, 756 F.2d at 1047.

A debtor cannot be ordered to assume an executory contract. *Stevens*, 271 B.R. at 412. *In re III Enterprises Inc. V*, 163 B.R. 453 (Bankr. E.D.Pa. 1994), aff'd., 169 B.R. 551(E.D. Pa. 1994). Nevertheless, the bankruptcy court, on the request of any party to such contract or lease, may order the trustee or debtor to determine within a specified period whether to assume or reject such executory contracts or unexpired lease. *Stevens*, 271 B.R. at 412.

The Bankruptcy Code does not define the term "executory contracts." *Laughlin vs. Nickless*, 190 B.R. 719, 722 (D. Mass. 1996). *In re Columbia Gas System Inc.*, 50 F.3d 233, 238 (3rd Cir. 1995) (*Columbia Gas*). *In re Resource Technology Corporation*, 254 B.R. 215, 222 (Bankr. N.D.Ill. 2000) (*Resource Technology*). What legislative history there is suggests a broad reading of the word "executory." Congressional reports state, "though there is no precise definition of what contracts are executory, it generally includes contracts on which performance remains due to some extent on both sides." *Columbia Gas*, 50 F.3d at 238. *Resource Technology*, 254 B.R. at 222 n3. Most courts have reached the conclusion that the definition of executory contracts emanating from this legislative history is too broad since it is the rare agreement that does not involve unperformed obligations on either side. *Columbia Gas*, 50 F.3d at 238. *Mitchell vs. Streets (In re Streets & Beard Farm Partnership)*, 882 F.2d 233, 235 (7th Cir. 1989) (*Mitchell*). As one commentator has put it, "All contracts to a greater or lesser extent are executory. When they cease to be so, they cease to be contracts." Vern Countryman, *Executory Contracts in*

*Bankruptcy: Part I.*, 57 Minn. L.Rev., 439, 450 (1973) (*Countryman*). Therefore, it has been left up to the courts to define what the term "executory contract" actually means. *Pharr-Mor*, 204 B.R. at 952. Courts agree, however, that Congress did not mean to allow a bankrupt debtor to reject any contract not fully performed. *In re Norquist*, 43 B.R. 224, 225 (Bankr. E.D.Wash. 1984). *Pharr-Mor*, 204 B.R. at 952.

In defining the term "executory contract," many circuits rely on what has been called the traditional definition, which provides that a contract is executory when "the obligations of both the bankrupt and the other party to the contract are so far unperformed that the failure of either to complete performance would constitute a material breach excusing the performance of the other." *In re Golden Books Family Entertainment Inc.*, 269 B.R. 300, 308 (Bankr. D.Del. 2001). *Countryman* at 460. *Cinicola*, 248 F.3d at 110. *Stevens*, 271 B.R. at 413.

Under this test, a court first evaluates the obligations of both parties and determines whether they are material. Next, the court determines whether, on the date that the bankruptcy petition was filed, either party's failure to perform its remaining obligations would give rise to a material breach and excuse performance. If either party has "substantially performed" its side of the bargain, such that the party's failure to perform further would not excuse performance by the other party, then the contract is not executory. The materiality of a remaining obligation and whether the failure to perform a remaining obligation is a material breach of the contract is an issue under state law. *In re Texscan Corporation*, 976 F.2d 1269, 1272 (9th Cir. 1992). *Mitchell*, 882 F.2d at 235.

The general rule is that a contract is not considered executory where the only obligation of a party to that contract is the payment of money. *In re Leibinger-Roberts Inc.*, 105 B.R. 208, 212-213 (Bankr. E.D.N.Y. 1989). *In re Chateaugay Corp.*, 102 B.R. 335, 344-345 (Bankr. S.D.N.Y. 1989). There are, however, some circumstances when a duty to pay money may constitute a material remaining obligation to the contract where there is a material obligation remaining on the other side. *Laughlin vs. Nicklass*, 190 B.R. 722. *In re Wegner*, 839 F.2d 533, 536-537 (9th Cir. 1988). In addition, just because the remaining obligations of one of the parties are a mere contingency does not prevent the contract in question from being executory. *Laughlin vs. Nicklass*, 190 B.R. at 722. *Lubrizol*, 756 F.2d at 1046.

Assumption imposes two important burdens on an estate. First, the estate takes on the debtor's obligations under the contract and these obligations become administrative expenses, which must be paid as a priority before the debtor's pre-bankruptcy obligations. *Resource Technology*, 254 B.R. at 221. *Columbia Gas*, 50 F. 3d at 238, 239. Second, under §365(b), the debtor may only assume the contract after demonstrating that the estate is able to meet the debtor's obligations by promptly curing any existing defaults and getting adequate assurance of future performance. *Resource Technology*, 254 B.R. at 221. *Metropolitan Airports Commission v. Northwest Airlines Inc., (In re Midway Airlines, Inc.)*, 6 F.3d 492, 496 (8th Cir. 1993).

If the debtor decides not to assume an executory contract, which the Bankruptcy Code calls rejection, there is no subsequent performance by the estate of the debtor's obligations under that contract and, under § 365(g), that contract or lease will be deemed breached by the debtor with a non-debtor party to that contract given a general, non-priority claim against the estate for the breach of that contract. *Resource Technology*, 254 B.R. at 221. *In re Lavigne*, 114 F.3d 379, 387 (2nd Cir. 1997).

During the period before the assumption or rejection of an executory contract or unexpired lease, the estate must pay the reasonable value of any contractual benefits the estate receives during that period, as an administrative expense. *Continental Energy Associates L.P. v. Hazelton Fuel Management Co. (In re Continental Energy Associates L.P.)*, 178 B.R. 405, 408 (Bankr. M.D.Pa. 1995). *Resource Technology*, 254 B.R. at 221.

Some courts have found that the traditional definition of executory contracts to "come up short." They believe that this definition is helpful, but not controlling in the resolution of what an executory contract actually is. *Pharr-Mor*, 204 B.R. at 952. These courts instead use what has been called a functional approach. Under this "functional approach," courts decide whether a contract is executory by investigating whether rejection of the contract would benefit the debtor's estate, an investigation intended to invoke the broader purposes of section 365. *Stevens* , 271 B.R. at 413.

When employing the functional approach, courts work backwards, proceeding from an examination of the goal, which the rejection of the contract is expected to accomplish. If those purposes have already been met, or if they cannot be satisfied through rejection, then the contract will not be deemed executory. *Laughlin v. Nicklass*, 190 B.R. at 723. *In re Jolly*, 574 F.2d 349, 351 (6th Cir. 1978), cert. denied, 439 U.S. 929 (1978). The purposes referred to in the functional approach include: (1) taking advantage of contracts that will benefit the estate; (2) relieving the estate of burdensome contracts; (3) promoting the debtor's fresh start; (4) permitting the determination of claims; and (5) clarifying the status of third parties with respect to their status as against the estate. *In re Bluman*, 125 B.R. 359, 363 (Bankr. E.D.N.Y. 1991). *Laughlin v. Nicklass*, 190 B.R. at 723. An executory contract should not extend to cases where the only effect of finding such a contract would be to prejudice other creditors in the estate. *In re Bluman*, 125 B.R. 363. *Laughlin v. Nicklass*, 190 B.R. at 723. *Countryman* at 450.

With the functional approach, courts look at the results that would be obtained if the contracts were held to be executory. Normally, a court should find a contract executory if such a determination allows the debtor to reject a burdensome or unfavorable contract. A court may find a contract is executory under the functional approach, even though it might not have found the very same contract to be executory using the traditional definition. *Pharr-Mor*, 204 B.R. at 952. *In re Jolly*, 574 F.2d at 351. *In re Drexel Burham Lambert Group Inc.*, 138 B.R. 687, 703 n. 24, 707-709 (Bankr. S.D.N.Y. 1992).

A contract need not be executory on both sides for it to be burdensome to the estate. Whether the non-debtor party has fully performed under the contract can be irrelevant as to whether breach or affirmation of the contract will be most beneficial to the estate. The ultimate purpose behind Section 365 is to allow a trustee to pick and choose among the debtor's agreements and assume those that benefit the estate and reject those that do not. *Pharr-Mor*, 204 B.R. at 953. *In re G-N Partners*, 48 B.R. 462, 465 (Bkrtcy. D.Minn. 1985).

In some bankruptcy cases, where the debtor has entered into multiple contracts, the courts have ruled that each of the agreements can be combined into one integrated transaction, under a three-part test that examines the following factors: (1) what is the nature and purpose of the contract and dispute; (2) what was the consideration for the contracts, i.e., are they separate and distinct; and (3) whether the obligations under the contracts are interrelated. *Byrd v. Gardinier (In re Gardinier)*, 831 F.2d 974, 976 (11th Cir. 1987). For this issue to be applicable, the contracts must be between the debtor and the same party. *In re Apache Products Company*, 293 B.R. 545-547 (Bankr. N.D.Fla. 2003).

## 5.    Confirmation Issues

Under the Bankruptcy Code, before a hearing on the confirmation of a plan of reorganization can occur, the bankruptcy court must approve a written disclosure statement, after notice and a hearing, which contains adequate information. A disclosure statement is a solicitation instrument—really just an information booklet—about the plan of reorganization that has been approved by the bankruptcy court as having adequate information so that an informed decision can be made as to whether to vote in favor of or against a plan of reorganization. *In re 266 Washington Associates*, 141 B.R. 275, 288 (Bankr. E.D.N.Y. 1992), aff'd 147 B.R. 827 (E.D.N.Y. 1992).

The primary purpose of a disclosure statement is to give creditors necessary information in order to determine whether to accept or reject the proposed plan of reorganization. The purpose of the disclosure statement is not to assure the acceptance or rejection of a plan, but rather, to provide the required amount of information to interested parties so that they can make the informed choice by themselves. *In re Dakota Rail Inc.*, 104 B.R. 138, 142 (Bankr. D.Minn. 1989). *In re Monroe Well Service Inc.*, 80 B.R. 324, 330 (Bankr. E.D.Pa. 1987). *In re United States Brass Corporation*, 194 B.R. 420, 423 (Bankr. E.D.Tex. 1996) (*Brass*).

The "genius" of Chapter 11 is to force a complete disclosure and quantification of all liabilities against the bankruptcy estate so that a meaningful reorganization plan can be negotiated and confirmed. *In re Diberto*, 164 B.R. 1, 4 (Bankr. D.N.H. 1993). The phrase "adequate information" has intentionally been held to be nebulous by the courts. *In re Ferretti*, 128 B.R. 16, 18 (Bankr. D.N.H. 1991).

When bankruptcy courts are called to determine whether there is adequate information present in a disclosure statement, they look to see whether certain factors are present, which include: (1) the history of the debtor and a description of the debtor's business; (2) a complete description of available assets and their value; (3) the anticipated future of the debtor; (4) the source of the information provided in the disclosure statement; (5) a disclaimer, which typically indicates that no statements of information concerning the debtor or its assets or securities are authorized, other than those set forth in the disclosure statement; (6) a recitation of the events precipitating the Chapter 11 filing; (7) the condition and performance of the debtor while in Chapter 11; (8) information regarding claims against the estate; (9) a liquidation analysis setting forth the estimated return that creditors would receive under Chapter 7; (10) a statement of the accounting method utilized to produce the financial information contained in the disclosure statement, and an identification of the accountants responsible for deriving the information as well as the valuation methods used to produce the financial information in the disclosure statement; (11) information regarding the future management of the debtor including the amount of compensation to be paid to any insiders, directors, and/or officers of the debtor; (12) a summary of the plan of reorganization; (13) an estimate of all administrative expenses, including attorneys' fees and accountants' fees; (14) the collectability of any accounts receivable; (15) any financial information, valuations or pro forma projections that would be relevant to a creditor's determination of whether to accept or reject the plan; (16) information relevant to the risks being taken by the creditors and interest holders; (17) the actual or projected value that can be obtained from avoidable transfers; (18) the existence, likelihood, and possible success of non-bankruptcy litigation; (19) the tax consequences and a statement of the tax attributes of the debtor and of a plan of reorganization; (20) the relationship of the debtor with affiliates; (21) a disclosure of transactions with insiders; (22) a statement as to how the plan is to be executed. *In re Dakota Rail Inc.*, 104 B.R. 138, 142-143. *In re Oxford Homes Inc.*, 204 B.R. 264, 269 (Bankr. D.Me. 1997). *Brass*, 194 B.R. at 424-425; Glen W. Merrick, *The Chapter 11 Disclosure Statement in a Strategic Environment*, 44 The Business Lawyer 103, 113-116 (November 1988) and the cases cited therein.

This list of factors to determine adequate information is not exhaustive, exclusive, or comprehensive. All of these factors do not have to be present in every single bankruptcy case. *In re Ferretti*, 128 B.R. at 19. *Brass*, 194 B.R. at 425. *In re Dakota Rail Inc.*, 104 B.R. at 143. When a disclosure statement contains adequate information, there is sufficient financial information provided so that a creditor, described as a "hypothetical reasonable investor," can make an informed judgment as to whether to accept or reject the proposed plan of reorganization. *In re Monroe Well Service Inc.*, 80 B.R. at 330. *In re Civitella*, 15 B.R. 206 (Bankr. E.D.Pa. 1981). *In re Northwest Recreational Activities Inc.*, 8 B.R. 10 (Bankr. N.D.Ga. 1980).

**Practice Pointer.** A bankruptcy court is entitled to deny approval of a disclosure statement when that disclosure statement describes a plan of reorganization that is incapable of being confirmed, on its face. *In re O'Leary*, 183 B.R. 338, 339 (Bank. D.Mass. 1995). *In re Felicity Associates Inc.*, 197 B.R. 12, 14 (D.R.I. 1996). *In re Gingerella*, 148 B.R. 157, 158 (Bankr. D.R.I. 1992). A plan of reorganization that is facially unconfirmable constitutes inadequate information and is misleading. *In re Pecht*, 57 B.R. 137, 139 (Bankr. E.D.Va. 1986). Therefore, when a disclosure statement describes an unconfirmable plan, for whatever reason, the confirmation hearing should be canceled to avoid the cost and delay because the disclosure statement hearing and the future confirmation hearing will be fruitless, since the plan is unconfirmable. *In re S.E.T. Income Properties III*, 83 B.R. 791, 792 (Bankr. N.D.Okla. 1988). *In re Pecht*, 57 B.R. at 139.

## Critical Legal Features of an Asset Sale

A strategy that is becoming more in vogue in reorganization cases is for the debtor to sell all, or a substantial portion of, its assets prior to a plan of reorganization. Section 363 does not establish a standard for determining when it is appropriate for a court to authorize the sale or disposition of a debtor's assets before confirmation. Courts have required that the decision to sell assets outside the ordinary course of business be based upon the sound business judgment of the debtor. *Licensing by Paolo Inc. v. Sinatra (In re Gucci)*, 126 F.3d 380, 387 (2nd Cir. 1997). *Committee of Equity Security Holders v. Lionel Corp. (In re Lionel Corp.)*, 722 F.2d 1063, 1071 (2nd Cir. 1983). *In re Chateaugay Corp.*, 973 F.2d 141 (2nd Cir. 1992). *Stephens Industries v. McClung*, 789 F.2d 386, 390 (6th Cir. 1986). *In re Phoenix Steel Corp.*, 82 B.R. 334, 335-336 (Bankr. D.Del. 1987). The "sound business judgment" test requires that a debtor set forth four factors to sell property outside the ordinary course of business: (1) that a "sound business purpose" justifies the sale of assets outside the ordinary course of business; (2) that adequate and reasonable notice has been provided to interested parties; (3) that the debtor has obtained a fair and reasonable price; and (4) that the debtor acted in good faith. *In re Phoenix Steel Corp.*, 82 B.R. at 335-336. When a debtor demonstrates a sound business justification, it does not have to provide an extraordinarily exhaustive investigation, but rather the debtor must "simply justify the proposed disposition with a sound business judgment." *In re Baldwin United Corp.*, 43 B.R. 888, 906 (Bankr. S.D.Ohio 1984).

In order to maximize asset sales, debtors make use of a number of features to bring in the highest sales price. One of these features is the employment of a "stalking horse." A stalking horse is a proposed buyer who takes the time and the effort to investigate the proposed purchase, and whose bid is then effectively shopped by the debtor. When a bidder agrees to be a stalking horse, in return and in consideration for having its bid shopped to other potentially interested purchasers, the debtor typically awards that proposed purchaser with the right to a "break-up fee." A break-up fee is a fee paid by the debtor to a prospective purchaser in the event that a contemplated sales transaction between them is not consummated, and is intended to compensate the prospective purchaser for the time, effort, and risk of being the stalking horse, and encourage that bidder to do the necessary due diligence with assurance that its efforts will be compensated if the transaction does not occur. *In re Dorado Marine Inc.*, 332 B.R. 637 (Bankr. M.D.Fla. 2005). *In re Diamonds Plus Inc.*, 233 B.R. 829 (Bankr. E.D.Ark. 1999). *In re President Casinos Inc.*, 314 B.R. 786 (Bankr. E.D.Mo. 2004).

Approval of break-up fees and/or expense reimbursement in connection with the sale of significant assets has become a regular practice in Chapter 11 asset sales because they enable a debtor to ensure a sale to a contractually committed bidder at a price the debtor believes is fair, while providing the debtor with the potential of obtaining even greater benefits for the estate through an auction process. There are numerous cases where this has been approved. *In re Worldwide Direct Inc.*, Case No. 99-108 (MFW) (Bankr. D. Del. February 26, 1999) (approving break-up fee of 3.1 percent of proposed purchase price and 4 percent of the actual purchase price). *In re Montgomery Ward Holding Corp., et al.*, Case No. 97-1409 (PUW) (Bankr.

D.Del. June 15, 1998) (approving 2.7 percent break-up fee). *In re Sfuzzi, Inc.*, Case No. 395-35195-HCA-11 (Bankr. N.D. Tex., November 27, 1996).

Another feature that debtors employ in asset sales is overbid protection. With overbid protection, the bids over and above the stalking horse bid must be at or above a certain level. This prevents competitive bidders from coming in over and above the stalking horse bid with de minimus amounts.

A topping fee, in the context of a sale of a debtor's assets, is a fee paid only in the event that a bidder other than the one to whom the debtor or trustee agrees to pay the topping fee is successful in purchasing the debtor's assets. It is different from a break-up fee. A break-up fee is a fee paid to the proposed purchaser of assets by the seller in the event that the transaction contemplated fails to be consummated for various reasons delineated in the purchase agreement, including the seller's acceptance of a later bid. Usually, the break-up fee covers reimbursement of the disappointed purchaser's out-of-pocket expenses related to the proposed acquisition and/or compensation for the time, efforts, resources, lost opportunity costs, and risks incurred by the disappointed purchaser. On the other hand, a topping fee is paid only in the event another bidder is the successful purchaser. The amount of the topping fee is typically a percentage of the amount over the unsuccessful purchaser's bid. Since topping fees are based on the amount of the overbid, they do not usually add a preset cost to the purchase price.

There are good reasons for having break-up and topping fees. From the buyer's point of view, these fees pay the initial bidder for its legal and other professional fees and expenses incurred in connection with obtaining financing commitments, completing legal due diligence, and negotiating and drafting agreements with the debtor. They compensate the initial bidder for its expenditure of time, efforts, and resources. The potential purchaser is being compensated for the risk of being used as a stalking horse to motivate other purchasers to bid higher. These fees also compensate the losing bidder for potentially losing other business and investment opportunities.

These fees also make sense from the buyer's perspective. They incentivize parties to become the stalking horse and start the bidding process. They discourage a bidding strategy based upon holding back competitive bids until very late in the game. They assist the seller in negotiating an initial bid that may be the bidder's highest and best offer. They establish a high floor early in the bidding process. They may also advance the bidding process by creating momentum toward the conclusion of a sale. *In re ADP Plus Inc.*, 223 B.R. 870, 874 (Bankr. E.D.N.Y. 1998).

All of the buyer's protections negotiated by the parties require the approval of the bankruptcy court. In deciding whether to permit a topping fee, courts look at the same factors for a break-up fee: (1) was the negotiation of the fee tainted by self-dealing and manipulation; (2) does the fee discourage rather than encourage bidding; and (3) is the fee unreasonable relative to the proposed purchase price?

There are two related types of objections that debtors need to watch for when they sell their assets outside of the ordinary course of business. If the debtor's sales are piecemeal and serial in nature, creditors may object based upon an alleged "creeping plan of reorganization," under which the debtor seeks to avoid the requirements of a disclosure statement and plan of reorganization by simply selling off its assets a little at a time. On the other hand, when all or substantially all of the debtor's assets are sold in one sale, instead of several spread out over time, the related objection is to a sub rosa plan of reorganization. Under this concept, when a proposed sale transaction specifies the terms for adopting a plan of reorganization, whether it is intentional or unintentional, the parties and the court must comply with the confirmation requirements of the Bankruptcy Code in any event. In other words, the bankruptcy court cannot allow a sale under § 363 to trump the requirements for confirmation under §§ 1125 and 1129. The circuits that have ruled on this issue have reached different results and have used different analyses. The seminal case in the Second Circuit is *Committee of Equity Securityholders v. The Lionel Corp., In re Lionel Corp.*, 722 F.2d 1063 (2nd Cir. 1983), where the court held that the bankruptcy judge is to be given wide-ranging discretion under the Bankruptcy Code, but that the judge is required to specify the sound business justifications for his decision. *Id.* at 1066.

The prominent case in the Third Circuit is *In re Abbotts Dairies of Pennsylvania Inc.*, 788 F.2d 143 (3rd Cir. 1986), where the case involved a sale of the debtor's assets under § 363 outside of a plan. The Third Circuit sent the case back to the bankruptcy court to make a specific finding that the buyer had acted in good faith in the course of the sale, and that there was no fraud, collusion, or attempt to take grossly unfair advantage of other bidders. *Id.* at 147. The Third Circuit required a showing that the purchase price was fair and reasonable, that the sale was in the best interests of the estate, and that the assets would substantially diminish if they were not sold immediately. *Id.* at 146.

## Those Industries or Commercial Sectors That Are Most Actively Pursing Bankruptcy Today

Today, there are a number of industries or commercial sectors that seem to be cresting the bankruptcy wave. This can be seen from the number of filings that occur on a daily, monthly, and annual basis. They include the automotive parts industry; the airline industry (most obvious are the bankruptcy cases of the major airlines such as United and Delta, but behind these, however, are the bankruptcy cases of the smaller non-commercial passenger airlines which are more freight-based in nature); natural resources; and the bankruptcy fallout from the subprime mortgage debacle. These cases are set forth in the charts below.

*Automotive Parts Industry*

| CASE NAME | CASE NUMBER | COURT | DATE OF FILING |
|---|---|---|---|
| Intermet Corporation | 04-67597 | ED-Michigan (Detroit) | 9/29/04 |
| Oxford Automotive Inc. | 04-74377 | ED-Michigan (Detroit) | 12/7/04 |
| Tower Automotive Inc. | 05-10578 | SD-New York (Manhattan) | 2/2/05 |
| Meridian Automotive Systems-Composites Operations Inc. | 05-11168 | District of Delaware | 4/26/05 |
| Collins & Aikman Corporation | 05-55927 | ED-Michigan (Detroit) | 5/17/05 |
| Delphi Corporation | 05-44481 | SD-New York (Manhattan) | 10/8/05 |

| | | | |
|---|---|---|---|
| Dana Corporation | 06-10354 | SD-New York (Manhattan) | 3/3/06 |
| MQVP Inc. | 06-51141 | ED-Michigan (Detroit) | 8/17/06 |
| Dura Automotive Systems Inc., et al. | 06-11202 | District of Delaware | 10/30/06 |
| Holley Performance Products Inc. | 08-10256 | District of Delaware | 2/11/08 |
| Diamond Glass Inc. | 08-10601 | District of Delaware | 4/1/08 |

*Airline Industry*

| CASE NAME | CASE NUMBER | COURT | DATE OF FILING |
|---|---|---|---|
| US Airways Inc., et al. | 04-13819 | ED-Virginia (Alexandria) | 9/12/04 |
| Aloha Airgroup Inc., et al. | 04-03063 | District of Hawaii (Honolulu) | 12/30/04 |
| Delta Airlines Inc., et al. | 05-17923 | SD-New York (Manhattan) | 9/14/05 |
| Northwest Airlines Corporation, et al. | 05-17930 | SD-New York (Manhattan) | 9/14/05 |
| Gemini Cargo Logistics Inc., et al. | 06-10870 | SD-Florida (Miami) | 3/15/06 |
| Kitty Hawk Inc. | 07-44536 | ND-Texas (Fort Worth) | 10/15/07 |
| Frontier Airlines Inc., et al. | 08-11297 | SD-New York (Manhattan) | 4/10/08 |

*Natural Resources*

| CASE NAME | CASE NUMBER | COURT | DATE OF FILING |
|---|---|---|---|
| ASARCO, et al. | 05-21207 | SD-Texas (Corpus Christi) | 8/9/05 |
| Scotia Pacific Co. LLC, et al. | 07-20027 | SD-Texas (Corpus Christi) | 1/18/07 |
| U.S. Energy Systems Inc., et al. | 08-10054 | SD-New York (Manhattan) | 1/9/08 |
| High Velocity Alternative Energy Corp. | 08-35285 | SD-New York (Poughkeepsie) | 2/20/08 |
| PRB Energy Inc., et al. | 08-12658 | District of Colorado (Denver) | 3/5/08 |
| Galaxy Energy Corporation, et al. | 08-13164 | District of Colorado (Denver) | 3/14/08 |
| Solano Well Services LLC, et al. | 08-32282 | SD-Texas (Houston) | 4/7/08 |
| Patman Drilling International Inc. | 07-34622 | ND-Texas (Dallas) | 9/25/07 |
| Reichman Petroleum | 06-20804 | SD-Texas (Corpus Christi) | 12/8/06 |

*Sub-prime Mortgage*

| CASE NAME | CASE NUMBER | COURT | DATE OF FILING |
|---|---|---|---|
| Ownit Mortgage Solutions Inc. | 06-12579 | CD-California (San Fernando Valley) | 12/28/06 |
| Mortgage Lenders Network USA Inc., et al. | 07-10146 | District of Delaware | 2/5/07 |

| | | | |
|---|---|---|---|
| Liquidating Trust of ResMAE Mortgage Corporation | 07-10177 | District of Delaware | 2/12/07 |
| New Century TRS Holdings, et al. | 07-10416 | District of Delaware | 4/2/07 |
| American Home Mortgage Holdings Inc., et al. | 07-11047 | District of Delaware | 8/6/07 |
| First Magnus Capital | 08-01494 | District of Arizona | 2/19/08 |

## Economic Factors That Influence the Number of Bankruptcies in a Particular Industry or Commercial Sector

From an industrial perspective, bankruptcies are cyclical in nature. In the mid to late 1980s, the business landscape was littered with bank failures and bankruptcy cases filed in the real estate and oil and gas industries. Today, with oil being sold at record amounts per barrel, the oil and gas industry is booming. Nevertheless, there are currently a surprising number of bankruptcies in the "oil patch." This may be due to the capital intensive nature of the industry, the inherent risks of the industry, extreme competition or the lack of significant barriers to entry into the business and the availability of investor capital or a combination of the above.

The high price being paid for oil demonstrates one of the economic factors that influence bankruptcies, and that is the ripple effect. With oil being sold at such a high dollar amount, this has negatively affected airlines that rely so heavily on the cost of fuel. This was particularly noted in the Delta bankruptcy case.

This ripple effect is also visible with respect to the vendors and support industry of large debtors that seek bankruptcy relief. If a major client of a vendor files for bankruptcy, this will, in all likelihood, negatively affect that vendor, and may well lead to that party seeking bankruptcy relief as well.

When the United States' economy does poorly, resulting in credit tightening, it becomes more and more difficult to borrow money. This makes it harder for companies to stay afloat or refinance their debts or restructure their balance sheet, and contributes to bankruptcy filings as well.

In addition, when there is competition from foreign companies that are subsidized by their governments, this also creates a challenge to American corporations.

## The Preparedness of Most Law Firms to Handle Bankruptcy Strategies, Specifically Restructuring

*Types of Bankruptcy Law Firms*

There are essentially three types of law firms that handle bankruptcy cases. First, there is the larger law firm that has a sizeable bankruptcy practice. In this scenario, the bankruptcy section not only has its own clients, but also exists to service the clients of the other sections of the firm, most notably the corporate and/or real estate sections. Second, there is the boutique law firm that is, for all intents and purposes, a bankruptcy practice standing alone. It may have other work, but this outside work is essentially incidental to servicing bankruptcy clients. A boutique law firm has its own clients, and lives by referrals from other law firms. Third, is the very small firm that services one or more bankruptcy clients including trustees. This firm is really nothing more than a "captive" of these clients.

Over the past several years, there has been a trend toward law firms merging and becoming more national or international in scope. This has resulted in the growth and sophistication of the bankruptcy practices of these merged law firms. However, boutique firms are now making a comeback.

It is becoming increasingly popular for larger law firms to "pitch" for committee representations and other bankruptcy work throughout the entire country, even in cities where they do not have an office or sizeable presence. If they are successful in obtaining such a representation, they then seek to obtain local counsel. In hiring local counsel, these larger firms want to employ a law firm that will not poach their client and are likely to look for a boutique law firm to be their presence in that venue. Besides marginalizing the larger law firms in that city, this has resulted in boutique law firms making a comeback and gaining an increasing presence in bankruptcy cases.

*Necessary Law Firm Features and Resources*

When a larger law firm has a bankruptcy section, this provides the bankruptcy attorneys in that firm with a reservoir of talent to draw from. Bankruptcy is, in many respects, an interdisciplinary field. Companies in all geographic areas and industries seek bankruptcy relief and a myriad of questions face bankruptcy attorneys on a daily basis, over and above the procedural and substantive elements of bankruptcy law. When a bankruptcy section has a law firm standing behind it which practices in other non-bankruptcy fields, this enables the bankruptcy attorneys to draw from their law firm's experience without having to hire outside or special counsel.

In contrast, boutique bankruptcy law firms may not have this breadth of experience to draw from and unless the bankruptcy attorneys have been in a similar bankruptcy case in the past, they may well be forced to hire outside special counsel. Consequently, it is extremely helpful when a bankruptcy firm has other attorneys with experience in the industry of the debtor. But that kind of experience, standing alone, is not helpful unless the law firm has seamless cross-referencing within it. In other words, the bankruptcy attorneys must know of the experience of the other lawyers in the firm, and have internal procedures established so that they can make use of those attorneys when needed. A law firm that is rigidly established and where it is difficult for attorneys to work on the projects of their colleagues makes it more difficult for bankruptcy lawyers to practice effectively and leverage the firm's resources. This can be especially true in larger, mega-firms, where lawyers do not know each other and are unfamiliar with the practice areas, expertise, and experience of their colleagues.

Bankruptcy is also an insular practice. It is has its own statute and its own courts. Locally, regionally, and nationally, it is easy for bankruptcy attorneys to become familiar with their counterparts at other firms. This is important from the prospective of networking, referrals, and conflicts of interest. Undoubtedly, conflicts of interest emerge and disqualify law firms from representations. Being well connected in the bankruptcy community often results in obtaining valuable cases. This networking is also true with respect to other professionals involved in the bankruptcy arena, such as restructuring officers, financial advisors, valuation specialists, and accountants.

**155**

## Best Practices for Handling Restructuring Needs of Bankruptcy Clients

In the best of all possible worlds, there are at least five separate and distinct practices that a law firm must tackle when handling the restructuring needs of its bankruptcy clientele. First, it is important to get to the client early. This is often a real challenge, because it is the client that seeks the attorney, not the attorney that seeks the client. Too often, the client gets to the attorney far too late, and the attorney is forced to make decisions under constricted time limitations. If the client gets to the attorney early enough, this gives the attorney enough time and flexibility to do the necessary research, consider and explore options, seek bankruptcy alternatives, and make the best possible decisions for the client.

Second, the attorneys need to speak to the personnel at the corporation who have personal knowledge of the particular problem at hand. Very often, the contact that brings the attorney the representation is not the person who is best suited to address the specific bankruptcy issues. Corporations are often large in size, and it is not uncommon for attorneys to have to speak with more than one individual to fully understand and appreciate the legal problems presented and their impact on the business operations of the client. Bankruptcy cases cover a diverse and broad spectrum of issues that may necessitate coming into contact with a large number of individuals at the debtor.

Third, review the client's documents. Your contacts at the debtor may have read these documents, and they will have their own personal interpretation. This should not be substituted for your own. It is essential that the attorney review and become familiar with a client's important documents. In large bankruptcy cases, this may be impossible, and the attorneys may have to employ accountants and other professionals to review documents, but it helps when the attorneys are hands-on and have personal knowledge of the documents.

Fourth, attorneys should understand the client's debt structure. Corporations will have obligations that are both secured and unsecured. For example, a bank creditor will be undersecured if the value of its collateral is less than the debt that it is owed. The bank will be secured in the amount of the value of its collateral and unsecured for the balance of the deficiency. It is imperative for the attorneys to be fluent with these issues. Secured creditors will undoubtedly take on a greater importance early in the case with respect to cash collateral and related issues.

Last, but not least, is a thorough understanding of a client's objectives. Companies go into bankruptcy for any number of reasons. Sometimes there is no choice, time is short, and bankruptcy is seen as a last resort. Other times, bankruptcy is a well thought-out, planned, almost surgical endeavor. Sometimes, companies want to jettison unprofitable affiliates, and sometimes the debtor is just looking for breathing space. Whatever the debtor's objectives are, the lawyers must know them, ensure they are realistic and achievable, and take them into account in formulating the overall strategy to achieve the desired results.

These practices are developed, prioritized, and implemented based upon the existing time schedule. If bankruptcy is impending due to an upcoming deadline—for example a loan payment is looming—there is often a mad scramble to right the ship and get the debtor on proper footing. When this happens, the corporation files for bankruptcy by simply filing its petition, matrix, and list of the twenty largest unsecured creditors, but it may not have had the time, pre-petition, to also prepare and file its schedules and statement of financial affairs and other important, but not necessarily critical, tasks. This results in the debtor filing a motion to extend time to file those additional documents. This means that the debtor is, for all practical purposes, playing catch-up during the early stages of the bankruptcy case. On the other hand, if the lawyer is involved with the corporation sooner, rather than later, and there is no impending deadline that has to be dealt with right away, the lawyers can undertake their examination of the debtor, with the help of not only the debtor's employees, but also the debtor's other professionals, such as accountants and financial advisers, and ensure that routine matters are under control so more critical actions can be focused on to ensure the debtor's success.

The attorneys involved in a corporate restructuring and/or bankruptcy depend upon the size of the debtor. Typically, when a corporation hires a law firm, the law firm puts together a "team" of attorneys to focus on that client. The team will be staffed pyramidically with senior lawyers at the top and junior lawyers at the bottom. Law firms that have represented debtors are, or should be, very sensitive to overburdening their representation because they have to file fee applications and obtain court approval of such fees in order to be paid. Law firms that overburden their representations with an ineffective or poorly managed team may have their fees cut.

## The Five Basic Steps Used to Evaluate Alternative Restructuring Strategies for Each Bankruptcy Client

*Restructuring Steps*

There are five basic steps used to evaluate alternative restructuring strategies for each bankruptcy client. First, the lawyer must know who his client is and who his client is not. When representing a corporation, the lawyer's client is the corporation. It is not an officer, director, shareholder, employee, guarantor, or the contact that brought the representation to the lawyer. This is extremely important because sometimes individuals have different agendas than their corporations—and lawyers often lose sight of this. The obligation of the lawyer is to the corporation and to no other entity or person. Conflicts often get in the way, and the corporation's lawyer can get caught in the resulting cross fire. For example, officers and directors may have breached their fiduciary duties to the corporation and may have liability to the corporation as a result and yet they are the people making day-to-day decisions in the bankruptcy proceeding for the corporation. Another example is if a corporate principal or director guarantees a corporate debt and wants the corporation to pay that debt first before other debts are paid. It is imperative for the lawyer not only to know who his client is, but also to make that perfectly clear to the corporate debtor and the corporate debtor's principals at the outset. At a minimum, there should be a provision in the law firm's retention agreement that sets out this principle.

An example of what can go wrong in this step is a decision in the case of *In re Kendavis Industries International Inc.* 91 B.R. 742 (Bankr. N.D.Tex. 1988). There, the corporate debtor's law firm was held to have been acting in the interests of the debtor's principals, and was sanctioned as a result. This type of a result needs to be avoided at all costs. That is why counsel for the debtor must go to whatever lengths it can to make certain that it represents the debtor corporation and no one else.

In extremely large bankruptcy cases, this principle comes into play in another way as well. Very large law firms not only represent debtors, but also creditors. A large bankruptcy case can involve thousands of creditors and it is not uncommon for a debtor's law firm to have represented creditors, pre-petition, in transactions that did not involve the debtor. This will be brought to the bankruptcy court's attention in the motion to employ the debtor's law firm and that law firm's affidavit of disinterestedness. Sometimes, however, the transaction under which the creditor employed the debtor's law firm might actually involve the debtor tangentially. When that happens, objections may be filed to the debtor's retention of its law firm. In this type of a scenario, at a minimum, transparency is very important, and the debtor's law firm must divulge all of its relationships so that the bankruptcy court can make a fully informed decision on whether that law firm can continue to represent the debtor.

Second, whatever restructuring strategy is employed, the debtor should be the party making that decision. All too often, it is the debtor's lender or creditors that may force the debtor into a specific course of action. At one extreme is the involuntary bankruptcy petition that is filed against the debtor. This usually occurs when three creditors of the debtor file the bankruptcy petition and the debtor is given an opportunity to challenge that filing. Until the bankruptcy court deems the filing appropriate, the debtor corporation is an "alleged debtor." Although involuntary bankruptcy petitions are not commonplace, they do occur, and they demonstrate the importance of having the debtor make the restructuring decision. Another example of this is when the debtor's lender uses its leverage to take more collateral or to have the debtor execute new loan documents which give the lender rights which it did not have before, in the form of higher interest rates, etc. Lenders need to be careful, because they should not be in the position of dictating how a debtor corporation runs its business, for fear of being a defendant in a lender liability lawsuit. Nevertheless, whatever restructuring strategy the debtor chooses, it is in the debtor's best interest for the debtor to make that decision—not the debtor's creditors and/or lenders.

Third, it is vitally important for the debtor to set the momentum when it institutes its restructuring strategy. For example, if the debtor is going to file for bankruptcy, the debtor should, at the same time that it files its petition, also file not only its schedules and statement of financial affairs, but should also file all of its first day pleadings along with a supporting affidavit. When this is done, the debtor obtains a hearing on its petition date, or soon thereafter, and is able to have the court rule on the multitude of issues encompassed by the first day pleadings. This gives the debtor a tremendous amount of momentum. Many creditors may be surprised by the bankruptcy filing and will not be in a position to contest, or contest vigorously, the relief that the debtor is seeking. An extreme example of this is when the debtor files, along with all of these other pleadings, a pre-packaged plan of reorganization, and seeks to obtain reorganization on an extremely fast track. This may not always be successful, because the bankruptcy court will want to enable the creditors to have enough time to respond, but it certainly gives the debtor a leg up very early on in its bankruptcy case.

Fourth, and related, is survival of the first day. If a debtor corporation is able to obtain a first day hearing on its first day pleadings, it is important that the debtor obtain its requested relief. A court ruling in contravention to what the debtor is asking for may derail or sidetrack a debtor's bankruptcy case and give the debtor's creditors an extra edge that they did not have before.

Often, this is not as bad as it sounds. First day hearings are sometimes interim hearings, with final hearings to occur later on, perhaps thirty days away. If a debtor gets an adverse ruling at the first day, interim hearing, it then has a period to regroup; reevaluate its sought-after relief; negotiate with its creditors; and then go back to the court.

Fifth, is having an exit strategy. It may seem, at first blush, counterintuitive, but when a debtor goes into bankruptcy, it must know how it is going to leave bankruptcy. All too often, debtors file for bankruptcy because they want some breathing room. They have no viable business or means to reasonably restructure their financial affairs. Experience teaches that breathing room dissipates quickly, and the debtor is then left with the difficult decision of how it is going to reorganize. Often, this happens because the debtor is forced into bankruptcy by events beyond its control, such as with creditors foreclosing on assets, or loans coming due with an inability to pay them. When a debtor goes into bankruptcy with a viable, well thought-out exit strategy, it makes bankruptcy that much easier. That is not to say that the exit strategy you go in with is the exit strategy that ultimately prevails. Bankruptcy is, after all, a form of litigation, and litigation is inherently unpredictable. You cannot be 100 percent sure of what other parties will do, or how a court will rule. Nevertheless, having an exit strategy enables the debtor to move its bankruptcy case forward, and establishes a platform from which to begin negotiations. A debtor that has and can articulate a viable exit plan is more likely to get the benefit of the doubt from the bankruptcy judge.

## Evaluation/Collection of Information/Analysis

With respect to understanding whom your client is and who your client is not, this is done, at least preliminarily, through a conflicts check. The debtor's principals and creditors are run through the law firm's databases in order to see whether the law firm has ever represented or been adverse to them. In making sure that bankruptcy is the client's choice, it is essential for the lawyer to go over each restructuring alternative with the debtor. When deciding on a reorganization, the exit strategy will have to be determined and evaluated. In other words, the debtor will need to be made aware of the different steps that it will have to undergo in order to emerge from Chapter 11. As for an exit strategy, the list of possibilities is limited only by the lawyer's imagination. Reorganizing companies emerge from bankruptcy under any number of scenarios including, without limitation, the sale of assets; the issuance of new stock; the prosecution of litigation; the sale of the debtor's operations as a going concern; refinancing; and paying creditors over time through the regular course of business.

## The Most Challenging Restructuring Strategy

The most challenging restructuring strategy is reorganization under Chapter 11 of the Bankruptcy Code. Pre-bankruptcy workouts can be complicated—there is no question about that. Refinancing, new loan documents, sale of assets, sale of affiliates or divisions, can all be extremely complicated depending upon the nature of the business, the size of the business, and the assets involved. But what makes reorganization that much more challenging is the fact that no matter what type of restructuring goes on pre-bankruptcy, the very same kind of a restructuring can go on in a bankruptcy case. Added to that is the fact that the corporation has to continue in the ordinary course of its business pending that restructuring. In other words, besides making certain that the corporation restructures, the debtor's lawyers must insure that the debtor continues in business.

Navigating these challenges requires attorneys that are fluent in a broad range of specialties. First, it is helpful if the debtor's counsel has experience in the industry that the debtor is in. For example, if the debtor contains franchisees, then its bankruptcy counsel should have a working knowledge of franchise law as well as experience in the unique attributes of a franchise business. Another example is if the debtor is involved in retail, then its bankruptcy counsel should have a working knowledge and experience in retail bankruptcies. Besides that, the bankruptcy counsel must have experience with the bankruptcy issues that will typically arise in its client's case. For example, in retail bankruptcies, an important issue will be the assumption and rejection of executory contracts and unexpired leases. A retail debtor's bankruptcy counsel must be fully conversant in this area. Furthermore, the debtor's counsel must have experience in all of the intricate legal matters that the debtor will likely run into on a day-to-day basis in running its business. This may well include areas of corporate governance, employment, taxes, finance, and contracts, and run the entire gamut of legal issues.

## The Questions to Ask Bankruptcy Clients When Developing Restructuring Strategies

Whenever a bankruptcy attorney counsels a corporate client, questions must be asked in order to develop appropriate restructuring strategies. These questions include, without limitation: (1) what are your goals/what does the debtor hope to accomplish; (2) how is the debtor going to restructure; (3) can the debtor achieve its goals without restructuring and, if so, how; (4) are there any existing time restrictions or limitations, or in other words, is there anything impending which requires that a restructuring take place immediately; (5) does the debtor's loan documents or corporate governance documents impose restrictions on restructuring; (6) who will benefit from the restructuring (e.g., the debtor's principles, guarantors, secured creditors, unsecured creditors); (7) what will happen if the debtor does not restructure; (8) has the debtor restructured in the past, and if so, how was this done; (9) will the debtor's lenders be cooperative with this restructuring; (10) will the debtor's unsecured creditors, the committee, be cooperative with this restructuring; (11) how will the restructuring impact the debtor's business (will the debtor's business be better off and will the debtor be more marketable and in a better position to survive in the economy); (12) how will the restructuring impact the debtor's creditors; (13) what are the tax implications for the proposed restructuring; (14) which creditors are the debtor's critical vendors; (15) what payments have been made over the past ninety days that would qualify for preferences, and what affirmative defenses exist, if any, to those preferences; (16) what causes of action exist against the debtor's lenders, secured creditors, unsecured creditors, other parties in interest; (17) what causes of action exist against the debtor, its shareholders, officers, directors, principles, and/or control personnel; (18) does the debtor have access to cash that does not qualify as cash collateral; and (19) will the debtor's lenders agree or consent to the use of cash collateral?

## The Corporate Individuals Most Involved in the Restructuring Process

There are a number of individuals within a corporate debtor's structure that will be most involved in the restructuring and/or bankruptcy process. Some corporations hire a restructuring officer, giving that individual the title CRO, or chief restructuring officer. This individual is given the responsibility for turning the debtor around and will be in charge of many, if not most, aspects of the restructuring process. There now exists, in the bankruptcy community, companies that make restructuring officers available to companies going into bankruptcy. This has become, to a large extent, a cottage industry within bankruptcy itself.

Besides a restructuring officer, another individual who will play a key and very important role in the restructuring and bankruptcy process is the debtor's chief financial officer. This individual is responsible for the debtor's money that goes in and goes out. Her presence will be key during the first day hearings when she testifies about the debtor's need for financing and use of cash collateral. A debtor's chief executive officer, to the extent she has not been replaced by the CRO, sits atop the operational pyramid and, by definition, will play an important role in addressing the overall operational and financial challenges facing the debtor. The size of this role will depend upon her involvement in the bankruptcy and restructuring process.

Corporations are faceless entities. Often vast in size, they do not have somebody that they can be readily identified with. Bankruptcy is a form of litigation that requires a presence in court. One of the most important people in the bankruptcy process for a corporation is the person who will show up at the hearings with the attorney and some as the key witness. It is this person that will humanize the corporate debtor and who the bankruptcy judge, and other parties in interest, will begin to identify the debtor with. Selecting the wrong person, or selecting the right person who happens to be a bad witness, can be a challenging task for any bankruptcy attorney.

### Security and Asset Issues in Bankruptcy Restructuring Strategies

A debtor's assets and the debtor's creditors' security interests in those assets are often at the forefront of bankruptcy restructuring strategies. There are a number of reasons for this. First, the debtor's assets may be the engine that generates income to keep the debtor in business or fund its reorganization. Second, the assets may be sold in order to generate funds to repay creditors in a reorganization. Third, the debtor's assets may be the collateral for a lender under which cash collateral is made available to a debtor in a Chapter 11 reorganization.

A creditor that has a lien on cash collateral will try to use its secured position as leverage against the debtor. In these situations, the secured creditor may make cash collateral available to the debtor only if the debtor agrees to any number of protections, including that the creditor's secured position is valid and not subject to any objection. A debtor in this type of a situation may feel trapped, but what the debtor will do is get the unsecured creditors' committee to make the objection that is necessary.

**Practice Pointer.** A savvy creditor will agree to the use of its cash collateral on the condition that it not be spent paying any professionals to contest the validity of its lien and establishing a reasonable deadline by which any such challenge must be commenced.

*Joseph J. Wielebinski is a shareholder and serves as chairman of Munsch Hardt Kopf & Harr's Reorganization and Corporate Finance practice group, which consists of more than twenty attorneys in Dallas, Houston, and Austin. He has focused his practice on bankruptcy, creditors' rights and financial restructuring for almost twenty-five years and he is active throughout the United States in a variety of complex restructuring, insolvency and bankruptcy cases.*

*Mr. Wielebinski received his Bachelor of Arts degree, magna cum laude, from Temple University in 1980. He received his Master of public affairs degree and his Juris Doctorate degree from Syracuse University in 1983, where he was the senior executive editor of the* Syracuse University Journal of International Law and Commerce.

*He was admitted to the State Bar of Texas in 1983 and is a member of the Dallas and American Bar Associations. Mr. Wielebinski is admitted to practice before the Supreme Court of Texas, all four districts in Texas, various United States districts throughout the country, as well as the Fourth and Fifth Circuit Courts of Appeals.*

*Mr. Wielebinski is the past president of the Bankruptcy & Commercial Law Sections of the Dallas Bar Association. He is also the past president of the Dallas/Ft. Worth Chapter of the Turnaround Management Association. Mr. Wielebinski is an active member in the American Bar Association and the American Bankruptcy Institute. He was named a Leader in his Field in 2005 through 2007 by* Chambers & Partners *and named a "Super Lawyer" by the* Texas Monthly *magazine in 2003 through 2007. He was also listed in* Euromoney's Experts' Guide *for insolvency and restructuring attorneys in 2006 to 2007. Recently, Mr. Wielebinski was selected for inclusion in the 2008 edition of* Best Lawyers in America.

*Mr. Wielebinski is a frequent author and speaker on a variety of topics including bankruptcy, asset sales, telecom insolvencies, fraud and commercial crime, asset recoveries, and financial reorganizations in the United States and internationally.*

*Mr. Wielebinski is a member of FraudNet, an invitation-only organization sponsored by the International Chamber of Commerce, which consists of professionals throughout the world who have significant experience in matters involving complex commercial fraud and offshore asset identification and recovery.*

***Seymour Roberts Jr.*** *is a senior associate with Munsch Hardt Kopf & Harr PC. Mr. Roberts has experience representing the interests of debtors, creditors, and committees in large and complex reorganizations. In addition, he is a receiver of multi-family housing properties. He also has seven years of judicial experience, as a municipal court judge, pro tem, for the city of Fort Worth, Texas. Mr. Roberts has attained the designation of Advocate with the National Institute of Trial Advocacy and is a certified mediator, family mediator and victim offender mediator and was a finalist two years in a row for the Mediator of the Year Award for Dispute Resolution Services of Tarrant County, Texas. He is also a graduate of Leadership Fort Worth, Texas.*

# Looking Ahead—and to the Past—in Developing Restructuring Strategies

## Stuart M. Brown

*Partner, Co-Chair Insolvency and Bankruptcy Department,*
*Partner-in-Charge Wilmington, DE Office*
Edwards Angell Palmer & Dodge LLP

ASPATORE

## Setting the Stage

Bankruptcy lawyers may be the last of the generalists. In an age of ever growing specialization, bankruptcy lawyers are called upon to transcend all areas of commercial law to spot and deal with issues of every nature, usually with an insolvency overview. They are transactional attorneys that litigate and litigators that negotiate and close transactions. They are equally at home in the courtroom as they are in the board room. They represent borrowers, guarantors, lenders, landlords, trade vendors, contract parties, owners of companies, purchasers of assets from bankruptcy estates, bondholders, indenture trustees and committees of unsecured creditors, equity holders, and a myriad of other parties-in-interest in the larger bankruptcy cases.

Bankruptcy cases are multi-party litigations. These cases may be resolved through litigation, or more often than not, as a result of a negotiated business transaction, with the bankruptcy laws utilized as a set of guiding principles for the structuring of a transaction. Many issues that are litigated involve parties' prospective rights and relationships, as various aspects of a debtor's business are subject to bankruptcy court supervision and approval. Bankruptcy cases differ from typical litigation in that the parties not only litigate over events that occurred years prior; rather, the litigation also involves questions of whether a particular transaction will be authorized by the bankruptcy court or to determine the relative rights and priorities of competing classes of creditors. Oftentimes parties with competing rights are fighting over a limited pool of assets and bankruptcy cases involve disputes over which classes of creditors will receive distributions before other classes of creditors. Furthermore, bankruptcy courts are courts of equity that weigh the differing classes' competing interests in determining disputes, also guided by the principles of the bankruptcy code. Bankruptcy lawyers, therefore, must exercise a great deal of judgment in predicting the outcome of disputes as there are many competing interests taken into consideration in the balance.

Bankruptcy lawyers add the most value through their experience in representing the various interests of parties in bankruptcy cases. They are guided by well-worn paths charted by others, as well as new avenues or techniques that might be effectively and efficiently taken to achieve a particular client's goal in a particular bankruptcy matter. For example, when the Seventh Circuit decided that the doctrine of necessity was not a sufficient underpinning for critical vendor payments in a large retail bankruptcy case, we started to think about other strategies that would permit debtors to recognize and treat their critical trade vendors. Since most critical trade vendor motions and payments to critical trade vendors under those motions are conditioned on such vendors providing trade credit on terms as good or better than they provide prior to the bankruptcy case, and since most bankruptcy cases involve the use of cash collateral or post-petition financing, which rely on cash flow projections that incorporate assumptions about the level and terms of trade credit, it was determined that critical trade vendor motions may find support under Section 364 of the Bankruptcy Code, the section authorizing post-petition credit. Essentially, critical vendor motions and the resulting trade credit extended to debtors are integral to post-petition financing and, therefore, authority for a debtor's desired preferential treatment of its critical vendors could be obtained under another bankruptcy provision. It is the flexible and creative bankruptcy lawyer that has a solid foundation of knowledge of the bankruptcy code that delivers valuable services to her clients.

## Restructuring Strategy Trends

The bankruptcy code is a federal statutory scheme that governs situations involving, among other things, insolvent enterprises and individuals. The code promotes various public policies through a careful balance of the rights of and protections for debtors and the rights of creditors. The bankruptcy code includes provisions in Chapter 7 for the liquidation of the assets of an enterprise and ratable distribution of the proceeds to creditors according to priorities set by state and federal law. The code also sets forth the laws permitting businesses to reorganize under Chapter 11, a process typically controlled by current management of the enterprise. The current bankruptcy laws were enacted in 1898, but have been amended several times and most recently were subject to change through the enactment of the Bankruptcy Abuse and Consumer Protection Act of 2005 ("BACPA"). Even though BACPA targeted substantial revisions to the consumer bankruptcy laws, the act included a number of changes pertaining to commercial bankruptcies. Two of those changes were quite significant. The first involves extensions a debtor might obtain to assume and assign non-residential unexpired real estate leases. Prior to the amendment in 2005 a debtor could seek permission from the bankruptcy court to extend its deadline to assume and assign such a lease until the effective date of a plan that may be confirmed at some time much later in the bankruptcy case. Oftentimes plans were not confirmed in cases for several years, leaving landlords insecure about the future of the occupancy at their properties, and in certain circumstances such uncertainty prevented landlords from selling or refinancing their properties at market prices and rates. The 2005 amendments now limit the bankruptcy court's authority to grant such extensions beyond 210 days following the filing of the bankruptcy case, unless the landlord consents to such an additional extension.

The second significant amendment imposes a limitation on a debtor's right to seek extension of the exclusive period granted to a debtor to propose a plan of reorganization or a plan of liquidation in its bankruptcy case and to solicit acceptances of its plan from the classes of creditors and equity holders entitled to vote on the plan. Exclusivity has long been touted as the great leveler of the playing field among the rights and leverage of competing constituencies in bankruptcy cases. Exclusivity acted to keep creditors at bay while debtors fixed fundamental operating issues or permitted debtors to wait out down business cycles while protected by the automatic stay. Delays in proposing and confirming a plan in a bankruptcy case delayed distributions to creditors, delayed the debtor's assumption of executory contracts and unexpired leases and the debtor's obligation to cure pre-bankruptcy defaults, delayed the determination of the value of secured lenders' collateral, and delayed the restructuring of the debtor, generally. As such, debtor's management that stayed in possession and control of the debtor, as a debtor in possession, was able to leverage such delays and threats of delays, as well as the incidental increased costs of the bankruptcy case due to the longer period during which the bankruptcy court and creditors would have oversight of the debtor and its operations, in their negotiations with the various constituencies in their bankruptcy case, often resulting in plans that involved compromises by all. In cases where parties were unyielding, extensions of exclusivity permitted debtors to propose a plan that sought to impose a compromise but might not be confirmed, and if unsuccessful, leaving debtors a second chance at exclusively proposing a confirmable plan. The 2005 amendments limit exclusivity extension to eighteen months following the beginning of a bankruptcy case. At the expiration of the eighteen-month exclusive period, the cases are not necessarily over, merely debtors' right exclusively to propose a plan terminates and ultimately, if no party in the case proposes and confirms a plan in the Chapter 11 case, the case will likely be converted to a liquidation under Chapter 7 or dismissed.

Both changes to the bankruptcy code in 2005 shorten debtors' abilities to benefit from the mere passage of time, or even the threat of the passage of time. As a result of Congress' limitations imposed by BACPA, debtors and their professionals will now be required to spend more time planning strategies for the administration of and exiting from their bankruptcy cases. For example, in retail bankruptcy cases debtors will be required to make store-by-store strategic decisions before a case is filed and be prepared to stand by those decisions by quickly assuming leases for profitable stores, while rejecting leases for marginal or unprofitable stores. These decisions are likely to be made when debtors are least able to focus their resources as they are not benefiting from the "breathing spell" occasioned by the automatic stay invoked by the commencement of a bankruptcy case. The automatic stay is abroad statutory injunction, preventing creditors from continuing to pursue collection activities. Furthermore, retailer debtors' estates will not derive the same value from below market leases as they did prior to BACPA, because the professionals and service providers that brokered the sale and assignment of those leases will have far less time to find buyer assignees willing to pay market rates for those leases.

BACPA's changes to the bankruptcy code are likely to result in fewer restructurings and reorganizations, instead funneling most bankruptcy cases into sale cases. Debtors will possibly lose the opportunity to fix fundamental business issues, like purchasing, pricing or distribution, while the bankruptcy case is pending. In retail cases, debtors will have only a brief period to ascertain the profitability of each location and the market value of the underlying lease for each location. Retailer debtors will have a very short time to implement business strategies to improve profitability, thereby permitting marginal stores to turn around operationally and economically. Retailer debtors seeking to reorganize may be forced to reorganize around a smaller number of stores and not benefit from economies of scale in purchasing, distribution and spreading overhead over a larger infrastructure.

During the wave of bankruptcies filed in the early 1990s, it was often the case that debtors would file bankruptcy with no real exit strategy in mind. Debtors would file for bankruptcy and operate as debtors in possession for an extended period. Debtors were able to deleverage their balance sheets immediately simply by filing—debtors were not permitted or required to pay their accounts payable and secured creditors whose collateral is worth less than the extent of their claims have somewhat limited rights in enforcing the full extent of the secured claim against the bankruptcy estate. In many cases that were pending during that period, debtors often obtained very long extensions of their exclusive right to propose a plan of reorganization, despite creditors' best efforts seeking termination or limitation of exclusivity, and eventually, there was a public outcry that these bankruptcy cases were going on far too long. Indeed, some debtors remained in bankruptcy for years and years, all the while the debtor is operating under bankruptcy with the protection of the automatic stay and creditors whose claims arose prior to the bankruptcy case sit and await a distribution. For example, in late 2006 the bankruptcy court confirmed the plan in the Owens Corning bankruptcy case. That case was filed in 2000. Under BACPA it is extremely unlikely that bankruptcy courts will permit cases to languish in bankruptcy so long. Whether BACPA is ultimately beneficial to the bankruptcy process or creditors' recoveries remains to be seen.

Consequently, since the enactment of BACPA, many bankruptcy cases have been filed either with pre-packaged or pre-negotiated plans of reorganization where existing lenders agree to convert debt to equity in order to exit the bankruptcy case in a matter of months with an enhanced position in the capital structure, or debtors file with a strategy of selling the businesses as going concerns under Section 363 of the Bankruptcy Code, but not necessarily with a strategy to propose and confirm a plan in the case. Notwithstanding these time tested bankruptcy strategies, with the capital markets now increasingly constricting it would appear that companies filing bankruptcies are going to be facing a very difficult restructuring strategy and climate in the years to come, simply because financial purchasers with liquidity seeking to buy at severe discounts are not meeting the recovery expectations of creditors, and parties are not willing to give up substantial value in the near term. Therefore, it is quite likely that many more of the bankruptcy cases that are filed will need to have longer durations, and there will be considerably more fighting involved in resolving them because of the time limits imposed by BACPA.

Certain industries have been more actively involved in these restructuring trends than others. In particular, it would appear that retailers, both traditional retailers with "bricks and sticks" distributions channels, as well as cyber retailers selling over the Internet and through catalogs, and restaurants, in particular, are experiencing a decline in sales and revenue and they have not been able effectively to reduce their expenses commensurate with their reduction in revenue, as many have considerable fixed costs typically resulting from over leveraged balance sheets. Other industries that have signs of distress are automobile manufacturers, auto parts manufacturers, trucking, airlines, and certain segments of media. Other industries that rely heavily on fossil fuels are also likely to be on the brink of distress as the macro economy weakens and customers are increasingly incapable of absorbing price increases. Finally, as a result of the vast liquidity in the capital markets during the last business cycle, many businesses were traded for increasing multiples of their earnings. Now that their earnings are shrinking and capital markets have become illiquid, the value of these enterprises has plummeted as both valuation factors declined simultaneously, yet these enterprises are saddled with leverage that as a multiple of their current earnings likely exceeds their value and their capacity to service such extraordinary debt. Consequently, the convergence of these factors will leave many companies in financial hardship.

## Evaluating Restructuring Strategies: Key Challenges

There is no "one size fits all" restructuring or bankruptcy strategy. Many situations may look alike at first blush, but each seems to possess its own degree of uniqueness, requiring a unique approach to the resolution of the cause of the distress. Some companies are distressed by the state of the macro economy, others by the obsolescence of their product or methods, and others simply by over leveraged balance sheets. Some matters are welcomed in by constituents expressing a common objective and acceptance of risk and loss sharing, while others are greeted by mutually exclusive competing objectives.

The first step in evaluating a restructuring strategy is to try to understand the client's business and the issue or issues that are causing the enterprise distress. This stage is much like the practice of medicine; lawyers too need to develop skills of diagnosis, including the enterprise's pain tolerance. The first questions to ask are "How much cash and liquidity does the company have and how long will it last?" Oftentimes management is in denial and the answer might be somewhat shocking, ranging from a couple weeks to a few months. The answers to these questions may materially limit the company's alternatives for reorganization and may necessitate a quick sale to preserve as much enterprise value as possible, or a straight Chapter 7 liquidation if the patient is dead on arrival with no prospects.

The second critical step in evaluating restructuring strategies is to understand and challenge the client's objectives. Questions to ask management include whether there is a reason for the company to exist, what analysis have they performed to determine the opportunity to reorganize the company, what goals have they developed for the restructuring, including whether job preservation, theirs, is a chief objective or whether they are focused on maximizing value while avoiding costs, at the cost of preserving value. Then ask the same questions to the board of directors, assuming there is some degree of independence on the board and synthesize the position of management and the board in order to attempt to develop a preliminary approach to the situation responsive to the proper objectives of the client.

The third step is to understand the enterprise's capital structure and the nature and objectives of the various constituencies involved—i.e., who are the lenders, are the lenders selling their holdings in the secondary markets, at par or for a discount, is the price trending up or down, do the current holders have common or divergent objectives and who are the owners of the company and their desire and ability to fund a restructuring? In addition to obtaining an appreciation of the various motivations and objectives of the several constituencies involved in a particular matter, this step also entails identifying what, if any, leverage—legal, economical, moral or structural—the client has over each of the other parties involved. Included in this part of the analysis is a review of intercreditor issues and the relationship of various obligations including whether there exist cross default or cross collateral provisions or other contractual triggers that might prematurely result in parties exercising rights before the debtor is prepared to file bankruptcy or otherwise respond. Finally, there should be some estimation of the value of the enterprise in order to ascertain which security issued by the debtor is the fulcrum security—the security last exhausting the value—as that is the party with which the debtor is most likely to negotiate its plan of reorganization.

The next step is to develop a plan to accomplish the company's objectives, while doing as little harm to the other constituencies' objectivities as possible, so that whatever form the restructuring takes—whether it be a sale, an exchange of debt for equity, or some other combination or capital restructuring of the company—it can be effectuated as efficiently and quickly as possible. For example, a bankruptcy case may be filed after the company and its senior creditors agree on a restructuring where all of the value of the enterprise is preserved for the senior lenders, and the senior lenders offer a distribution to junior classes of creditors even though the enterprise value is insufficient to result in any distribution to the junior creditors and equity concedes that its holdings will be extinguished. If the distribution offered by the senior debt holders is acceptable to a group of the junior debt holders, the debtor has the makings of a prepackaged bankruptcy case where the debtor discloses the facts and circumstances of its distress, proposes its plan, and solicits votes on the plan. If the debtor obtains the requisite votes to confirm its plan, the debtor may file the bankruptcy case and seek confirmation of its plan the very first day of the case. As straightforward as a consensual case might be, situations involving warring factions of members holding the same securities because their objectives are divergent interests present much different challenges requiring unique strategies depending on the source of the dispute. Some of these disputes arise because certain holders are traditional institutional lenders whose goal might be to liquidate the collateral in a commercially reasonable manner as quickly as possible, while others may desire to hold the securities for a period of time to permit the value of the enterprise to recover to the point where the holders may recover a predetermined return on their investment, and yet other such holders may desire ultimately to own the enterprise with a longer investment strategy and a higher required or desired return on their investment. Disputes among parties in the same class usually arise from different investment strategies and differing opinions of current and potential value.

## Plan Confirmation – Absolute Priority Rule

Facilitating a scenario where pre-bankruptcy ownership remains intact post-confirmation is one of the most challenging aspects of the restructuring process, because one of the predominate reasons why companies file bankruptcy is because there is a decline in value. If creditors are not paid in full, it is likely to be objectionable to them that the owners get to keep their ownership of the company. The bankruptcy code requires that all classes of creditors vote to accept a plan to avoid what is known as a "cram-down". If any class rejects a plan, then the plan may still be confirmed or crammed down over that class' objection. In order to effect a cram-down, each senior class must be paid in full before any junior class is entitled to receive or retain anything of value under the plan—this is known as the absolute priority rule. If the value of the enterprise is insufficient to pay all creditors in full, equity will not be permitted to retain their interests.

## New Value Exception to the Absolute Priority Rule

Nevertheless, there is one circumstance where current equity may retain its interest in the enterprise, which involves current ownership making a substantial contribution to the reorganization in order essentially to buy back the company from the creditors; this is known as the new value exception to the absolute priority rule. The nature and sufficiency of their contribution will be determined on a case-by-case basis, taking into consideration the extent of the claims that are subordinate to the secured claims, the value of the enterprise currently, the enterprise's prospects, and the degree of contribution by equity relative to their overall net worth as compared to the treatment of rejecting classes under the plan. Most significantly, the sufficiency of new value will subjected to a market valuation in order that the bankruptcy court may ascertain whether the market would pay more for the right to possess and control the equity of the enterprise under the plan.

Very few firms are willing or capable of making that contribution. The old adage, "Your first loss is your best loss" still holds true, as equity investors shy away from investing good money to rescue a bad investment. Financial investors are loath to reinvest their capital into a distressed company. Strategic, as opposed to financial, investors have been more willing to consider sponsoring a new value bankruptcy reorganization plan. They perceive that making another investment in the enterprise to finance the exit from bankruptcy is the best utilization of their limited resources as such an investment will be the last to consummate the plan and made at a time when the other challenges facing the enterprise have been resolved through the case and the restructuring plan and the enterprise is benefiting from the discounted treatment offered to creditors.

## Key Players in the Restructuring Process

On the corporate side, the key players in the restructuring process typically include the board of directors, and key management primarily involving the president and the CFO. The board is charged with the fiduciary duty of maximizing value and many times includes independent directors with no personal stake in the decision. Short of a shareholder vote required in limited circumstances, the board of directors, or like governing body in alternative entity forms, is empowered to authorize a bankruptcy filing, the sale of substantially all assets, and a restructuring. The president is chief manager charged with the responsibility to implement the board's will. The president is usually the person at the client company that focuses on the big picture—someone who is elevated above the nitty-gritty, day-to-day operations of the company, but who has a very good understanding of the company's capital structure, as well as the competitive market in which the company exists. The CFO tends to be the person who is more grounded in the details of the company and understands what the company can and cannot afford in terms of negotiating contracts and structuring transactions. He or she also has as an appreciation for the tax attributes that the company either enjoys or is burdened by, as well as those attributes that might come up in any transaction. For example, the CFO will appreciate the impact of a particular transaction that might result in a high recovery for creditors but laden the company with taxable income that the company will not be able to pay because all the proceeds went to creditors. In addition to the board, president, and CFO, the restructuring team might include a chief restructuring officer or CRO, communications consultants, investment bankers, financial and tax advisors, special litigation, SEC, corporate or regulatory counsel, and bankruptcy counsel. A CRO may be engaged to replace key management, or on a more limited basis, to work with management to mange through the crisis that is the restructuring, while management remains focused on the fundamentals of operating the business.

Key players in a case usually include the agent for the secured creditor group, any indenture trustee for secured or unsecured notes or bonds, and either post-petition funding sources or asset purchasers. Creditors of the company will also be represented by counsel and frequently by their own investment bankers and financial advisors. Companies contemplating filing for bankruptcy also must understand that in bankruptcy cases unsecured creditors are entitled to form a committee and engage professionals, whose fees are paid by the bankruptcy estate, and to the extent provided for in the pre-petition agreements, it is typical for secured creditors to engage professionals and seek payment of their fees from the estate. Finally, the Office of the United States Trustee within the United States Department of Justice is a party in interest in bankruptcy cases and is charged with the responsibility of overseeing the administration of the bankruptcy process from an executive branch perspective and to protect creditors' rights prior to the formation of official committees. Each of these players has a role in a bankruptcy case; the significance of the role in any particular case, however, depends on the strategy of the debtor in the case as well as whether the class of creditors is "in the money" given the perceived value of the enterprise.

## The Role of the Attorney

The primary role of an attorney in a restructuring process is to listen and counsel. Counseling involves understanding what the other person is saying to you, and being able to effectively communicate with that person in such a way that they can understand why their objectives may or may not be achievable; as well as whether there are any available alternatives that might permit the achievement of comparable, if not identical, goals. For example, bankruptcy laws permit a debtor to sell or lease its property and also to abandon property. If certain property is marginally valuable or burdensome, it may be disposed of through a sale or lease transaction or abandonment. The outcome is the same, to rid the estate of the property, but the path very different. A bankruptcy attorney should also draw upon her experience to guide the client to an efficient and effective course of action. For example, occasionally particularly aggressive clients want to sue various parties in the case before spending the energy of investigating a possible settlement. Through the counseling of bankruptcy lawyers a dispute like this is often capable of resolution, thus avoiding the costs and risks of litigation for the benefit of a debtor's estate.

In order to effectively counsel and persuade the client, it is essential to have a complete understanding of the Bankruptcy Code, and an appreciation of the intricacies of how its various sections and code policies work together. With that understanding bankruptcy lawyers are able to educate both the client and persuade the other parties in interest as to what the likely outcomes are, and be in a position to better negotiate a resolution of various issues that might come up between the parties.

It is also important to be familiar with the rulings and temperament of the judiciary; an appreciation of what is happening in the market; and lots of experience. Notwithstanding such knowledge and experience, bankruptcy lawyers can never be absolutely certain about the outcome of any particular strategy, because disputes are subject to determination by a bankruptcy court sitting in equity. Most notably, parties usually disagree on the valuation of an enterprise. Valuation is not a precise science and is subject to expert opinions based on assumptions and judgment about the hypothetical price a willing seller would sell to a willing buyer. Accordingly, despite the bankruptcy lawyer's best efforts, if the parties cannot agree to a value or strategy to determine the actual, as opposed to hypothetical, value, it is likely that the parties will seek a determination of that dispute from the court. The bankruptcy lawyer's role is critical to the presentation of the case for valuation.

### Key Documentation in the Implementation of a Bankruptcy Strategy

Prior to filing for bankruptcy on behalf of an insolvent client, you need to prepare the voluntary bankruptcy petition, which includes the name, address, and tax payer identification number of the debtor. Well before filing a case, bankruptcy counsel should begin to work on the bankruptcy schedules of liabilities and assets, and statements of the debtor's financial affairs. Bankruptcy counsel will also typically work with the board of directors and senior management of the debtor and other professionals for the company in performing due diligence, in order to develop a list of relief the company would need in order to have a soft landing into bankruptcy. Because the filing of a bankruptcy precludes a debtor from paying any pre-petition claims, certain relief from the bankruptcy court is required for smooth transition into bankruptcy, known as a "soft landing." In order to obtain that relief, bankruptcy counsel should prepare various motions to be filed on the first day of the bankruptcy case and a supporting affidavit of the senior management of the company. Typical first-day motions include a motion to pay pre-petition claims that are not permitted to be paid upon a strict application of the bankruptcy code, but which are necessary to be paid in order to permit the debtor to continue to operate its business in the ordinary course and minimize any disruption to its operations resulting from the commencement of the bankruptcy case. For example, debtors usually seek to pay accrued pre-petition wages in order to maintain its employees; accrued charges of entities in the distribution chain of its products like warehousemen, customs and others whose delay in releasing or moving the debtor's inventory may have a material negative impact on the viability of the enterprise. Critically, debtors usually obtain post-petition financing or the consent of its lenders for the use of cash collateral, both of which permit the debtor to continue to operate in the ordinary course, and which require bankruptcy court approval. Debtors may also seek orders from the bankruptcy court confirming the bankruptcy code's prohibitions of actions by others, in order that the debtor may have an order in hand to send to offending creditors, rather than direct creditors to read a particular bankruptcy code section.

Bankruptcy counsel's primary role at the beginning of the case is to develop a strategy for the initiation of the case to facilitate the orderly transition into the bankruptcy case, consistent with the overall objectives of the case, while also engendering confidence of creditors in the debtor and its continued ordinary course operations. Bankruptcy courts understand the stress debtors are under at the beginning of a case and tend to accommodate debtors' requests for hearings on their first-day motions with very little notice to creditors or other parties in interest in the bankruptcy cases. Bankruptcy courts' consideration of these motions balances the immediate emergent needs of the debtor with the rights of creditors. Bankruptcy counsel's role is to merge the debtor's needs with reasonable expectations of the extent of the relief that the bankruptcy court would be willing to grant during that first hearing, oftentimes tempering the desire and expectations of the debtor, as a successful soft landing into bankruptcy, having the bankruptcy court approve all requested relief, usually is the first step to a successful bankruptcy case.

Equally important to the preparation of the schedules and statements and proper motions seeking appropriate first-day relief is the development of a communication plan by the debtor among the company's officers and employees, and the company's vendors and customers. Such plans include both internal meetings and memoranda, with messages communicated, timed, and staged with a view of instilling confidence in management and the bankruptcy process and objectives. They also involve the dissemination of press releases developed with the same goals in mind. For example, for a debtor that has missed payments to creditors because of tightening liquidity, and a debtor that has obtained the commitment of lenders to provide substantial new liquidity, the communication plan should focus on the positive aspects of the filing, substantial liquidity to pay creditors going forward, and the new opportunities to be exploited by the debtor. If the bankruptcy case is a pre-negotiated or pre-packaged case, then bankruptcy counsel would also prepare the disclosure statement and plan of reorganization, and all of the supporting schedules and motions, prior to the commencement of the case.

An important aspect to be looked at in many cases after the first day hearing is an analysis of the debtor's executory contracts and unexpired leases. At this stage the debtor has the opportunity under the bankruptcy code to shed unfavorable contracts and leases. Therefore, a debtor whose case is likely to be administered for a period of time should continuously evaluate the benefit of its contracts and leases, and either try to negotiate favorable amendments or negotiate replacement contracts which are more beneficial to the company going forward. In the event any transaction is accomplished that is not in the ordinary course of the debtor's business, such transactions must be disclosed to the bankruptcy court and creditors and approved by the court. It is not unusual for a debtor to have leased more space expecting growth or to shrink its operations post-petition in either case leaving the debtor with more space than it requires. Debtors typically try to negotiate with their landlords to return a portion of the unused space in order to reduce their costs for the benefit of the bankruptcy estate. Agreements between the landlord and debtor are not usually in the ordinary course of the debtor's business and require court approval after counsel prepares and files a motion. Furthermore, in Chapter 11 cases a debtor is required to file monthly reports detailing the results of its operations and financial reports.

Finally, in a bankruptcy case that culminates in confirmation of a plan of reorganization, bankruptcy counsel with the debtor and its other professionals would draft a disclosure statement, akin to a securities prospectus, describing the debtor, its history, its capital structure, the markets in which it transacts business, the major events occurring during the bankruptcy case, and the plan for the restructuring. A plan is a contract among the debtor and its creditors and equity holders that provides for the treatment of creditors' claims and the means for the implementation of the restructuring. For example, a plan may provide for the sale of the enterprise as a going concern and for the distribution of the proceeds of the sale to creditors in order of priority until the proceeds are exhausted. In asbestos bankruptcy cases, cases filed by current or former manufacturers of asbestos products are the defendants in the mass of asbestos personal injury or property damage asbestos litigation, however, a plan may be extremely complex and provide for a channeling injunction, forcing all asbestos litigation to one forum and providing that each claimant of a particular type receive its proportionate share of a fixed pot or simply a fixed sum depending on the nature of the injury sustained. By virtue of the plan's significance to the culmination of the bankruptcy case and establishing the rights of the many constituencies involved in a case going forward, it and its collateral documents, is an extremely important document that is key to the successful exit from bankruptcy.

**Security and Asset Issues**

Value is everything in a bankruptcy case. Its determination is critical to secured parties' rights at the beginning of the bankruptcy case as well as at the end. Under the Bankruptcy Code a secured creditor's rights vary considerably, depending on whether the value of its collateral exceeds or is less than the extent of its claim. Therefore, having a rational view of the value of the collateral in the client's bankruptcy case permits you to have a rational negotiation with its lenders with respect to what they will be willing to agree to that assists in the reorganization efforts or whether their interests and objectives significantly diverge from the debtor's. The value of the secured lender's collateral determines whether the lender is fully secured, whether the lender is entitled to payment of post-petition interest and reimbursement of expenses, and whether the lender will realize a full recovery on its claim.

Typically, most debtors and secured creditors—especially in situations where a secured creditor is willing to provide debtor-in-possession financing—do not engage in a contest over value during the bankruptcy case, and especially not at the beginning of a case, but instead choose to put it off for another day. This strategy is usually preferable, because it permits the debtor to accomplish a soft landing into bankruptcy, both by deferring a confrontation with its lenders and by providing often critically needed liquidity. Commencing a bankruptcy case with such accommodations engenders confidence of creditors, vendors, and customers, and whatever the value of the secured lenders' collateral package, acts to preserve or enhance that value. Alternatively, bankruptcy cases that begin with the bang of clashes between the secured lenders and the debtor are rife with key management and vendor departures, loss of customers, and the debtors experience additional stress, rather than a much appreciated "breathing spell." The lack of confidence of customers, creditors, and employees likely will have a material detrimental effect on the opportunity for the company to successfully reorganize. Therefore, postponing significant disputes with important constituencies at the beginning of a bankruptcy case respecting value of the collateral promotes security and comfort among the parties in interest in a case, because they will perceive that the company's lenders, vendors, and customers will continue to do business with the company post-bankruptcy, much as they did pre-bankruptcy.

## The Client's Goals During Negotiations

A client's goals during negotiations leading up to and during a bankruptcy case will often vary and depend largely on whether the client is a lender or the debtor. A client may enter into negotiations sometimes with unreasonable expectations and counsel's perception of whether such expectations are attainable will tend to instruct counsel on how negotiations should be conducted. It is important to vary the approach. It is ineffective to yell over every issue and it is ineffective to make issues personal.

However, varying your approach to negotiations by demanding more on important issues and yielding on less important issues, whether as a result of lengthy discussions or quick resolution, often yields the best—most effective and efficient—results for the client. Some clients are happy to always meet somewhere in the middle, while others are much more demanding, never yielding. Knowing your client instructs counsel on how to participate in a negotiation. Bankruptcy counsel must always enter into a negotiation after first understanding the client and its objectives.

Of course, it is sometimes important to counsel your client that a negotiated result, whatever it might be, is not in the client's best interest. For example, you might have negotiated some very general principle terms of a settlement, and then during the course of the negotiation over the details of the permutations of the deal make the general settlement far less valuable to your client. For example, the parties to a dispute may have agreed generally on which party would pay the party money and how much. However, during the negotiation of the release, the party receiving the money in the settlement is unwilling to agree to certain provisions favoring the paying party, leaving the paying party exposed to the assertion of similar claims that the paying party believed were being settled and compromised. At that point, it is important to recognize that the settlement has not taken on a life of its own and the paying party should not settle for settlement's sake. This is especially true where the client has fiduciary duties to other parties in interest.

Value is typically the hardest aspect of a negotiation, while the boilerplate issues are usually easier to negotiate. Indeed, the general core of the business issues that are being negotiated are generally those which are the most difficult to resolve, especially where the two parties have very different views of the world, and very different objectives for the negotiation. For example, one party may be looking for performance, while the other is looking for payment. They are not even talking about the same thing and settlement may prove illusive.

In addition, negotiations involving any third parties to a transaction that do not necessarily appreciate the difficulty that went into the original negotiations tend to be more difficult to resolve. Plans of reorganization typically involve the simultaneous negotiation of the distribution of value among various classes of creditors that hold different rights. In a recent experience, one class of secured creditors held a lien on the working capital assets, while another class of secured creditors held a lien on the property, plant, and equipment. A third class held yet another lien, subordinate to both of the other classes, on all of the assets. The value of the different collateral packages was perceived to be sufficient to pay the working capital lien holders in full and provide a substantial recovery to the junior lien holders from the working capital assets, while the fixed asset lien holders were perceived to be woefully undersecured. The debtor was trying to negotiate a plan that fairly treated all secured creditors and suggested that the working capital lien holders should agree to give up some value to the fixed asset lien holders in order to preserve the going concern value for all. These negotiations involved many moving parts simply by virtue of the number of parties engaged in the discussions. Nevertheless, all parties finally realized that a consensual transaction created more value for all and an agreement ultimately was achieved that left all parties unhappy, which is usually the sign a fair settlement.

## Benchmarks for a Good Restructuring Strategy

The benchmark of any successful restructuring strategy is accomplishing the client's goals—confirming a plan of reorganization that maximizes value for all parties-in-interest, or in those rare circumstances where the plan permits debtor's equity to retain its ownership of the debtor following confirmation, for example. Furthermore, accomplishing a negotiated result among the various constituencies is generally a higher benchmark than accomplishing a litigated result, as value is generally preserved or enhanced to a greater degree through amicable resolutions, than exhausting value through litigation. Indeed, it is often said that one should litigate when a resolution cannot be agreed upon. Litigation is expensive, both in terms of dollars and focus of resources, and litigants cannot control the outcome—a judge or a jury decides the result. Therefore, most businesspeople will tell you that they much prefer to make their own decision with respect to what happens in a bankruptcy case, as opposed to having a court impose a result on them by ordering what they *have* to do.

Notwithstanding, sometimes litigation is an effective tool, and sometimes it is a necessary evil. When engaged in negotiations with a party that is more of the demanding unyielding type, it may be necessary to commence litigation to demonstrate the fortitude of your client's position and subject the other party to the exposure of the downside risks of litigation, including discovery. While bankruptcy lawyers should not always sue and ask questions later, keeping that tool in the bag without fear of calling upon it may prove helpful to the flexible and creative bankruptcy lawyer in difficult negotiations.

## Essential Resources in Developing a Restructuring Strategy

Perhaps the most essential resource for any bankruptcy lawyer in developing a bankruptcy strategy is her colleagues' and her experience. Having a client with vast economic and time resources are nice, too, but unlike other practices, clients involved in bankruptcy cases or other insolvency situations are looking to a recovery of their investment, not the vast expectancy of a sound return on investment. The best path forward is typically the road well traveled, but an experienced bankruptcy lawyer knows not to dart off down such roads ill-prepared or without consideration of the consequences, those intended, and trying to minimize exposure to unintended consequences. Working with various businesspeople and professionals in various parts of the country, in various market segments, during various economic times, are experiences from which bankruptcy lawyers may draw in counseling clients. Most progress has some historical roots; and having a group of experienced professional colleagues from which to draw emboldens bankruptcy attorneys to approach new situations with the confidence of experience, plus the flexibility and creativity to devise new techniques to accomplish results.

## Final Thoughts

Young bankruptcy attorneys should observe and contemplate the styles, mannerisms, communication styles, and techniques of the senior attorneys to whom they have access in order to develop the skills and styles that best suit their personalities. Each of us should represent a collage of skills and styles that a successful bankruptcy practitioner brings to bear in any effective representation. It is important to remember that there is no "one size fits all" strategy for how successful bankruptcy lawyers practice in this area.

*Stuart M. Brown is a partner with the global law firm of Edwards Angell Palmer & Dodge LLP. In addition to being a member of the firm's Policy Board, Mr. Brown is partner-in-charge of the firm's Wilmington, DE office and co-chair of EAPD's growing Insolvency Department. An accomplished bankruptcy attorney, Mr. Brown's practice encompasses the representation of various types of institutional lenders, investors and business enterprises in diverse matters, including general business, transactions with bankruptcy estates, anti-bankruptcy transactional consultation, bankruptcy litigation, substantive non-consolidation, securitization and servicing, and bankruptcy fraud. Mr. Brown also represents traditional and non-traditional funding sources with respect to workouts, claim realization and asset recovery. He is certified by the American Bankruptcy Board of Certification as a business bankruptcy law specialist.*

*Mr. Brown received his J.D. from Temple University James E. Beasley School of Law, with honors, where he was member of the* Law Review, *and received his B.S. from Boston University. He is a member of the American Bankruptcy Institute and the Delaware Bankruptcy Inns of Court.*

***Acknowledgment:*** *I would like to thank my partner, William E. Chipman for his essential help in preparing these materials.*

**187**

# Appendices

## Appendix A

## PRE-WORKOUT LETTER

[LETTERHEAD]

[Date]
[Address]

Re: Pre-Workout Letter
Ladies and Gentlemen:

Reference is made to that certain [ ] (the "**Credit Agreement**") dated as of [ ] by and among [ ], the Guarantors from time to time parties thereto, the various financial institutions from time to time parties thereto (the "**Lenders**"),[ ], as the Administrative Agent for the Lenders (in such capacity, the "**Administrative Agent**"), [ ], as the Syndication Agent, [ ], each as a Co-Documentation Agent, and [ ], each as a Co-Lead Arranger and Joint Book Runner (the "**Credit Agreement**"). Each capitalized term not otherwise defined herein shall have the meaning ascribed to such term in the Credit Agreement.

The Borrower has asked to meet with the Administrative Agent and one or more of the Lenders to discuss the Loans and obligations under the Loan Documents and matters pertaining thereto. The Administrative Agent and the Lenders have agreed to meet with the Borrower and its advisors to discuss the Loans, the Loan Documents and such matters, subject to the execution and delivery of this letter by the Borrower, the Guarantors and the Administrative Agent for itself and on behalf of the Lenders. When signed by each of us, this letter shall be the binding agreement by the Borrower, the Guarantors, the Administrative Agent and the Lenders (collectively, the "**Parties**") with respect to such discussions relating to the Loans and the status of matters pertaining thereto.

1.      Negotiations.   The Parties are about to commence discussions, which may be lengthy and complex, concerning the Loans, the Loan Documents, the status of matters pertaining thereto and a request by the Borrower to modify the Credit Agreement and obtain certain waivers

from by the Lenders of certain covenants contained therein. None of the Parties shall have any obligation to modify or amend any of the Loan Documents or agree to any waivers thereof as a result of such discussions or otherwise. Each of the Parties may terminate the discussions at any time, in its sole discretion, without prior notice of its intention to terminate and without any liability whatsoever. Unless a written agreement as described in Paragraph 2 hereof is executed and delivered by the Parties, none of the Parties shall have any obligation or liability by virtue of the commencement or termination of discussions concerning the Loans and the Loan Documents. The Parties each acknowledge and agree that the discussions are in the nature of settlement discussions and negotiations. Accordingly, statements made in the course of such discussions may not be used for any other purpose, including, without limitation, proof of admissions of liability or for other evidentiary purposes. Notwithstanding anything to the contrary contained in this letter, the Parties may exercise any right or remedy available to them pursuant to the Loan Documents or by applicable law or in equity during the pendency of the discussions contemplated herein, and nothing herein shall operate to restrict, impair or prohibit the Parties from exercising any such right or remedy, all of which are expressly reserved; provided, however, that if, as and when the parties enter into a Modification Agreement (defined below) the terms thereof shall apply to such exercise of rights and remedies.

2.     Only Written Agreements and Amendments. Although a number of issues are expected to be discussed, the Parties may reach agreement on one or more issues that are under discussion, the Parties have agreed that none of them shall be bound by any agreement on any of the issues until such agreement has been reduced to a definitive written agreement executed and delivered by each of them (each such agreement is hereinafter referred to as a "**Modification Agreement**"). Furthermore, in order to avoid any confusion or misunderstanding, the Parties also agree that this letter may only be amended in writing, signed by each of the Parties.

Without limiting the generality of the foregoing, any of the Parties may prepare or cause to be prepared term sheets or memoranda outlining or describing our discussions and/or proposals made in connection with these discussions. The preparation, distribution or response to, or failure to respond to, any such document shall not constitute an agreement or the basis by which any of the Parties may claim reliance on any agreement unless and until a Modification Agreement is executed and delivered by the Parties hereto and such agreement is contained in such Modification Agreement.

3.  Loan Documents Not Affected by this Letter. The primary purpose of this letter is to preserve the *status quo* legally as to the Loan and the Loan Documents (but subject in all events to the last sentence of Paragraph 1 hereof) during such negotiations and discussions so that none of the Parties waives or relinquishes any rights or incurs any obligations unless and until a Modification Agreement is executed and delivered by the Parties, and none of the Loan Documents shall be affected in any manner whatsoever unless and until a Modification Agreement modifying one or more of the Loan Documents is executed and delivered by the Parties hereto and then only to the extent the Modification Agreement actually modifies the Loan Documents. No negotiations or other action undertaken pursuant to this letter shall constitute a waiver or expansion of, or be deemed to prejudice, any Party's rights under the Loan Documents, including, without limitation, any rights or remedies conferred on the Parties, except to the extent specifically stated in a Modification Agreement that is executed and delivered by the Parties.

4.  Material Inducement. The Parties understand that the Administrative Agent and the Lenders would not enter into discussions with the Borrower without this letter clarifying the nature and terms of such negotiations.

5.  Alternative Opportunities. As negotiations may not produce a Modification Agreement, the Borrower should not forgo any attractive alternative opportunities during negotiations, including, but not limited to, refinancing, sale, lease or obtaining additional equity infusions, subject, however, to the terms of the Loan Documents.

6.  Costs and Expenses. The discussions contemplated by the Parties will require the engagement by the Administrative Agent of attorneys and other professionals. The applicable provisions of the Credit Agreement will apply thereto.

7.       <u>Miscellaneous</u>. This letter constitutes our entire agreement and understanding concerning the discussions relating to the Loans and the Loan Documents and the legal implications thereof, and all prior or contemporaneous understandings, oral representations or agreements by and among the Parties with respect thereto are merged in, and are contained in, this letter. The agreement of the Parties as set forth in this letter shall inure to the benefit of, and be binding upon, the Parties hereto and their respective successors and assigns, and shall be governed by, and interpreted in accordance with the internal laws of the State of Illinois. This letter may be executed in one or more counterparts, each of which shall constitute an original and all of which taken together shall constitute one agreement. Each Party executing this letter represents that such party has the full authority and legal power to do so.

If the foregoing accurately summarizes the terms of our agreement, please sign this letter in the acknowledged and acceptance space provided below and return one copy to the Borrower at your earliest convenience.

Very truly yours,

[ ]

By:_____
    Name:
    Title:

Acknowledge and Accepted:

By:_____
    Name:
    Title:

cc: Raniero D'Aversa, Jr.
    Mayer Brown LLP

*Courtesy of Raniero D'Aversa Jr., Mayer Brown LLP*

## Appendix B

## NOTICE OF DEFAULT

[LETTERHEAD]

[Date]

BY FAX AND
BY REGISTERED MAIL

[Address]

Re:     Notice of Default and Reservation of Rights

Ladies and Gentlemen:

Reference is made to that certain [Credit Agreement]. Capitalized terms used herein but not otherwise defined shall have the meaning assigned to such terms in the Credit Agreement.

This letter is to notify you that, as of the close of the Business Day on the date hereof, an Event of Default has occurred and is continuing under section [ ] of the Credit Agreement as a result of [describe default].

The Lender Agent hereby informs you that it has not waived any Default or Event of Default under the Credit Agreement or any other Loan Document and by this letter informs you that the Lender Agent, for itself and on behalf of the Lender, expressly reserves all rights, remedies and powers under the Credit Agreement and the other Loan Documents, including, but not limited to, the Lender Agent's right to declare all of the Loans and other amounts due and payable under the Credit Agreement and the other Loan Documents due and payable. In addition, the Lender Agent, on behalf of the Lender, expressly reserves all rights and remedies available to it whether at law or equity or otherwise. Any failure by the Lender or the Lender Agent to exercise, or any delay by the Lender or Lender Agent in exercising any such right or remedy, whether at this time or in the future, shall not constitute a waiver of such right or remedy or of any Default or Event of Default under the Credit Agreement or any other Loan

Document. Any prior or current discussions or course of conduct between the Lender and the Borrower shall not (and has not been intended to) constitute a waiver of any Default or Event of Default under the Credit Agreement or any other Loan Document or any rights or remedies or an amendment or other modification of the Credit Agreement or any other Loan Document.

Very truly yours,

[]

By: _____

cc: Raniero D'Aversa, Jr.
   Mayer Brown LLP

*Courtesy of Raniero D'Aversa Jr., Mayer Brown LLP*

## Appendix C

## AMENDMENT TO CREDIT AGREEMENT

THIS AMENDMENT TO THE CREDIT AGREEMENT, dated as [ ] (this "Amendment"), is entered into by [ ] (the "Issuer") and [ ], (the "Senior Noteholder").

## R E C I T A L S

A. The Issuer and the Senior Noteholder are parties to the Credit Agreement, dated as of [ ] (as amended on [ ] and as may be amended, supplemented or otherwise modified from time to time, the "Agreement");

B. The parties hereto desire to amend the Agreement on the terms and conditions set forth herein.

**NOW THEREFORE**, for good and valuable consideration, the receipt and sufficiency of which are hereby acknowledged, the parties agree as follows:

1. Certain Defined Terms. Capitalized terms used but not defined herein shall have the meanings set forth for such terms in Section 1.1 of the Agreement.

2. Amendment to the Agreement.

(a) Section 1.1 of the Agreement is hereby amended by deleting the definition of "Borrowing Base" in its entirety and inserting in lieu thereof the following:

""Borrowing Base" means, at any time of determination (i) [insert tighter borrowing base formula]

(b) Article II of the Agreement is hereby amended by inserting the following section 2.6 at the end thereof:

"Section 2.6.     Sale of Collateral.     Prior to an Event of Default and so long as no Borrowing Base deficit would be caused thereby, the Issuer shall sell or otherwise transfer part or all of the Collateral.  Proceeds of any such sale or transfer shall be distributed in accordance with the Priority of Payments (as defined in the Intercreditor Agreement).

(c)      Section 3.1(a) of the Agreement is herby amended by deleting such subsection (a) its entirety and inserting in lieu thereof the following:

"(a)      at a rate per annum equal to [higher interest rate]."

3.      Conditions Precedent.     The effectiveness of this Amendment is expressly conditioned upon (a) the execution and delivery by all of the parties hereto of this Amendment,  and (b) the Senior Noteholder shall have received payment in full in cash of its invoiced and unpaid expenses incurred in connection with preparation, negotiation, execution and delivery of this Amendment, and all other related documents (this amendment, the amended and restated Senior Note, the amendment to the Intercreditor Agreement and such other related documents (this amendment, the amended and restated Senior Note, the amendment to the Intercreditor Agreement and such other related documents, collectively, the "Transaction Document Amendments"), including all reasonable fees and disbursements of counsel.

4.      Consent, No Waiver; Other Defaults or Events of Default. Except as provided in the Transaction Document Amendments, nothing contained in this Amendment shall be construed or interpreted or is intended as a waiver of any rights, powers, privileges or remedies that the Senior Noteholder has or may have under the Agreement and the other Transaction Documents, including, on account of any default, Unmatured Event of Default or Event of Default, except as expressly provided herein. Except to the extent provided herein, nothing contained in this Amendment shall be construed or interpreted, nor is it intended, as a waiver of or limitation on any rights, powers privileges or remedies that the Senior

Noteholder has in connection with any other agreements other than the Agreement or any Transaction Document

5.     Release of Claims by the Issuer. The Issuer hereby releases and forever discharges (the "Release") the Senior Noteholder and/or its direct and indirect affiliates, subsidiaries, partners of subsidiaries, its successors and assigns, (and each of such entities' or persons' officers, directors, employees, representatives, attorneys, and agents, collectively, the "Releasees") of and from any and all claims, liabilities, demands, losses, costs, damages, expenses, attorneys' fees and causes of action whatsoever from the beginning of the World to the date of this Amendment, whether individual, class or derivative in nature, whether at law or in equity, whether based on federal, state or foreign law or right of action, foreseen or unforeseen, matured or unmatured, known or unknown, accrued or not accrued, which the Issuer has against the Releasees, arising out of or relating to (i) the Agreement, (ii) any other Transaction Documents or (iii) any action taken by any Releasee in connection with the foregoing agreements and documents, including without limitation any action taken by any Releasee to enforce its rights and remedies under the foregoing agreements and documents and any exercise of setoff or similar remedy heretofore undertaken by any Releasee (the "Released Claims"), and covenant not to institute, maintain, or prosecute any action, claim, suit, proceeding or cause of action of any kind to enforce any of the Released Claims. The Issuer expressly waives all rights of setoff, deduction, counterclaim, crossclaim or defense against the Releasees in connection with the Released Claim. In any litigation arising from or related to an alleged breach of the Release, the Release may be pleaded as a defense, counterclaim or crossclaim, and shall be admissible into evidence without any foundation testimony whatsoever. The Issuer expressly covenants and agrees that the Release shall be binding in all respects upon its respective successors, assigns and transferees, and shall inure to the benefit of the successors and assigns of the Releasees.

6.     Acknowledgment of Debt. The Issuer hereby acknowledges, confirms and declares that, as of [ ], (a) (i) the aggregate outstanding principal balance of the Term Loan Advances equals $[ ], plus accrued and unpaid uncapitalized interest, (b) the amounts set forth in this paragraph and all other amounts owing to the Senior Noteholder under the Agreement (including without limitation accrued and unpaid interest, fees

and reimbursement obligations) are owing to the Senior Noteholder and (c) all payments by the Issuer shall be made without setoff, deduction or counterclaim.

7.    Acknowledgement of Security Interest and Attorney General Action.  The Issuer hereby confirms, reaffirms and acknowledges that pursuant to Article XIII of the Agreement, the Senior Noteholder has valid, perfected, enforceable, first-priority liens and security interests in the Collateral.

8.    Effect of Amendment.  Except as expressly amended and modified by this Amendment, all provisions of the Agreement shall remain in full force and effect.   After the date hereof, all references in the Agreement to "this Agreement", "hereof", or words of similar effect referring to such Agreement shall be deemed to be references to the Agreement as amended by this Amendment. This Amendment shall not be deemed to expressly or impliedly waive, amend or supplement any provision of the Agreement other than as set forth herein.

9.    Counterparts.  This Amendment may be executed in any number of counterparts and by different parties on separate counterparts, each of which shall be deemed to be an original and all of which when taken together shall constitute but one and the same instrument.

10.    Governing Law.  This Amendment shall be governed by, and construed in accordance with, the law of the State of New York without regard to any otherwise applicable principles of conflicts of law.

11.    Section Headings.  The various headings of this Amendment are included for convenience only and shall not affect the meaning or interpretation of this Amendment, the Agreement or any provision hereof or thereof.

[Signature pages follow]

IN WITNESS WHEREOF, the parties have executed this Amendment as of the date first written above.

[ ] as Issuer

By:_____

Name:_____

Title:_____

[ ]
as Senior Noteholder

By:_____

Name:_____

Title:_____

By:_____

Name:_____

Title:_____

*Courtesy of Raniero D'Aversa Jr., Mayer Brown LLP*

## Appendix D

## CONSENT AGREEMENT

THIS CONSENT AGREEMENT (this "Agreement"), dated as of [ ], among [ ], a [ ] corporation (the "Borrower"), the various financial institutions from time to time parties to the Credit Agreement (as defined below) as lenders (collectively, the "Lenders"), and [ ], as administrative agent (the "Administrative Agent," together with the Syndication Agent, the "Agents"). Capitalized terms used herein and not otherwise defined herein shall have the meanings assigned to such terms in the Credit Agreement (as defined below).

W I T N E S S E T H:

WHEREAS, the Borrower, the Lenders, and the Administrative Agent are parties to a Credit and Guaranty Agreement, dated as of [ ] (as heretofore amended, modified and supplemented and in effect as the date hereof, the "Credit Agreement");

WHEREAS, the Borrower has failed to make the interest payment on the Term Loans that was due and payable on [ ] and [ ], and the principal payments on the Term Loans that was due [ ] (collectively, the "Payment Defaults"), and such failures constitute Events of Default under [ ] of the Credit Agreement;

WHEREAS, Events of Default exist and are continuing under the Credit Agreement as a result of Borrower's breach of certain financial covenants by failing to satisfy the minimum fixed charge coverage covenant and the minimum EBITDA covenant for the fiscal period ending [ ] (the "Covenant Defaults");

WHEREAS, Events of Default exist and are continuing under the Credit Agreement as a result of the Borrower's failure to make mandatory prepayment of certain Net Asset Sale Proceeds from the sale of the [ ] as set forth in the Notices of Continuing Default and Reservation of Rights, dated [ ] (the "Prepayment Default");

WHEREAS, certain other Events of Default exist and are continuing under the Credit Agreement (together with the Payment Defaults, the Covenant Defaults and the Prepayment Default, the "Existing Defaults");

WHEREAS, the Borrower has requested the use of proceeds of Collateral to pay professional fees incurred in connection with the transaction contemplated by the Asset Purchase Agreement (the "APA"), dated [ ];

WHEREAS, the Lenders have agreed, on the terms and conditions set forth herein, to enter into this Consent Agreement, effective upon satisfaction of the conditions precedent set forth herein.

NOW, THEREFORE, in consideration of the agreements herein contained, and for other good and valuable consideration, the receipt and sufficiency of which are hereby acknowledged, the parties hereto agree as follows:

## PART I

## CONSENT

Each Lender party to this Agreement hereby consents that notwithstanding the Existing Events of Default, the Borrower may access $[ ] of proceeds of Collateral to pay professional fees incurred in connection with the transaction contemplated by the APA, provided that the Borrower provides that Administrative Agent with evidence that such professional fees have actually been incurred.

## PART II

## CONDITIONS TO EFFECTIVENESS

This Agreement shall be and become effective upon the prior or concurrent satisfaction or waiver of each of the conditions precedent set forth in this Part II (the "Agreement Effective Date").

**SUBPART 2.1.** Execution of Counterparts. The Agents shall have received counterparts of this Agreement duly executed by the Borrower and the Requisite Lenders (or evidence thereof satisfactory to the Agents).

**SUBPART 2.2.** Payment of Fees and Expenses. The Borrower shall have paid and reimbursed the Agents for all of their reasonable fees and expenses incurred in connection with the negotiation, preparation, execution and delivery of this Agreement and related documents, including all reasonable fees and disbursements of counsel to the Agents.

**SUBPART 2.3.** Satisfactory Legal Form. The Administrative Agent and its counsel shall have received all information, and such counterpart originals or such certified or other copies of such materials, as the Administrative Agent or its counsel may reasonably request, and all legal matters incident to the effectiveness of this Agreement shall be satisfactory to the Administrative Agent and its counsel. All documents executed or submitted pursuant hereto or in connection herewith shall be reasonably satisfactory in form and substance to the Administrative Agent and its counsel.

**SUBPART 2.4.** Representations and Warranties. Each of the representations and warranties contained in this Part II of this Agreement, both before and after giving effect to this Agreement, shall be true and correct as if made on the Agreement Effective Date.

**SUBPART 2.5.** Additional Representations and Warranties.

(A) Power and Authority. Each Loan Party who is party to this Agreement has all requisite power and authority to enter into this

Agreement and to carry out the transaction contemplated by this Agreement.

(B) <u>Authorization of Agreements</u>. The execution and delivery of this Agreement and the performance of the Loan Parties hereunder has been duly authorized by all necessary corporate action on the part of each Loan Party thereto.

(C) <u>Binding Obligation</u>. This Agreement is the legally valid and binding obligation of the Loan Parties party hereto, each enforceable against each such Loan Party in accordance with their respective terms, subject to the effect of any applicable bankruptcy, insolvency, reorganization, moratorium or similar laws affecting creditors generally and general principles of equity.

(D) <u>Accuracy of Recitals</u>. The Recitals to this Agreement are true and correct in all respects on and as of the date hereof, and are incorporated hereby as if fully set forth herein.

(E) <u>Incorporation of Representations and Warranties</u>. The representations and warranties contained in Section 5 of the Credit Agreement are and will be true, correct and complete in all material respects on and as of the date hereof to the same extent as though made on and as of such date, except to the extent such representations and warranties specifically relate to an earlier date, in which case they were true, correct and complete in all material respects on and as of such earlier date.

## PART III

## MISCELLANEOUS

**SUBPART 3.1.** <u>Cross-References</u>. References in this Agreement to any Part or Subpart are, unless otherwise specified, to such Part or Subpart of this Agreement. References in this Agreement to any Article or Section are, unless otherwise specified, to such Article or Section of the Credit Agreement.

**SUBPART 3.2.** Loan Document. This Agreement is a Loan Document executed pursuant to the Credit Agreement and shall (unless otherwise expressly indicated therein) be construed, administered and applied in accordance with the terms and provisions of the Credit Agreement, including [ ] of the Credit Agreement.

**SUBPART 3.3.** Counterparts, etc. This Agreement may be executed by the parties hereto in several counterparts, each of which shall be deemed to be an original and all of which shall constitute together but one and the same Agreement.

**SUBPART 3.4.** Limitation. The consents set forth herein shall be limited precisely as provided for herein, and shall not be deemed to be a waiver of, amendment of, consent to or modification of any other term or provision of the Credit Agreement or of any term or provision of any other Loan Document or other instrument referred to therein or herein, or of any transaction or further or future action on the part of the Parent, the Borrower or any other Person which would require the consent of the Agents or any of the Lenders under the Credit Agreement or any such other Loan Document or instrument. The Credit Agreement and the other Loan Documents shall remain in full force and effect and are hereby ratified and confirmed.

**SUBPART 3.5.** Governing Law. THIS AGREEMENT SHALL BE GOVERNED BY AND CONSTRUED IN ACCORDANCE WITH THE LAWS OF THE STATE OF NEW YORK.

[INTENTIONALLY LEFT BLANK – SIGNATURE TO FOLLOW]

IN WITNESS WHEREOF, the parties hereto have caused this Agreement to be executed by their respective officers hereunto duly authorized as of the day and year first above written.

[ ]

By: _____
Name:
Title:

[ ]

By: _____
Name:
Title:

[ ]

By: _____
               Authorized Signatory

_____
[Print Name of Lender]

By: _____
Name:
Title:

*Courtesy of Raniero D'Aversa Jr., Mayer Brown LLP*

## Appendix E

## LOCK-UP AND VOTING AGREEMENT

This Forbearance, Lock-Up and Voting Agreement (the "Agreement"), dated as of [ ], is by and among [Company], a Delaware corporation ("[Company]") and the undersigned holders (each, a "Consenting Holder") of [Company]'s Senior Subordinated Notes ("Notes").

WITNESSETH:

WHEREAS, [ ], the Consenting Holders have engaged in good faith negotiations with the objective of reaching an agreement to restructure Company's obligations under the Notes, and to recapitalize Company in accordance with the terms set forth in this Agreement and the Term Sheet attached hereto as Exhibit A (the "Restructuring Transactions");

WHEREAS, in order to implement the Restructuring Transactions, Company (together with its parent corporation and certain of its operating subsidiaries) has determined to commence a case (the "Chapter 11 Case") under chapter 11 of the United States Bankruptcy Code (the "Bankruptcy Code") in the United States Bankruptcy Court for the District of Delaware (the "Bankruptcy Court"), to prepare and file therein a disclosure statement (the "Disclosure Statement") and plan of reorganization (the "Reorganization Plan") implementing the Term Sheet and the Restructuring Transactions, and to use its reasonable best efforts to have such Disclosure Statement approved and such Reorganization Plan confirmed by the Bankruptcy Court as expeditiously as possible under the Bankruptcy Code and the Federal Rules of Bankruptcy Procedure (the "Rules");

WHEREAS, the Consenting Holders own or control, in the aggregate, the principal amount of Notes (as identified in the signature page hereto) which constitutes at least 66 ⅔% of all outstanding Notes.

WHEREAS, each Consenting Holder is prepared to commit, on the terms and subject to the conditions of this Agreement, during the period commencing on the date hereof and ending on the date of an

Agreement Termination Event (as defined herein) not to sell, transfer or assign any of the Consenting Holder's Notes except as permitted herein.

WHEREAS, in order to expedite the implementation of the Restructuring Transactions, each Consenting Holder is prepared to commit, on the terms and subject to the conditions of this Agreement, and applicable bankruptcy law, to support only a reorganization plan which in all respects contains the terms set forth in the Term Sheet.

NOW, THEREFORE, in consideration of the premises and the mutual covenants and agreements set forth herein, and for other good and valuable consideration, the receipt and sufficiency of which are hereby acknowledged, Company and each Consenting Holder hereby agree as follows:

1.      Forbearance.  So long as no "Agreement Termination Event" (as defined in Section 6 of this Agreement) shall have occurred and be continuing, each Consenting Holder hereby agrees commencing on the date hereof to forbear from the exercise of (or causing any other person or entity to exercise on its behalf) any rights or remedies it may have under the Consenting Holder's Notes, applicable law or otherwise with respect to any default existing or arising hereafter.

2.      Consenting Holder Support.  Each Consenting Holder represents and warrants that, as of the date hereof, it is the beneficial owner of, and/or the investment adviser or manager for the beneficial owners of (with the power to vote and dispose of such Consenting Holder's Notes, and any and all rights and claims relating thereto or arising thereunder or in connection therewith, on behalf of such beneficial owners) the Note Claims.  Each Consenting Holder agrees that, subject to the condition that no Agreement Termination Event has occurred, it shall (i) support (without out-of-pocket expense or court appearance) Company in seeking confirmation of a Reorganization Plan and approval of the Disclosure Statement that contains in all respects, the terms set forth in and contemplated by the Term Sheet and the Restructuring Transactions, as described herein. Pursuant to the requirements of 11 U.S.C. § 1125(b), nothing in this Agreement shall be construed as either (i) a solicitation of an acceptance or rejection of the Reorganization Plan or any plan of

reorganization, or (ii) an acceptance or rejection of the Reorganization Plan or any plan or reorganization.

3.     <u>Restriction on Transfer</u>. Each Consenting Holder hereby agrees that, so long as this Agreement has not been terminated, it shall not sell, transfer or assign any of the Notes, Note Claims, Claims or any option thereon or any right or interest (voting or otherwise) therein, unless the transferee thereof agrees in writing to be bound by all the terms of this Agreement by executing a counterpart signature page of this Agreement and the transferor provides Company with a copy thereof, in which event Company shall be deemed to have acknowledged that its obligations to each Consenting Holder and Lender hereunder shall be deemed to constitute obligations in favor of such transferee, and Company shall confirm that acknowledgment in writing.

4.     <u>Company's Agreements</u>. Company hereby agrees (i) to use its reasonable best efforts promptly to prepare a draft Disclosure Statement and Reorganization Plan implementing the Restructuring Transactions contemplated by and provided for in the Term Sheet; (ii) commence the Chapter 11 Case on or prior to July 13, 2000 and to use its reasonable best efforts to obtain an order of the Bankruptcy Court approving the Disclosure Statement and thereafter to take all reasonable steps necessary and desirable to obtain an order of the Bankruptcy Court confirming the Reorganization Plan, in each case, as expeditiously as possible under the Bankruptcy Code and Rules.

5.     <u>Support of the Reorganization Plan</u>. As long as this Agreement remains in effect, Company will (i) use its reasonable best efforts to obtain confirmation of the Reorganization Plan in accordance with the Bankruptcy Code as expeditiously as possible and (ii) take all necessary and appropriate actions to achieve confirmation including, upon approval of the Disclosure Statement, recommending to the holders of impaired claims and interests that they vote to approve the Reorganization Plan. As long as an Agreement Termination Event has not occurred and this Agreement remains in effect, each Consenting Holder and Lender shall not (a) object to confirmation of the Reorganization Plan or otherwise commence any proceeding to oppose or alter the Reorganization Plan or any other reorganization related documents or agreements (the "<u>Plan</u>

Documents"), (b) vote for, consent to, support or participate in the formulation of any other plan of reorganization or liquidation proposed or filed or to be proposed or filed in any chapter 11 or chapter 7 case commenced in respect of Company, (c) directly or indirectly seek, solicit, support or encourage any other plan, sale, proposal or offer of dissolution, winding up, liquidation, reorganization, merger or restructuring of Company or any of its subsidiaries that could reasonably be expected to prevent, delay or impede the successful implementation of the Restructuring Transactions as contemplated by the Reorganization Plan, or (d) object to the Disclosure Statement (except to the extent it does not contain adequate information as required by § 1125) or the solicitation of consents to the Reorganization Plan.

6.      Termination of Agreement. Except as set forth in Section 13 hereof, this Agreement shall terminate automatically immediately upon the occurrence of any "Agreement Termination Event" (as hereinafter defined), unless the occurrence of such Agreement Termination Event is waived in writing by the Consenting Holders.  If any Agreement Termination Event occurs (and has not been waived) at the time when permission of the Bankruptcy Court shall be required for the Consenting Holders to change or withdraw (or cause to be changed or withdrawn) its votes to accept the Reorganization Plan, Company shall not, subject to its fiduciary duties as a debtor-in-possession, oppose any attempt by the Consenting Holders to change or withdraw (or cause to be changed or withdrawn) such votes at such time.

An "Agreement Termination Event" shall mean any of the following:

(a)     The Chapter 11 Case to implement the Restructuring Transactions contemplated by and provided for in the Term Sheet shall not have been commenced on or before [Date] (the "Commencement Date");

(b)     The Disclosure Statement with respect to the Reorganization Plan shall not have been approved by the Bankruptcy Court within 90 days after the Commencement Date;

(c) The Reorganization Plan or any plan of reorganization or liquidation proposed by Company shall contain terms inconsistent with the Restructuring Transactions contemplated by and provided for in the Term Sheet or shall have been changed or amended in any respect which makes it inconsistent with the terms of the Restructuring Transactions and the Term Sheet;

(d) The Reorganization Plan shall not have been confirmed by the Bankruptcy Court and substantially consummated in accordance with its terms within 120 days after the Commencement Date;

(e) Company breaches any other material provision of this Agreement, including, but not limited to, ceasing to use its best efforts to obtain approval of the Disclosure Statement and/or confirmation of the Reorganization Plan;

(f) The provisions of documents to be prepared to implement the Restructuring Transactions contemplated by the Term Sheet are not in a form fully in accordance with the provisions of the Term Sheet; or

(g) Any Consenting Holder fails to approve the form and content of provisions of the documents prepared to implement the Restructuring Transactions which are not set forth in the detail in the Term Sheet or which provisions are referenced in the Term Sheet as "To be Negotiated", referenced as "Customary" or referenced as "Covenants", by no later than 60 days after the Commencement Date.

Upon the occurrence of any Agreement Termination Event, unless such Agreement Termination Event is waived in accordance with the terms hereof, this Agreement shall terminate and no party hereto shall have any continuing liability or obligation to any other party hereunder, except as otherwise provided in Section 13, provided, that, no such termination shall relieve any party from liability for its breach or non-performance of its obligations hereunder prior to the date of such termination.

8. <u>Representations and Warranties</u>. Company, on the one hand, and each Consenting Holder on the other, represents and warrants to each other that the following statements are true, correct and complete as of the date hereof:

(a) <u>Corporate Power and Authority</u>. It has all requisite corporate power and authority to enter into this Agreement and to carry out the transactions contemplated by, and perform its respective obligations under this Agreement;

(b) <u>Authorization</u>. The execution and delivery of this Agreement and the performance of its obligations hereunder have been duly authorized by all necessary corporate action on its part;

(c) <u>No Conflicts</u>. The execution, delivery and performance by it of this Agreement do not and shall not (i) violate any provision of law, rule or regulation applicable to it or any of its subsidiaries or its Certificate of Incorporation or by-laws or those of any of its subsidiaries or (ii) conflict with, result in a breach of or constitute (with due notice or lapse of time or both) a default under any material contractual obligation to which it or any of its subsidiaries is a party or under its certificate of incorporation or by-laws;

(d) <u>Governmental Consents</u>. The execution, delivery and performance by it of this Agreement do not and shall not require any registration or filing with, consent or approval of, or notice to, or other action to, with or by, any Federal, state or other governmental authority or regulatory body, except such filings as may be necessary and/or required for disclosure by the Securities and Exchange Commission and in connection with the commencement of the Chapter 11 Case, the approval of the Disclosure Statement and confirmation of the Reorganization Plan; and

(e) <u>Binding Obligation</u>. This Agreement is the legally valid and binding obligation of it, enforceable against it in accordance with its terms, except as enforcement may be limited by bankruptcy, insolvency, reorganization, moratorium or other similar laws relating to or limiting creditors' rights generally or by equitable principles relating to enforceability.

(f)     Acknowledgment.  This Agreement and the terms of the Term Sheet are the product of good faith negotiations between the Company, Consenting Holders and Lenders.  This Agreement is not, and shall not, be deemed to be a solicitation for consents to the Reorganization Plan.  Each Consenting Holders' and Lenders' acceptance of the Reorganization Plan will not be solicited until it has received a disclosure statement approved by the Bankruptcy Court.

9.     Further Acquisition of Securities.  This Agreement shall in no way be construed to preclude any Consenting Holder from acquiring additional Notes.  Any and all rights and claims obtained by any Consenting Holder with respect to, on account of or pursuant to such subsequently acquired Notes shall automatically be deemed to be Note Claims and to be subject to the terms of, and the obligations of the Consenting Holder under, this Agreement.

10.     Effectiveness; Amendments; Consenting Holder.  This Agreement shall not become effective and binding on the parties hereto unless and until counterpart signature pages hereto shall have been executed and delivered, by Company and by the Holders of Notes constituting in the aggregate at least sixty-six and two-thirds (66-2/3 percent) of the principal amount of the Notes.  Once effective, this Agreement may not be modified (except as provided in Section 3), amended or supplemented except in writing signed by Company and all Consenting Holders and Lenders.

11.     Impact of Appointment to Creditors Committee.  Notwithstanding anything herein to the contrary, in the event that any Consenting Holder is appointed to and serves on a committee of creditors in Company's Chapter 11 Case, the terms of this Agreement shall not be construed so as to limit such Consenting Holder's exercise (in its sole discretion) of its fiduciary duties to any person arising from its service on such committee, and any such exercise (in the sole discretion of such

Consenting Holder) of such fiduciary duties shall not be deemed to constitute a breach of the terms of this Agreement.

12. <u>Disclosure of Individual Holdings.</u> Unless required by applicable law or regulation, Company shall not disclose the Consenting Holder's holdings of Note Claims, without the prior written consent of the Consenting Holder; and if such announcement or disclosure is so required by law or regulation, Company shall afford the Consenting Holder a reasonable opportunity to review and comment upon any such announcement or disclosure prior to Company's making such announcement or disclosure. The foregoing shall not prohibit Company from disclosing the approximate aggregate holdings of Company Notes by all holders that have agreed, in writing, to vote to accept the Reorganization Plan.

13. <u>Governing Law; Jurisdiction.</u> This Agreement shall be governed by and construed in accordance with the internal laws of the State of New York, without regard to any conflicts of law provision which would require the application of the law of any other jurisdiction. By its execution and delivery of this Agreement, each of the parties hereto hereby irrevocably and unconditionally agrees for itself that any legal action, suit or proceeding against it with respect to any matter under or arising out of or in connection with this Agreement or for recognition or enforcement of any judgment rendered in any such action, suit or proceeding, may be brought in the U.S. District Court for the District of New York. By execution and delivery of this Agreement, each of the parties hereto hereby irrevocably accepts and submits itself to the nonexclusive jurisdiction of such court, generally and unconditionally, with respect to any such action, suit or proceeding. Notwithstanding the foregoing consent to jurisdiction, upon the commencement of Company's Chapter 11 Case, each of the parties hereto hereby agrees that the Bankruptcy Court shall have exclusive jurisdiction of all matters arising out of or in connection with this Agreement.

14. <u>Specific Performance.</u> It is understood and agreed by each of the parties hereto that money damages would be an insufficient remedy for any breach of this Agreement by any party, and each non-breaching

party shall be entitled to specific performance and injunctive or other equitable relief as a remedy of any such breach.

15. <u>Fees and Expenses</u>. In the event any party brings an action against any other party based upon a breach by such other party of its obligations hereunder, the prevailing party shall be entitled to all reasonable expenses incurred, including reasonable attorneys' accountants' and financial advisers' fees in connection with such action.

16. <u>Headings</u>. The headings of the sections, paragraphs and subsections of this Agreement are inserted for convenience only and shall not affect the interpretation hereof.

17. <u>Successors and Assigns</u>. This Agreement is intended to bind and inure to the benefit of the parties and their respective successors, assigns, heirs, executors, administrators and representatives.

18. <u>Prior Negotiations</u>. This Agreement supersedes all prior negotiations with respect to the subject matter hereof.

19. <u>Counterparts</u>. This Agreement may be executed in one or more counterparts, each of which shall be deemed an original and all of which shall constitute one and the same Agreement.

20. <u>No Third-Party Beneficiaries</u>. Unless expressly stated herein, this Agreement shall be solely for the benefit of the parties hereto and no other person or entity shall be a third-party beneficiary hereof.

21. <u>Consideration</u>. It is hereby acknowledged by the parties hereto that no consideration shall be due or paid to any Consenting Holder for their agreement (i) to vote the Claims; (ii) to accept the Reorganization Plan in accordance with the terms and conditions of this Agreement other than Company's agreements to commence the Chapter 11 Case; (iii) to use its best efforts to obtain approval of the Disclosure Statement and; (iv) to take all steps necessary and desirable to confirm the Reorganization Plan in accordance with the terms and conditions of this Agreement.

IN WITNESS WHEREOF, each of the parties hereto has caused this Agreement to be executed and delivered by its duly authorized officer as of the date first above written.

COMPANY

By: _____

      Name:
      Title:

CONSENTING HOLDER

By: _____

      Name:
      Title:
      Entity:

_____

Principal Amount of Claim

*Courtesy of Raniero D'Aversa Jr., Mayer Brown LLP*

## Appendix F

# FORBEARANCE AGREEMENT

THIS FORBEARANCE AGREEMENT (this "Agreement"), dated as of [ ], among: [ ]. Capitalized terms used herein and not otherwise defined herein shall have the meanings assigned to such terms in the Loan Documents (as defined below).

W I T N E S S E T H:

WHEREAS, the Borrower and the Lender are parties to the [Loan Agreement] and the [Security Agreement].

WHEREAS, pursuant to the Loan Agreement, the Lenders have made loans and other financial accommodations (the "Loans") to the Borrower which remain outstanding;

WHEREAS, certain Events of Default have occurred and are continuing as a result of [describe defaults] (the "Existing Defaults");

WHEREAS the Loan Parties have requested that the Lender, and the Lender has agreed to forbear from exercising remedies in respect of the Existing Defaults during the First Forbearance Period (as defined below), and, if applicable, the Second Forbearance Period (as defined below), but only on the terms and conditions set forth herein;

NOW, THEREFORE, in consideration of the premises and for other good and valuable consideration, the receipt and sufficiency of which is hereby acknowledged, the parties hereto hereby agree as follows:

## ARTICLE 1
## DEFINITIONS

"Collateral" is defined the Security Agreement and the [ ] Security Agreement.

"Deferred Interest" is defined in [ ].

"Effective Date" is defined in [ ].

"Existing Defaults" is defined in the third recital.

"First Forbearance Termination Date" is defined in [ ].

"First Forbearance Period" is defined in [ ].

"Forbearance Default" is defined in the [ ].

"Forbearance Events" is defined in [ ].

"Forbearance Period" shall mean the First Forbearance Period and the Second Forbearance Period.

"[ ] Security Agreement" shall mean the Security Agreement between the Lender and [ ] dated as of [ ].

"Loans" is defined in the second recital.

"Loan Documents" shall mean the Loan Agreement, the Promissory Note, the Consignment Agreement, the Facility Letter, the Security Agreement, the [ ] Security Agreement, the General Liability Agreement, the Guaranties and any documents related thereto.

"Loan Parties" is defined in the preamble.

"Monthly Flash Report" shall mean the report furnished to the Lender pursuant to [ ], substantially in the form attached hereto as Exhibit A.

"Overadvance" shall be the amount equal to (i) the amount of Loans from time to time outstanding under the Loan Documents minus (ii) the Facility Letter Borrowing Base.

"Second Forbearance Period" is defined in [ ].

"Second Forbearance Termination Date" is defined in [ ].

# ARTICLE 2
# FORBEARANCE

Section 2.1 First Forbearance Period. For the period commencing on the Effective Date (as defined in Article 5) and ending on the Forbearance Termination Date (as defined below) (the "First Forbearance Period"), the Lender will not take any action to exercise its rights and remedies under the Loan Documents or applicable law. Upon the earlier of the occurrence of (i) any Forbearance Default and (ii) [ ] (the "First Forbearance Termination Date"), the First Forbearance Period shall be deemed null and void and of no further effect, and shall automatically and without any action by the Lender, terminate and expire and the Lender shall be entitled (but not required) to exercise any of its rights and remedies under any of the Loan Documents or applicable law, including without limitation, the right to enforce the liens on, and security interest in, the Collateral described in the Security Agreement. Nothing in this Agreement shall be deemed to constitute a waiver of the Existing Defaults or a forbearance by the Lender with respect to any other term, provision or condition of the Loan Documents or any other instrument or agreement referred to herein or relating to the Loans.

Section 2.2 Second Forbearance Period. If, on the First Forbearance Termination Date, (i) no Forbearance Default shall have occurred and be continuing, (ii) the Overadvance shall be in an amount less than $5,000,000, and (iii) the Borrower shall pay all accrued Deferred Interest in cash on or before the First Forbearance Termination Date, then, for the period commencing on the First Forbearance Termination Date and ending on the Second Forbearance Termination Date (as defined below) (the "Second Forbearance Period") the Lender will not take any action to exercise their rights and remedies under the Loan Documents or applicable law. Upon the earlier of the occurrence of (i) any Forbearance Default and (ii) [ ] (the "Second Forbearance Termination Date"), the Second Forbearance Period shall be deemed null and void and of no further effect, and shall automatically and without any action by the Lender, terminate and expire and the Lender shall be entitled (but not required) to exercise any of its rights and remedies under any of the Loan Documents or applicable law, including without limitation, the right to enforce the liens on, and security interest in, the Collateral described in the Security Agreement. Nothing in this Agreement shall be deemed to constitute a waiver of the Existing Defaults or a forbearance by the Lender with respect to any other term, provision or condition of the Loan Documents or any other instrument or agreement referred to herein or relating to the Loans.

## ARTICLE 3
## AGREEMENTS

Section 3.1 <u>Interest</u>. (a) During the Forbearance Period, the Borrower shall pay interest on the principal amount from time to time unpaid under the Note at the rate per annum equal to [ ] *plus* the Prime Rate, payable in arrears monthly in cash on the last business day of each month and on the date the Loans shall be paid in full.

(b) In addition to the interest provided in <u>subsection (a)</u> above, at any time when an Overadvance shall exist, additional interest shall accrue and accumulate on such Overadvance at a rate per annum equal to [ ] (the "<u>Deferred Interest</u>").

Section 3.2 <u>Reporting</u>. During the Forbearance Period, the Borrower shall furnish to the Lender:

(a) as soon as available and in any event within 15 days of the end of each month, a Monthly Flash Report, including all of the information called for by the form thereof for such month, together with a certificate of the chief financial officer of the Borrower duly certifying that no Forbearance Event shall have occurred and attaching a schedule of the computations used by the Borrower in determining compliance with the covenants contained in <u>Section 3.4</u>; and

(b) as soon as available, and in any event no later than

(i) 45 days following the Effective Date, for each month beginning on [ ] and ending on [ ], and

(ii)   [ ], for each month beginning on [ ] and ending on [ ],

forecasts prepared by management of the Borrower, in the form attached hereto as Exhibit B and otherwise satisfactory to the Lender, of balance sheets, income statements, cash flow statements, Borrowing Base and a written description of significant assumptions for the applicable period.

Section 3.3  Mandatory Payments.  The Borrower shall pay to the Lender for account of the principal amount of the Loans, the following amounts no later than the date set forth below:

| Payment Date | Amount |
|---|---|
| [] | [] |
| [] | [] |
| [] | [] |
| [] | [] |
| [] | [] |
| [] | [] |
| [] | [] |
| [] | [] |

Section 3.4  Overadvance.  (a)  The Borrower shall not permit, for any month, the actual Overadvance as reported on the Monthly Flash Report to exceed the amount of the Overadvance set forth in the Forecast for such month by ten percent (10%).

(b)     So long as the Overadvance shall remain unpaid, the Borrower shall not permit the Overadvance to be more than the amount set forth opposite each period at any time during such period:

| Period | Amount |
|---|---|
| Effective Date to [ ] | [] |
| [ ] to [ ] | [] |
| [ ] to [ ] | [] |
| [ ] to [ ] | [] |
| [ ] to [ ] | [] |
| [ ] to [ ] | [] |

| | |
|---|---|
| [ ] to [ ] | [ ] |
| [ ] to [ ] | [ ] |
| [ ] to [ ] | [ ] |
| [ ] to [ ] | [ ] |
| [ ] and thereafter | $      0 |

Section 3.5 <u>Payment of Fees and Expenses</u>. The Borrower shall, within two days following such request from the Lender, reimburse the Lender for all of its reasonable fees and expenses incurred in connection with the negotiation, preparation, execution and delivery of this Agreement, the Loan Documents and related documents, including all reasonable fees and disbursements of counsel to the Lender and advisors to Lender.

## ARTICLE 4
## FORBEARANCE DEFAULTS

Section 4.1 If any of the following events ("<u>Forbearance Events</u>") shall occur:

(a)      the Loan Parties shall default, breach or fail to observe any term, covenant or agreement applicable to it contained in this Agreement; or

(b)      the occurrence of an Event of Default under any Loan Document (other than the Existing Defaults);

then, such Forbearance Event shall constitute a "<u>Forbearance Default</u>." The occurrence of any Forbearance Default shall constitute an Event of Default under the Loan Agreement.

## ARTICLE 5
## CONDITIONS TO EFFECTIVENESS

This Agreement shall not be effective unless and until the date (the "<u>Effective Date</u>") when each of the following conditions shall have been satisfied or waived by the Lender, for whose sole benefit such condition exist:

Section 5.1 Execution of Counterparts. The Lender shall have received counterparts of this Agreement duly executed by the Loan Parties.

Section 5.2 Resolutions. Authorizing resolutions of the Borrower, [ ] and [ ] approving the terms of this Agreement, in each case, in form and substance satisfactory to the Lender.

## ARTICLE 6
## RELEASE AND ACKNOWLEDGEMENTS

Section 6.1 Release of Claims by the Loan Parties. Each Loan Party hereby releasees and forever discharges (the "Release") the Lender and its respective direct and indirect affiliates, subsidiaries, partners of subsidiaries, their successors and assigns, (and each of such entities' or persons' officers, directors, employees, representatives, attorneys, and agents, collectively, the "Releases") of and from any and all claims, liabilities, demands, losses, costs, damages, expenses, attorneys' fees and causes of action whatsoever from the beginning of the world to the date of this Agreement, whether individual, class or derivative in nature, whether at law or in equity, whether based on federal, state or foreign law or right of action, foreseen or unforeseen, matured or unmatured, known or unknown, accrued or not accrued, which the each Loan Party had against the Releasees, arising out of or relating to (i) the Loan Documents or (ii) any action taken by any Releasee in connection with the foregoing agreements and documents, including without limitation any action taken by any Releasee to enforce its rights and remedies under the foregoing agreement and documents and any exercise of set off or similar remedy heretofore undertaken by any Releasee (the "Released Claims"), and covenant not to institute, maintain, or prosecute any action, claim, suit, proceeding or cause of action of any kind to enforce any of the Released Claims. In any litigation arising from or related to an alleged breach of the Release, the Release may be pleaded as a defense, counterclaim or crossclaim, and shall be admissible into evidence without any foundation testimony whatsoever. Each Loan Party expressly covenants and agrees that the Release shall be binding in all respects upon its respective successors, assigns and transferees, and shall inure to the benefit of the successors and assigns of the Releasees.

Section 6.2 <u>Acknowledgment of Debt</u>. The Loan Parties hereby acknowledge, confirm and declare that, as of the Effective Date, and after giving effect to this Agreement and the transactions contemplated hereby (i) the aggregate outstanding principal balance of the Loans is equal to $ [ ] under the Loan Agreement, plus accrued and unpaid interest, fees and reimbursement obligations on the Loans, and (ii) the amounts set forth in this paragraph and all other amounts due to the Lender under the Loan Agreement and the other Loan Documents are unconditionally due and owing to the Lender, without any setoff, deduction, counterclaim, or defense of any kind or nature to the payment thereof.

Section 6.3 <u>Acknowledgement of Liens</u>. The Borrower and [ ] hereby confirms, reaffirms and acknowledges that pursuant to the Security Agreement, the Lender has an enforceable, valid and perfected first priority lien on the security interest in the Collateral.

Section 6.4 <u>Acknowledgement of Loan Documents</u>. The Borrower and each Guarantor hereby ratifies and confirms that the terms, provisions and conditions of the Loan Agreement and the other Loan Documents remain in full force and effect and that the Loan Agreement and each other Loan Document is enforceable in accordance with its terms.

## ARTICLE 7
## MISCELLANEOUS

Section 7.1 <u>Loan Documents</u>. This Agreement is a Loan Document, executed pursuant to the Loan Agreement and shall (unless otherwise expressly indicated therein) be construed, administered and applied in accordance with the terms and provisions of the Loan Agreement.

Section 7.2 <u>Counterparts</u>. This Agreement may be executed by the parties hereto in several counterparts, each of which shall be deemed to be an original and all of which shall constitute together but one and the same agreement.

Section 7.3 <u>Survival</u>. All representations, warranties, covenants, agreements and undertakings of the Loan Parties contained herein shall survive the termination of the limited forbearance granted pursuant to Article 2.

Section 7.4 <u>Representations and Warranties</u>. (a) Each Loan Party hereby represents and warrants as of the date hereof that (i) the recitals set forth in this Agreement are true and correct and (ii) after giving effect to this Agreement, (A) no default or Event of Default has occurred and is continuing under the Loan Documents, except the Existing Defaults, and (B) all representations and warranties of the Borrower contained in the Loan Documents (with such term being deemed to include this Agreement) are true and correct in all material respects with the same effect as if made on and as of such date, except that any representation and warranty as to the nonexistence of defaults or Events of Default shall be deemed to exclude any Existing Default.

Section 7.5 <u>Limitation</u>. The amendments and modifications set forth herein shall be limited precisely as provided for herein, and shall not be deemed to be a waiver of, amendment of, consent to or modification of any other term or provision of the Loan Agreement or any term or provision of any other Loan Document or instrument referred to therein or herein, or of any transaction or further or future action on the part of any Loan Party or any other person which would require the consent of the Lender under the Loan Agreement, the Consignment Agreement or any such other Loan Document or instrument. The Loan Agreement, Consignment Agreement and the other Loan Documents shall remain in full force and effect and are hereby ratified and confirmed.

Section 7.6 <u>Notices</u>. All notices and other communications provided for hereunder shall be in writing or by facsimile and addressed, delivered or transmitted to the appropriate party at the address or facsimile number of such party specified below or at such other address or facsimile number as may be designated by such party in a notice to the other party. Any notice or other communication, if mailed and properly addressed with postage prepaid or if properly addressed and sent by pre-paid courier service, shall be deemed given when received; any such notice or other communication, if transmitted by facsimile, shall be deemed given when transmitted and electronically confirmed.

[ ]

With a copy to:

[ ]

[ ]

With a copy to:

Raniero D'Aversa, Jr.
Mayer Brown LLP

Section 7.7 <u>Governing Law</u>. THIS AGREEMENT SHALL BE GOVERNED BY AND CONSTRUED IN ACCORDANCE WITH THE LAWS OF THE STATE OF NEW YORK.

Section 7.8 <u>JURY TRIAL WAIVER</u>. EACH LOAN PARTY AND THE LENDER EACH WAIVE ANY RIGHT TO HAVE A JURY PARTICIPATE IN RESOLVING ANY DISPUTE, WHETHER SOUNDING IN CONTRACT, TORT OR OTHERWISE, AMONG ANY LOAN PARTY AND THE LENDER, OR ANY THEREOF, ARISING OUT OF, IN CONNECTION WITH, RELATED TO, OR INCIDENTAL TO THE RELATIONSHIP ESTABLISHED AMONG THEM IN CONNECTION WITH THIS AGREEMENT OR ANY NOTE OR OTHER INSTRUMENT, DOCUMENT OR AGREEMENT EXECUTED OR DELIVERED IN CONNECTION HEREWITH OR THE TRANSACTIONS RELATED THERETO. THIS WAIVER SHALL NOT IN ANY WAY AFFECT, WAIVE, LIMIT, AMEND OR MODIFY THE LENDER'S ABILITY TO PURSUE REMEDIES PURSUANT TO ANY CONFESSION OF

JUDGMENT OR COGNOVIT PROVISION CONTAINED IN ANY NOTE OR OTHER INSTRUMENT, DOCUMENT OR AGREEMENT AMONG BORROWER AND THE LENDER, OR ANY THEREOF.

*Courtesy of Raniero D'Aversa Jr., Mayer Brown LLP*

## Appendix G

## NOTICE OF TERMINATION OF COMMITMENT

[LETTERHEAD]

[Date]

BY FAX AND
BY REGISTERED MAIL

[Address]

Re:     Notice of Termination of Commitment and Acceleration of
        Amounts Due

Ladies and Gentlemen:

Reference is made to [Credit Agreement]. Capitalized terms used herein and not defined shall have the meanings ascribed thereto in the Credit Agreement.

Please be advised that Events of Default have occurred and are continuing under Section [ ] of the Credit Agreement as a result of [describe default] (collectively, the "Known Existing Defaults").

Accordingly, please be informed that:

- Pursuant to Section [ ] of the Credit Agreement, the Commitment is hereby terminated, the Obligations and all other amounts payable under the Credit Agreement or the Loan Documents are hereby immediately due and payable and the Administrative Agent hereby demands immediate payment in full in cash of the same.

- Pursuant to Section [ ] of the Credit Agreement, the Borrower shall automatically and immediately Cash Collateralize all Letter of Credit Outstanding.

- Pursuant to Section [ ] of the Credit Agreement, any and all amounts due under the Credit Agreement or the Loan Documents shall bear interest at a rate per annum equal to (i) in the case of overdue principal on any Loan, the rate of interest that is otherwise applicable to such Loan plus 2% per annum and (ii) in the case of overdue interest, fees, and other monetary Obligations, the Alternate Base Rate plus 2% per annum.

- Pursuant to Section [ ] of the Credit Agreement, the Administrative Agent and each Secured Party hereby exercises their right to set-off all deposits, credits, collateral and property in the possession, custody, safekeeping or control of the Administrative Agent or any Secured Party. This letter shall constitute notice to the Borrower, pursuant to Section [ ] of the Credit Agreement of such setoff.

The Administrative Agent, on behalf of the Lenders, hereby informs you that neither it nor any of the Lenders waive or has waived the Known Existing Defaults or any other Default or Event of Default and by this letter informs you that the Lenders and the Administrative Agent expressly reserve all rights, remedies and powers under the Credit Agreement and the other Loan Documents. In addition, the Administrative Agent and the Lenders expressly reserve all rights and remedies available at law or equity or otherwise. Any failure by the Administrative Agent or any Lender to exercise, or any delay by the Administrative Agent or any Lender in exercising, any such right or remedy, whether at this time or in the future, shall not constitute a waiver of such right or remedy or of any Default or Event of Default. Any prior or current discussions or course of conduct between the Administrative Agent and the Lenders, on the one hand, and the Borrowers and/or any affiliates, on the other hand, shall not (and has not been intended to) constitute a waiver of any Default or Event of Default or any rights or remedies or an amendment or other modification of the Credit Agreement or any other Loan Document.

Very truly yours,

[ ],

as Administrative Agent

By:_____
        Name:
        Title:

cc: Raniero D'Aversa, Jr.
    Mayer Brown LLP

*Courtesy of Raniero D'Aversa Jr., Mayer Brown LLP*

## Appendix H

### SELLERS' SALE ORDER

### UNITED STATES BANKRUPTCY COURT
### DISTRICT OF MAINE

| | | |
|---|---|---|
| In re: | ) | Chapter 11 |
| | ) | |
| PEGASUS SATELLITE TELEVISION, | ) | Case No. 04-20878 |
| INC. | | |
| | ) | |
| Debtors. | ) | (Jointly Administered) |
| | ) | |

**ORDER PURSUANT TO SECTIONS 105(a), 363, 365, AND 1146(c) OF THE BANKRUPTCY CODE (i) AUTHORIZING THE SALE OF THE PURCHASED ASSETS FREE AND CLEAR OF LIENS, CLAIMS, ENCUMBRANCES AND OTHER INTERESTS; (ii) APPROVING ASSET PURCHASE AGREEMENTS; AND (iii) APPROVING THE ASSIGNMENT OF CERTAIN EXECUTORY CONTRACTS AND UNEXPIRED LEASES IN CONNECTION WITH SUCH SALE**

Upon the motion (the "Sale Motion") dated June 15, 2006, of Pegasus Satellite Communications, Inc., Pegasus Broadcast Television, Inc., WTLH License Corporation, WDSI License Corporation, WOLF License Corporation, HMW, Inc., Pegasus Broadcast Associates, L.P. – each a Reorganized Debtor in the above-captioned chapter 11 case (collectively, the "Debtor Sellers") – the Liquidating Trustee of The PSC Liquidating Trust, and non-debtors WGFL License Corporation and WGFL Corporation (collectively, the "Non-Debtor Sellers")[1] for entry of an order pursuant to sections 105(a), 363(b), 365 and 1146(c) of title 11 of the United States Code (the "Bankruptcy Code") and Rules 2002, 6004 and 6006 of the Federal Rules of Bankruptcy Procedure (the "Bankruptcy

---

[1] WGFL License Corporation and WGFL Corporation are non-debtor affiliates of the Reorganized Debtors.

Rules") approving (i) the sale (the "Sale") of the Purchased Assets[2] free and clear of all Encumbrances (defined below), other than Permitted Encumbrances, to CP Media, LLC and MPS Media of Portland LLC (collectively, the "Buyers"), and (ii) the assignment to the Buyers of the contracts and leases listed on Exhibit F to the Sale Motion, as amended (the "Assigned Contracts and Leases"), all as described in the Sale Motion; and this Court having reviewed the Sale Motion, the Asset Purchase Agreement dated August 7, 2006, by and among the Debtor Sellers, the Non-Debtor Sellers (the Debtor Sellers and Non-Debtor Sellers are collectively referred to as the "Sellers") and CP Media, LLC (the "Broadcasting Agreement"), and the Asset Purchase Agreement dated August 7, 2006, by and among Pegasus Broadcast Television, Inc., HMW, Inc., and MPS Media of Portland LLC (together with the Broadcasting Agreement, the "Agreements"); and upon this Court's prior order, dated June 29, 2006, approving the Bidding Procedures (the "Bidding Procedures Order"); and due notice of the Sale Motion, the Bidding Procedures Order and the auction conducted in connection therewith (the "Auction") having been given to all parties entitled thereto; and the Auction having been held on August 7, 2006; and a hearing on the Sale (the "Sale Hearing") having been held on August 8, 2006;

**NOW, THEREFORE**, upon the entire record of the Sale Hearing and these cases, and after due deliberation thereon and good cause appearing therefor

**IT IS HEREBY FOUND AND DETERMINED THAT:**

A.      This Court has jurisdiction over the Sale Motion and the relief requested therein pursuant to 28 U.S.C. §§ 157 and 1334, and over the Purchased Debtor Assets pursuant to the First Amended Plan of Reorganization (the "Plan") and confirmation order (the "Confirmation Order") entered in the Reorganized Debtors' chapter 11 cases. This matter is a core proceeding pursuant to 28 U.S.C. § 157(b). Venue of these cases in this district is proper under 28 U.S.C. §§ 1408 and 1409.

---

[2] Capitalized terms not otherwise defined herein shall have the meaning ascribed to them in the Agreements (defined below). The Purchased Assets subject to the Agreements include assets of the Debtor Sellers (the "Purchased Debtor Assets") as well as assets of the Non-Debtor Sellers.

B.    The statutory predicates for the relief sought in the Sale Motion are sections 105(a), 363(b), 365 and 1146(c) of the Bankruptcy Code and Bankruptcy Rules 2002, 6004 and 6006.

C.    Proper, timely, adequate and sufficient notice of the Sale Motion and the relief requested therein, the Auction, the Sale Hearing, the Sale, the assignment of the Assigned Contracts and Leases, and related transactions described in the Agreements (all such transactions are hereafter collectively referred to as the "Sale Transaction") has been provided in accordance with sections 102(1) and 363 of the Bankruptcy Code and Bankruptcy Rules 2002, 6004 and 6006, and in compliance with the Bidding Procedures Order, to all interested persons and entities. Such notice constitutes good and sufficient notice of the Sale Motion, the Auction and the Sale Hearing, and was appropriate under the circumstances. No other or further notice of the Sale Motion, the relief requested therein and all matters relating thereto, the Auction, the Sale Hearing, the Sale Transaction or entry of this Order is or shall be required.

D.    As demonstrated by (i) the Sale Motion, (ii) the testimony and/or other evidence proffered or adduced at the Sale Hearing, and (iii) the representations of counsel made on the record at the Sale Hearing, the Sellers have adequately marketed the Purchased Assets and conducted the sale process in compliance with the Bidding Procedures Order.

E.    Creditors, parties-in-interest and other entities have been afforded a reasonable opportunity to bid for the Purchased Assets and a reasonable opportunity to object or be heard with respect to the Sale Motion and the relief requested therein.

F.    The Sellers have full corporate power and authority to consummate the Sale Transaction pursuant to the Agreements, and to consummate all other documents contemplated thereby, and no consents or approvals, other than those expressly provided for in the Agreements, are required for the Sellers to consummate the Sale Transaction.

G.     The Sellers have demonstrated good, sufficient, and sound business purpose and justification for the Sale pursuant to section 363(b) of the Bankruptcy Code. The terms and conditions of the Agreements are fair and reasonable. The Agreements represent the highest or otherwise best offer received by the Sellers for the Purchased Assets, and will provide a greater recovery for the Debtor Sellers' creditors than would be provided by any other practical use of the Purchased Debtor Assets. Approval of the Agreements and consummation of the Sale Transaction are in the best interests of the Debtor Sellers, their creditors, their estates, The PSC Liquidating Trust (the "Liquidating Trust") and its beneficiaries, and other parties-in-interest.

H.     The Agreements were negotiated, proposed and entered into by and among the Sellers and the Buyers without collusion, in good faith, and from arm's-length bargaining positions. Neither the Sellers nor the Buyers have engaged in any conduct that would cause or permit the avoidance of the Agreements or of the consummation of the Sale Transaction, or the imposition of costs or damages under section 363(n) of the Bankruptcy Code.

I.     The transactions contemplated by the Agreements are undertaken by the Buyers and the Sellers at arm's length, without collusion and in good faith within the meaning of section 363(m) of the Bankruptcy Code, and such parties are entitled to the protections of section 363(m) of the Bankruptcy Code with regard to the sale of the Purchased Debtor Assets.

J.     The consideration provided by the Buyers for the Purchased Assets pursuant to the Agreements is fair and reasonable, and constitutes reasonably equivalent value and fair consideration under the Bankruptcy Code and under the laws of the United States, any state, territory, possession, or the District of Columbia.

K.     The Sellers have demonstrated that assigning the Assigned Contracts and Leases pursuant to the Agreements is an exercise of their sound business judgment and is in the best interests of the Debtor Sellers, their estates, the Liquidating Trust and its beneficiaries, and other parties-in-interest.

L.      The Buyers have provided adequate assurance of their future performance under the Assigned Contracts and Leases within the meaning of sections 365(b) and (f) of the Bankruptcy Code.

M.      Any non-Seller party to an Assigned Contract or Lease that has not objected to the assignment to the Buyers of that agreement, or that has withdrawn its objection, is deemed to have consented to the assignment of such Assigned Contract or Lease.

N.      The Purchased Assets constitute property of the Debtor Sellers' estates or of the Non-Debtor Sellers, as the case may be. The transfer of the Purchased Assets to the Buyers will be a legal, valid, and effective transfer of the Purchased Assets, and will vest the Buyers with all right, title, and interest of the Sellers in, to and under the Purchased Assets, including all right, title, and interest of the Debtor Sellers in, to and under the Purchased Debtor Assets free and clear of all Liens (as defined in the Agreements), claims (including claims arising under the Assigned Contracts and Leases on or prior to the Closing), encumbrances and other interests arising on or prior to the Closing (collectively, "Encumbrances"), other than Permitted Encumbrances.

O.      The Debtor Sellers may sell the Purchased Debtor Assets free and clear of all Encumbrances, except as expressly provided in the Agreements, because one or more of the standards set forth in section 363(f)(1) – (5) have been satisfied with regard to each such Encumbrance. Those non-Seller parties with Encumbrances or adverse claims in or with respect to the Purchased Debtor Assets that did not object, or that withdrew their objections to the Sale Transaction or the Sale Motion, are deemed to have consented to the sale of the Purchased Debtor Assets free and clear of those non-Seller parties' Encumbrances in the Purchased Debtor Assets pursuant to section 363(f)(2) of the Bankruptcy Code.

P.      The transfer of the Purchased Assets to the Buyers (i) does not constitute an avoidable transfer under the Bankruptcy Code or under applicable bankruptcy or non-bankruptcy law and (ii) except as expressly set forth in the Agreements, does not and will not subject the Buyers to any liability whatsoever with respect to the operation of the Sellers' business prior to the closing of the Sale Transaction (the "Closing") or by reason of such transfer under the laws of the United States, any state, territory, or possession thereof, or the District of Columbia, based, in whole or in part, directly or indirectly, in any theory of law or equity including, without limitation, any laws affecting antitrust, successor, transferee or vicarious liability.

Q.     The Buyers have provided the Sellers with a $2,500,000 deposit (the "Deposit") in accordance with the Agreements, which Deposit is currently being held by an escrow agent pursuant to the Agreements.

**NOW THEREFORE, IT IS HEREBY ORDERED, ADJUDGED, AND DECREED THAT:**

### General Provisions

1.     The Sale Motion is hereby approved to the extent provided in this Order.

2.     The findings of fact set forth above and conclusions of law stated herein shall constitute this Court's findings of fact and conclusions of law pursuant to Bankruptcy Rule 7052, made applicable to this proceeding pursuant to Bankruptcy Rule 9014. To the extent any finding of fact later shall be determined to be a conclusion of law, it shall be so deemed, and to the extent any conclusion of law later shall be determined to be a finding of fact, it shall be so deemed.

3.     All objections, if any, to the Sale Motion or the relief requested therein that have not been withdrawn, waived, or settled, and all reservations of rights included in such objections, are hereby overruled on the merits with prejudice.

4.     The bid of the Buyers is hereby approved as the highest and best offer at the Auction for the Purchased Assets (the "Winning Bid"). The bid of MM Broadcasting, LLC ("MM Broadcasting") and Bluenose Television of Portland LLC ("Bluenose") (the "Backup Bidders") is hereby approved as the second highest and best bid (the "Backup Bid") and shall remain open for sixty (60) days following the entry of this Sale Order or the closing of the Agreements, whichever is earlier. If the Buyers fail to consummate the sale of the Purchased Assets because of

a breach or failure to perform on the part of such Buyers, the Backup Bid shall be automatically deemed to be the successful bid and the Backup Bidders shall be obligated to consummate the transaction in accordance with the Backup Bid if the Backup Bid remains open. The Sellers and the Backup Bidders may consummate such a Sale without further order of the Bankruptcy Court pursuant to the terms of the agreements between the Sellers and the Backup Bidders as the same may have been amended at the Auction. In the event the Agreements fail to close, this Sale Order shall apply in all respects to the agreements between the Sellers and the Backup Bidders and all references in this Sale Order to "Buyers" and "Agreements" shall be deemed to refer and apply to the Backup Bidders and the agreements between the Sellers and the Backup Bidders.

5. All amounts to be paid to MM Broadcasting and Bluenose pursuant to the Bidding Procedures Order or to the Asset Purchase Agreement dated June 15, 2006, by and among the Sellers and MM Broadcasting, LLC and the Asset Purchase Agreement dated June 15, 2006, by and among Pegasus Broadcast Television, Inc., HMW, Inc., and Bluenose Television of Portland LLC (collectively, the "Stalking Horse Agreements") shall be paid pursuant to the terms set forth in the Bidding Procedures Order and the Stalking Horse Agreements if and when any such obligations of the Sellers arise under the Bidding Procedures Order and the Stalking Horse Agreements without any further order of this Court.

**Approval of the Agreements**

6. The Sale Transaction and all of the terms and conditions and transactions contemplated by the Agreements are hereby authorized and approved pursuant to sections 105(a), 363(b) and 365 of the Bankruptcy Code.

7. Pursuant to section 363(b) of the Bankruptcy Code, the Debtor Sellers are authorized and directed to sell the Purchased Debtor Assets to the Buyers upon the terms and subject to the conditions set forth in the Agreements.

8. The Sellers and the Liquidating Trustee of The PSC Liquidating Trust are authorized and directed to execute and deliver,

and empowered to perform under, consummate, and implement the Agreements, together with all additional instruments and documents that may be reasonably necessary or desirable to implement the Agreements and effectuate the provisions of this Order and the transactions approved hereby, and to take all further actions as may be reasonably requested by the Buyers for the purpose of assigning, transferring, granting, conveying and conferring to the Buyers, or reducing to possession, the Purchased Assets, or as may be necessary or appropriate to the performance of the Sellers' obligations as contemplated by the Agreements.

9. As promptly as practicable, but no later than ten (10) business days after the entry of this Order, the Sellers shall cause to be prepared and delivered to the Buyers revised schedules to the Agreements detailing any changes to the subject matter of the Schedules subsequent to the execution of the Agreements. If the Buyers disagree with the Sellers' revisions to the Schedules, the Buyers may, within ten (10) business days after delivery of the revised Schedules, deliver a notice to the Sellers disagreeing with the revisions and specifying those items or amounts as to which the Buyers disagree, and the Buyers shall be deemed to have agreed with all other items and amounts contained in the revised Schedules. The Buyers and Sellers shall, and shall cause their respective representatives to, cooperate and assist in the preparation of revised Schedules acceptable to the Sellers and the Buyers.

10. The Sellers and the Buyers may agree, in writing and in their sole discretion, to waive or extend any deadline or time period set forth in the Agreements without the need to obtain further court approval.

11. Schedule 5.14 to the Broadcasting Agreement is hereby amended to include the contract between Pegasus Broadcast Television, Inc. and Steven Kovacs dated January 2, 2003 as a Material Contract.

**Transfer of the Purchased Assets**

12. Except as expressly provided in the Agreements, upon the Closing the Purchased Debtor Assets shall be transferred to the

Buyers free and clear of all Encumbrances (other than Permitted Encumbrances) pursuant to sections 105(a) and 363(f) of the Bankruptcy Code, with all such Encumbrances to attach to the net proceeds of the Sale Transaction attributable to the Purchased Debtor Assets with the same validity, priority, force and effect as such Encumbrances had upon the Purchased Debtor Assets immediately prior to the Closing, subject to any claims and defenses, setoffs or rights of recoupment the Sellers may possess with respect thereto.

13.     The transfer of the Purchased Assets to the Buyers pursuant to the Agreements constitutes a legal, valid, and effective transfer of the Purchased Assets, and shall vest the Buyers with all right, title, and interest of the Sellers in and to the Purchased Assets, including good and marketable title to the Purchased Assets.

14.     Except as expressly provided in the Agreements, all persons and entities (and their respective successors and assigns) including, but not limited to, all debt security holders, equity security holders, governmental, tax, and regulatory authorities, lenders, trade and other creditors, holding Encumbrances (whether legal or equitable, secured or unsecured, matured or unmatured, contingent or non-contingent, senior or subordinated) against, in or with respect to the Debtor Sellers and/or the Purchased Debtor Assets and arising under or out of, in connection with, or in any way relating to the Debtor Sellers, the Purchased Debtor Assets, the operation of the Debtor Sellers' business prior to the Closing, or the transfer of the Purchased Debtor Assets to the Buyers, hereby are forever barred, estopped, and permanently enjoined from asserting such persons' or entities' Encumbrances against the Buyers and/or their Affiliates, except as otherwise expressly provided in the Agreements.

15.     The Buyers are not acquiring or assuming any of the Sellers' or any other Person's Liabilities except as expressly provided in the Agreements, and in no event shall the Buyers have any Liability or responsibility for any Liability of the Sellers not included in the Assumed Liabilities as defined in the Agreements.

16.     All Persons are hereby enjoined from taking any action against the Buyers or any Affiliates of the Buyers (as they existed

immediately prior to the Closing) to recover any claim that such Person has solely against a Debtor Seller or its Affiliates (other than claims related to Assumed Liabilities).

17.    The Buyers shall not have any successor or transferee liability, or otherwise be derivatively liable, for liabilities of any Seller or any Subsidiary of a Seller (whether under federal or state law or otherwise) as a result of the sale, purchase, transfer or assignment of the Purchased Assets.

18.    The sale of the Purchased Assets to the Buyers pursuant to the Agreements will constitute a transfer for reasonably equivalent value and fair consideration under the Bankruptcy Code, the laws of the United States, any state, territory, or possession thereof, or the District of Columbia.

19.    The Debtor Sellers and the Liquidating Trustee of The PSC Liquidating Trust are hereby authorized and directed, in accordance with section 365 of the Bankruptcy Code, and subject to the terms of the Agreements, to (a) assign to the Buyers, and have the Buyers accept assignment of, the Assigned Contracts and Leases and (b) execute and deliver to the Buyers such documents or other instruments as may be necessary to assign and transfer to the Buyers such Assigned Contracts and Leases.  In accordance with sections 365(b)(2) and (f) of the Bankruptcy Code, upon transfer of the Assigned Contracts and Leases from the Debtor Sellers to the Buyers (a) the Buyers shall have all of the rights of the Debtor Sellers thereunder and each provision of such Assigned Contracts and Leases shall remain in full force and effect for the benefit of the Buyers notwithstanding any provision in any such Assigned Contract or Lease or in applicable law that prohibits, restricts or limits in any way any such assignment or transfer and (b) no Assigned Contract or Lease may be terminated, or the rights of any party modified in any respect, including pursuant to any "change of control" clause, by any other party thereto as a result of the transactions contemplated by the Agreements.

20.    There shall be no rent accelerations, assignment fees, increases, or any other fees charged to the Buyers as a result of the assignment of the Assigned Contracts and Leases, and the validity of the

assignment and sale to the Buyers of the Assigned Contracts and Leases shall not be affected by any dispute between any Debtor Seller and another party to an Assigned Contract or Lease regarding the payment of a "cure" amount pursuant to section 365(b) of the Bankruptcy Code. All parties to the Assigned Contracts and Leases are forever barred and enjoined from raising or asserting against the Buyers any assignment fee, default or breach under, or any claim or pecuniary loss, or condition to assignment, arising under or related to those Assigned Contracts and Leases existing as of the Closing or arising by reason of the Closing.

21.     The Buyers shall not be liable for any claims of the non-Seller parties to the Assigned Contracts and Leases in respect of any claim or breach of an Assigned Contract or Lease that accrued prior to the Closing.

22.     The Sellers shall not have any Liability for any obligations under the Assigned Contracts and Leases upon and after the Closing pursuant to section 365(k) of the Bankruptcy Code other than with respect to the Liabilities not included in Net Working Capital at the time of the Closing, as defined and described in the Agreements.

23.     The transfer of the Purchased Assets pursuant to the Sale Transaction is a transfer pursuant to the Plan and necessary for the consummation of the Plan and, accordingly, shall not be taxed and/or shall not be subject to any tax under any federal, state, local, municipal or other law imposing or claiming to impose a Transfer Tax or any other similar tax on any of the Sellers' transfers or sales of real estate, personal property or other assets owned by the Sellers or transferred in connection with the Sale Transaction pursuant to section 1146(c) of the Bankruptcy Code. Each and every federal, state and local government agency or department is hereby directed to accept any and all documents and instruments necessary and appropriate to consummate the transfer of any of the Purchased Assets, all without imposition or payment of any stamp tax, transfer tax, or similar tax.

24.     All obligations of the Sellers relating to Taxes, whether arising under law, by the Agreements, or otherwise, shall be fulfilled by the Sellers.

## Additional Provisions

25.    The Buyers are hereby granted the protections provided to a good-faith purchaser under section 363(m) of the Bankruptcy Code with regard to the sale of the Purchased Debtor Assets. Accordingly, any reversal or modification on appeal of the authorization provided herein to consummate the Sale Transaction shall not affect the validity of the Sale Transaction to the Buyers, unless such authorization is duly stayed pending such appeal.

26.    All amounts to be paid to the Buyers pursuant to the Agreements shall constitute administrative expenses under sections 503(b) and 507(a)(1) of the Bankruptcy Code, and shall be immediately payable if and when any such obligations of the Sellers arise under the Agreements without any further order of this Court.

27.    No bulk sales law, or similar law of any state or other jurisdiction shall apply in any way to the transactions contemplated by the Agreements, the Sale Motion or this Order.

28.    Prior to or upon the Closing of the Sale Transaction, each of the Sellers' creditors is authorized and directed to execute such documents and take all other actions as may be necessary to release their interests, if any, in the Purchased Assets as such interests may have been recorded or may otherwise exist.

29.    Except as expressly provided in the Agreements, this Order (a) shall be effective as a determination that, upon the Closing, all Encumbrances existing with respect to the Debtor Sellers and/or the Purchased Debtor Assets prior to the Closing have been unconditionally released, discharged and terminated as to the Buyers and the Purchased Debtor Assets, and that the conveyances described herein have been effected, and (b) shall be binding upon all filing agents, filing officers, title agents, title companies, recorders of mortgages, recorders of deeds, registrars of deeds, administrative agencies, governmental departments, secretaries of state, federal, state, and local officials, and all other persons and entities who may be required by operation of law, the duties of their office, or contract, to accept, file, register or otherwise record or release any

documents or instruments, or who may be required to report or insure any title or state of title in or to any of the Purchased Assets.

30. Each and every federal, state, and local governmental agency, department or office is hereby directed to accept this Order and any and all documents and instruments necessary and appropriate to consummate the transactions contemplated by the Agreements.

31. If any person or entity that has filed financing statements, mortgages, mechanic's liens, lis pendens or other documents or agreements evidencing interests with respect to the Sellers and/or the Purchased Assets that have been released pursuant to this Order, the Plan or the Confirmation Order shall not have delivered to the Sellers prior to the Closing, in proper form for filing and executed by the appropriate parties, termination statements, instruments of satisfaction, releases of all interests which the person or entity has with respect to the Sellers, the Purchased Assets or otherwise, then (a) the Buyers and/or Sellers are hereby authorized (and, in the case of the Sellers, directed) to execute and file such statements, instruments, releases and other documents on behalf of the person or entity with respect to the Purchased Assets and (b) the Buyers and/or the Sellers are hereby authorized to file, register, or otherwise record a certified copy of this Order, which, once filed, registered, or otherwise recorded, shall constitute conclusive evidence of the release of all Encumbrances in, against or with respect to the Debtor Sellers and/or the Purchased Debtor Assets. This Order is deemed to be in recordable form sufficient to be placed in the filing or recording system of each and every federal, state, and local governmental agency, department, or office.

32. All entities that are presently, or on the Closing may be, in possession of some or all of the Purchased Debtor Assets are hereby directed to surrender possession of the Purchased Debtor Assets to the Buyers upon the Closing.

33. Except as otherwise set forth in the Agreements to the contrary with respect to the Purchase Price adjustments set forth in Sections 2.4 and 2.5 of the Broadcasting Agreement, this Court shall retain

exclusive jurisdiction to interpret and enforce the provisions of the Agreements, the Bidding Procedures Order, and this Order in all respects; provided, however, that in the event this Court abstains from exercising or declines to exercise jurisdiction with respect to any matter provided for in this paragraph or is without jurisdiction, such abstention, refusal, or lack of jurisdiction shall have no effect upon and shall not control, prohibit or limit the exercise of jurisdiction of any other court having competent jurisdiction with respect to any such matter.

34.     The terms and provisions of the Agreements and this Order shall be binding in all respects upon, and shall inure to the benefit of, the Sellers, the Debtor Sellers' estates, their creditors, their shareholders, the Liquidating Trustee of The PSC Liquidating Trust, the beneficiaries of the Liquidating Trust, the Buyers, and any of such parties' respective affiliates, designees, successors, and assigns, and shall be binding in all respects upon any affected third parties notwithstanding any subsequent appointment of any trustee(s), examiner(s), or receiver(s) under any chapter of the Bankruptcy Code or any other law, and all such provisions and terms shall likewise be binding on such trustee(s), examiner(s), or receiver(s) and shall not be subject to rejection or avoidance by the Sellers, the Debtor Sellers' estates, their creditors, their shareholders, the Liquidating Trustee of The PSC Liquidating Trust, or any other trustee(s), examiner(s), or receiver(s).

35.     The failure specifically to include any particular provision of the Agreements in this Order shall not diminish or impair the effectiveness of such provision, it being the intent of this Court that the Agreements be authorized and approved in their entirety.

36.     The Agreements and any related agreements, documents, or other instruments may be modified, amended, or supplemented by the parties thereto, in a writing signed by both parties, and in accordance with the terms thereof, without further order of this Court, provided that any such modification, amendment or supplement does not have a material adverse effect on the Debtor Sellers' estates or the Liquidating Trust.

37.     This Order shall be effective and enforceable immediately upon its entry, and its provisions shall be self-executing. The provisions of this Order are non-severable and mutually dependent.

38.     As provided by Bankruptcy Rule 7062, and notwithstanding Bankruptcy Rules 6004(g) and 6006(d), this Order shall not be automatically stayed, but shall be effective and enforceable immediately upon the signing of this Order.

Dated:          _____, 2006
            Portland, Maine


                    _____
                    HONORABLE JAMES B. HAINES, JR.
                    UNITED STATES BANKRUPTCY
                    JUDGE


                    *Courtesy of Kenneth A. Rosen, Lowenstein Sandler PC*

## Appendix I

## MOTION TO SELL BROADCAST ASSETS

Bidding Procedures Hearing: June 29, 2006
Time: 10:30 a.m.
Place: Portland
Bidding Procedures Objection Deadline: June 26, 2006
Time: 4:00 p.m.

Sale Hearing: August 8, 2006
Time: 9:00 a.m.
Place: Portland
Objection Deadline: July 31, 2006
Time: 4:00 p.m.

## UNITED STATES BANKRUPTCY COURT
## DISTRICT OF MAINE

| | | |
|---|---|---|
| In re: | : | Chapter 11 |
| PEGASUS SATELLITE TELEVISION, INC., et al., [1] | : | |
| Case No. 04-20878 | : | |
| | : | :(Jointly Administered) |
| Debtors. | : | |

---

[1] The Reorganized Debtors are: Argos Support Services Company, Bride Communications, Inc., B.T. Satellite, Inc., Carr Rural TV, Inc., DBS Tele-Venture, Inc., Digital Television Services of Indiana, LLC, DTS Management, LLC Golden Sky DBS, Inc., Golden Sky Holdings, Inc., Golden Sky Systems, Inc., Henry Country MRTV, Inc., HMW, Inc., Pegasus Broadcast Associates, L.P., Pegasus Broadcast Television, Inc., Pegasus Broadcast Towers, Inc., Pegasus Media & Communications, Inc., Pegasus Satellite Communications, Inc., Pegasus Satellite Television of Illinois, Inc., Pegasus Satellite Television, Inc., Portland Broadcasting, Inc., Primewatch, Inc., PST Holdings, Inc., South Plains DBS, LP., Telecast of Florida, Inc., WDSI License Corp., WILF, Inc., WOLF License Corp., and WTLH License Corp.

## MOTION OF THE REORGANIZED DEBTORS AND LIQUIDATING TRUSTEE FOR ORDERS (1) AUTHORIZING AND APPROVING SALE OF REORGANIZED DEBTORS' BROADCAST ASSETS FREE AND CLEAR OF ANY LIENS, CLAIMS AND ENCUMBRANCES; (2) AUTHORIZING BID PROCEDURES FOR SOLICITATION OF HIGHER AND BETTER OFFERS IN CONNECTION WITH SUCH SALE INCLUDING BIDDING INCENTIVES; (3) APPROVING FORM AND MANNER OF NOTICE OF SALE; (4) SETTING HEARING DATE FOR FINAL SALE APPROVAL; (5) AUTHORIZING THE ASSIGNMENT OF CERTAIN EXECUTORY CONTRACTS AND UNEXPIRED LEASES; AND (6) GRANTING RELATED RELIEF

Pegasus Satellite Communications, Inc. ("PSC"), Pegasus Broadcast Television, Inc., WTLH License Corp., WDSI License Corp., WOLF License Corp., HMW, Inc., Pegasus Broadcast Associates, L.P., each a Reorganized Debtor in the captioned chapter 11 cases, the Liquidating Trustee of The PSC Liquidating Trust (the "Liquidating Trustee"), and nondebtors WGFL License Corporation and WGFL Corporation (collectively the "Movants"), hereby file this motion (the "Sale Motion") pursuant to the Plan, Confirmation Order, sections 105(a), 363, 365 and 1146(c) of Title 11 of the United States Code (the "Bankruptcy Code"), Rules 2002, 6004, 6006, 9007 and 9014 of the Federal Rules of Bankruptcy Procedure (the "Bankruptcy Rules") and D. Me. LBR 2002-1 and 6004-1, for entry of orders: (1) authorizing and approving sale of certain of the Reorganized Debtors' assets free and clear of any liens, claims and encumbrances; (2) authorizing bidding procedures for solicitation of higher and better offers in connection with such sale, including the bidding incentives; (3) approving form and manner of notice of sale; (4) setting a hearing date for final sale approval; (5) authorizing the assignment of certain executory contracts and unexpired leases; and (6) granting related relief. In support of the Sale Motion, the Movants respectfully represents as follows:

## SUMMARY OF RELIEF REQUESTED[2]

1.      By this Motion, the Movants request authorization, pursuant to sections 105, 363, 365 and 1146 of the Bankruptcy Code, and Bankruptcy Rules 2002, 6004, 6006, 9007, and 9014 and D. Me. LBR 2002-1, 6004-1, and 6006-1, to auction, and thereafter sell, the Purchased Assets as a single lot to one bidder or in separate lots to more than one bidder. In order to facilitate the orderly sale of its Purchased Assets, the Movants further request that this Court approve various bidding procedures and guidelines.

2.      Specifically, by this Sale Motion, the Movants request that the Court enter the following orders:

- The Bidding Procedures Order: The Movants request that the Court enter an order, substantially in the form attached hereto as Exhibit D (the "Bidding Procedures Order"), approving (i) the auction bidding procedures described herein (the "Bidding Procedures"), in connection with the Movants' solicitation of higher and better offers including bidding incentives; (ii) notice of the auction (the "Auction") and the sale hearing (the "Sale Hearing"), in the form and manner consistent with the Bidding Procedures Order as described herein; and (iii) establishing the dates, times and places of the Auction and the Sale Hearing.

- The Sale Order(s): The Movants further request that the Court enter one or more orders, substantially in form attached hereto as Exhibit E (the "Sale Order(s)") following the Auction, approving and authorizing (i) the proposed sale of assets of the Reorganized Debtors and the Liquidating Trustee (the "Purchased Debtor Assets") pursuant to the terms of the Agreements or an alternative agreement or agreements (obtained in accordance with the bidding procedures that provides the estate with greater

---

[2] Defined terms used in this Summary shall have the meaning assigned to them in the Sale Motion.

consideration than that provided for by the Agreements), free and clear of all liens, claims, encumbrances and other interests; (ii) the assignment(s) of certain executory contracts and unexpired leases in connection with such sale(s) as set forth in Exhibit F hereto (the "Assigned Contracts and Leases"); and (iii) the exemption of the sale(s) of the Purchased Assets from state and local transfer taxes pursuant to section 1146(c) of the Bankruptcy Code.

3.      The Sale Motion is divided into two parts. Part I constitutes the Movants' request for approval of the Bidding Procedures Order. Part II constitutes the Movants' request for approval of the Sale to the highest and best bidder or bidders, including the assignment of any executory contracts and unexpired leases, as well as other related relief.[3]

## CASE BACKGROUND

4.      On June 2, 2004 (the "Petition Date"), the Reorganized Debtors filed petitions for relief under chapter 11 of the Bankruptcy Code in the United States Bankruptcy Court for the District of Maine (the "Court"). On June 4, 2004, the Court entered an order directing joint administration of the Reorganized Debtors' cases for procedural purposes only.

5.      The Reorganized Debtors continued in possession of their respective property and continued to operate their businesses as debtors in possession pursuant to sections 1107(a) and 1108 of the Bankruptcy Code throughout their chapter 11 cases until the Plan became effective on May 5, 2005.

6.      On April 15, 2005, the Court entered an order ("Confirmation Order") confirming the Reorganized Debtors' First Amended Joint Plan of Reorganization (the "Plan"), as modified by the Confirmation Order (Docket # 1236). Pursuant to the Plan and Confirmation Order, Ocean Ridge Capital Advisors, LLC was appointed

---

[3] The Movants reserves their rights to reject any agreement not to be assumed or assigned.

the Liquidating Trustee of The PSC Liquidating Trust established under the Plan.

7. Movants WGFL License Corporation and WGFL Corporation (the "WGFL Entities") are each wholly-owned subsidiaries of Reorganized Debtor Pegasus Satellite Communications, Inc. and were not Debtors and are not Reorganized Debtors.

## THE REORGANIZED DEBTORS' BUSINESS

8. As of the Petition Date, the Reorganized Debtors' principal operating business was their direct broadcast satellite ("DBS") business. At that time, the Reorganized Debtors were the largest independent distributor of DIRECTV® DBS services with approximately 1.1 million subscribers and the exclusive right to distribute certain DIRECTV® services to approximately 8.4 million rural households in certain territories within 41 states. During the chapter 11 proceedings, this Court entered an order dated August 26, 2004, authorizing the Reorganized Debtors to sell the DBS business to DIRECTV® for approximately $988 million (Docket # 504). The closing of this sale occurred on or about August 27, 2004.

9. The Reorganized Debtors (through the Broadcast Debtors[4]) and the WGFL Entities also owned and/or operated several broadcast television stations and related property (collectively, the "Broadcast Assets"). The Broadcast Assets are, generally, assets necessary to the operation of the Reorganized Debtors' broadcast television business, and include, but are not limited to, certain Federal Communications Commission ("FCC") authorizations, permits, and licenses, real property, agreements to operate television stations, rights to purchase television stations, time brokerage agreements, lease agreements with respect to studio facilities and other contract rights and working capital. The stations owned or programmed by the Reorganized Debtors and the WGFL Entities were affiliated with the CBS, FOX, UPN and WB networks, and reach

---

[4] The Broadcast Debtors are: Pegasus Satellite Communications, Inc., Bride Communications, Inc., BT Satellite Inc., HMW, Inc., Pegasus Broadcast Associates, L.P., Pegasus Broadcast Television, Inc., Pegasus Broadcast Towers, Inc., Portland Broadcasting, Inc., Telecast of Florida, Inc., WDSI License Corp., WILF, Inc. WOLF License Corp., and WTLH License Corp.

approximately 2% of the U.S. television households in five designated market areas ("DMAs"): Wilkes Barre-Scranton, Pennsylvania; Portland, Maine; Chattanooga, Tennessee; Tallahassee, Florida; and Gainesville, Florida.

10. Included among the Broadcast Assets are relationships and agreements that grant the Reorganized Debtors and the WGFL Entities the right to program and receive advertising revenues from multiple television stations within the same DMA, including stations the licenses of which are owned directly by other entities.[5] Pursuant to FCC rules and regulations, a single entity within a DMA may only own a specified number of television station licenses depending upon the overall number of independently owned stations operating in the DMA. The Reorganized Debtors are or will be able to receive economic benefits from programming multiple stations in the Wilkes-Barre-Scranton, Pennsylvania and Tallahassee, Florida DMAs pursuant to agreements with Mystic Television of Scranton LLC and Mystic Television of Tallahassee LLC (collectively, "Mystic"). While the Reorganized Debtors own a FCC license and operate a television station in these markets, the FCC local television ownership rules do not prohibit separate licensees in one DMA, such as the Reorganized Debtors and Mystic, from consolidating operations through time brokerage agreements ("TBAs") or similar agreements provided that the licensee of the brokered station retains ultimate control over its station. Additionally, certain Reorganized Debtors operate multiple stations in the Portland, Maine DMA pursuant to a waiver of the FCC's local television ownership rules.

## THE DEBTORS' PLAN OF REORGANIZATION

11. On January 31, 2005, the Reorganized Debtors filed their Plan and Disclosure Statement in connection with the solicitation of acceptances of the Plan. On April 15, 2005, the Court confirmed the Plan and the Plan became effective on May 5, 2005 (the "Effective Date").

12. Presently, in addition to the net proceeds from a prior sale of the Reorganized Debtors' direct broadcast satellite business,

---

[5] The Broadcast Debtors and the WGFL Entities operate multiple television stations in all of these DMAs except Chattanooga, Tennessee.

the Broadcast Assets comprise the vast majority of all the remaining tangible assets being administered by the Reorganized Debtors and/or the Liquidating Trustee established under the Plan.[6] The Plan and Confirmation Order contemplate the sale of the Broadcast Assets by the Liquidating Trustee and anticipate that the Liquidating Trustee would identify a buyer for the Broadcast Assets, seek the required approvals of the Bankruptcy Court, seek the required approvals of the FCC, and take such actions as necessary to consummate the transfer of the Broadcast Assets to the ultimate buyer. Paragraph 21 requires the Liquidating Trustee to "obtain order(s) from the Bankruptcy Court to sell or otherwise dispose of all or a portion of the Broadcast Assets including the Debtors' FCC licenses and broadcast television stations." Similarly, paragraph 26(q) of the Confirmation Order preserves the jurisdiction of the Bankruptcy Court to consider and enter orders approving the sale of assets after the Effective Date. See also Liquidating Trust Agreement, §§ 3.01, 3.02(ee), 4.02.

13.     In an effort to maximize the marketable value of the Broadcast Assets, the Plan and Confirmation Order also maintained the Reorganized Debtors' ability to assign certain executory contracts or unexpired leases to meet the needs of any buyer that may emerge from the marketing of the Broadcast Assets. Section 8.2 of the Plan, captioned "Assumption," provides, in part, that on the Effective Date, the Reorganized Debtors would assume certain executory contracts and unexpired leases listed on Schedule 8.2(a) of the Amended Plan Supplement and that "the Debtors may also assume, assume and assign or reject certain executory contracts and unexpired leases that are the subject of motions filed with the Bankruptcy Court and pending on the Confirmation Date for which the Bankruptcy Court shall retain exclusive jurisdiction to determine such motions." Plan, §8.2(a). Pursuant to Section 13.1 of the Plan, the Court retained jurisdiction over of all matters related to the assumption, assumption and assignment, or rejection, of any executory contract or

---

[6] The Plan, as amended by the Confirmation Order, empowers the Liquidating Trustee with the authority to make all operating decisions and exercise all control over the Broadcast Assets including the Debtors' broadcast television stations, subject to the jurisdiction of the Bankruptcy Court. Specifically, paragraph 21 of the Confirmation Order authorizes the Liquidating Trustee to "exercise all control over the assets of the Reorganized Debtors and the Liquidating Trust, including, without limitation, the Broadcast Assets including the Debtors' broadcast television stations, subject to the jurisdiction of the Bankruptcy Court."

unexpired lease of the Debtors, including, without limitation, determination of one or motions to assume, assume and assign or reject executory contracts and unexpired leases of the PBT Debtors and/or PSC used in the operation of the Broadcast Business Filed on or before and pending on the Confirmation Date.

14.    The Plan and Confirmation Order also provided that any transfer of assets pursuant to the Plan or contemplated by the Plan, including the transfer of the Broadcast Assets or the stock of the Reorganized Debtors, shall not be subject to any stamp tax, sales and use tax or similar tax pursuant to section 1146(c) of the Bankruptcy Code. See Confirmation Order, ¶ 28; Plan, §5.12. The Confirmation Order directs the appropriate state or local governmental officials or agents to forego the collection of any such tax or governmental assessment and to accept for filing and recordation any applicable instruments or documents without the payment of any such tax or governmental assessment. Confirmation Order, ¶ 28. The Bankruptcy Court specifically retained jurisdiction to enforce this direction, by contempt or otherwise. Id. at ¶26.

## PRIOR ASSUMPTION OF EXECUTORY CONTRACTS

15.    On or about April 13, 2005, prior to the April 15, 2005 Confirmation Date, the Reorganized Debtors filed a "Motion for Order Authorizing the Assumption or Assumption and Assignment of Certain Executory Contracts or Unexpired Leases" (Docket # 1217) (the "Global 365 Motion"). Through the Global 365 Motion, the rights of the Reorganized Debtors and Liquidating Trustee to assume, assume and assign, or reject various executory contracts and leases relating to the operation of the Broadcast Assets were preserved. On June 29, 2005, an order granting the Global 365 Motion was entered (Docket # 1532) that provided that "[t]he Reorganized Debtors retain their rights, subject to appropriate notice and opportunity to object and Bankruptcy Court approval, to assign any of the Assumed Contracts pursuant to and in accordance with the requirements of § 365 of the Bankruptcy Code."

16.    The Reorganized Debtors have also assumed contracts pursuant to other orders of the Bankruptcy Court as authorized by the Plan and the order on the Global 365 Motion. In particular, on June

24, 2005, the Court entered a stipulated order agreed to by the Reorganized Debtors, the Liquidating Trustee and Twentieth Television, Inc. ("Twentieth") (Docket # 1518) that authorized the assumption of all contracts subject to the Global 365 Motion listing Twentieth as a party. The order retained the ability or the Reorganized Debtors and the Liquidating Trustee to assign any of the assumed contracts pursuant to § 365 of the Bankruptcy Code.[7] Additionally, pursuant to a June 29, 2005 order, the Reorganized Debtors assumed certain executory contracts and unexpired leases with KB Prime Media LLC (Docket # 1533) and, pursuant to the order, the Court retained jurisdiction over the assignment of any of the assumed contracts pursuant to § 365 of the Bankruptcy Code.

17.    Additionally, on June 10, 2005, the Bankruptcy Court entered an order authorizing the assumption of an asset purchase agreement between Pegasus Satellite Communications, Inc. and KB Prime Media LLC for television station WSWB-TV (Channel 38), in Scranton/Wilkes-Barre, Pennsylvania (the "KB Scranton Agreement") and the assignment of the KB Scranton Agreement to Mystic (Docket # 1453). On March 16, 2006, the Reorganized Debtors and the Liquidating Trustee filed a Motion to Enforce Prior Orders of the Court, to Compel Closing of Sale by KB Prime Media, LLC and Related Relief (the "KB Enforcement Motion") (Docket # 1837). The Enforcement Motion was settled pursuant to a stipulation entered on April 10, 206 (Docket # 1866).

## SALE OF ASSETS

18.    As discussed above, the Broadcast Assets are the primary tangible property being administered by the Liquidating Trustee.

---

[7] On June 10, 2005, the Court entered a stipulated order on the Reorganized Debtors and the Liquidating Trustee's Motion for an Order Authorizing the Assumption of Certain Executory Contracts Between Pegasus Broadcast Television, Inc. and Fox Broadcasting Company and/or Fox News Network, L.L.C. (Docket #1454) that authorized the Reorganized Debtors to assume certain contracts with Fox Broadcasting Company and/or Fox News Network, L.L.C. The assignment of the Fox contracts was permitted with the express, written consent of Fox Broadcasting and/or Fox News and the approval of the Court. By entering into the Stipulated Order, the parties agreed that the Agreements expired by their terms on June 30, 2005 and that any subsequent agreements would "be deemed to be new agreements between the parties thereto and shall not be deemed to relate to, modify, amend, arise from, or have any relationship and/or affiliation to or with the Agreements."

The Plan expressly authorizes the Liquidating Trustee to sell all or a portion of the Broadcast Assets to generate funds to distribute to creditors. The Liquidating Trustee, in consultation with its investment banker and financial advisor, Miller Buckfire & Co., LLC ("Miller Buckfire"), has considered and evaluated a variety of factors to determine whether it is appropriate to retain ownership of all or a portion of the Broadcast Assets or to dispose of all or a portion of the Broadcast Assets to maximize the value of recoveries to creditors. These factors include, but are not limited to, whether the particular Broadcast Assets are being operated, the amount of capital expenditures associated with the respect to maintaining and preserving each of the Broadcast Assets, the profitability of any operating Broadcast Assets, the range of valuation for each Broadcast Asset and the marketability of the Broadcast Assets.

19.     In connection with the potential sale of the Broadcast Assets, the Liquidating Trustee utilized the services of Miller Buckfire to identify, educate and negotiate with potential acquirers, including preparation of sale memoranda and presentation materials. Miller Buckfire was retained by the Debtors shortly after the Petition Date to evaluate and market the Broadcast Assets, and, in August 2004, began assisting the Debtors in the preparation of an offering memorandum for the Broadcast Assets. At the request of the Reorganized Debtors, Miller Buckfire began contacting a broad group of over 125 strategic and financial buyers in March 2005. After executing non-disclosure agreements with prospective buyers, Miller Buckfire distributed over 50 information memoranda. Prospective buyers were given the option of bidding on the entire Broadcast Asset group or individual stations. In April, May and June 2005, Miller Buckfire received 10 indications of interest, including an indication from Silver Point Capital Advisors, LLC ("Silver Point").[8]

---

[8] This marketing process also resulted in the sale of certain other Broadcast Assets relating to a permit to construct a television station in Hammond, LA (the "Hammond Station") to Mayavision, Inc. ("Mayavision"). Upon the receipt of an indication of interest for the Hammond Station, Miller Buckfire distributed final bidding instructions and a form asset purchase agreement to Mayavision in June 2005, and over the next month, negotiated the final purchase price and terms of the asset purchase agreement. The Court approved transfer of the Hammond Station to Mayavision by order dated March 20, 2006 (Docket # 1842).

20.     At the direction of the Liquidating Trustee and the Reorganized Debtors, Miller Buckfire suspended negotiations with potential acquirers, until November 2005, when Miller Buckfire was asked to return to the market to solicit bids on the entire Broadcast Asset group. Miller Buckfire contacted all of the bidders that were interested in the entire Broadcast Asset group and received revised indications of interest from four bidders. After consultation with the Liquidating Trustee and the Reorganized Debtors, Miller Buckfire selected two bidders to complete legal and business due diligence and to submit final bids. Based on these bids, in March 2006, the Liquidating Trustee, in consultation with Miller Buckfire, selected Silver Point as the stalking horse bidder for the Broadcast Assets.

21.     Notwithstanding the prior service of Silver Point on the Debtors' creditors committee, the negotiations between Silver Point and the Reorganized Debtors and the Liquidating Trustee have been strictly at arm's length. Virtually every conceivable issue was negotiated in the Agreements as the parties attempted to resolve their competing and divergent views on the Sale of the Purchased Assets. On June 15, 2006, after weeks of extensive and, at times, difficult negotiations, the Reorganized Debtors and the Liquidating Trustee agreed to enter into asset purchase agreements with MM Broadcasting, LLC and Bluenose Television of Portland LLC (collectively, the "Buyers") and to seek an order approving the procedures for an auction sale of the Purchased Assets with the Buyers acting as a "stalking horse bidder."

22.     The Movants believe, in their reasonable business judgment, that it is in the best interests of the Liquidating Trust to sell the Purchased Assets via an auction either as a whole to one bidder, or in parts to more than one bidder. In furtherance of such interests, the Movants have entered into two asset purchase agreements dated June 15, 2006 (the "Agreements") for the sale of substantially all of the Broadcast Assets for an aggregate price of $49.5 million (the "Purchase Price"), subject to higher and better offers that may be submitted in accordance with Court approved Bidding Procedures. Pursuant to the main agreement (the "Broadcasting Agreement") by and between the Movants as sellers and MM Broadcasting, LLC ("MM Broadcasting") as buyers, the Movants seek to sell certain authorizations issued by the FCC and certain other assets used and useful to

operate television stations WOLF, Hazelton, Pennsylvania; WILF, Williamsport, Pennsylvania; WPXT, Portland, Maine; WPME, Lewiston, Maine; WDSI, Chattanooga, Tennessee; WTLH, Bainbridge, Georgia; WGFL, High Springs, Florida. A copy of the Broadcasting Agreement is attached hereto as Exhibit A.

23.     Because the Movants are selling multiple stations in the Portland, Maine DMA, the FCC's local television ownership rules preclude the sale of both of the Movants' television stations in that area, WPME, Lewiston, Maine and WPXT, Portland, Maine, to MM Broadcasting. Accordingly, Pegasus Broadcast Television, Inc. and HMW, Inc. entered into a second asset purchase agreement on June 15, 2006, with Bluenose Television of Portland LLC as buyer for the sale of certain assets used and useful to operate WPME (the "WPME Agreement"). A copy of the WPME Agreement is attached hereto as Exhibit B.

24.     In light of the interrelated nature of these Agreements, the Movants seek by this Motion to sell all assets subject to the Agreements (the "Purchased Assets") together at Auction. The Purchased Assets subject to the Agreements include assets of the Reorganized Debtors (the Purchased Debtor Assets") and assets of the WGFL Entities.[9]

25.     The Movants do not seek Bankruptcy Court approval of a third related agreement by and between Mystic Television of Scranton LLC and Mystic Television of Tallahassee LLC as sellers, and Bluenose Television of Scranton LLC and Bluenose Television of Tallahassee LLC, as buyers for the sale of assets used and useful to operate television stations WSWB(TV), Scranton, Pennsylvania and WTLF-DT, Tallahassee, Florida (the "Mystic Agreement"). The assets being sold by Mystic include those that are the subject of certain TBAs or similar agreements that enable the Reorganized Debtors to receive or be able to receive economic benefits from programming multiple stations in the Wilkes-Barre-Scranton, Pennsylvania and Tallahassee, Florida DMAs. The closing of the Broadcasting Agreement and the WPME Agreement are

---

[9] The WGFL Entities seek to sell their assets in the ordinary course and do not seek the protections of section 363 of the Bankruptcy Code with respect to such assets. Because the WGFL Entities are wholly-owned subsidiaries of Reorganized Debtor Pegasus Satellite Communications, Inc., the sale of their assets will avail to the benefit of the Liquidating Trust.

conditions precedent to the closing on the Mystic Agreement. A copy of the Mystic Agreement is attached hereto as Exhibit C.

## SUMMARY OF PROPOSED SALES

26. The Agreements can be summarized as follows:[10]

a. **Purchased Assets.** The Agreements provide that the Buyers shall acquire and assume all of the Purchased Assets and Assumed Liabilities from the Movants, pursuant to Sections 363 and 365 of the Bankruptcy Code, to the extent applicable, on the terms and subject to the conditions set forth in the Agreements.

b. **Purchase Price.** The aggregate consideration for the Purchased Assets to be paid by the Buyers is (a) an amount in cash equal to $49,500,000 less certain amounts due for certain assets set forth in the Agreements and subject to adjustments for Post-Closing Working Capital and Digital Capital Projects, and (b) the assumption of the Assumed Liabilities. The Purchase Price shall be subject to a cash reduction of $2,000,000 in the event the Sale Order has not been entered by the Bankruptcy Court within one hundred (100) days after the date hereof.

c. **Break Up Fee.** The Sellers have agreed to pay Buyers a break-up fee of $1,500,000 (the "Break-Up Fee") and an expense reimbursement for Buyer's reasonable out-of-pocket expenses, not to exceed $700,000, incurred in connection with, or arising from, the transactions contemplated by the Agreements and the financing thereof (the "Expense Reimbursement"). The Break-Up Fee and Expense Reimbursement will be payable pursuant to the Bidding Procedures and the Sale Motion in various circumstances, including, without limitation, if the Movants enter into a definitive agreement providing for an Alternative Transaction prior to a date twelve months following the date of termination of the Broadcasting Agreement and such transaction is subsequently consummated.

---

[10] Interested parties should not rely on this summary, and should instead consult the Agreements attached as Exhibits A and B and incorporated herein by reference for the specific terms of the proposed sale.

d. **Conditions Precedent.** The Agreements contain a number of conditions precedent. The following is a list of some of the more relevant conditions precedent:

(i) **Bidding Procedures Order.** The Bankruptcy Court shall enter the Bidding Procedures Order.

(ii) **Sale Order in the Chapter 11 Case.** The Sale Order shall be a Final Order and notice of approval of the Sale Order shall be served on all Taxing Authorities and Governmental Authorities having jurisdiction over the Purchased Assets, and the attorneys general of all states in which the Purchased Assets are located.

e. **Solicitation of Overbids.** The Agreements specifically recognize the solicitation of overbids for the Purchased Assets in accordance with the bidding procedures to be established by the Bankruptcy Court.

27. The obligations of the Buyers are explicitly conditioned upon receiving the prior consent and approval of the FCC (the "FCC Consent"). Because FCC approval is required, in addition to approval of the Bankruptcy Court, the Reorganized Debtors have filed applications with the FCC for approval of the transfers embodied in the Agreements.

## RELIEF REQUESTED

28. The Movants respectfully request, pursuant to sections 105, 363, 365 and 1146 of the Bankruptcy Code, Rules 2002, 6004, 6006, 9007 and 9014 of the Bankruptcy Rules, and D. Me. LBR 2002-1, 6004-1, and 6006-1, (A) entry of the Bidding Procedures Order approving (i) the Bidding Procedures, break-up fee, and expense reimbursement, and thereafter (ii) the Auction and Hearing Notice; and (B) entry of the Sale Order approving (i) the sale of the Purchased Debtor Assets free and clear of liens, claims, encumbrances and other interests (other than Permitted Encumbrances), (ii) the assignment of certain executory contracts and unexpired leases in connection with the sale of the Purchased Debtor Assets, and (iii) the exemption of the sale of the Purchased Assets from stamp or similar taxes.

29. The Movants believe, in an exercise of their sound business judgment, that entering into the Agreements with the Buyers and then proceeding with the Auction in accordance with the proposed Bidding Procedures will result in the highest and best offer for the Broadcast Assets. Furthermore, the Movants believe that selling the Broadcast Assets under Bankruptcy Code §§ 363(b) and (f) is the best way to ensure an orderly and equitable sale process and distribution of proceeds.

30. The Liquidating Trustee expressly reserves the right to modify the relief requested in the Sale Motion, including the proposed Bidding Procedures, prior to or at the applicable hearings, subject to the consent of the Buyers.

## JURISDICTION

31. This Court has jurisdiction to consider this Motion pursuant to 28 U.S.C. §§ 157 and 1334 and (ii) and the Plan and Confirmation Order (as those terms are defined later herein). This matter is a core proceeding pursuant to 28 U.S.C. § 157(b)(2). Venue is proper in this Court pursuant to 28 U.S.C. §§ 1408 and 1409. This Court expressly retained jurisdiction over the post-confirmation sale of the Broadcast Assets and the assumption or assumption and assignment of the certain executory contracts and unexpired leases pursuant to the Bankruptcy Code, section 13.1 of the Plan, and paragraphs 21 and 26 of the Confirmation Order.[11] Section 1142(b) of the Bankruptcy Code provides that a bankruptcy court

---

[11] Paragraph 21 of the Confirmation Order requires the Liquidating Trustee to "obtain order(s) from the Bankruptcy Court to sell or otherwise dispose of all or a portion of the Broadcast Assets including the Debtors' FCC licenses and broadcast television stations." See Confirmation Order at ¶ 21. Similarly, paragraph 26(q) of the Confirmation Order preserves the jurisdiction of the Bankruptcy Court to consider and enter orders approving the sale of assets after the Effective Date and explicitly provides that:

> For the avoidance of doubt, the Liquidating Trustee shall be required to obtain, and the Bankruptcy Court hereby retains jurisdiction to adjudicate and implement, orders pursuant to sections 363 and 365 of the Bankruptcy Code for the sale or other disposition of all or a portion of the Broadcast Assets including, without limitation, the Debtors' FCC licenses and the Debtors' broadcast television stations.

See id.

retains jurisdiction to ensure that the terms and provisions of a confirmed chapter 11 plan are carried out. See In re Boston Regional Medical Center, Inc., 410 F.3d 100 (1st Cir. 2005); In re Johns-Manville Corp., 97 Bankr. 174, 180 (Bankr. S.D.N.Y. 1989) (clear intent of section 1142(b) is to assure that the terms and provisions of a confirmed chapter 11 plan are carried out until the plan is completed and the case is closed). More specifically, prior cases have held that the bankruptcy court retains jurisdiction to approve the sale of a debtor's assets, and that such retention is particularly appropriate where, as here, the Plan expressly provides for the court's continued jurisdiction. See, e.g., In re Bicoastal Corp., 164 B.R. 1009, 1014-15 (Bankr. M.D. Fl. 1993); see also In re Chateaugay Corp., 201 B.R. 48, 66 (Bankr. S.D.N.Y. 1996). Accordingly, this Court retains jurisdiction to approve any post-confirmation sale of the Broadcast Assets, including the assignment to the Buyers of the Assigned Contracts and Leases.

## ARGUMENT

## PART I

32.    In order to facilitate an orderly sale of the Purchased Assets, the Movants request that the Court approve the following Bidding Procedures, including the manner in which notice of the Auction and Sale Hearing is provided.

## THE BIDDING PROCEDURES

33.    In an effort to insure that maximum value is obtained for the Purchased Assets, the Movants request that this Court approve the following Bidding Procedures. The Movants believe that entering into the Agreements with the Buyers and then proceeding with the Auction of the Purchased Assets conducted in accordance with the Bidding Procedures will maximize the value of the Purchased Assets. While all interested bidders should read the Bidding Procedures in their entirety, a summary of the Bidding Procedures follows:[12]

---

[12] This summary is qualified in its entirety by the Bidding Procedures.

(a)     At least twenty (20) days prior to the Sale Hearing, the Movants shall serve copies of the Sale Motion without the Agreements, the Bidding Procedures Order, the Notice of Sale and Auction Procedures, and the proposed Sale Order, by first class mail, postage prepaid, to (i) all potential purchasers identified by the Reorganized Debtors and the Liquidating Trustee or their agent, (ii) the Office of the United States Trustee, (iii) each entity designated on the All Notices List in this case, (iv) all entities known to the Reorganized Debtors and the Liquidating Trustee to claim a lien, security interest, or other interest in any of the Purchased Debtor Assets, (v) each contracting party to the Assumed Contracts, (vi) all Taxing Authorities and Governmental Authorities having jurisdiction over the Purchased Assets, and (vii) the attorneys general of all states in which the Purchased Assets are located. The Movants, in their discretion, may publish the Sale Notice or otherwise advertise the Sale in the national edition of *The Wall Street Journal* or such other publications or on the website of the Liquidating Trust. Copies of the Sale Motion, the exhibits thereto, or other pleadings in connection with the Sale Motion by submitting a written request to counsel for the Reorganized Debtors and the Liquidating Trustee. The Sellers, in their discretion, may publish copies of the Agreements on the website of the Liquidating Trust.

(b)     Prior to the Auction, the Movants may qualify potential bidders by, *inter alia*, examining potential bidders' current financial statements and ability to consummate the purchase of the Purchased Assets ("Qualified Bidders"). After executing a confidentiality agreement in a form to be determined by the Movants, Qualified Bidders will be allowed to perform reasonable due diligence on the Purchased Assets, including reasonable access to the books, records and executives of the Movants. Any interested bidders should contact Miller Buckfire & Co., LLC, 250 Park Avenue, 19th Floor, New York, NY 10177,

Attention: Stuart Erickson, Telephone: 212-895-1812, Facsimile: 212-895-1862, e-mail:

stuart.erickson@millerbuckfire.com to seek to become Qualified Bidders and, thereafter, to request information in connection with their due diligence.

(c)　　Alternative Transactions bids shall contain firm bids in excess of $51,950,000 which shall include the sum of (i) the Purchase Price plus the purchase prices under the Other Station Agreements, (ii) the initial overbid increment of $250,000, (iii) the Break-Up Fee of $1,500,000, and (iv) the Expense Reimbursement of $700,0000, or in the case of Piecemeal Bids (as defined below), provide for consideration payable at closing in excess of such amount when considered in the aggregate with other Piecemeal Bids; thereafter, bidding increments shall be equal to at least $250,000, or such other lesser amount as the Liquidating Trustee shall announce from time to time at the Auction, until the Liquidating Trustee declares a winner.

(d)　　In order for any Alternative Transaction to be a Qualified Bid, it must be: (i) in writing; (ii) firm, unconditional bid to purchase some or all of the Purchased Assets, together with a firm, unconditional bid of one or more other Qualified Bidders to purchase some or all of the assets under the Other Station Agreements not subject to any contingencies (other than closing conditions consistent with the closing conditions contained in the Agreements) as to the validity, effectiveness and/or binding nature of the offer, including, without limitation, further due diligence review or financing; (iii) accompanied by sufficient information to demonstrate that the competing bidder or bidders, has the financial wherewithal and ability to timely consummate the acquisition of the Purchased Assets on terms and conditions substantially the same or better than those contained in the Agreements, including evidence of adequate financing and a financial guaranty, if appropriate; (iv) accompanied by a signed contract, or contracts, substantially in the form of the Agreements, as appropriate, and marked to show any changes made to the Agreement(s), provided, however, that the Movants reserve the right to reject a competing bid in the event that any proposed changes to the Agreement(s) are not satisfactory to the Movants as determined in their sole business judgment; (v) accompanied by the name and telephone number(s) of a contact person who will be available to answer questions regarding the bid, as well as the names and telephone numbers of any financial and legal advisors retained by the competing bidder, as applicable; (vi) accompanied by evidence of the Qualified Bidder's ability to provide adequate assurance of future performance with respect to the Assigned Contracts and Leases if the bid is conditioned on the assignment of any such Assigned Contracts and Leases; (viii) accompanied by a good faith cash deposit in an amount equal to the Purchase Price Deposit, as set forth below; and (ix) such other information as reasonably may be requested by the Movants.

(e)      All Qualified Bids must be submitted in writing so that they are *actually received* by no later than August 2, 2006, at 5:00 p.m. prevailing Eastern Time, (the "Bid Deadline") by Miller Buckfire & Co., LLC, at the address set forth in paragraph four (4) above, with copies to the following parties:(i) Ocean Ridge Capital Advisors, LLC, 56 Harrison Street, Suite 203A, New Rochelle, NY  10801, Attn: Bradley E. Scher (ii) Akin Gump Strauss Hauer & Feld LLP, Robert S. Strauss Building, 1333 New Hampshire Avenue, NW, Washington, DC 20036, Attn: Russell W. Parks, Jr. , Esq.; and (iii) Lowenstein Sandler PC, 65 Livingston Avenue, Roseland, NJ 07068, Attn: Jeffrey A. Kramer, Esq.

(f)     Any Qualified Bids must be accompanied by a good faith cash Purchase Price Deposit in an amount equal to $2,500,000, provided however, any person that seeks to purchase a part of the Purchased Assets shall deposit a good faith cash Purchase Price Deposit in an amount equal to five percent (5%) of the Qualified Bid.  Such deposits shall be held by the Movants, without interest, and shall be forfeited in the event that any bidder for an accepted bid defaults.

(g)     The Movants shall promptly provide Buyer with a copy of any Qualified Bid received by the Movants and such other information regarding Alternative Transactions as provided for in Section 3.2.3(b) of the Agreements.

(h)     If the Movants determine in good faith and in their reasonable discretion that they have not received a Qualified Bid by the Bid Deadline that, singly or in combination with a series of Qualified Bids for portions of the Purchased Assets, is a higher or better bid than the one represented by the Agreements, the Movants shall seek approval of the Agreements at the Sale Hearing without conducting an Auction and without further motion.  The Agreements executed by the Buyers shall constitute a Qualified Bid for all purposes.

(i)     The Purchased Assets and the assets under the Other Station Agreements need not be sold in a single lot; provided, that the aggregate consideration to be received for the Purchased Assets and the assets under the Other Station Agreements to be sold shall be in accordance with in paragraph (c) above.  If the Movants receive Piecemeal Bids that qualify *en toto* as a Qualified Bid, the Movants shall be permitted to first conduct an auction on each of the assets or groups of assets that are the subject of Piecemeal Bids (the "Piecemeal Auctions").  Upon the completion of the Piecemeal Auctions, the aggregate consideration to be received pursuant to the Piecemeal

Auctions shall be considered the Starting Auction Bid unless another Qualified Bid provides for greater consideration than the aggregate consideration to be received pursuant to the Piecemeal Auctions. Thereafter, the Movants shall be permitted to conduct the Auction of the Purchased Assets in accordance with the terms herein.

(j)     If at least one timely Qualified Bid that meets all of the requirements herein is timely received, the Auction will be conducted at the offices of Akin Gump Strauss Hauer & Feld, LLP, 590 Madison Avenue, New York, NY 10022 on August 7, 2006 at 10:00 a.m. or such later time or other place as the Movants shall notify all Qualified Bidders who have submitted Qualified Bids. Only (i) the Buyers, (ii) the Movants, and (iii) any Qualified Bidders who have timely submitted Qualified Bids shall be entitled to attend the Auction, and only the Buyers and the Qualified Bidders will be entitled to make any subsequent Qualified Bids at the Auction. The Movants may select the winning bid at the conclusion of the Auction, and the winning bidder will be required to enter into a definitive agreement (as modified by the bids submitted at the Auction) before the Auction is adjourned. When determining the highest or best bid, the Movants shall include the Bidding Incentives in the Buyers' last bid, which Bidding Incentives would otherwise be payable to the Buyers.

(k)     The Movants shall have the right and discretion to (i) reject any bid (other than the Buyers') the Movants deem to be inadequate, (ii) adjourn the Auction by announcing such adjournment prior to or during the Auction without further notice, (iii) modify the terms and conditions of the Auction by announcing such modifications at or prior to the commencement of the Auction, or during the Auction, and (iv) extend the deadlines set forth in the Bidding Procedures.

(l)     If the Winning Bidder fails to consummate the sale of the Purchased Assets because of a breach or failure to perform on the part of such Winning Bidder, the Backup Bid, as approved at the Sale Hearing, shall be automatically deemed to be the successful bid and the Backup Bidder, which may be the Buyers, shall be obligated to consummate the transaction in accordance with the Backup Bid for 120 days following the acceptance of the Winning Bid, except if the Buyers' bid is the Backup Bid, in which case the Buyers will be obligated to consummate the transaction in accordance with the Backup Bid for 60 days following acceptance of the Winning Bid, and, thereafter, shall not be obligated to consummate the Backup Bid. The Movants and Backup Bidder may consummate such a Sale without further order of the Bankruptcy Court. If the Buyers are the Backup Bidder, the Buyers may terminate the Agreements after 60 days following the acceptance of the Winning Bid in accordance with Section 11.1(g) of the Agreements.

**THE BID OF ANY BIDDER FAILING TO COMPLY WITH THESE REQUIREMENTS MAY NOT BE CONSIDERED BY THE MOVANTS, IN THEIR REASONABLE DISCRETION.**

**THE FOREGOING IS ONLY A SUMMARY OF THE BIDDING PROCEDURES AND ALL INTERESTED PARTIES SHOULD CAREFULLY REVIEW THE BIDDING PROCEDURES ORDER.**

34.     The Movants believes that these Bidding Procedures provide an appropriate framework for selling the Purchased Assets in a uniform fashion and will enable the Movants to review, analyze and compare all bids received to determine which bid(s) is/are in the best interests of the Liquidating Trust and creditors. Therefore, the Movants respectfully request that this Court approve the Bidding Procedures.

## APPROVAL OF BIDDING INCENTIVES

35.     As part of the Bidding Procedures Order, the Movants respectfully request that the Court approve the Break-up Fee and Expense Reimbursement provisions of the Agreements (collectively, the "Bidding Incentives") in order to maximize the value that the Movants may obtain for the Purchased Assets. The Agreements provide for the payment of a break-up fee of $1,500,000 (the "Break-Up Fee") and reimbursement for Buyers' reasonable out-of-pocket expenses, not to exceed $700,000, incurred in connection with, or arising from, the transactions contemplated in the Agreements and the financing thereof (the "Expense Reimbursement"), in the event that a successful bidder other than the Buyers purchase the Purchased Assets that are the subject of the Agreements or upon the occurrence of certain other events as set forth in section 3.2.1 of the Broadcasting Agreement. The Movants further request that the Bidding Procedures Order, as required under section 3.2.2 of the Broadcasting Agreement, provide that the Bidding Incentives be treated as allowed administrative expenses with priority over all administrative expenses of the kind specified in Sections 503(b) and 507(b) of the Bankruptcy Code and that the Buyers be entitled to bid the Break-Up Fee and Expense Reimbursement as part of any bid made at the Auction.

36.     Break-up fees such as those provided for in the Agreement "are important tools to encourage bidding and to maximize the value of the debtor's assets" and serve a number of useful functions: (1) they attract bidders, (2) they help to insure that a bidder does not withdraw its bid, and (3) they help to establish a bid standard for other bidders. See Official Committee of Subordinated Bondholders v. Integrated Resources, Inc. (In re Integrated Resources, Inc.), 147 B.R. 650, 659-62 (S.D.N.Y. 1992), appeal dismissed, 3 F.3d 49 (2d Cir. 1993) (because a corporation has a duty to encourage bidding, fees can be necessary to discharge such duties to maximize value of the estate). Specifically, "breakup fees and other strategies may be legitimately necessary to convince a 'white knight' bidder to enter the bidding by providing some form of compensation for the risks it is undertaking." In re 995 Fifth Ave. Assocs., L.P., 96 B.R. 24, 28 (Bankr. S.D.N.Y. 1989) (internal quotations omitted); see also, Integrated Resources, 147 B.R. at 660-61 (break-up fees can prompt bidders to commence negotiations and "ensure that a bidder does not retract its bid");

In re Hupp Industries, 140 B.R. 191, 194 (Bankr. N.D. Ohio 1992) ("without such fees, bidders would be reluctant to make an initial bid for fear that their first bid will be shopped around for a higher bid from another bidder who would capitalize on the initial bidder's . . . due diligence").

37.     The Buyers have expended considerable time and expense in connection with the Agreements and the negotiation thereof and the identification and assessment of assets of Movants. The Movants submit that the amount of the Bidding Incentives embodied in the Agreements is reasonable in these circumstances. The Bidding Incentives were and are a material inducement for, and condition of, the Buyers' entry into the Agreement. The Buyers are unwilling to commit to hold open their offer to purchase the Purchased Assets without these bidding incentives. Thus, the Bidding Incentives will promote more competitive bidding by inducing the Buyers' bid that otherwise would not have been made, and without which any bidding might be limited. Absent authorization of the Bidding Incentives, the Movants may lose the opportunity to obtain the highest and best offer for the Purchased Assets.

38.     Although the First Circuit has not yet addressed the issue of break-up fees in a written opinion, other circuits have found that the approval of break-up fees depends on whether awarding such fees and expenses is within the reasonable "business judgment" of the debtor, see Integrated Resources, 147 B.R. at 659-60; 995 Fifth Ave. Assocs., 96 B.R. at 28, or is in the best interest of the estate, see Calpine Corp. v. O'Brien Environmental Energy, Inc. (In re O'Brien Environmental Energy, Inc.), 181 F.3d 527 (3d Cir. 1999); In re S.N.A. Nut Co., 186 B.R. 98 (Bankr. N.D. Ill. 1995).

39.     In approving or denying break-up fees, numerous bankruptcy courts have applied a standard that is based on the business judgment rule. See 995 Fifth Ave. Assocs., 96 B.R. at 28 (finding that the business judgment rule had "vitality by analogy" to the bankruptcy context, and should be used to analyze whether to approve a break-up fee). In In re Integrated Resources, Inc., 147 B.R. 650 (S.D.N.Y. 1992), the district court affirmed a bankruptcy court decision approving a break-up fee finding that the fees were entitled to the same presumption of validity as in other

corporate actions such as mergers. The business judgment rule, as defined by the court, "shields corporate decision-makers and their decisions from judicial second-guessing when the following elements are present: (1) a business decision, (2) disinterestedness, (3) due care, (4) good faith, and (5) according to some courts and commentators, no abuse of discretion or waste of corporate assets." Id. at 656. See also In re Global Crossing Ltd., 295 B.R. 726, 744 n.58 (Bankr. S.D.N.Y. 2003) (declaring that the court "does not believe that it is appropriate for a bankruptcy court to substitute its own business judgment for that of the Debtors and their advisors" so long as they meet case law requirements); In re Great Northern Paper, Inc., Case No. 03-10048-LHK (Bankr. D. Me. February 18, 2003) (finding that the debtor's agreement to pay a break-up fee was, under the circumstances, a proper exercise of the debtor's business judgment as a fiduciary for its chapter 11 bankruptcy estate).

40.     In Integrated Resources, the court noted that prior decisions regarding break-up fees suggest three questions for courts to consider in assessing whether break-up fees are appropriate exercise of a debtor's business judgment "(1) is the relationship of the parties who negotiated the break-up fee tainted by self-dealing or manipulation; (2) does the fee hamper, rather than encourage, bidding; (3) is the amount of the fee unreasonable relative to the proposed purchase price?" See Integrated Resources, 147 B.R. at 657. See also In re RSL COM Primecall, Inc., 2002 Bankr. LEXIS 367 at *29-31 (Bankr. S.D.N.Y. Apr. 11, 2002) (affirming the reasonableness of a break-up fee using the tripartite test factors set forth in Integrated Resources). In this matter, this standard is easily met. The Bidding Incentives are the product of extended good faith, arm's-length negotiations between the Movants and the Buyers and have encouraged meaningful bidding by (i) attracting and retaining the Buyers' bid, and (ii) establishing a benchmark against which the Movants can evaluate other bids. Moreover, the Movants submit that the amount of the Bidding Incentives is fair and reasonable relative to the amount to be paid to the Movants based on the amount of the Buyers' offer prior to any adjustments relating to market fluctuations. Under the Agreements, the largest potential amount to be paid pursuant to the Bidding Incentives, $2,200,000, is 4.44% of the consideration to be paid for the Purchased Assets and is within the range of break-up fees approved in the context of section 363 sales. See, e.g., Integrated Resources, 147 B.R. at 662 ("A break-up fee should

constitute a fair and reasonable percentage of the proposed purchase price, and should be reasonably related to the risk, effort, and expenses of the prospective purchaser."). Accordingly, the Movants should be authorized to offer the Bidding Incentives as is necessary in the Movants' business judgment.

41.     Rather than rely on business judgment, other courts have held that, to be approved, bidding incentives must provide some benefit to a debtor's estate. In Calpine, the Third Circuit held that even though bidding incentives are measured against a business judgment standard in nonbankruptcy transactions, the administrative expense provisions in § 503(b) of the Bankruptcy Code govern in the bankruptcy context. 181 F.3d at 533. The O'Brien Court identified at least two instances in which bidding incentives may provide the requisite benefit to the estate. First, benefit may be found if "assurance of a break-up fee promoted more competitive bidding, such as by inducing a bid that otherwise would not have been made and without which bidding would have been limited." Id. at 537. Second, where the availability of bidding incentives induces a bidder to research the value of the subject assets and submit a bid that serves as a minimum or floor bid on which other bidders can rely, "the bidder may have provided a benefit to the estate by increasing the likelihood that the price at which the debtor is sold will reflect the true worth." Id.

42.     In In re S.N.A. Nut Co., 186 B.R. 98 (Bankr. N.D. Ill. 1995), the court applied the "best interest of the estate" test to determine whether the payment of a break-up fee to an unsuccessful bidder in a liquidating chapter 11 case was appropriate. In so doing, the court expressed the view that "the proper standard for evaluating a break-up fee should be whether the interests of all concerned parties are best served by such a fee." Id. at 104. In this case, the Bidding Incentives is in the "best interest of the estate," and the "interests of all concerned parties" are best served by approving the provision for the Bidding Incentives, because the provisions are integral parts of a transaction that represents the highest and best proposal for the purchase of the Purchased Assets and the best means of increasing the likelihood of competitive bidding.

43.     Under either of the standards set forth in O'Brien and S.N.A. Nut Co., the Break-Up Fee should be approved. The Movants' ability to persuade the Buyers to proceed is dependent on an assurance that the Buyers would receive protection, in the event a third party submits a higher and better offer, which would enable the Buyers to recover at least some reimbursement for the cost of its efforts. Further, by moving forward with the Buyers' offer, the Movants have been able to set a floor bid, which should increase the likelihood of attracting competitive bids. Finally, the fact that the Buyers are prepared to proceed with this transaction after having conducted its due diligence maximizes the likelihood that third parties interested in the Purchased Assets will participate in the sale process, thereby increasing the possibility of achieving the highest realizable value under the circumstances. Finally, the mere existence of the Bidding Incentives permits the Movants to insist that competing bids for the Purchased Assets be higher or otherwise better than the Purchase Price under the Agreements, a clear benefit to the Movants. For the foregoing reasons, Movants submit that the standards set forth in O'Brien and S.N.A. Nut Co. are satisfied.

44.     Accordingly, the Movants request that the Court approve the Bidding Incentives as defined in, and pursuant to, the terms and conditions of the provisions of the Bidding Procedures.

## THE NOTICE OF SALE AND AUCTION PROCEDURES AND NOTICE OF THE SALE MOTION

45.     A proposed form of notice with respect to the sale of the Purchased Assets and the assignment or the Assigned Contracts and Leases (as defined herein), and the objection, Bid Deadline, Auction and Hearing dates is attached hereto as Exhibit G (the "Notice of Sale and Auction Procedures"). The Movants respectfully request this Court approve the Notice of Sale and Auction Procedures.

46.     The Order Establishing Case Management Procedures and Hearing Schedule entered in the Reorganized Debtors' bankruptcy cases on July 9, 2004 (the "Case Management Order") requires notice of the proposed use, sale, or lease of property of the estate other than in the ordinary course of business to be served on each entity on the

All Notices List and each entity known to the Reorganized Debtors to claim a lien, security interest, or other interest in the property.[13] The Case Management Order also requires notice of a motion to assign a contract or lease to be served on each contracting party to the contract or lease and each entity designated on the All Notices List. The Notice of Sale and Auction Procedures complies with Bankruptcy Rule 2002(c) and the Case Management Order and includes information on the Bidding Procedures necessary to enable interested parties to participate in the Auction and the Sale Hearing.

47.     At least twenty (20) days prior to the Sale Hearing (the "Mailing Date"), the Movants shall serve a copy of the Sale Motion without copies of the Agreements, the Notice of Sale and Auction Procedures, the Bidding Procedures Order, and the proposed Sale Order, by first class mail, postage prepaid, to (i) all potential purchasers previously identified by the Reorganized Debtors and the Liquidating Trustee or their agent, (ii) the Office of the United States Trustee, (iii) each entity designated on the All Notices List in this case, (iv) all entities known to the Reorganized Debtors and the Liquidating Trustee to claim a lien, security interest, or other interest in any of the Purchased Debtor Assets, (v) each contracting party to the Assumed Contracts, (vi) all Taxing Authorities and Governmental Authorities having jurisdiction over the Purchased Assets, and (vii) the attorneys general of all states in which the Purchased Assets are located (the "Service List").

48.     The Bidding Procedures Order will also provide that the Movants, in their discretion, may publish the Notice of Sale and Auction Procedures or otherwise advertise the Sale in the national edition of *The Wall Street Journal* or such other publications or on the website of the Liquidating Trust. Such publication shall be deemed proper notice to any other interested parties whose identities are unknown to the Movants.

49.     The Notice of Sale and Auction Procedures provides that any party that wishes to obtain a copy of this Sale Motion, the exhibits thereto (including the Agreements), or other pleadings in

---

[13] The Case Management Order provides that "[n]otice in accordance with this Order shall be deemed adequate pursuant to Bankruptcy Rule 2002 and the Local Rules." Case Management Order, ¶ 7.

connection with the Sale Motion, may make such a request in writing to counsel for the Reorganized Debtors and the Liquidating Trustee prior to July 31, 2006 at 4:00 p.m. prevailing Eastern Time. Requests must include a street address for delivery.

50.     Additionally, the Bidding Procedures Order and the Notice of Sale and Auction Procedures will also provide that any person may request notification of the winning bid by submitting a written request including either an e-mail address or facsimile number so that such request is actually received by counsel for the Reorganized Debtors and the Liquidating Trustee by 4:00 p.m. prevailing Eastern Time on August 5, 2006 (a "Notice Request"). Notice of the winning bid(s) shall be sent by email or facsimile, as the case may be, only to those persons who submitted a Notice Request.

51.     The Movants further request that objections, if any, to the portion of the relief requested in the Sale Motion with respect to the Sale of the Purchased Assets or the assignment of Assigned Contracts and Leases, including the assignment of the Assigned Contracts and Leases to a purchaser or purchasers other than the Buyers, must be: (a) in writing; (b) conform to the requirements of the Bankruptcy Code, the Federal Rules of Bankruptcy Procedure, and the Local Rules of the United States Bankruptcy Court for the District of Maine; (c) set forth the name and address of the objector and shall contain requisite information respecting the objecting party's status; (d) state with particularity the legal and factual bases of the objection and the specific grounds therefor; and (e) filed with the Court on or before July 31, 2006 at 4:00 p.m. prevailing Eastern Time and served so that same are received on or before July 31, 2006 at 4:00 p.m. prevailing Eastern Time by (1) Office of the Clerk of the United States Bankruptcy Court, 527 Congress Street, Portland, Maine 04101; (2) Lowenstein Sandler, PC, Attn: Jeffrey A. Kramer, Esq., 65 Livingston Avenue, Roseland, New Jersey 07068; (3) Preti, Flaherty, Beliveau, Pachios & Haley, LLP, Attn: John P. McVeigh, Esq., One City Center, PO Box 95465, Portland, Maine 04112-9546; and (4) Weil, Gotshal & Manges, LLP, Attn: George A. Davis, Esq., 767 Fifth Avenue, New York, New York 10153. The Movants further request that the Bidding Procedures Order provide that unless a party to the Assigned Contracts and Leases timely files an objection to assignment of the Assigned Contract or Lease to which it is

a party in accordance with this Order, it shall be deemed to have consented to the assignment of such Assigned Contract or Lease to the Buyers or to any purchaser or purchasers other than the Buyers.

52. The Movants submit that the notice to be provided through the Notice of Sale and Auction Procedures, the Sale Motion and the Supplement and the method of service proposed herein constitutes good and adequate notice of the sale of the Purchased Assets and the proceedings to be had with respect thereto. The Movants hereby seek approval of the Notice of Sale and Auction Procedures to ensure that no questions about the adequacy of the content of the Notice of Sale and Auction Procedures cloud the sale, or delay its consummation, and also seek to ensure that the Bidding Procedures contained in the Notice of Sale and Auction Procedures and the Agreements meet with the approval of the Court. As set forth above, Rules 2002, 6004, and 9007 and D. Me. LR 2002-1 and 6004-1 provide the Court with flexibility in regulating notice of an intended sale. Rule 9007 in particular authorizes the Court to regulate and approve not only the time within which the notice is to be served and the parties to be served, but the form and manner of the proposed notice. Therefore, for the reasons articulated in more detail above, and pursuant to Code section 105(a)'s broad grant of equitable powers, the Movants respectfully request that the Court approve the Notice of Sale and Auction Procedures attached hereto as Exhibit G.

## PART II

## THE SALE OF THE MOVANTS' ASSETS SHOULD BE APPROVED

53. The Movants submit that ample authority exists for the proposed sales of the Purchased Debtor Assets. Most significant, the Plan and Confirmation Order provide express authority for the Liquidating Trustee to exercise its discretion to sell all or a portion of the Broadcast Assets, subject to the jurisdiction and approval of the Bankruptcy Court. In addition, a debtor or trustee in a chapter 11 proceeding are authorized to sell property outside the ordinary course of business is section 363(b)(1) of the Bankruptcy Code which provides: "[t]he Trustee, after notice and a hearing, may use, sell or lease, other than in the ordinary

course of business, property of the estate." 11 U.S.C. § 363(b). See also Fed. R. Bankr. P. 6004(f)(1) ("All sales not in the ordinary course of business may be by private sale or by public auction."). Similarly, section 1123(a)(5)(D) provides that a chapter 11 plan may provide for the sale of property of the estate.

54. A bankruptcy court's power to authorize a sale under section 363(b) is to be exercised at the court's discretion. See In re WPRV-TV, Inc., 983 F.2d 336, 340 (1st Cir. 1993); New Haven Radio, Inc. v. Meister (In re Martin-Trigona), 760 F.2d 1334, 1346 (2d Cir. 1985); Committee of Equity Sec. Holders v. Lionel Corp. (In re Lionel Corp.), 722 F.2d 1063, 1069 (2d Cir. 1983). Courts have authorized the sale of a debtor's assets pursuant to section 363(b) of the Bankruptcy Code where there is a "sound business purpose" for doing so. See Titusville Country Club, v. Penn Bank (In re Titusville Country Club), 128 B.R. 396, 399 (Bankr. W.D. Pa. 1991); In re Delaware & Hudson Ry. Co., 124 B.R. 169, 176 (D. Del. 1991); In re Industrial Valley Refrig. & Air Conditioning Supplies, Inc., 77 B.R. 15, 20 (Bankr. E.D. Pa. 1987). See also Stephens Indus., Inc. v. McClune, 789 F.2d 386, 390 (6th Cir. 1986) ("bankruptcy court can authorize a sale of all a Chapter 11 debtor's assets under §363(b)(1) when a sound business purpose dictates such action"); Committee of Equity Security Holders v. Lionel Corp. (In re Lionel Corp.), 722 F.2d 1063, 1071 (2d Cir. 1983) (setting forth the "sound business purpose" test in the context of a sale of assets under section 363(b)). The same test should apply here to a sale in furtherance of a confirmed chapter 11 plan.

55. The "sound business purpose" test requires a debtor to establish four elements to sell property outside the ordinary course of business; namely, (a) that a "sound business purpose" justifies the sale of assets outside the ordinary course of business, (b) that adequate and reasonable notice has been provided to interested persons; (c) that the debtor has obtained a fair and reasonable price; and (d) good faith. See In re Abbotts Dairies of Pa., 788 F.2d 143, 147-50 (3d Cir. 1986); Titusville Country Club, 128 B.R. at 399; In re Sovereign Estates, Ltd., 104 B.R. 702, 704 (Bankr. E.D. Pa. 1989); Industrial Valley, 77 B.R. at 21. Courts have made it clear that a debtor's showing of a sound business justification need not be unduly exhaustive but, rather, a debtor is "simply required to justify

the proposed disposition with sound business reasons." In re Baldwin United Corp., 43 B.R. 888, 906 (Bankr. S.D. Ohio 1984).

56. The Movants submit that the proposed sale of the Purchased Debtor Assets is reasonable, an exercise of sound business judgment, and should be approved. In this case, the "sound business purpose" test is easily met because the only purpose for the continued existence of the Reorganized Debtors and the Liquidating Trust is to wind-down the Reorganized Debtors' affairs and liquidate the Liquidating Trust Assets, by conversion to cash or other methods, as expeditiously as reasonably possible in order to maximize the recovery of the Holders of Liquidating Trust Interests. See Plan, § 5.4(b)(1). The Movants submit that it is in the best interests of the Holders of Liquidating Trust Interests for the Purchased Debtor Assets to be sold to the Buyers pursuant to the Agreement or, as contemplated herein, to another purchaser(s) who offers to the Movants greater consideration than that provided under the Agreement. Moreover, the proposed Bidding Procedures provided for adequate and reasonable notice of the Sale and will assure that the price offered for the assets is reasonable and fair under the circumstances. Finally, the Sale is proposed in good faith because the purpose of the Sale is to maximize the value of the Purchased Debtor Assets for the benefit of creditors.

## SALE FREE AND CLEAR OF LIENS, CLAIMS AND ENCUMBRANCES

57. In order to facilitate the sale of the Purchased Debtor Assets, the Movants require authorization to sell them free and clear of all Liens (as defined in the Agreements), claims (including claims arising under the Assigned Contracts and Leases on or prior to the Closing), encumbrances and other interests arising on or prior to the Closing (collectively, "Encumbrances") (other than Permitted Encumbrances) pursuant to Section 363(f) of the Bankruptcy Code, to the extent applicable. Section 363(f) of the Bankruptcy Code authorizes a trustee to sell property under section 363(b) "free and clear of any interest in such property of an entity other than the estate" if one of the following is satisfied:

(1) applicable nonbankruptcy law permits the sale of such property free and clear of such interest;

(2) such entity consents;

(3) such interest is a lien and the price at which such property is to be sold is greater than the aggregate value of all liens on such property;

(4) such interest is a bona fide dispute; or

(5) such entity could be compelled, in a legal or equitable proceeding, to accept a money satisfaction of such interest.

11 U.S.C. § 363(f). Furthermore, courts have held that they have the equitable power to authorize sales free and clear of interests that are not specifically covered by section 363(f). See, e.g., In re Trans World Airlines, 322 F.3d 283, 290 (3d Cir. 2003); Volvo White Truck Corp. v. Chabersburg (In re White Motor Credit Corp.), 75 B.R. 944, 948 (Bankr. N.D. Ohio 1987). The Plan also authorizes the Liquidating Trustee to sell the Broadcast Assets free and clear of liens, claims, and other interests except as may be expressly set forth in a sale order. See Plan, §5.2(a).

58. With respect to any Encumbrance (other than Permitted Encumbrances) or claim on the Purchased Debtor Assets, each Encumbrance satisfies at least one of the five conditions set forth in section 363(f) and will be adequately protected by having such Encumbrances attach to the proceeds of the Sale with the same priority, validity, force and effect as they now have in or against the Purchased Debtor Assets, subject to any claims and defenses that the Movants' may possess with respect thereto. Accordingly, the Movants submit that the sale of the Purchased Debtor Assets free and clear of Encumbrances (other than Permitted Encumbrances) satisfies the statutory prerequisites of section 363(f) of the Bankruptcy Code.

## GOOD FAITH PURSUANT TO § 363(m)

59.     The Movants respectfully requests that the Buyers or other high bidders are entitled to the protections afforded by section 363(m) of the Bankruptcy Code.     In this matter, the transactions contemplated by the Agreements are undertaken by the Buyers and the Movants at arm's length, without collusion and in good faith within the meaning of Section 363(m) of the Bankruptcy Code.

60.     Section 363(m) of the Bankruptcy Code provides:

> The reversal or modification on appeal of an authorization under subsection (b) or (c) of this section of a sale or lease of property does not affect the validity of a sale or lease under such authorization to an entity that purchased or leased such property in good faith, whether or not such entity knew of the pendency of the appeal, unless such authorization and such sale or lease were stayed pending appeal.

11 U.S.C. § 363(m).  While the Bankruptcy Code does not define "good faith," the Seventh Circuit in In re Andy Frain Services, Inc., 798 F.2d 1113 (7th Cir. 1986), held that:

> The requirement that a purchaser act in good faith ... speaks to the integrity of his conduct in the course of the sale proceedings. Typically, the misconduct that would destroy a purchaser's good faith status at a judicial sale involves fraud, collusion between the purchaser and other bidders or the trustee, or an attempt to take grossly unfair advantage of other bidders.

798 F.2d at 1125 (emphasis omitted) (quoting In re Rock Industries Machinery Corp., 572 F.2d 1195, 1198 (7th Cir. 1978) (interpreting Bankruptcy Rule 805, the precursor of section 363(m)). In connection with section 363 sales, courts have required that the sale price be fair and reasonable and that the sale be the result of good faith negotiations with the buyer. Abbotts Dairies, 788 F.2d at 147-50; In re Tempo Technology Corp., 202 B.R. 363, 367 (D. Del. 1996), aff'd sub nom. Diamond Abrasives Corp. v. Temtecho, Inc. (In Re Temtecho, Inc.), 141 F.3d 1155 (3d Cir. 1998); In re Industrial Valley Refrig. & Air Conditioning Supplies, Inc., 77 B.R. 15, 22 (Bankr. E.D. Pa. 1987); In re Stroud Ford, Inc., 163 B.R. 730, 733 (Bankr. M.D. Pa. 1983); see also, e.g., In re Ewell, 958 F.2d 276, 281 (9th Cir. 1992) (declining to set aside or modify a sale pursuant to section 363 of the Bankruptcy Code because the price was fair and reasonable and the buyer was a good faith purchaser pursuant to section 363(m) of the Bankruptcy Code).

61.     While Silver Point is a creditor of the Reorganized Debtors and served as the chair of the Creditors' Committee in the Reorganized Debtors' bankruptcy cases, the Movants submit, and will present evidence at the Sale Hearing, if necessary, that (i) the Agreements were intensely negotiated over a four month period and constitute an arm's-length transaction, in which the Buyers have acted in good faith; (ii) the consideration to be paid is fair and reasonable under the circumstances; and (iii) the Broadcast Assets have been exposed to the marketplace by means of an exhaustive marketing effort. The Movants further note that the Buyers have made no offers of continued employment to any of the Movants' representatives. The Movants therefore request that the Court make a finding that the Buyers have purchased the Purchased Assets, including the Assumed Contract, in good faith within the meaning of § 363(m) of the Bankruptcy Code.

## ASSIGNMENT OF EXECUTORY CONTRACTS AND UNEXPIRED LEASES

62.     The assignment of certain executory contracts and unexpired leases of the Reorganized Debtors to the Buyers is an integral part of the proposed sale and should be approved by the Court. The executory contracts and unexpired leases sought to be assigned to the

Buyers pursuant to Section 365 of the Bankruptcy Code (the "Assigned Contracts and Leases") are set forth in Exhibit F hereto.[14] Each of the Assigned Contracts and Leases has been previously assumed by the Reorganized Debtors pursuant to either the Plan or an order of this Court and all prior defaults on the Assigned Contracts and Leases have been previously cured.

      63.     Section 365 of the Bankruptcy Code authorizes a debtor to assign its executory contracts and unexpired leases subject to the approval of the Bankruptcy Court only if:

> (A) the trustee assumes such contract or lease in accordance with the provisions of this section; and
>
> (B) adequate assurance of future performance by the assignee of such contract or lease is provided, whether or not there has been a default in such contract or lease.

See 11 U.S.C. § 365(f)(2). Accordingly, because the Assigned Contracts and Leases were previously assumed by the Reorganized Debtors,[15] section 365 authorizes the proposed assignments provided that adequate assurance of future performance is provided.

      64.     The meaning of "adequate assurance of future performance" depends on the facts and circumstances of each case, but should be given "practical, pragmatic construction." See Carlisle Homes, Inc. v. Arrari (In re Carlisle Homes, Inc.), 103 B.R. 524, 538 (Bankr. D.N.J. 1989); see also In re Natco Indus., Inc., 54 B.R. 436, 440 (Bankr. S.D.N.Y.

---

[14] The Movants reserve the right to modify Exhibit F at any time up to the Sale Hearing upon notice to the contracting parties thereto. Certain other executory contracts and leases being assigned in connection with the Sale are not being assigned pursuant to section 365. Exhibit H hereto includes a list of all known Material Contracts and Real Property Leases with respect to Stations being so assigned.

[15] The Reorganized Debtors and the Liquidating Trustee themselves have been materially performing their postpetition obligations under the contracts and leases previously assumed.

1985) (adequate assurance of future performance does not mean absolute assurance that debtor will thrive and pay rent); In re Bon Ton Rest. & Pastry Shop, Inc., 53 B.R. 789, 803 (Bankr. N.D. Ill. 1985) ("Although no single solution will satisfy every case, the required assurance will fall considerably short of an absolute guarantee of performance.").

65.     Among other things, adequate assurance may be given by demonstrating the assignee's financial health and experience in managing the type of enterprise or property assigned. In re Bygaph, Inc., 56 B.R. 596, 605-06 (Bankr. S.D.N.Y. 1986) (adequate assurance of future performance is present when prospective assignee of a lease from debtor has financial resources and has expressed a willingness to devote sufficient funding to business in order to give it strong likelihood of succeeding; chief determinant of adequate assurance is whether rent will be paid).

66.     In connection with the Sale Hearing, the Movants will provide evidence that all requirements for the assignment of the Assigned Contracts and Leases will be satisfied. As part of the marketing of the Purchased Assets pursuant and the Auction, the Movants will evaluate the financial wherewithal and ability to timely consummate the acquisition of the Purchased Assets of all potential bidders before qualifying such bidders as a potential purchaser. The Movants will provide all parties to executory contracts and unexpired leases to be assigned pursuant to the Sale Motion with notice of the Sale Motion and an opportunity to be heard. To the extent a party to an Assigned Debtor Agreement does not object to the assignment of that agreement, the party should be deemed to have consented to such assignment. Thus, the Movants respectfully submit that by the conclusion of the Sale Hearing, assignment of the executory contracts and unexpired leases should be approved.

67.     Additionally, the Reorganized Debtors and the Liquidating Trustee respectfully request that any form of Final Sale Order expressly relieve the Reorganized Debtors and the Liquidating Trust from any further obligations under the Assigned Contracts and Leases after the assignment, other than with respect to the liabilities not included in Net Working Capital occurring prior to the Closing; Section 365(k) of the Bankruptcy Code provides that an "[a]ssignment by the trustee to an entity of a contract or lease assumed under [section 365 of the Bankruptcy Code]

relieves the trustee and the estate from any liability for any breach of such contract or lease occurring after such assignment." Accordingly, any Final Sale Order should expressly grant the Reorganized Debtors and the Liquidating Trust the protections provided for in § 365(k) of the Bankruptcy Code.

## APPLICABILITY OF § 1146(C) OF THE BANKRUPTCY CODE

68.    Finally, pursuant to paragraph 28 of the Confirmation Order and section 1146(c) of the Bankruptcy Code, the transfer of the Purchased Assets should not be subject to any stamp tax, sale or use tax or similar tax.  Section 1146(c) of the Bankruptcy Code provides:

> The issuance, transfer, or exchange of a
> security, or the making or delivery of an
> instrument of transfer under a plan
> confirmed under section 1129 of this title,
> may not be taxed under any law imposing
> a stamp tax or similar tax.

11 U.S.C. § 1146(c).  As discussed above, the sale of the Purchased Assets to the Buyers is under the Plan as confirmed by the Court pursuant to the Confirmation Order. Accordingly, the sale and/or transfer of the Purchased Assets under the Agreements is exempt from state and local transfer taxes under section 1146(c) of the Bankruptcy Code.  See City of New York v. Jacoby-Bender, Inc. (In re Jacoby-Bender), 758 F.2d 840, 841 (2d Cir. 1985); In re Hechinger Inv. Co. of Del., Inc., 254 B.R. 306, 313-14 (Bankr. D. Del. 2000), rev'd on other grounds 335 F.3d 243 (3d Cir. 2003).  In addition, the transfer of assets by the WGFL Entities is also exempt from state and local transfer taxes under section 1146(c) as such transfers are both pursuant to the Plan and necessary to the consummation of the Plan.  See In re T.H. Orlando Ltd., 391 F.3d 1287, 1295 (11th Cir. 2004), rehearing and rehearing en banc den'd, 129 Fed.Appx. 603, --- F.3d ---- (11th Cir. 2005) ("We conclude, however, the plain language of § 1146(c) exempts from stamp taxes or similar taxes any transfer that is necessary to the consummation of a Chapter 11 plan.  Nothing in the plain language of § 1146(c) restricts the exemption to transactions involving the debtor and estate property.").  The Movants are not aware of any transfer taxes that would be applicable to

these sales. Out of an abundance of caution, the Movants have served a copy of the Sale Motion on all Taxing Authorities.

69.      Accordingly, in accordance with Bankruptcy Code § 1146(c), the making or delivery of any instrument to effectuate the transfer of the Purchased Assets, including the Agreements, and the transactions contemplated thereby may not be taxed under any law imposing a stamp tax or a sale, transfer, or any other similar tax, and the recordation of any instruments (including bills of sale, leases, assignments and amendments thereto) to evidence the sale of the Purchased Assets is not subject to any such tax.

## FINALITY OF ORDER

70.      The Movants further seek, pursuant to Federal Rules of Bankruptcy Procedure 6004(g) and 6006(d), that the Court expressly provide that the effectiveness of any order approving of the sale of the Purchased Debtor Assets and/or assignment of any contracts in conjunction with the sale of the Purchased Debtor Assets not be stayed for any period of time after the entry of such order(s).

## REQUEST FOR EXPEDITED RELIEF

71.      The Movants have filed, contemporaneously with this Motion, a Motion for Expedited Hearing (the "Expedited Hearing Motion") with respect to that portion of the Sale Motion concerning the proposed Bidding Procedures and the proposed Bidding Procedures Order. In the Expedited Hearing Motion, the Movants have requested a hearing on the proposed Bidding Procedures and the proposed Bidding Procedures Order as soon as the Bankruptcy Court's calendar allows. The Movants hereby incorporate by reference the Expedited Hearing Motion into this Motion.

## NO PRIOR REQUEST AND RESERVATION OF RIGHTS

72.      No prior motion for the relief requested herein has been made to this or any other court. The Movants reserve their rights to withdraw and/or modify this Motion.

## NOTICE

73.     Notice of this Motion has been provided to (i) all potential purchasers identified by the Reorganized Debtors and the Liquidating Trustee or their agent, (ii) the Office of the United States Trustee, (iii) each entity designated on the All Notices List in this case, (iv) all entities known to the Reorganized Debtors and the Liquidating Trustee to claim a lien, security interest, or other interest in any of the Purchased Debtor Assets, (v) all Taxing Authorities and Governmental Authorities having jurisdiction over the Purchased Assets, and (vi) the attorneys general of all states in which the Purchased Assets are located.

## CONCLUSION

For the reasons stated above, the Movants respectfully request the entry of an order granting the Motion and such other related relief as may be just and proper.

Respectfully submitted,

**LOWENSTEIN SANDLER PC**
Paul Kizel, Esq. (PK 4176)
Jeffrey A. Kramer, Esq. (JK 8278)
65 Livingston Avenue
Roseland, New Jersey 07068
(973) 597-2500 (telephone)
(973) 597-2400 (facsimile)

-and-

**PRETI, FLAHERTY, BELIVEAU, PACHIOS & HALEY, LLP**

By:_____ /s/     DRAFT
John P. McVeigh (JM )
One City Center, P.O. Box 9546
Portland, Maine 04112-9546

(207) 791-3000 (telephone)
(207) 791-3111 (facsimile)

*Counsel to The Reorganized Debtors and Liquidating Trustee of The PSC Liquidating Trust*

Dated: June 15, 2006

*Courtesy of Kenneth A. Rosen and Paul Kizel, Lowenstein Sandler PC*

## Appendix J

## PROPOSED BIDDING PROCEDURES ORDER

### UNITED STATES BANKRUPTCY COURT
### DISTRICT OF MAINE

|  |  |
|---|---|
| | : |
| In re: | :      **Chapter 11** |
| | : |
| | |
| **PEGASUS SATELLITE TELEVISION, INC., et al.,** [1] | :   **Case** |
| **No. 04-20878** | |
| | : |
| | :**(Jointly Administered)** |
| **Debtors.**     | : |
| | : |

## ORDER (i) APPROVING BIDDING PROCEDURES; (ii) APPROVING FORM AND MANNER OF NOTICE OF SALE; AND (iii) SCHEDULING AUCTION AND FINAL HEARING ON APPROVAL OF SALE

This matter having come before the Court on the motion dated June 15, 2006 (the "Sale Motion") filed by Pegasus Satellite Communications, Inc. ("PSC"), Pegasus Broadcast Television, Inc., WTLH License Corp., WDSI License Corp., WOLF License Corp., HMW, Inc., Pegasus Broadcast Associates, L.P., each a Reorganized Debtor in the captioned chapter 11 cases, the Liquidating Trustee of The PSC Liquidating

---

[1] The Reorganized Debtors are: Argos Support Services Company, Bride Communications, Inc., B.T. Satellite, Inc., Carr Rural TV, Inc., DBS Tele-Venture, Inc., Digital Television Services of Indiana, LLC, DTS Management, LLC Golden Sky DBS, Inc., Golden Sky Holdings, Inc., Golden Sky Systems, Inc., Henry Country MRTV, Inc., HMW, Inc., Pegasus Broadcast Associates, L.P., Pegasus Broadcast Television, Inc., Pegasus Broadcast Towers, Inc., Pegasus Media & Communications, Inc., Pegasus Satellite Communications, Inc., Pegasus Satellite Television of Illinois, Inc., Pegasus Satellite Television, Inc., Portland Broadcasting, Inc., Primewatch, Inc., PST Holdings, Inc., South Plains DBS, LP., Telecast of Florida, Inc., WDSI License Corp., WILF, Inc., WOLF License Corp., and WTLH License Corp.

Trust (the "Liquidating Trustee"), and nondebtors WGFL License Corporation and WGFL Corporation (collectively, the "Sellers") requesting the entry of orders pursuant to the Plan, Confirmation Order, sections 105(a), 363, 365 and 1146(c) of the United States Code (the "Bankruptcy Code"), Rules 2002, 6004, 6006, 9007 and 9014 of the Federal Rules of Bankruptcy Procedure (the "Bankruptcy Rules") and D. Me. LBR 2002-1, 6004-1, and 6006-1: (1) authorizing and approving the sale of certain of the Reorganized Debtors' assets free and clear of any liens, claims, encumbrances, and other interests; (2) authorizing bidding procedures for the solicitation of higher and better offers in connection with such sale, including the Bidding Incentives (as defined below); (3) approving form and manner of notice of sale; (4) setting a hearing date for final sale approval; (5) authorizing the assignment of certain executory contracts and unexpired leases; and (6) granting related relief; and it appearing that the Sellers entered into an asset purchase agreement, dated June 15, 2006, by and between the Sellers and MM Broadcasting, LLC (the "Broadcast Agreement") and an asset purchase agreement, dated June 15, 2006, by and between Pegasus Broadcast Television, Inc. and HMW, Inc. and Bluenose Television of Portland LLC (the "WPME Agreement") (collectively, the "Agreements") to sell certain of the Reorganized Debtors' assets (the "Purchased Debtor Assets") free and clear of liens, claims, encumbrances, and other interests and certain assets of WGFL License Corporation and WGFL Corporation (together with the Purchased Debtor Assets, the "Purchased Assets") in the ordinary course (the "Sale"); and it appearing that notice of the Sale Motion was adequate and proper under the circumstances of the case; and it appearing that no other or further notice need be given; and it appearing that the relief requested in the Sale Motion is in the best interests of the Reorganized Debtors and The PSC Liquidating Trust (the "Liquidating Trust"); and the Court having conducted an expedited hearing on June 29, 2006 on that portion of the Sale Motion concerning the proposed Bidding Procedures and the proposed Bidding Procedures Order; (the "Bidding Procedures Hearing"); and upon the Sale Motion and all of the proceedings before the Court; and after due deliberation and sufficient cause appearing therefore, it is:

# FOUND AND DETERMINED THAT:

A. All capitalized terms not otherwise defined herein shall have the meanings ascribed to such terms in the Sale Motion or the Agreements.

B. On June 2, 2004 (the "Petition Date"), the Reorganized Debtors filed petitions for relief under chapter 11 of the Bankruptcy Court in the United States Bankruptcy Court for the District of Maine (the "Court").

C. On April 15, 2005, the Court entered an order ("Confirmation Order") confirming the Reorganized Debtors' First Amended Joint Plan of Reorganization (the "Plan"), as modified by the Confirmation Order (Docket # 1236). Pursuant to the Plan and Confirmation Order, Ocean Ridge Capital Advisors, LLC was appointed the Liquidating Trustee of The PSC Liquidating Trust established under the Plan.

D. The Court has jurisdiction over this matter and over the property of the Reorganized Debtors and the Liquidating Trust pursuant to 28 U.S.C. § 1334 and § 157(a).

E. This is a core proceeding pursuant to 28 U.S.C. § 1334 and § 157(b)(2)(A), (N) and (O).

F. The Bidding Procedures set forth herein are reasonable and appropriate and represent a fair and reasonable method for maximizing the value of the Purchased Assets.

G. The Notice of Sale and Assignment of Certain Contracts and Leases and Auction Procedures in Connection Therewith (the "Notice of Sale and Auction Procedures") provides due, adequate and timely notice of the sale of the Purchased Assets and the assignment of the contracts and leases listed on Exhibit F to the Sale Motion (the "Assigned Contracts and Leases") in accordance with Bankruptcy Rules 2002, 6004 and 6006, D. Me. LBR 2002-1 and 6004-1, the Case Management Order, and the applicable provisions of the Bankruptcy Code to all persons, entities and other parties-in-interest.

H.     Based on the record adduced before the Court at the Bidding Procedures Hearing, the Bidding Procedures, including the Break-Up Fee and Expense Reimbursement (collectively, the "Bidding Incentives"), are fair and reasonable, reflect the Reorganized Debtors and the Liquidating Trustee's exercise of prudent business judgment consistent with their fiduciary duties, and represent the best method for maximizing the value to the Broadcast Assets. The Bidding Procedures and the Bidding Incentives were and are material inducements for, and condition of, the Buyers' entry into the Agreements. The Buyers are unwilling to commit to hold open their offers to purchase the Purchased Assets without the Bidding Incentives. Thus, the Bidding Procedures and the Bidding Incentives will promote more competitive bidding by inducing the Buyers' bids that otherwise would not have been made, and without which any bidding might be limited. Absent authorization of the Bidding Procedures and the Bidding Incentives, the Reorganized Debtors and the Liquidating Trustee may lose the opportunity to obtain the highest and best offer for the Purchased Assets.

I.     In particular, payment of the Bidding Incentives are (i) actual and necessary costs and expenses of preserving the Reorganized Debtors' estates within the meaning of 11 U.S.C. §§ 503(b) and 507(a)(1), (ii) of substantial benefit to the Reorganized Debtors' estates, (iii) reasonable and appropriate in light of the size and nature of the proposed sale and the efforts that have been and will be expended by the Buyers notwithstanding that the proposed sale is subject to higher or better offers for the Purchased Assets, and (iv) necessary to ensure that the Buyers will continue to pursue their proposed acquisition of the Purchased Assets.

J.     The entry of this Order is in the best interest of the Reorganized Debtors and the Liquidating Trust and its beneficiaries as it will, among other things, retain for the benefit of the estate the prospect of a successful sale to the Buyers, while enabling the Sellers to solicit higher and better offers in accordance herewith.

K.     Expedited relief is justified in these circumstances pursuant to D. Me. LBR 9013-1(i).

L. Based upon the foregoing findings and conclusions, and upon the record made before this Court at the Bidding Procedures Hearing, and good and sufficient cause appearing therefore;

## NOW, THEREFORE, IT IS HEREBY ORDERED:

1. The relief requested in the Motion with respect to the Bidding Procedures and the Sale Notice is granted, subject to the terms and conditions set forth in this Order, and any and all objections thereto are hereby overruled on the merits.

2. This order shall be deemed to be the "Bidding Procedures Order."

3. The Sellers are authorized to take all steps necessary to perform under this Order, and the following procedures ("Bidding Procedures") shall govern the form, submission and consideration of bids and any Auction held in connection therewith.

### QUALIFICATION OF BIDDERS AND DUE DILIGENCE

4. Prior to the Auction, the Sellers may qualify potential bidders by, *inter alia*, examining potential bidders' current financial statements and ability to consummate the purchase of the Purchased Assets ("Qualified Bidders"). After executing a confidentiality agreement in a form to be determined by the Sellers, Qualified Bidders will be allowed to perform reasonable due diligence on the Purchased Assets, including reasonable access to the books, records and executives of the Sellers. Any interested bidders should contact Miller Buckfire & Co., LLC, 250 Park Avenue, 19th Floor, New York, NY 10177, Attention: Stuart Erickson or Kevin Haggard, Telephone: 212-895-1812, Facsimile: 212-895-1862, e-mail: stuart.erickson@millerbuckfire.com or kevin.haggard@millerbuckfire.com to seek to become Qualified Bidders and, thereafter, to request information in connection with their due diligence.

5. All Qualified Bidders shall be deemed to have consented to the core jurisdiction of the Bankruptcy Court and to have

waived any right to a jury trial in connection with any dispute involving or related to the Auction or Sale.

## SUBMISSION OF QUALIFIED BIDS

6.    The Sellers shall be entitled to consider higher or better competing bids (each an "Alternative Transaction") for the Purchased Assets and will consider only those Alternative Transactions that constitute Qualified Bids under this Order and the Agreements.   In order for any Alternative Transaction to be a Qualified Bid, it must be:

a.    in writing;

b.    received by Sellers at the addresses set forth below no later than the Bid Deadline set forth below;

c.    a firm, unconditional bid to purchase some or all of the Purchased Assets, together with a firm, unconditional bid of one or more other Qualified Bidders to purchase some or all of the assets under the Other Station Agreements not subject to any contingencies (other than closing conditions consistent with the closing conditions contained in the Agreements) as to the validity, effectiveness and/or binding nature of the offer, including, without limitation, further due diligence review or financing;

d.    contain firm bids in excess of $51,950,000 (i.e., the sum of (i) the Purchase Price plus the purchase prices under the Other Station Agreements, (ii) the initial overbid increment of $250,000, (iii) the Break-Up Fee of $1,500,000, and (iv) the Expense Reimbursement of $700,0000) payable at the closing, or in the case of Piecemeal Bids (as defined below), provide for consideration payable at closing in excess of such amount when considered in the aggregate with other Piecemeal Bids;

e.    accompanied by sufficient information to demonstrate that the competing bidder or bidders has the financial wherewithal and ability to timely consummate the acquisition of the Purchased Assets on terms and conditions substantially the same or better than those contained in the Agreements, including evidence of adequate financing and a financial guaranty, if appropriate;

f. accompanied by a signed contract, or contracts, substantially in the form of the Agreements, as appropriate, and marked to show any changes made to the Agreement(s); provided, however, that the Sellers reserve the right to reject a competing bid in the event that any proposed changes to the Agreement(s) are not satisfactory to the Sellers as determined in their sole business judgment;

g. accompanied by the name and telephone number(s) of a contact person who will be available to answer questions regarding the bid, as well as the names and telephone numbers of any financial and legal advisors retained by the competing bidder, as applicable;

h. accompanied by evidence of the Qualified Bidder's ability to provide adequate assurance of future performance of the Assigned Contracts and Leases if the bid is conditioned on the assignment of any such Assigned Contracts and Leases;

i. accompanied by a good faith cash deposit in an amount equal to the Purchase Price Deposit, as set forth below, to be deposited with Sellers on or before the Bid Deadline;

j. such other information as reasonably may be requested by the Sellers.

7. Any Qualified Bids must be accompanied by a good faith cash Purchase Price Deposit in an amount equal to $2,500,000, provided however, any person that seeks to purchase a part of the Purchased Assets shall deposit a good faith cash Purchase Price Deposit in an amount equal to five percent (5%) of its Qualified Bid. Such deposits

shall be held by the Sellers, without interest, and shall be forfeited in the event that any bidder for an accepted bid defaults.

8.      All Qualified Bids must be submitted in writing so that they are actually received by no later than August 2, 2006, at 5:00 p.m. prevailing Eastern Time, (the "Bid Deadline") by Miller Buckfire & Co., LLC, at the address set forth in paragraph four (4) above, with copies to the following parties: (i) Ocean Ridge Capital Advisors, LLC, 56 Harrison Street, Suite 203A, New Rochelle, NY 10801, Attn: Bradley E. Scher (ii) Akin Gump Strauss Hauer & Feld LLP, Robert S. Strauss Building, 1333 New Hampshire Avenue, NW, Washington, DC 20036, Attn: Russell W. Parks, Jr., Esq.; and (iii) Lowenstein Sandler PC, 65 Livingston Avenue, Roseland, NJ 07068, Attn: Jeffrey A. Kramer, Esq. The Sellers after consultation with the Buyers may extend the Bid Deadline once or successively, but are not obligated to do so. If the Sellers extend the Bid Deadline, they shall promptly notify all other Qualified Bidders of such extension.

9.      The Sellers shall promptly provide the Buyers with a copy of any Qualified Bid received by the Sellers and such other information regarding Alternative Transactions as provided for in Section 3.2.3(b) of the Agreements.

10.     If Sellers determine in good faith and in their reasonable discretion that they have not received a Qualified Bid by the Bid Deadline that, singly or in combination with a series of Qualified Bids for portions of the Purchased Assets, is a higher or better bid than the one represented by the Agreements, the Sellers shall seek approval of the Agreements at the Sale Hearing without conducting an Auction and without further motion. The Agreements executed by the Buyers shall constitute a Qualified Bid for all purposes.

11.     If the Sellers receive bids that seek to purchase parts of the Purchased Assets ("Piecemeal Bids"), the Sellers shall evaluate all such Piecemeal Bids and determine whether the aggregate consideration to be received for the Purchased Assets and the assets under the Other Station Agreements to be sold pursuant to such Piecemeal Bids is in an amount at least equal to that in paragraph 6(d) above. In such a

circumstance, the Sellers shall be permitted to consider the Piecemeal Bids together as a Qualified Bid.

## THE AUCTION

12.    If at least one Qualified Bid that meets all of the requirements herein is timely received, the Auction will be conducted at the offices of Akin Gump Strauss Hauer & Feld, LLP, 590 Madison Avenue, New York, NY 10022 on August 7, 2006 at 10:00 a.m. or such later time or other place as the Sellers shall notify all Qualified Bidders who have submitted Qualified Bids. Only (i) the Buyers, (ii) the Sellers, and (iii) any Qualified Bidders who have timely submitted Qualified Bids shall be entitled to attend the Auction, and only the Buyers and the Qualified Bidders will be entitled to make any subsequent Qualified Bids at the Auction.

13.    The Purchased Assets and the assets under the Other Station Agreements need not be sold in a single lot; provided, that the aggregate consideration to be received for the Purchased Assets and the assets under the Other Station Agreements to be sold shall be in accordance with in paragraph 6(d) above. If the Sellers receive Piecemeal Bids that qualify *en toto* as a Qualified Bid, the Sellers shall be permitted to first conduct an auction on each of the assets or groups of assets that are the subject of Piecemeal Bids (the "Piecemeal Auctions"). Upon the completion of the Piecemeal Auctions, the aggregate consideration to be received pursuant to the Piecemeal Auctions shall be considered the Starting Auction Bid unless another Qualified Bid provides for greater consideration than the aggregate consideration to be received pursuant to the Piecemeal Auctions. Thereafter, the Sellers shall be permitted to conduct the Auction of the Purchased Assets in accordance with the terms herein.

14.    The Sellers shall evaluate all Qualified Bids received and shall determine which Qualified Bid reflects the highest or best offer as the starting bid at the Auction contemplated by this Order ("Starting Auction Bid"). The Sellers shall announce their determination of the Starting Auction Bid at the commencement of the Auction. Notwithstanding anything to the contrary contained within the Agreements,

the Buyers shall not be entitled to increase their offer to a level in excess of any Qualified Bid to be eligible to become the Starting Auction Bid.

15.     The first incremental competitive bid at the Auction shall be at least $250,000 over the Starting Auction Bid, with any subsequent increases of bids to be made in increments equal to as least $250,000, or such other lesser amount as the Liquidating Trustee shall announce from time to time at the Auction, until the Liquidating Trustee declares a winner.

16.     No bids shall be considered by the Sellers unless a party submitted a Qualified Bid and participates in the Auction.

17.     The Sellers shall have the right and discretion to (i) reject any bid (other than the Buyers') the Sellers deem to be inadequate, (ii) adjourn the Auction by announcing such adjournment prior to or during the Auction without further notice, (iii) modify the terms and conditions of the Auction by announcing such modifications at or prior to the commencement of the Auction, or during the Auction, and (iv) extend the deadlines set forth in the Bidding Procedures.

18.     When determining the highest or best bid, the Sellers shall include the Bidding Incentives in the Buyers' bid, which Bidding Incentives would otherwise be payable to the Buyers.

19.     The Sellers may select the winning bid at the conclusion of the Auction and the winning bidder will be required to enter into a definitive agreement (as modified by the bids submitted at the Auction) before the Auction is adjourned.

20.     If the Sellers select a bid from an entity other than the Buyers that the Buyers believe is not the highest or best bid, the Bankruptcy Court shall determine which is the successful bidder.

21.     Any person may request notification of the winning bid by submitting a written request including either an e-mail address or facsimile number so that such request is actually received by (1) Lowenstein Sandler, PC, Attn: Jeffrey A. Kramer, Esq., 65 Livingston

Avenue, Roseland, New Jersey 07068 or (2) Preti, Flaherty, Beliveau, Pachios & Haley, LLP, Attn: John P. McVeigh, Esq., One City Center, PO Box 95465, Portland, Maine 04112-9546 by 4:00 p.m. prevailing Eastern Time on August 5, 2006 (a "Notice Request"). Notice of the winning bid(s) shall be sent by email or facsimile, as the case may be, only to those persons who submitted a Notice Request.

## BIDDING INCENTIVES

22.     The Break-Up Fee in the amount of $1,500,000 and the Expense Reimbursement in an amount not to exceed $700,000 for the Buyers' reasonable out-of-pocket expenses incurred in connection with, or arising from, the transactions contemplated hereby and the financing thereof (collectively, the "Bidding Incentives") are hereby approved and shall be payable to the Buyers in accordance with the terms of the Agreements.

23.     If the Bidding Incentives become payable under the terms of the Agreements, then the Sellers shall pay to the Buyers, as the Buyers' sole remedy under the Agreements, the Bidding Incentives on the first (1st) Business Day after the earliest occurrence of any of the events giving rise to the payment of such Bidding Incentives as set forth in the Agreements.

24.     The Bidding Incentives shall be administrative priority expenses under Sections 503(b) and 507(a)(1) of the Bankruptcy Code.

## THE SALE HEARING

25.     A hearing (the "Sale Hearing") shall be held before the Honorable James B. Haines, Jr., United States Bankruptcy Judge, in his courtroom in the United States Bankruptcy Court for the District of Maine (the "Bankruptcy Court"), 537 Congress Street, 2nd Floor, Portland, Maine 04101 on August 8, 2006 at 9:00 a.m., prevailing Eastern time, or as soon thereafter as counsel may be heard to consider approval of the Sale to

the Buyers or such other successful bidder(s) as may be selected by the Sellers, and any objections thereto.

26.     If bidding for the Purchased Assets occurs at the Auction, the successful bidder(s), if other than the Buyers, shall: (a) prior to the conclusion of the Auction, execute and deliver to the Sellers its sale agreement which shall reflect the name of the successful bidder(s)and the successful bid price(s) (the "Bid Price") submitted at the Auction by the successful bidder(s) and which shall be substantially in the form of the Agreement(s), or on terms no less favorable to the Sellers, as amended to reflect the Bid Price; and (b) use its best efforts to demonstrate to the satisfaction of the Sellers, and the Court at the Sale Hearing its ability to: (i) satisfy all requirements of the sale agreement for purchase of the Purchased Assets and assignment of the Assigned Contracts and Leases or other agreements to be assigned pursuant to the Agreement(s) including, but not limited to, establishing "adequate assurance of future performance" with respect to such agreements; and (ii) prove its status, by admissible evidence, as a good faith purchaser pursuant to section 363(m) of the Bankruptcy Code.

27.     At the Sale Hearing, the Sellers shall present to the Bankruptcy Court the bid, or combination of bids in the case of Piecemeal Bids, which the Sellers view as the "highest and best" bid as well as the bid, or combination of bids in the case of Piecemeal Bids, which the Sellers view as the next highest and best bid (the "Backup Bid"). Subject to Bankruptcy Court approval, the Sellers shall consummate the sale of the Purchased Assets with the bidder, or bidders, approved by the Bankruptcy Court as having made the highest and best bid for the Purchased Assets (the "Winning Bidder").

28.     If the Winning Bidder fails to consummate the sale of the Purchased Assets because of a breach or failure to perform on the part of such Winning Bidder, the Backup Bid, as approved at the Sale Hearing, shall be automatically deemed to be the successful bid and  the Backup Bidder, which may be the Buyers, shall be obligated to consummate the transaction in accordance with the Backup Bid for 120 days following the acceptance of the Winning Bid, except if the Buyers' bid is the Backup Bid, in which case the Buyers will be obligated to consummate the

transaction in accordance with the Backup Bid for 60 days following acceptance of the Winning Bid, and, thereafter, shall not be obligated to consummate the Backup Bid. The Sellers and Backup Bidder may consummate such a Sale without further order of the Bankruptcy Court. If the Buyers are the Backup Bidder, the Buyers may terminate the Agreements after 60 days following the acceptance of the Winning Bid in accordance with Section 11.1(g) of the Agreements.

29.     If the Winning Bidder or the Backup Bidder, as the case may be, fails to consummate the Sale, and such failure is the result of a breach by the Winning Bidder or the Backup Bidder, as the case may be, then the Purchase Price Deposit tendered by such breaching bidder shall be forfeited to the Sellers and the Sellers specifically reserve the right to seek all available damages from such entity or person, except to the extent that the Sellers have agreed to limit its damages to the Purchase Price Deposit (in the case of the Buyers).

30.     As soon as the Bankruptcy Court has identified and approved the Winning Bidder and Backup Bidder, respectively, the Sellers shall immediately return all Purchase Price Deposits other than those provided by the Winning Bidder and the Backup Bidder. The Purchase Price Deposit tendered by the Winning Bidder (other than the Buyers), while still refundable, shall be held pending the closing on the Winning Bidder's bid at which time it will be applied as a credit against the purchase price. Any deposit from the Backup Bidder, while still refundable, shall be held by Sellers until the earlier of (i) closing on the Sale occurs, and (ii) 120 days following the acceptance of the Winning Bid, except if the Buyers' bid is the Backup Bid, in which case the deposit shall be held for 60 days following acceptance of the Winning Bid. If the Backup Bidder buys the Purchased Assets, then the deposit tendered by the Backup Bidder shall be applied as a credit against the purchase price.

## NOTICE

31.     The Notice of Sale and Auction Procedures, a copy of which is annexed hereto as Exhibit A, is hereby approved, and notice of the Sale Motion and the Sale Hearing shall be good and sufficient, and no other notice shall be required, if given as set forth herein.

32.     At least twenty (20) days prior to the Sale Hearing, the Sellers shall serve a copy of the Sale Motion without the Agreements, the Notice of Sale and Auction Procedures, this Bidding Procedures Order, and the proposed Sale Order, by first class mail, postage prepaid, to (i) all potential purchasers identified by the Reorganized Debtors and the Liquidating Trustee or their agent, (ii) the Office of the United States Trustee, (iii) each entity designated on the All Notices List in this case, (iv) all entities known to the Reorganized Debtors and the Liquidating Trustee to claim a lien, security interest, or other interest in any of the Purchased Debtor Assets, (v) each contracting party to the Assumed Contracts, (vi) all Taxing Authorities and Governmental Authorities having jurisdiction over the Purchased Assets, and (vii) the attorneys general of all states in which the Purchased Assets are located.

33.     Any party may request copies of the Sale Motion, the exhibits thereto (including the Agreements), or other pleadings in connection with the Sale Motion by submitting a written request that is actually received by (1) Lowenstein Sandler, PC, Attn: Jeffrey A. Kramer, Esq., 65 Livingston Avenue, Roseland, New Jersey 07068 or (2) Preti, Flaherty, Beliveau, Pachios & Haley, LLP, Attn: John P. McVeigh, Esq., One City Center, PO Box 95465, Portland, Maine 04112-9546 prior to July 31, 2006 at 4:00 p.m. prevailing Eastern Time. Requests must include a street address for delivery. The Sellers, in their discretion, may publish copies of the Sale Motion, the exhibits thereto (including the Agreements), or other pleadings in connection with the Sale Motion on the website of the Liquidating Trust.

34.     The Sellers, in their discretion, may publish the Sale Notice or otherwise advertise the Sale in the national edition of *The Wall Street Journal* or such other publications or on the website of the

Liquidating Trust. Such publication shall be deemed proper notice to any other interested parties whose identities are unknown to the Sellers.

35.    Objections to the portion of the relief requested in the Sale Motion with respect to the Sale of the Purchased Assets, if any, must be: (a) in writing; (b) conform to the requirements of the Bankruptcy Code, the Federal Rules of Bankruptcy Procedure, and the Local Rules of the United States Bankruptcy Court for the District of Maine; (c) set forth the name and address of the objector and shall contain requisite information respecting the objecting party's status; (d) state with particularity the legal and factual bases of the objection and the specific grounds therefor; and (e) filed with the Court on or before July 31, 2006 at 4:00 p.m. prevailing Eastern Time and served so that same are received on or before July 31, 2006 at 4:00 p.m. prevailing Eastern Time by (1) Office of the Clerk of the United States Bankruptcy Court, 527 Congress Street, Portland, Maine 04101; (2) Lowenstein Sandler, PC, Attn: Jeffrey A. Kramer, Esq., 65 Livingston Avenue, Roseland, New Jersey 07068; (3) Preti, Flaherty, Beliveau, Pachios & Haley, LLP, Attn: John P. McVeigh, Esq., One City Center, PO Box 95465, Portland, Maine 04112-9546; and (4) Weil, Gotshal & Manges, LLP, Attn: George A. Davis, Esq., 767 Fifth Avenue, New York, New York 10153.

36.    Objections by any party to the Assigned Contracts and Leases to such assignment, if any, including the assignment of the Assigned Contracts and Leases to a purchaser or purchasers other than the Buyers, must be: (a) in writing; (b) conform to the requirements of the Bankruptcy Code, the Federal Rules of Bankruptcy Procedure, and the Local Rules of the United States Bankruptcy Court for the District of Maine; (c) set forth the name and address of the objector and shall contain requisite information respecting the objecting party's status; (d) state with particularity the legal and factual bases of the objection and the specific grounds therefor; and (e) filed with the Court on or before July 31, 2006 at 4:00 p.m. prevailing Eastern Time and served so that same are received on or before July 31, 2006 at 4:00 p.m. prevailing Eastern Time by (1) Office of the Clerk of the United States Bankruptcy Court, 527 Congress Street, Portland, Maine 04101; (2) Lowenstein Sandler, PC, Attn: Jeffrey A. Kramer, Esq., 65 Livingston Avenue, Roseland, New Jersey 07068; (3) Preti, Flaherty, Beliveau, Pachios & Haley, LLP, Attn: John P. McVeigh,

Esq., One City Center, PO Box 95465, Portland, Maine 04112-9546; and (4) Weil, Gotshal & Manges, LLP, Attn: George A. Davis, Esq., 767 Fifth Avenue, New York, New York 10153.

37.     The failure of any person or entity receiving notice to file an objection on a timely basis shall be a bar to the assertion of an objection to the Sellers' consummation and performance of the Agreement at the Sale Hearing or thereafter.

38.     Unless a party to the Assigned Contracts and Leases timely files an objection to assignment of the Assigned Contract or Lease to which it is a party in accordance with this Order, it shall be deemed to have consented to the assignment of such Assigned Contract or Lease to the Buyers or to any purchaser or purchasers other than the Buyers.

39.     The Sellers shall be authorized to modify the list of Assigned Contracts and Leases set forth in Exhibit F to the Sale Motion at any time prior to the Sale Hearing upon notice to the contracting parties thereto.

## RETENTION OF JURISDICTION

40.     This Court shall retain jurisdiction over any matters related to or arising from the implementation of this Order, including, but not limited to the right to amend this Order.

_____

UNITED STATES BANKRUPTCY JUDGE

Portland, Maine
Dated: June ___, 2006

*Courtesy of Kenneth A. Rosen and Paul Kizel, Lowenstein Sandler PC*

## Appendix K

# SAMPLE SALE AND BID PROCEDURES MOTION

UNITED STATES BANKRUPTCY COURT
EASTERN DISTRICT OF WISCONSIN

---

In re _____     Chapter 11

Debtor.     Case No. _____

---

**DEBTOR'S MOTION FOR AN ORDER (A) AUTHORIZING THE SALE OF FOODSERVICE AND NOVELTY ASSETS OUTSIDE THE ORDINARY COURSE OF BUSINESS PURSUANT TO § 363 OF THE BANKRUPTCY CODE, (B) APPROVING AUCTION TERMS AND PROCEDURES, (C) APPROVING FORM OF ASSET PURCHASE AGREEMENT, AND (D) SETTING AUCTION DATE**

---

_____ (the "Debtor"), by its attorneys, hereby moves the Court pursuant to 11 U.S.C. § 363(b) for authority to sell certain assets of its foodservice division (the "Foodservice Division") and novelty division (the "Novelty Division") outside the ordinary course of business, free and clear of all liens, claims and encumbrances, and for approval of terms, conditions and procedures for an auction sale of such assets. In support of its Motion, the Debtor states as follows:

## Background

1.     On _____ (the "Petition Date"), the Debtor filed a voluntary petition for relief under Chapter 11 of the United States Bankruptcy Code, 11 U.S.C. § 101 *et seq.* (the "Code").

2.     No trustee has been appointed. The Debtor remains in possession of its Assets and is operating its business pursuant to § 1107 and § 1108 of the Code.

3.     The Debtor is a _____ corporation engaged primarily in the business of manufacturing _____.

4.     The Debtor employs more than 500 people, and has operations in Milwaukee and Boston. The Debtor closed its manufacturing operations in Atlanta, Chicago and Dallas prior to the Petition Date.

5.     In _____, the Debtor had sales in excess of $200,000,000. It is the largest manufacturer of _____ in the United States.

## Sale of Assets

6.     The Debtor operated the Foodservice Division out of its Atlanta, Chicago and Dallas facilities. Through the Foodservice Division, the Debtor supplied _____ primarily to restaurants and vendors of food products. Customers of the Foodservice Division included _____. Prior to the Petition Date, due to a lack of working capital, the Debtor ceased operating the Foodservice Division and closed its manufacturing facilities in Atlanta, Dallas and Chicago.

7.     The Novelty Division operates out of the Debtor's facilities in Milwaukee and Boston. The Novelty Division primarily supplies _____ and related products to manufacturers of _____ products. The Novelty Division also manufactures _____ for private label sales in grocery stores and similar retail outlets. The Debtor continues to operate the Novelty Division in the ordinary course of business.

8.     The assets of the Foodservice and Novelty Divisions which the Debtor proposes to sell (the "Assets") consist primarily of the Atlanta, Chicago, Dallas, and Milwaukee real estate, all inventory, machinery, equipment, molds, vehicles, furniture and fixtures located at each of the foregoing facilities, and all customer lists, trademarks and

brands and other intellectual property associated with the Foodservice and Novelty Divisions.

9. _____ Bank, individually and as agent for _____ (collectively, the "Banks") claims valid, perfected and enforceable liens and security interests (the "Liens") in and to the Assets. The Banks have consented to a sale of the Assets as set forth in this Motion.

10. The Debtor proposes to sell the Assets free and clear of all liens, claims and encumbrances, with such liens, claims and encumbrances attaching to the proceeds. The proceeds of the sale of the Assets, net of the costs of the sale (other than professional fees and costs), will be paid to _____ Bank on a provisional basis, subject to disgorgement.

11. Because the Foodservice Division is no longer operating, an immediate sale of the Foodservice Division is imperative in order to maximize the value of the Foodservice Division assets for the following reasons:

(a) The Foodservice Division is in immediate danger of losing its customer base due to its inability to meet orders going forward. Losing the customer base would likely have a substantial adverse affect on the value of the Foodservice Division assets.

(b) As each day passes, the former employees of the Foodservice Division are more likely to have found other employment opportunities, thus hampering any potential buyer's ability to reassemble the workforce.

(c) In order for a potential buyer to meet the demands for the summer season, it is imperative that it begin manufacturing inventory now. The inability to manufacture sufficient inventory for the summer season substantially diminishes the value of the Foodservice Division to any potential buyer. A number of potential purchasers have informed the Debtor that if the assets are not conveyed on or before the end _____, the summer production season will be missed and such buyers will not be interested in purchasing the Foodservice Division assets.

12.    The Debtor believes the sale of the Novelty Division Assets at the Auction is imperative for the following reasons:

(a)    The Novelty Division is in immediate danger of losing customers and employees due to the negative publicity associated with this bankruptcy proceeding.    Losing customers and/or employees would likely have a substantial adverse effect on the value of the Novelty Division assets.

(b)    In order for a potential buyer to meet the demands for the summer season, it is imperative that it begin manufacturing inventory now.    The inability to manufacture sufficient inventory for the summer season substantially diminishes the value of the Novelty Division assets to any potential buyer.    A number of potential purchasers have informed the Debtor that if the assets are not conveyed on or before the end of _____, the Summer production season will be missed and such buyers will not be interested in purchasing the Novelty Division assets.

13.    Based upon the foregoing, the Debtor believes that it is in the best interest of this estate and its creditors that the Assets be offered for sale pursuant to the procedures outlined in this Motion as soon as possible and that the ten-day stay of the order approving the sale set forth in Rule 6004(g) of the Federal Rules of Bankruptcy Procedure be waived.

### Bid Procedures

14.    In order to expedite the sale of the Assets, the Debtor has determined that it is in the best interest of this estate and its creditors to sell the Assets at an auction sale (the "Auction") to be conducted before the Court, pursuant to the terms, conditions and procedures set forth on Exhibit A attached hereto (the "Bid Procedures").

15.    The Debtor further believes that it is in the best interest of this estate and its creditors that in the event the Debtor receives prior to the Auction an offer to purchase all or substantially all of the Assets, the Debtor have the right to seek Court approval of a sale pursuant to such offer, in lieu of the Auction.

16.    As set forth in the Bid Procedures, the Debtor proposes to sell the Assets on an "AS IS-WHERE IS" basis, with no representations or warranties of any kind.

17.    The Bid Procedures provide, inter alia, that all buyers shall execute and deliver to the Debtor an asset purchase agreement in a form approved by the Court. Attached hereto as Exhibit B is a form of asset purchase agreement (the "Asset Purchase Agreement") the Debtor proposes to utilize in connection with the sale of the Assets.

WHEREFORE, the Debtor respectfully requests that this Court enter an order (1) authorizing the Debtor to sell the Assets, free and clear of all liens, claims and encumbrances, with such liens, claims and encumbrances attaching to the proceeds, on the terms, conditions and procedures set forth herein, (2) approving the Bid Procedures, (3) setting a date for the Auction not later than _____ (4) approving the Asset Purchase Agreement, (5) waiving the ten-day stay of such order set forth in Rule 6004(g) of the Federal Rules of Bankruptcy Procedure, and (6) granting such other relief as it deems appropriate.

Dated    at    Milwaukee,    Wisconsin,    this    _____    day    of
_____.

Reinhart Boerner Van Deuren s.c.        Peter C. Blain
1000 North Water Street, Suite 2100     State Bar ID No. _____
P.O. Box 2965                           Michael D. Jankowski
Milwaukee, WI 53201-2965                State Bar ID No. _____
Phone: 414-298-1000
Fax: 414-298-8097                       BY_____
                                        Attorneys for _____

*Courtesy of Peter C. Blain, Reinhart Boerner Van Deuren s.c.*

**307**

## Appendix L

## FORBEARANCE AGREEMENT

THIS FORBEARANCE AGREEMENT is by and among _____ ("Lender"), _____, a _____ [corporation] [limited liability company] ("Borrower") and _____ and _____ (each, a "Guarantor," collectively, "Guarantors").

## RECITALS

A. Borrower is indebted to Lender under a certain _____ Note (as amended, the "Revolving Note") from Borrower to Lender, dated _____, in the stated principal amount of $_____. As of _____, the outstanding principal balance of the Revolving Note was $_____.

B. Borrower is indebted to Lender under a certain _____ Note (as amended, the "Term Note") from Borrower to Lender, dated _____, in the stated principal amount of $_____. As of _____, the outstanding principal balance of the Term Note was $_____. The Revolving Note and Term Note are hereinafter referred to as "Notes."

C. The Notes were issued in connection with a _____ Agreement (as amended, the "Credit Agreement") between Borrower and Lender dated _____.

[Borrower and Lender have entered into that certain ISDA Master Agreement dated _____ and any schedules to such agreement, together with all confirmations provided thereunder (collectively, the "Swap Agreement"). **[If the swap provider is an affiliate, the affiliate must be party to the agreement]**

D. To secure all of the indebtedness and obligations of Borrower to Lender (collectively, the "Obligations"), including, without limitation, Borrower's obligations under the Notes and the Credit Agreement [and the Swap Agreement], Borrower executed and delivered to Lender (i) a certain _____ Agreement (the " Security Agreement"), dated _____, granting to Lender a security interest in all of the personal property and fixtures of Borrower and (ii) a certain _____ Mortgage (the "Mortgage"), dated _____, granting to Lender a mortgage on the land and improvements located at _____ (the "Real Estate").

All property of Borrower in which Borrower has granted to Lender a security interest, mortgage, or lien, or which Borrower has assigned or pledged to Lender as collateral, including, without limitation, the property described in the Security Agreement and Mortgage, is hereinafter referred to collectively as the "Collateral." The Security Agreement, Mortgage and all other documents pursuant to which Borrower has granted to Lender a security interest, mortgage, or lien, or pursuant to which Borrower has assigned or pledged property to Lender as collateral, are hereinafter referred to collectively as the "Security Documents."

E.      As a condition to Lender extending credit to Borrower, each Guarantor executed and delivered to Lender a certain _____ Guaranty (each a "Guaranty," collectively, the "Guaranties"), dated _____, unconditionally guarantying to Lender payment of the Obligations.

The Notes, the Credit Agreement, [the Swap Agreement,] the Security Agreement, the Mortgage, the other Security Documents, the Guaranties, and all other agreements, instruments and other documents executed in connection with or relating to any of the Obligations or any of the Collateral are hereinafter referred to collectively as the "Loan Documents."

F.      Borrower is in default under the Loan Documents.

G.      Borrower and Guarantors have requested that Lender forbear from exercising its rights and remedies to collect the Obligations.

H.     Upon the terms and conditions contained herein, Lender is prepared to forbear from the exercise of such rights and remedies for a limited period of time as set forth herein.

## AGREEMENTS

NOW THEREFORE, in consideration of the agreements and undertakings contained herein and for other good and valuable consideration the receipt and sufficiency is hereby acknowledged, the parties hereby agree as follows:

1.     Acknowledgments.     Borrower     and     Guarantors acknowledge and agree as follows:

(a)     Recitals. The above recitals are true and correct.

(b)     Borrower in Default. An event of default has occurred and is continuing under each of the Loan Documents by reason of _____ (the "Existing Default").

(c)     Right to Immediate Payment. As a result of the Existing Default, [the Obligations have been accelerated and are now due and payable] or [Lender is entitled to demand immediate payment of the Obligations without restriction].

(d)     No Obligation to Lend. As a result of the Existing Default, [Lender's obligation to make loans to Borrower under the Loan Documents has terminated and Lender has no obligation to make loans or otherwise extend credit to Borrower] or [Lender has no obligation to make loans or otherwise extend credit to Borrower].

(e)     Notice of Defaults. To the extent required under the Loan Documents or applicable law, Borrower and Guarantors have received timely, adequate and proper notice of the Existing Default[, the acceleration of the Obligations, and the termination of Lender's obligation to make loans to Borrower under the Loan Documents,] and hereby waive their rights (if any) to any further notice thereof.

(f)     Default Rate of Interest. As a result of the Existing Default, Lender is entitled to and did, as of _____, increase the interest rates under the Notes. Effective _____, the per annum interest rate under the Revolving Note is _____ and the per annum interest rate under the Term Note is _____.

(g)     No Waiver of Defaults under Loan Documents. Neither this Agreement nor any course of dealing between or among any of the parties hereto is intended to operate, nor shall they be construed, as a waiver of the Existing Default or any other existing or future defaults or events of default under any of the Loan Documents, as to which all rights of Lender shall remain reserved.

(h)     Preservation of Rights and Remedies. Except as expressly provided to the contrary herein, (i) all of Lender's rights and remedies available under the Loan Documents and at law and in equity remain unchanged and available without restriction; (ii) the terms of the Loan Documents remain unchanged and in full force and effect and have not been amended, modified, or changed, whether orally or in writing; and (iii) the obligations and duties of Borrower and each Guarantor to Lender are not released, impaired, diminished, or amended as a result of the execution and delivery of this Agreement or by any subsequent undertakings of the parties.

(i)     Obligations, Liens, Etc. The Obligations are due and owing without offsets, deductions, counterclaims, or defenses of any kind or character whatsoever, and the security interests, mortgages, and liens of Lender in the Collateral constitute valid, enforceable and perfected security interests, liens, and mortgages as to which neither Borrower nor any Guarantor has any offsets, deductions, counterclaims, or defenses of any kind or character whatsoever.

(j)     Loan Documents. The Loan Documents are valid, binding and enforceable against Borrower and Guarantors in accordance with their respective terms, and Borrower and Guarantors each hereby ratify each of the Loan Documents to which they are a party. There have been no modifications to any of the Loan Documents except pursuant to a writing signed by Lender and each other party to such Loan Document.

(k)     Lender's Compliance With Loan Documents. Lender has (i) fully and timely performed all of its obligations and duties to Borrower and each Guarantor under the Loan Documents; (ii) no obligation to (nor has it made any representation of any kind that it will) extend any financial accommodations to Borrower or any Guarantor not expressly contemplated under the Loan Documents or this Agreement; (iii) not made any agreements, representations, or commitments, other than those expressly set forth in this Agreement or in the Loan Documents; and (iv) acted reasonably, in good faith, and appropriately under the circumstances, and within Lender's rights under the Loan Documents and applicable law, in all actions taken by Lender with respect to Borrower, each Guarantor and all Collateral.

(l)     Purpose of Forbearance Period. The purpose of this Agreement is to give Borrower a period of time within which to attempt to [obtain new financing and pay the Obligations in full] or [sell its assets and pay the Obligations in full] or [improve its operating and financial performance to Lender's satisfaction].

(m)     Benefit to Parties. The forbearance by Lender as provided herein was requested by Borrower and Guarantors and shall result in a direct and substantial benefit to Borrower and Guarantors.

2.     Forbearance by Lender.

(a)     Forbearance Period. Lender agrees to forbear from exercising its rights and remedies against Borrower and Guarantors until the earliest to occur of the following: (i) _____ (the "Termination Date") and (ii) the occurrence of any Event of Default under this Agreement. The period of time from the date hereof until the earlier to occur of (i) or (ii), above is referred to as the "Forbearance Period." The Forbearance Period shall terminate immediately and automatically, as provided above, without notice to or action by any party.

(b) <u>Termination of Forbearance Period</u>. Upon the termination of the Forbearance Period, any obligation of Lender to (i) forbear from the exercise of its rights and remedies as provided in section 2(a) or (ii) extend loans, credit, or other financial accommodations to Borrower shall terminate automatically and immediately without notice or further action and Lender shall be free to exercise immediately against Borrower and each Guarantor any and all of its rights and remedies, including, without limitation, any rights and remedies under the Loan Documents, this Agreement, or applicable law. Lender's acceptance of any payment on account of the Obligations or other performance by Borrower or any Guarantor after the termination of the Forbearance Period shall not constitute an extension or reinstatement of the Forbearance Period or a waiver of any Event of Default or any of Lender's rights or remedies.

(c) <u>Preservation of Interests by Lender</u>. Notwithstanding its agreement to forbear as set forth herein, Lender may at any time, in its sole discretion, take any action reasonably necessary to preserve its interest in any Collateral against the actions of Borrower, any Guarantor, or any third party (including any executions, levies, injunctions, conversion, theft, commingling, waste, misuse, neglect, misappropriation, fraud, or any of the like) without notice to or the consent of any party.

(d) <u>Renewal/Extension of Forbearance Period</u>. Lender has no obligation to, has not agreed to, nor has it made any representation that it will, and this Agreement shall not constitute an agreement by or require Lender to, renew or extend the Forbearance Period, grant additional forbearance periods, extend the time for payment of any of the Obligations, make any loans or otherwise extend credit to Borrower or any Guarantor, or allow Borrower to use any of the Collateral after termination of the Forbearance Period.

3. <u>Conditions Precedent to Lender's Obligations</u>. The obligations of Lender under this Agreement (including, without limitation, the obligation to forbear) are contingent upon the occurrence of the following on or before the date of this Agreement:

(a)     Lender shall have received the following from Borrower and Guarantors, all in form, detail and content satisfactory to Lender:

(i)     <u>Secretary's Certificate</u>. Copies, certified by the [Secretary] [manager/a member] of Borrower to be true and correct and in full force and effect on the date hereof, of [1] Borrower's [articles of incorporation and bylaws] [articles of organization and operating agreement], [2] the resolutions of Borrower's [board of directors] [members] authorizing the execution and delivery of this Agreement and all documents required to be delivered in connection herewith and [3] a statement containing the names and titles of the [officer or officers] [member or members/manager or managers] of Borrower authorized to sign such Loan Documents, together with true signatures of each such [officer] [member/manager]. **[include any corporate/LLC guarantors]**

(ii)     <u>Budget</u>. A detailed cash budget through _____ setting forth on a weekly basis Borrower's projected weekly expenses, as amended or supplemented from time to time pursuant to section 9(a) (the "Budget"). A copy of the Budget is attached hereto as Exhibit __.

(iii)     <u>Cash Flow Forecast</u>. A cash flow forecast through _____ that includes a detailed cash flow, collateral, loan balance and borrowing base analysis.

(iv)     <u>Recovery Plan</u>. A written report detailing Borrower's plan for liquidating its excess assets (the "Recovery Plan"), a copy of which is attached hereto as Exhibit__, which Plan shall be acceptable to Lender in its sole discretion.

(v)     <u>New Collateral Documents</u>. Such additional instruments, agreements, and other documents as Lender may require, in its sole discretion, , duly executed by the appropriate parties, including, without limitation, the following:

[1]     _____;

[2] _____; and

[3] _____.

        (vi)    <u>Additional Guaranties</u>. Continuing and unlimited guaranties of payment of the Obligations, duly executed by _____.

        (vii)    <u>Subordination Agreements</u>. Subordination agreements in favor of Lender, duly executed by _____, pursuant to which _____ agrees to subordinate (i) any obligations owed it by Borrower to the Obligations and (ii) any liens granted it by Borrower to the liens of Lender.

        (viii)    <u>Guarantor Financial Statements</u>. Current financial statements from each Guarantor, certified by such Guarantor.

        (ix)    <u>Foreclosure Stipulation</u>. A stipulation for entry of a judgment of foreclosure and sale with respect to the Real Estate and replevin of all personal property Collateral, in the form of Exhibit _____ attached hereto, duly executed by _____ (the "Foreclosure Stipulation").

        (x)    <u>Chapter 128 Assignment</u>. An assignment for the benefit of creditors, duly executed by Borrower, assigning to _____ (the "Assignee"), for the benefit of Borrower's creditors, all of Borrower's assets (the "Chapter 128 Assignment"). Lender shall hold the Chapter 128 Assignment until such time as Lender chooses to deliver the Chapter 128 Assignment to the Assignee under section 13(f) herein; provided, however, that the Chapter 128 Assignment shall not be effective until delivered by Lender to the Assignee and Lender shall have no duty to deliver the Chapter 128 Assignment to Assignee.

        (xi)    <u>Other Documents</u>. Such other agreements, instruments and other documents as Lender may reasonably request to carry out the terms or intent of this Agreement.

(b)      Forbearance Fee.  Borrower shall have paid to Lender, in good and available funds, a forbearance fee in the amount of $_____.

(c)      Engagement of Turnaround Consultant. Borrower shall have retained and continued to retain, at its own expense, the services of a turnaround consultant reasonably acceptable to Lender, on terms and conditions acceptable to Lender.

[      4.      Extension of Credit During Forbearance Period. Notwithstanding the Existing Default and the acceleration of the Obligations, during the Forbearance Period, Lender shall continue to make loans to Borrower as provided in the Credit Agreement (as amended herein); provided, however, that Borrower shall use the proceeds of such loans solely to pay Borrower's expenses in accordance with the Budget. The obligation of Lender to make such loans to Borrower shall automatically terminate, without notice to or action by any party, upon termination of the Forbearance Period. **[If not currently in existence, consider setting up a lock box or cash collateral account and applying all collections to revolver. Would require amendments to the Credit Agreement.]]**

**or**

[      4.      Use of Cash Collateral During Forbearance Period. Borrower shall deposit all cash, cash equivalents, checks, notes, drafts, instruments, refunds, rebates, deposits, and other proceeds from the sale of goods or services in the ordinary course of business ("Cash Collateral"), into account no. _____ (the "Cash Collateral Account") maintained by Borrower with Lender.  Borrower is hereby authorized to use Cash Collateral only in accordance with the Budget; provided that Borrower's authority to use Cash Collateral shall terminate immediately and automatically upon the termination of the Forbearance Period.  Borrower shall not use any proceeds from the sale, transfer, or collection by Borrower of any of its property outside the ordinary course of business, and instead shall deliver such proceeds to Lender for application to the Obligations as provided in section 9(f).]

5.    Payments.    Notwithstanding anything in the Loan Documents to the contrary, and in lieu of any payments required under the Loan Documents, during the Forbearance Period, Borrower shall make the following payments to Lender:

(a)    Interest. _____.

(b)    Principal. _____.

(c)    Late Fees.    Borrower shall pay to Lender on demand a late fee of 5% of the amount of any principal or interest not paid on or before the date due.

6.    Amendments to Credit Agreement.    The Credit Agreement is hereby amended as follows:

(a)    _____.

(b)    _____.

(c)    _____.

7.    Loan Documents Cross-Defaulted and Obligations Cross-Collateralized.    Notwithstanding anything in the Loan Documents to the contrary, (a) a default or event of default under any Loan Document shall constitute a default and event of default under each and every Loan Document and an Event of Default hereunder shall constitute a default and event of default under each and every Loan Document and (b) the indebtedness and obligations secured by the Security Documents include all Obligations.

8.    Representations and Warranties. Borrower and Guarantors represent and warrant to Lender as follows:

(a)    Organization; Corporate Power.    Borrower is a [corporation] [limited liability company] validly existing under the laws of the State of _____.    Borrower has the [corporate] [limited liability company] power to own its properties and carry on its business as currently being conducted. **[include any corporate/LLC guarantors]**

(b) <u>Authorization and Binding Effect</u>. The execution and delivery by Borrower of this Agreement and all other documents contemplated by or related to this Agreement, and the performance by Borrower of its obligations thereunder: (i) are within its [corporate] [limited liability company] power, (ii) have been duly authorized by proper action on the part of Borrower, (iii) are not in violation of any applicable law, the [articles of incorporation or by-laws] [articles of organization or operating agreement] of Borrower or the terms of any agreement, restriction, or undertaking to which Borrower is a party or by which it is bound, and (iv) do not require the approval or consent of the [shareholders] [members] of Borrower, any governmental authority or any other party, other than those obtained and in full force and effect. **[include any corporate/LLC guarantors]** This Agreement, when executed and delivered, will constitute the valid and binding obligation of Borrower and Guarantors enforceable in accordance with its terms, except as limited by bankruptcy, insolvency or similar laws of general application affecting the enforcement of creditors' rights and except to the extent that general principles of equity might affect the specific enforcement of this Agreement.

(c) <u>Litigation</u>. There is no litigation or administrative proceeding pending or, to the knowledge of Borrower or Guarantors, threatened, against or affecting Borrower or any Guarantor or the properties of Borrower or any Guarantor.

(d) <u>Accuracy of Information</u>. All information furnished by Borrower or any Guarantor to Lender is true, correct, and complete in all material respects as of the date furnished and does not contain any untrue statement of a material fact or omit to state a material fact necessary to make such information not misleading.

9. <u>Covenants During the Forbearance Period</u>. As a condition to the continuation of the Forbearance Period, Borrower and Guarantors each covenant and agree that at all times during the Forbearance Period:

(a)     Compliance with Budget.  Borrower shall make only such expenditures as are specifically identified in the Budget.  The maximum amount of expenditures that Borrower may make for each line item for each particular week is specified in the Budget.  Expenditures stated for each line item for a particular week may be carried over and added to the amount set forth in such specific line item for the following week if such expenditure is not made during the week specified in the Budget.  In addition, Borrower shall be permitted on a weekly basis to shift between line items as specified in the Budget an amount not to exceed 10% of any such line item.  The Budget may be modified only by written agreement between Borrower and Lender.

(b)     Compliance with Loan Documents.  Except with respect to the Existing Default, Borrower and Guarantors each shall comply with all covenants, terms and conditions of all of the Loan Documents (as expressly modified herein) and this Agreement; provided, however, that nothing herein shall be construed as a waiver of the Existing Default.

(c)     Financial Covenants.

(i)     _____.

(ii)    _____.

(d)     Turnaround Consultant.  Borrower shall retain, at its own expense, the services of a turnaround consultant reasonably acceptable to Lender, at a level and on terms and conditions acceptable to Lender.

(e)     Bank Accounts.  Borrower shall maintain all of its checking, operating, transaction, deposit, and other similar accounts with Lender and, except as expressly provided in section 9(f) with respect to the payment to Lender of the proceeds from the sale of assets outside the ordinary course of business, shall deposit all cash, cash equivalents, checks, notes, drafts, instruments, refunds, deposits, and proceeds of Collateral in such accounts.

(f) <u>Sale of Assets</u>. Borrower and Guarantors shall use their best efforts to implement and execute the sale of Borrower's assets pursuant to the Recovery Plan; provided, however, that Borrower shall not sell, lease, transfer, or dispose of any of its assets outside the ordinary course of business (whether pursuant to the Recovery Plan or otherwise) without the prior written consent of Lender. Borrower shall provide to Lender [1] not less than five days written notice of any proposed sale, transfer, or other disposition of any of its assets outside the ordinary course of business and [2] a written accounting of each such sale, transfer, or other disposition, in form and content satisfactory to Lender, within 30 days of the consummation thereof. In the event a sale is approved by Lender, Borrower shall cause all proceeds of such sale to be paid by the buyer directly to Lender for application to the Obligations.

(g) <u>Perfection of Lender's Liens</u>. Borrower and Guarantors shall execute such documents and take such actions as Lender shall request from time to time to perfect or protect any security interests, mortgages, or liens granted by Borrower or any Guarantor to Lender.

(h) <u>Weekly Financial Reporting</u>. In addition to any weekly financial reporting required under the Loan Documents, on or before _____ _.m. (Central Time) on _____ of each calendar week, Borrower shall deliver to Lender the following, all in form, content and detail satisfactory to Lender:

(i) <u>Borrower's Certificate</u>. A completed Borrower's Certificate, in the form of Exhibit ____ attached hereto, accurately calculating the borrowing base under the Credit Agreement as of the close of business for the immediately preceding calendar week and containing a statement sworn to by an officer of Borrower indicating whether Borrower is [1] in compliance with the terms and conditions of this Agreement and the Loan Documents, and [2] current with respect to the payment of all wages, benefits, taxes and insurance, duly executed by an authorized officer of Borrower.

(ii)     Accounts Receivable Aging Report.  An accounts receivable aging report, including information regarding all outstanding credit memos, setoffs, and expected setoffs against Borrower's outstanding accounts receivable and the names and addresses of all account debtors, as of the close of business for the immediately preceding calendar week.

(iii)    Cash Receipts and Expenditures Report. A report summarizing Borrower's cash receipts and disbursements as of the close of business for the immediately preceding calendar week, including a comparison of actual to budgeted amounts on a weekly and cumulative basis.

(iv)     Accounts Payable Report.  A report summarizing Borrower's accounts payable, including, without limitation, an aging thereof and a summary of any payment plans with creditors as of the close of business for the immediately preceding calendar week.

(i)      Monthly Financial Reporting.  In addition to any monthly financial reporting required under the Loan Documents, within 30 days after the end of each calendar month, Borrower shall deliver to Lender the following information as of the end of such month, all in form, content and detail satisfactory to Lender:

(i)      Financial Statements.  A balance sheet and related statements of income and cash flows for the period from the beginning of the fiscal year through the end of such month, certified, subject to normal year-end adjustments, by the chief financial officer of Borrower.

(ii)     Cash Flow Forecast.  A current rolling 13-week cash forecast that includes a detailed cash flow, collateral, loan balance and borrowing base analysis.

(iii)    Litigation Report.  A report summarizing the status of all litigation involving Borrower and any disputes between Borrower and any other party.

(iv)  <u>Recovery Plan Report</u>.  A report summarizing the status of the execution of the Recovery Plan.

(v)  <u>Employee Report</u>.  A report detailing by employee all unpaid wages and benefits, including, without limitation, salaries, commissions, bonuses, overtime pay, holiday pay, severance pay, vacation pay, sick pay, health benefits, pension benefits, and profit sharing benefits.

(j)  <u>Other Financial Information</u>.  Borrower and Guarantors each shall furnish to Lender such other financial information as Lender may from time to time request.

(k)  <u>Notice of Adverse Claims</u>.  Borrower and Guarantors each shall notify Lender in writing of any lawsuits, judgments, levies, attachments, garnishments, liens, or other actions brought against any of them or against any of their property (each, an "Adverse Claim"), immediately upon discovering same, and shall provide to Lender all such documentation and other information Lender may request regarding such Adverse Claim.

(l)  <u>Transfers to Insiders</u>.  Borrower shall not make any payments, distributions, loans, or other transfers of property to (i) any direct or indirect shareholder or member of Borrower, or any person or entity in control of Borrower, (ii) any Guarantor or any relative of any Guarantor, (iii) any affiliate of Borrower, any Guarantor, any direct or indirect shareholder or member of Borrower, or person in control of Borrower, or (iv) any entity owned in whole or part, or controlled by, Borrower, any Guarantor, or any shareholder, member, or person in control of Borrower, except standard base salary payable in the ordinary course of Borrower's business for services actually rendered and reimbursement of reasonable business expenses incurred in the ordinary course of Borrower's business.

(m)  <u>Restricted Payments</u>.  Borrower shall not (i) pay any dividends or make any other distributions or transfers based upon the [stock] [membership interests] of Borrower or (ii) purchase, redeem, or acquire, directly or indirectly, any of the [stock] [membership interests] of Borrower. **[include any corporate/LLC guarantors]**

(n) <u>Liens and Encumbrances</u>. Borrower shall not create, assume, or permit to exist any mortgage, security interest, lien, execution, garnishment, charge, or encumbrance of any kind upon any of its property ("Liens"), whether such property is now owned or hereafter acquired, other than Liens in favor of Lender **[add any other applicable exceptions per Credit Agreement]**.

(o) <u>Property Taxes</u>. Borrower shall pay before they become delinquent all taxes, assessments, and other charges which may be assessed or levied against the Real Estate or any other Collateral, and upon request, shall deliver written proof to Lender of such timely payment.

(p) <u>Payments to Creditors</u>. Borrower shall pay all of its liabilities arising in the ordinary course of business during the Forbearance Period as contemplated by the Budget.

(q) <u>Indebtedness</u>. Borrower shall not create, incur, assume, or permit to exist any indebtedness except (i) indebtedness owed to the Lender; (ii) indebtedness which is fully subordinated, in a manner satisfactory to Lender, to the prior payment of the Obligations; (iii) trade credit incurred to acquire goods, services and supplies in the ordinary course of business; and (iv) wages or other compensation due to employees for services actually performed **[add any other applicable exceptions per Credit Agreement]**.

(r) <u>Further Assurances</u>. Borrower and Guarantors shall take such further action and execute and deliver such additional documents as Lender shall request in connection with this Agreement and the transactions contemplated herein.

(s) <u>No Defaults to Third Parties</u>. Borrower shall not be in default with respect to any of its obligations to third parties.

(t)　　Lender's Access. Lender at all times shall have reasonable access to Borrower's places of business, the Collateral, and all of Borrower's books, records, and documents for the purpose of inspecting, examining, verifying, appraising, or valuing same or exercising any of Lender's rights or remedies under this Agreement, any of the Loan Documents, any documents executed in connection with this Agreement or any Loan Document, or applicable law.

The foregoing covenants are in addition to any covenants of Borrower or any Guarantor contained in the Loan Documents.

10.　　Reaffirmation of Guaranties. Each Guarantor hereby:

(a)　　Acknowledges that pursuant to his Guaranty, he has unconditionally guarantied payment of the Obligations to Lender;

(b)　　Acknowledges that the reaffirmation of his Guaranty is a material inducement to Lender to enter into this Agreement; and

(c)　　Reaffirms that his obligations under his Guaranty remain in full force and effect, without offsets, deductions, counterclaims, or defenses of any kind or character whatsoever.

**11.　　Waiver, Release of Claims, and Indemnification. Borrower and each Guarantor, for themselves and each and all of their respective officers, employees, agents, shareholders, members, directors, heirs, successors, and assigns, do hereby fully, unconditionally, and irrevocably waive and release Lender and its officers, employees, agents, directors, shareholders, affiliates, attorneys, successors, and assigns (each a "Released Party"), of and from any and all claims, liabilities, obligations, causes of action, defenses, counterclaims, and setoffs, of any kind, whether known or unknown and whether in contract, tort, statute, or under any other legal theory, arising out of or relating to any act or omission by Lender or any other Released Party, on or before the date of this Agreement. Borrower and each Guarantor agree to defend,**

indemnify, and hold Lender and each other Released Party harmless from and against any and all losses, costs, expenses, damages, or liabilities (including reasonable attorneys' fees) incurred in connection with any demand, claim, counterclaim, cause of action, or proceeding brought as a result of, or arising out of, or in any way related to the Obligations, the Collateral, any of the Loan Documents, this Agreement, any documents executed in connection with or related to this Agreement or any of the Loan Documents, the performance by Lender under any of the Loan Documents, this Agreement, or any documents executed in connection with or related to this Agreement or any of the Loan Documents, or any transaction financed or to be financed, in whole or in part, directly or indirectly, with the proceeds of any loans from Lender to Borrower. Notwithstanding the foregoing, neither Borrower nor Guarantors shall have any obligation to defend, indemnify, or hold Lender or any other Released Party harmless with respect to any loss, cost, expense, damage, or liability resulting solely from willful misconduct on the part of Lender or such other Released Party.

12. <u>Events of Default</u>. Each of the following shall constitute an "Event of Default" under this Agreement:

(a) The occurrence of the Termination Date;

(b) Borrower or any Guarantor fails to comply with any term, covenant, agreement, or other provision contained in this Agreement, or any document executed in connection with or related to this Agreement;

(c) A default or event of default shall occur under any Loan Document or any documents executed in connection with or related to this Agreement or any of the Loan Documents (other than the Existing Default), including, without limitation, any Guaranty, or any Guarantor dies, ceases to exist, or revokes or terminates his liability under any Guaranty, or any Guarantor contests in any manner the validity or enforceability of such Guaranty or denies that such Guarantor has any further liability or obligation thereunder, or any party to any Loan

Document fails to timely comply with any term, covenant or agreement contained therein;

(d) Borrower or any Guarantor becomes insolvent (as such term is defined in section 101(32) of the United States Bankruptcy Code) or the subject of state insolvency proceedings, fails generally to pay its debts as they become due, or makes an assignment for the benefit of creditors; or Borrower or any Guarantor ceases to conduct business in the ordinary course; or a receiver, trustee, custodian, or other similar official is appointed for, or takes possession of any substantial part of the property of, Borrower or any Guarantor;

(e) The taking of action by Borrower or any Guarantor to authorize such organization or individual to become the subject of proceedings under the United States Bankruptcy Code; or the execution by Borrower or any Guarantor of a petition to become a debtor under the United States Bankruptcy Code; or the filing of an involuntary petition against Borrower or any Guarantor under the United States Bankruptcy Code; or the entry of an order for relief under the United States Bankruptcy Code against Borrower or any Guarantor;

(f) A tax lien, warrant, or levy is served, filed, or recorded with respect to Borrower or any Collateral;

(g) An action, whether in law or equity, is commenced by Borrower, any Guarantor, or any of their respective creditors against Lender in respect of any of the Loan Documents, this Agreement, any agreement or document executed in connection with or related to this Agreement or any of the Loan Documents, or any action or omission by Lender or its agents in connection with any of the foregoing;

(h) Any action is commenced by any of Borrower's or any Guarantor's creditors against Borrower or any Guarantor to collect any debt, obligation, or liability;

(i) Any representation, warranty, or other statement made to Lender by Borrower or any Guarantor in connection with this Agreement is false in any material respect when made; or

(j)     Any action is taken by Borrower or any Guarantor which is in the reasonable judgment of Lender inconsistent in any material respect with any provision of this Agreement.

13.     Remedies.  Upon the occurrence of any Event of Default:

(a)     The Forbearance Period shall terminate automatically and immediately without notice to, or action by, any party;

(b)     Lender shall have any and all rights and remedies under the Loan Documents, this Agreement, the Foreclosure Stipulation, any other documents executed in connection with or related to this Agreement or any of the Loan Documents, or applicable law;

(c)     [Any obligation of Lender to make loans or otherwise extend credit or other financial accommodations to Borrower shall terminate automatically and immediately without notice to or action by any party] or [Borrower's authority to use Cash Collateral shall terminate automatically and immediately without notice to or action by any party];

(d)     Borrower shall surrender to Lender, immediately upon Lender's request, at the time and place designated by Lender, all personal property Collateral and cooperate with Lender's repossession of same; and

(e)     Lender may, in its sole discretion, elect to commence foreclosure actions with respect all or a portion of the Real Estate and replevin actions with respect to any of the other Collateral, and enforce the Foreclosure Stipulation;

(f)     Lender may, in its sole discretion, elect to remove the Chapter 128 Assignment from escrow and deliver it to the Assignee, at which time the Chapter 128 Assignment shall become effective and the Assignee shall have the right to file the Chapter 128 Assignment with the Wisconsin Circuit Court for _____ County and request to be appointed as receiver for Borrower pursuant to Chapter 128 of the Wisconsin Statutes.

(g)     Lender may set-off all or any part of the Obligations against any deposit balances or other money now or hereafter owed Borrower by Lender.

(h)     Lender may, in its sole discretion, terminate the Swap Agreement, and upon termination of the Swap Agreement, the termination payment thereunder shall be immediately due and payable.

**14.     Relief from the Automatic Stay.   As a material inducement to Lender to enter into this Agreement, Borrower hereby stipulates and agrees that Lender shall be entitled to relief from the automatic stay imposed by 11 U.S.C. § 362 or any similar stay or suspension of remedies under any other federal or state law in the event Borrower becomes subject to a bankruptcy or other insolvency proceeding, to allow Lender to exercise its rights and remedies with respect to the Collateral.**

15.     Notices.   All notices required or permitted by this Agreement shall be in writing and shall be (a) delivered; (b) sent by express or first class mail; or (c) sent by facsimile transmission and confirmed in writing provided to the recipient in a manner described in (a) or (b); and each such notice shall be addressed as follows, unless and until such party notifies the other parties in accordance with this paragraph of a change of address; such notices shall be deemed given when delivered, mailed or so transmitted:

    If to Lender:          _____

                           _____

                           _____

                           Attn: _____
                           Facsimile No. _____

    with a copy to:_____

                           _____

                           _____

                           Attn: _____
                           Facsimile No. _____

If to Borrower: _____

_____

_____

Attn: _____
Facsimile No. _____

with a copy to:_____

_____

_____

Attn: _____
Facsimile No. _____

If to
a Guarantor: _____

_____

_____

Attn: _____
Facsimile No. _____

with a copy to: _____

_____

_____

Attn: _____
Facsimile No. _____

16. <u>Miscellaneous</u>.

(a) <u>Entire Agreement</u>. This Agreement reflects the entire understanding of the parties with respect to the subject matter herein contained, and supersedes any prior agreements (whether written or oral) between the parties. The terms of this Agreement may not be waived, amended, or supplemented except in a writing signed by all parties hereto. This Agreement shall not be construed against the drafter hereof.

(b) <u>Severability</u>. In the event any provision of this Agreement shall be held invalid or unenforceable by any court of competent jurisdiction, such holding shall not affect the validity or enforceability of any other provision hereof.

(c) <u>Full Force and Effect/Assigns</u>. Except as expressly modified herein, all terms of the Loan Documents shall remain unchanged and in full force and effect. This Agreement shall be binding upon and inure to the benefit of the parties hereto and their respective successors and permitted assigns, provided that Borrower's and Guarantors' rights under this Agreement are not assignable. Lender's rights under and interests in this Agreement, the Loan Documents, and all documents executed in connection with or related to this Agreement or the Loan Documents, may be assigned at any time by Lender without the consent of or notice to Borrower or any Guarantor. Borrower and Guarantors hereby authorize Lender to provide to any prospective assignee such information concerning the Collateral, Borrower and/or Guarantors as Lender, in its sole discretion, deems necessary. Upon consummation of such assignment by Lender, the assignee shall have all rights, powers and interests of Lender under the Loan Documents, this Agreement and all documents executed in connection with or related to this Agreement or the Loan Documents.

(d) <u>Governing Law</u>. This Agreement shall be governed by, and shall be construed in accordance with, the laws of the State of Wisconsin (irrespective of such state's choice of laws rules).

(e) <u>No Waiver</u>. No delay or omission of Lender in exercising any of its rights, remedies, or powers arising from the Existing Default or any Event of Default shall be construed as a waiver or an acquiescence thereof, nor shall any single or partial exercise of any such rights, remedies, or powers preclude any further exercise thereof or the exercise of any other right, remedy, or power arising from the Existing Default or any Event of Default. Lender's acceptance of any payment on account of the Obligations or other performance by Borrower or any Guarantor after the occurrence of an Event of Default shall not constitute a waiver of such Event of Default, any other Event of Default, or any of Lender's rights or remedies.

(f) <u>Application of Payments</u>. Lender may apply any and all payments it receives from Borrower, any Guarantor, or any other party, and any proceeds of any Collateral, to such portion of the Obligations as Lender shall determine in its sole discretion.

(g)     Recommendation of Counsel.  Borrower and Guarantors acknowledge and understand that Lender has recommended that they each consult with legal counsel prior to the execution of this Agreement.  Borrower and Guarantors represent that they have either consulted with legal counsel prior to executing this Agreement and any documents delivered in connection herewith or related hereto or have knowingly waived the right to do so notwithstanding the express recommendation of Lender.

**(h)     Submission to Jurisdiction; Service of Process.** As a material inducement to Lender to enter into this Agreement:

**(i)     Borrower and Guarantors each hereby agree that all actions or proceedings in any manner relating to or arising out of this Agreement or any of the Loan Documents may be brought only in courts of the State of Wisconsin located in _____ County or the Federal District Court for the _____ District of Wisconsin and Borrower and Guarantors each hereby consent to the jurisdiction of such courts. Borrower and Guarantors each waive any objection they may now or hereafter have to the venue of any such court and any right they many now or hereafter have to claim that any such action or proceedings is in an inconvenient court.  The foregoing notwithstanding, Lender may bring actions or proceedings against Borrower, any Guarantor, or any Collateral in any other courts for the purpose of protecting or exercising any of Lender's rights or remedies; and**

**(ii)     Borrower and Guarantors each hereby consent to the service of process in any such action or proceeding by certified mail sent to the address in section 15.**

**(i)     Waiver of Right to Jury Trial.  As a material inducement to Lender to enter into this Agreement, Borrower and Guarantors each hereby waive trial by jury and consent to the granting of such legal or equitable relief as is deemed appropriate by a judge of a court of competent jurisdiction.**

(j)     <u>Reimbursement of Costs and Expenses</u>. Borrower and Guarantors shall reimburse Lender for all costs and expenses (including attorneys' fees) incurred by Lender with respect to the Obligations or the Collateral, including, without limitation, attorneys' fees, costs and expenses incurred in the preparation, negotiation, administration, implementation and enforcement of this Agreement, the Loan Documents, or any documents executed in connection with or related to this Agreement or the Loan Documents, and all fees, costs and expenses incurred in connection with any insolvency proceeding. The obligations of Borrower and Guarantors under this section 16(j) are joint and several.

(k)     <u>Titles</u>. The titles of sections in this Agreement are for convenience only and do not limit or construe the meaning of any section.

(l)     <u>Execution in Counterparts</u>. This Agreement may be executed in several counterparts, each of which shall be an original and all of which shall constitute but one and the same instrument.

(m)     <u>Electronic and Facsimile Signatures</u>. Electronic or facsimile copies of any party's signature hereto shall be deemed effective execution of this Agreement by such party.

(n)     <u>Time is of the Essence</u>. Time is of the essence with respect to the terms and conditions of this Agreement.

Dated as of the _____ day of _____, _____.


LENDER:


_____

BY_____

_____

BORROWER:

_____

BY_____
_____

GUARANTORS:

_____
_____

_____
_____

*Courtesy of Peter C. Blain, Reinhart Boerner Van Deuren s.c.*

## Appendix M

## SAMPLE BID PROCEDURES

## AUCTION TERMS AND PROCEDURES

**In re** _____

**Bankruptcy Case No.** _____


I.     AUCTION TERMS

A.     <u>Assets</u>. _____ (the "Debtor") will conduct an auction (the "Auction") of substantially all of its assets consisting primarily of the Debtor's owned real estate in Atlanta (the "Atlanta Facility"), Chicago (the "Chicago Facility"), Dallas (the "Dallas Facility") and Milwaukee (the "Milwaukee Facility"), machinery, equipment, molds, vehicles, furniture, fixtures, intellectual property, customer lists and inventory, all as more particularly described herein (collectively, the "Assets") at the Pfister Hotel, Imperial Ballroom, 424 East Wisconsin Avenue, Milwaukee, Wisconsin 53202 on _____, beginning at 9:00 a.m. (Central Time). The Assets will be sold in lots (each, a "Lot") as described herein.

B.     <u>"As Is-Where Is."</u> The Assets will be sold on an "AS IS-WHERE IS" basis, without any representations or warranties of any kind.

C.     <u>Free and Clear of Liens</u>. _____ Bank, individually and as agent for _____ (collectively, the "Secured Lenders"), claims valid, perfected and enforceable liens and security interests in and to the Assets. Other parties may assert liens, claims, or encumbrances against the Assets as well. All sales of Assets shall be free and clear of all liens, claims and encumbrances, with such liens, claims and encumbrances attaching to the proceeds.

D.     <u>Due Diligence</u>. The Debtor shall grant reasonable access to the Assets and make financial and maintenance information available to any prospective purchaser who executes and delivers to the Debtor a confidentiality agreement acceptable to the Debtor.

E.      Taxes. Buyers (as defined herein) will be responsible for any sales, transfer or other taxes, if any, applicable to its purchase of any Assets and shall pay the same to the Debtor at the time of the closing of the sale in question.

F.      Asset Purchase Agreement. All Buyers shall execute and deliver to the Debtor prior to or at closing an asset purchase agreement substantially in the form of that approved by the Court (the "Asset Purchase Agreement"). Interested parties may obtain the form of Asset Purchase Agreement by contacting the Debtor's counsel (see below).

G.      Closing. Except as set forth below, the closing of all sales shall be within fifteen business days of the Auction, unless (i) a later date is agreed to in writing by the Debtor and the Buyer or (ii) the expiration or early termination of all waiting periods required by the Hart-Scott-Rodino Antitrust Improvements Act of 1976, as amended (the "HSR Act") is required, in which case, the parties shall file all required forms and information on an expedited basis and close promptly upon expiration or early termination of all applicable waiting periods. Notwithstanding the foregoing, at the option of the Debtor, the closing of a sale of any Assets in Lots 10, 11, 12 or 13 shall be within up to 60 calendar days of the Auction. The appeal of the order approving a particular sale shall not, absent a stay pending appeal or an injunction enjoining the sale, relieve either party of its obligation to close such sale. All sales shall be final and for cash or cash equivalents.

H.      Removal of Assets. In the event there is a Winning Bid (as defined herein) for Lot 14, 15, 16, 17, 18, 19, 20, 21 or 22, and the Buyer of such Lot has not also submitted a Winning Bid for the real estate upon which the Assets in such Lot are located, the Buyer of such Lot shall remove the Assets from the premises within, at the Debtor's option, the later of (i) ten business days of the closing date of the sale of the Assets in Lot 14, 15, 16, 17, 18, 19, 20, 21 or 22, as the case may be, or (ii) ten days prior to the closing date of the sale of the real estate in question. The Buyer for each such Lot shall (1) be responsible for all costs and expenses in connection with the removal of the Assets and (2) repair all damage to the premises from which the Assets were removed resulting from the removal of such Assets. In addition, prior to removing any Assets, the Buyer shall provide to the Debtor evidence, satisfactory to the Debtor, that the purchaser has adequate insurance against claims for personal injury and property damage resulting from the removal of the Assets. Such insurance shall be in an amount satisfactory to the Debtor. Notwithstanding the foregoing, in the event the Assets in Lot 14, 15, 16, 17, 18, 19, 20, 21 or 22 are not sold at the Auction, and a party other than the Secured Lenders has submitted a Winning Bid for the real estate upon which the Assets in such Lot are located, the Secured Lenders shall have twenty business days after the closing date for the sale of the real estate to remove the Assets from the premises.

## II.    BID PROCEDURES

A.    <u>Bidder Qualification</u>. All persons or entities, or their counsel, wishing to participate in the Auction shall (1) be present in person, (2) register by signing the "Official Sign-in Sheet" acknowledging their interest in participating in the Auction and their familiarity with and acceptance of the terms and procedures, and (3) on or before _____ at 2:00 p.m. (Central Time) present to the Debtor's counsel (see address below), a cashier's or certified check in the amount of $100,000 (the "Participation Deposit"), together with financial statements evidencing, to the satisfaction of the Debtor, such party's ability to consummate a purchase. In lieu of submitting financial statements, a party may present to the Debtor's counsel a cashier's or certified check in the amount of $500,000 (the "Qualifying Deposit"). All checks shall be made payable to "Reinhart Boerner Van Deuren s.c. Trust Account." Parties may submit a deposit via wire transfer in lieu of a cashier's or certified check. Wire transfer instructions may be obtained by contacting the Debtor's counsel. The Secured Lenders may participate in the Auction by credit bidding their liens pursuant to section 363(k) of the Bankruptcy Code, without the requirement of a Participation Deposit, financial statements, or a Qualifying Deposit. Only those parties meeting the foregoing requirements (hereinafter, a "Bidder") shall be entitled to bid at the Auction.

B.        Bids. All bids shall be unconditional. Without limiting the generality of the foregoing, no bid may be conditioned (i) upon the acceptance of one or more other bids or (ii) the assumption or assignment of one or more Contracts (as defined herein). Bids may only be made for whole Lots. Bids for a portion of the Assets in any Lot will not be considered.

The Debtor reserves the right to reject the final highest and best bid for any particular Lot ("Tentative Winning Bid") and to decline to sell the Assets in such Lot at the Auction. If the Debtor agrees to accept a Tentative Winning Bid for a Lot (a "Winning Bid"), it shall do so by the conclusion of the Auction, and the Debtor will seek to have the Court enter an order authorizing the Debtor to consummate the sale at the Winning Bid to the Bidder making such Winning Bid (hereinafter, a "Buyer"), and to execute such additional reasonable documentation as is necessary to complete the sale. A Winning Bid shall be binding on the Buyer and may be withdrawn only in the event it is not approved by the Court. No Winning Bid is binding on the Debtor until the Court enters an order approving the sale pursuant to such Winning Bid.

C.        Identification of Lots. Upon registering for the Auction, each Bidder intending to bid on Lots 1, 2, or 3 shall indicate such intention to the Debtor. At that time, all Bidders expressing an interest in bidding on Lots 1, 2, or 3 will be interviewed in private by the Debtor and shall disclose to the Debtor their opening bid for such Lots. The highest and best of such opening bids for Lots 1, 2 and 3 (each, a "Stalking Horse Bid") shall be recorded by the Debtor.

D.        Order of Sale; Opening Bids. The Auction will proceed in rounds. The first round of bidding will begin with Lot 4 through Lot 22, with such Lots being offered in such order as the Debtor may elect. With respect to Lots 4 through 22, an opening bid will be suggested. If there are no bids at the suggested opening bid, such opening bid shall be reduced until a bid is made. The bidding for Lots 4 through 22 shall proceed (using the established minimum bid increments for each such Lot) until the highest and best bid for each such Lot is achieved.

Lots 2 and 3 (in that order) shall be offered for bidding after the conclusion of the bidding on Lots 4-22. The minimum opening bid for each of Lots 2 and 3 shall be the Stalking Horse Bid for such Lot. The bidding for Lots 2 and 3 shall proceed (using the established minimum bid increments for each Lot) until the highest and best bid for each such Lot is achieved.

Upon the conclusion of the bidding for Lot 3, Lot 1 will be offered for bidding at a minimum opening bid equal to the higher and better of (1) the Stalking Horse Bid for Lot 1 and (2) the aggregate of the highest and best bids for Lots 2 and 3. The bidding on Lot 1 will then proceed (using the established minimum bid increments for Lot 1) until the highest and best bid is achieved for Lot 1. Round 1 of bidding will end upon the conclusion of the bidding for Lot 1.

Upon the completion of round 1, and following a short recess, round 2 of bidding shall commence. The Lots shall be offered for bidding in the same order as in round 1, and bidding will proceed until the highest and best bid is achieved for each Lot. Each Lot will be offered at a minimum opening bid equal to the highest and best bid for such Lot in round 1 If no bid was received in round 1 for a particular Lot, the opening bid shall be as determined by the Debtor.

In the event no combination of bids for the Assets in round 2 is higher and better than the highest and best combination of bids in round 1, the Auction shall conclude after round 2. If, on the other hand, there is a combination of bids in round 2 which is higher and better than the highest and best combination of bids in round 1, the Auction will proceed to round 3. Thereafter, the Auction will proceed in a similar fashion, with the final round occurring when no combination of bids in such round is higher and better than the highest and best combination of bids from the prior round.

E.     Court Approval.     Upon conclusion of all bidding, the Debtor will present the results of the Auction to the Court and ask the Court to approve the Winning Bid(s) and to authorize the Debtor to consummate the sale(s) to the Buyer(s).

F.     Purchase Deposits.   Unless otherwise agreed to by the Buyer and the Debtor, each Buyer shall be required to deposit with the Debtor such additional funds, that when added to its Participation Deposit and Qualifying Deposit (if any), equals a sum of not less than 20% of the amount of the Winning Bid (together with the Participation Deposit and Qualifying Deposit, the "Purchase Deposit") in the form of cash or cash equivalents, within 24 hours of the conclusion of the Auction, which Purchase Deposit shall be deposited into a separate interest-bearing account at _____ Bank (a "Deposit Account").   In the event that the Secured Lenders submit a Winning Bid, they are excused from making a Purchase Deposit.   In the event of a default by any Buyer, the Purchase Deposit shall, at the option of the Debtor, be treated as liquidated damages or as a partial contribution toward damages to be determined at a later date. The Purchase Deposits shall not be transferred from the Deposit Accounts except pursuant to further order of the Court.   Any Bidder making a Participation Deposit or Qualifying Deposit, who does not become a Buyer, shall have its Participation Deposit and Qualifying Deposit (if any) returned to it by the Debtor within ten business days of the date of the Auction.   In the event a Buyer defaults, then the Bidder who submitted the next highest and best bid for the Lot in question shall be invited to proceed as a Buyer, and if such Bidder elects within 48 hours of the invitation to so proceed, then its bid will be treated as the Winning Bid and it must post the requisite Purchase Deposit within 24 hours of such election, and the parties shall proceed under the terms hereof.

G.     Preemptive Offers.   The Debtor reserves the right, in the event it receives prior to the Auction an offer to purchase substantially all of the Assets, to seek Court approval of a sale pursuant such offer, in lieu of the Auction.

H.     Auction Rules.   At the Auction the Debtor will adopt rules for the Auction that are not inconsistent with terms and procedures set forth herein.

III.    ASSETS AVAILABLE FOR PURCHASE

    A.    <u>Lots</u>. The Assets will be sold in the following Lots:

        1.    <u>Lot 1 - All Assets</u>. The Atlanta, Chicago, Dallas and Milwaukee Facilities, all machinery, equipment, molds, vehicles, furniture and fixtures located at the Atlanta, Chicago, Dallas, or Milwaukee Facilities, or at the properties leased by the Debtor in Boston or Milwaukee, all packaging inventory (wherever located), including finished goods, work-in-process and raw materials ("inventory"), all customer lists, patents, patent applications, trademarks and brands and other intellectual property, and such contracts and leases of personal or real property of the Debtor (hereinafter referred to collectively as the "Contracts") as the Buyer designates in writing to be included (as set forth below).

        2.    <u>Lot 2 - All Foodservice Assets</u>. The Atlanta, Chicago and Dallas Facilities, all machinery, equipment, molds, vehicles, furniture and fixtures located at the Atlanta, Chicago and Dallas Facilities, all inventory of the Foodservice Division (wherever located), all machinery, equipment, furniture, fixtures and inventory located at the property leased by the Debtor in Boston related to the Foodservice Division, all customer lists, patents, patent applications, trademarks and brands and other intellectual property associated with the Debtor's foodservice division (the "Foodservice Division"), all customer lists, patents, patent applications, trademarks and brands and other intellectual property used in the Debtor's packaging operations and associated solely with the Foodservice Division and, subject to perpetual nonexclusive licenses of the rights

thereunder (as described below), U.S. Patent Nos. _____ and _____, and such Contracts as the Buyer designates in writing to be included (as set forth below).

3. <u>Lot 3 - All Novelty Assets</u>. The Milwaukee Facility, all machinery, equipment, molds, vehicles, furniture, fixtures and inventory located at the Milwaukee Facility, or at the properties leased by the Debtor in Milwaukee, all machinery, equipment, furniture, fixtures and inventory located at the property leased by the Debtor in Boston related to the Novelty Division, all customer lists, patents, trademarks and brands and other intellectual property associated with the Debtor's novelty division (the "Novelty Division"), all customer lists, patents, patent applications, trademarks and brands and other intellectual property used in the Debtor's packaging operations and associated solely with the Novelty Division and perpetual nonexclusive licenses (as described below) of U.S. Patent Nos. _____ and _____, and such Contracts as the Buyer designates in writing to be included (as set forth below).

4. <u>Lot 4 - All Packaging Assets</u>. All machinery, equipment, furniture, fixtures and inventory located at the property leased by the Debtor in Boston, all customer lists, patents, patent applications, trademarks and brands and other intellectual property used in the Debtor's packaging operations (the "Packaging Intellectual Property") and such Contracts as the Buyer designates in writing to be included (as set forth below).

4(a).   Lot 4(a) - Foodservice Packaging Assets. All machinery, equipment, furniture, fixtures and inventory located at the property leased by the Debtor in Boston and all Packaging Intellectual Property, associated solely with the Foodservice Division, and, subject to perpetual nonexclusive licenses of the rights thereunder (as described below), U.S. Patent Nos. _____ and _____, and such Contracts as the Buyer designates in writing to be included (as set forth below).

4(b).   Lot 4(b) - Novelty Packaging Assets. All machinery, equipment, furniture, fixtures and inventory located at the property leased by the Debtor in Boston and all Packaging Intellectual Property, associated solely with the Novelty Division, and perpetual nonexclusive licenses (as described below) of U.S. Patent Nos. _____ and _____, and such Contracts as the Buyer designates in writing to be included (as set forth below).

5.      Lot 5 - Atlanta Assets. The Atlanta Facility, all machinery, equipment, molds, vehicles, furniture and fixtures located at the Atlanta Facility and such Contracts as the Buyer designates in writing to be included (as set forth below).

6.      Lot 6 - Chicago Assets. The Chicago Facility, all machinery, equipment, molds, vehicles, furniture and fixtures located at the Chicago Facility and such Contracts as the Buyer designates in writing to be included (as set forth below).

7.      Lot 7 - Dallas Assets. The Dallas Facility, all machinery, equipment, molds, vehicles, furniture and fixtures located at the Dallas Facility and such

Contracts as the Buyer designates in writing to be included (as set forth below).

8. Lot 8 - Milwaukee Assets. The Milwaukee Facility, all machinery, equipment, molds, vehicles, furniture and fixtures located at the Milwaukee Facility and such Contracts as the Buyer designates in writing to be included (as set forth below).

9. Lot 9 - All Real Estate. The Atlanta, Chicago, Dallas and Milwaukee Facilities.

10. Lot 10 - Atlanta Real Estate. The Atlanta Facility.

11. Lot 11 - Chicago Real Estate. The Chicago Facility.

12. Lot 12 - Dallas Real Estate. The Dallas Facility.

13. Lot 13 - Milwaukee Real Estate. The Milwaukee Facility.

14. Lot 14 - All Machinery and Equipment. All machinery, equipment, molds, vehicles, furniture and fixtures located at the Atlanta, Chicago, Dallas or Milwaukee Facilities, and such Contracts as the Buyer designates in writing to be included (as set forth below).

15. Lot 15 - Atlanta Machinery and Equipment. All machinery, equipment, molds, vehicles, furniture and fixtures located at the Atlanta Facility, and such Contracts as the Buyer designates in writing to be included (as set forth below).

16. Lot 16 - Chicago Machinery and Equipment. All machinery, equipment, molds, vehicles, furniture

and fixtures located at the Chicago Facility, and such Contracts as the Buyer designates in writing to be included (as set forth below).

17. <u>Lot 17 - Dallas Machinery and Equipment</u>. All machinery, equipment, molds, vehicles, furniture and fixtures located at the Dallas Facility, and such Contracts as the Buyer designates in writing to be included (as set forth below).

18. <u>Lot 18 - Milwaukee Machinery and Equipment</u>. All machinery, equipment, molds, vehicles, furniture and fixtures located at the Milwaukee Facility, or at the properties leased by the Debtor in Milwaukee, and such Contracts as the Buyer designates in writing to be included (as set forth below).

19. <u>Lot 19 - Foodservice Intellectual Property</u>. All customer lists, patents, patent applications, trademarks and brands and other intellectual property associated with the Foodservice Division.

20. <u>Lot 20 - Novelty Intellectual Property</u>. All customer lists, patents, patent applications, trademarks and brands and other intellectual property associated with the Novelty Division.

21. <u>Lot 21 - All Foodservice Inventory</u>. All inventory of the Foodservice Division remaining as of the date of the Auction (wherever located), but excluding all inventory located at the property leased by the Debtor in Boston.

22. <u>Lot 22 - All Novelty Inventory</u>. All inventory of the Novelty Division remaining as of the date of the Auction (wherever located), but excluding all

inventory located at the property leased by the Debtor in Boston.

B.     Trademarked Inventory.  The sale of any inventory bearing a trademark owned by a third party shall be conditioned upon the Buyer obtaining the consent to the sale from the owner of the trademark.  In the event a Buyer is unable to obtain consent from the owner of a trademark, any inventory bearing such trademark shall be removed from the Lot being sold; provided, however, that the amount of the Winning Bid shall not be reduced and the Buyer shall be obligated to purchase the remaining assets in such Lot for an amount equal to the Winning Bid submitted by the Buyer for such Lot.

C.     Intellectual Property Subject to Licenses.  The sale of any patents or trademarks owned by the Debtor shall be subject to any existing licenses of such patent or trademark.

D.     Temporary License of "_____" Trademark.  In the event the Buyer of Lots 5, 6, 7, 14, 15, 16 or 17 is not also the Buyer of Lot 19, prior to the closing of the sale of the Assets in Lot 5, 6, 7, 14, 15, 16 or 17, as the case may be, the Debtor shall grant to each such Buyer of the Assets in Lot 5, 6, 7, 14, 15, 16 or 17 a non-exclusive license to manufacture product bearing the "_____" trademark for a period of six months from the date of such closing and to sell such product for a period of twelve months from the date of such closing.  In that event, the Buyer of Lot 19 shall purchase such the "_____" trademark subject to the aforementioned license(s).

E.     Perpetual Licenses of Patents to Buyer of Lot 3.  In the event the Buyer of Lot 3 is not also the Buyer of Lot 2, the Debtor shall grant to the Buyer of Lot 3 perpetual, nonexclusive licenses to use the rights pursuant to U.S. Patent No. _____ and U.S. Patent No. _____ (the "Shared Patents") in manufacturing and selling products which are of the type manufactured and sold by the Novelty Division.  The Debtor shall grant such licenses prior to conveying the Shared Patents to any other party.  The licensee under such licenses shall have no obligation to pay any royalties or other amounts for the use of the rights under the

Shared Patents. The Buyer of Lot 2 shall purchase the Shared Patents subject to the aforementioned licenses.

F.      Contracts.

1.      Designation of Contracts. Within five business days after the date of the Auction, any Buyer of Lots 1, 2, 3, 4, 5, 6, 7 8, 14, 15, 16, 17 or 18 shall designate the Contracts it desires to acquire by completing a Lease and Contract Designation Form (the "Lease/Contract Designation"). As soon as practicable after the closing of a sale containing a Contract(s) included on a Lease/Contract Designation, the Debtor shall file with the Court a motion seeking authority to assume such Contract(s) and assign the same to the Buyer. In the event a Contract is designated by more than one Buyer, the Debtor reserves the right to assign such Contract as the Debtor deems to be in the best interest of the Debtor's bankruptcy estate. The failure of the Court to approve the assumption or assignment of any Contract, or the assignment of a Contract by the Debtor to another Buyer, shall not relieve a Buyer of its obligation to purchase the Assets for which it submitted a Winning Bid.

2.      Postpetition Liabilities and Cure Amounts. The Buyer shall be responsible for all postpetition liabilities owing on the Contracts before and after the date of closing, as well as the cost of any cure relating to prepetition liabilities as required under § 365 of the Bankruptcy Code.

G.      Allocation of Purchase Price. In the event (i) there is a Winning Bid for Lots 1, 2, 3, 5, 6, 7, 8, 9 or 14 and (ii) it becomes necessary to allocate the purchase price for any such Lot in order to determine the value of any lien on any of the Assets in such Lot, then the allocation of the purchase price between the Assets in such Lots shall be pro rata, based on the highest combination of aggregate Tentative Winning Bids for Lots 4, 10 through 13, and 15 through 22, as applicable. In the event there are not sufficient Tentative Winning Bids to allocate the purchase price, the allocation shall be determined by the Court. In any event, the Secured Lenders reserve the right to object to any allocation of the purchase price and to move the Court to approve an alternative allocation.

## IV.    ASSETS EXCLUDED FROM AUCTION

All assets of the Debtor not designated herein as included in the Auction are excluded, including, but not limited to, the following expressly excluded assets:

A.    Cash;

B    Accounts receivable, notes receivable and other rights to payment;

C.    Causes of Action (both prepetition and postpetition);

D.    Books and records; and

E.    Insurance policies.

Debtor's Counsel:        Reinhart Boerner Van Deuren s.c.
1000 North Water Street, Suite 2100
P.O. Box 2965
Milwaukee, WI 53201-2965
Attn: Peter C. Blain
Telephone No: 414-298-1000
Facsimile No.:414-298-8097
Email: pblain@reinhartlaw.com

*Courtesy of Peter C. Blain, Reinhart Boerner Van Deuren s.c.*

## Appendix N

## ENRON ADMINISTRATIVE ORDER

## UNITED STATES BANKRUPTCY COURT SOUTHERN DISTRICT OF NEW YORK

| | |
|---|---|
| In re | Chapter 11 |
| ENRON CORP., ET AL, | Case No. 0146034 (AJG) |
| | Jointly Administered |
| Debtors. | |

———————————————————————X

## ADMINISTRATIVE ORDER PURSUANT TO SECTIONS 105(a) AND 331 OF THE BANKRUPTCY CODE ESTABLISHING PROCEDURES FOR INTERIM COMPENSATION AND REIMBURSEMENT OF EXPENSES OF PROFESSIONALS

Upon consideration of the Motion of the Debtors for Administrative Order Pursuant to Sections 105(a) and 331 of the Bankruptcy Code Establishing Procedures for Interim Compensation and Reimbursement of Expenses of Professionals, dated December 3, 2001 ("Motion"), filed by Enron Corp. and certain of its affiliated debtors (collectively, the "Debtors"), as debtors and debtors in possession, seeking entry of an order pursuant sections 105(a) and 331 of the Bankruptcy Code establishing procedures for interim compensation and reimbursement of expenses of professionals, as more fully set forth in the Motion; and it appearing that the Court has jurisdiction to consider the Motion; and it appearing that the relief requested in the Motion is in the best interests of the Debtors, their estates and creditors; and it appearing that due and appropriate notice of the Motion has been given and no further notice need be given; and upon the proceedings before the Court; and good and sufficient cause appearing;

IT IS HEREBY ORDERED THAT:

1.      The Motion is granted.

2.      Except as may otherwise be provided in Court orders authorizing the retention of specific professionals, all professionals in this case may seek interim compensation in accordance with the following procedure:

Commencing on February 20, 2002, on or before the twentieth (20th) day of each month following the month for which compensation is sought (provided, however, that the first monthly statement shall pertain to the first two months of these chapter 11 cases), each professional seeking compensation under this Motion will serve a monthly statement, by hand or overnight delivery on (1) Ray Bowen, Jr., as the officer designated by the Debtors to be responsible for such matters;(ii) Weil, Gotshal & Manges (attention: Brian S. Rosen), as counsel for the Debtors; (iii) the Office of the United States Trustee; the attorneys for the statutory committee of unsecured creditors once appointed; and (iv) each of Shearman & Sterling (attention: Frederick Sosnick) and Davis Polk & Wardell (attention: Marshall S. Huebner), as counsel to Citicorp USA, Inc. and JPMorgan Chase Bank, respectively, in their capacities as co-administrative agents under the Debtors' post-petition Revolving Credit and Guaranty Agreement.

a.      The monthly statement shall be filed with the Court. A courtesy copy need not be delivered to the presiding judge's chambers. This Order is not intended to alter the fee application requirements outlined in sections 330 and 331 of the Bankruptcy Code. Professionals are still required to serve and file interim and final applications for approval of fees and expenses in accordance with the relevant provisions of the Bankruptcy Code, the Federal Rules of Bankruptcy Procedure and the Local Rules for the United States Bankruptcy Court for the Southern District of New York;

b.      Each monthly fee statement must contain a list of the individuals and their respective titles (e.g.

attorney, accountant, or paralegal) who provided services during the statement period, their respective billing rates, the aggregate hours spent by each individual, a reasonably detailed breakdown of the disbursements incurred (No professional should seek reimbursement of an expense which would otherwise not be allowed pursuant to the Court's Administrative Orders dated June 24, 1991 and April 21, 1995 or the United States Trustee Guidelines for Reviewing Applications for Compensation and Reimbursement of Expenses Filed under 11 U.S.C. § 330 dated January 30, 1996), and contemporaneously maintained time entries for each individual in increments of tenths (1/10) of an hour;

c.    Each person receiving a statement will have at least fifteen (15) days after service to review such statement and, in the event that he or she has an objection to the compensation or reimbursement sought in a particular statement, he or she shall, by no later than the thirty-fifth (35th) day following the month for which compensation is sought, serve upon the professional whose statement is objected to and the other persons designated to receive statements in paragraph (a), a written "Notice Of Objection To Fee Statement," setting forth the nature of the objection and the amount of fees or expenses at issue;

d.    At the expiration of the thirty-five (35) day period, the Debtors shall promptly pay eighty percent (80%) of the fees and one hundred percent (100%) of the expenses identified in each monthly statement to which no objection has been served in accordance with paragraph (d);

e.     If the Debtors receive an objection to a particular fee statement, they shall withhold payment of that portion of the fee statement to which the objection is directed and promptly pay the remainder of the fees and disbursements in the percentages set forth in paragraph (e);

If the parties to an objection are able to resolve their dispute following the service of a Notice Of Objection To Fee Statement and if the party whose statement was objected to serves on all of the parties listed in paragraph (a) a statement indicating that the objection is withdrawn and describing in detail the terms of the resolution, then the Debtors shall promptly pay, in accordance with paragraph (e), that portion of the fee statement which is no longer subject to an objection;

All objections that are not resolved by the parties, shall be preserved and presented to the Court at the next interim or final fee application hearing to be heard by the Court (See paragraph (j), below);

h.     The service of an objection in accordance with paragraph (d) shall not prejudice the objecting party's right to object to any fee application made to the Court in accordance with the Bankruptcy Code on any ground whether raised in the objection or not. Furthermore, the decision by any party not to object to a fee statement shall not be a waiver of any kind or prejudice that party's right to object to any fee application subsequently made to the Court in accordance with the Bankruptcy Code;

i.  Approximately every 120 days, but no more than every 150 days, each of the professionals shall serve and file with the Court an application for interim or final Court approval and allowance, pursuant to sections 330 and 331 of the Bankruptcy Code (as the case may be) of the compensation and reimbursement of expenses requested;

Any professional who fails to file an application seeking approval of compensation and expenses previously paid under this Motion when due shall (1) be ineligible to receive further monthly payments of fees or expenses as provided herein until further order of the Court and (2) may be required to disgorge any fees paid since retention or the last fee application, whichever is later;

k.  The pendency of an application or a Court order that payment of compensation or reimbursement of expenses was improper as to a particular statement shall not disqualify a professional from the future payment of compensation or reimbursement of expenses as set forth above, unless otherwise ordered by the Court;

1. Neither the payment of, nor the failure to pay, in whole or in part, monthly compensation and reimbursement as provided herein shall have any effect on this Court's interim or final allowance of compensation and reimbursement of expenses of any professionals; and

Counsel for any official committee may, in accordance with the foregoing procedure for monthly compensation and reimbursement of professionals, collect and submit statements of expenses, with supporting vouchers, from members of the committee he or she represents; provided, however, that such committee counsel ensures that these reimbursement requests comply with the Court's Administrative Orders dated June 24, 1991 and April 21, 1995.

3. Each member of the Committee in this case is permitted to submit statements of expenses and supporting vouchers to counsel (and co-counsel, if appointed) for the Committee who will collect and submit such requests for reimbursement in accordance with the foregoing procedure for monthly and interim compensation and reimbursement of professionals.

4. Sending notice of hearing to consider interim applications to: (i) the Office of the United States Trustee; (ii) counsel for the Committee; and (iii) all parties who have filed a notice of appearance with the Clerk of this Court and requested such notice shall be good and sufficient notice.

5. To the extent that any affiliates of the Debtors subsequently commence chapter 11 cases which are jointly administered with these chapter 11 cases, the relief requested herein shall apply to such debtors, their respective estates, and their Court-approved professionals.

Dated: New York,
New York January 17, 2002

**s/Arthur J. Gonzalez**
UNITED    STATES    BANKRUPTCY
JUDGE

*Courtesy of Joseph J. Wielebinski, Munsch Hardt Kopf & Harr PC*

## Appendix O

## ENRON ORDER OF EMPLOYEE RETENTION

## UNITED STATES BANKRUPTCY COURT SOUTHERN DISTRICT OF NEW YORK

- - - - - - - - - - - x

In re

ENRON CORP., et al.,

Debtors.

Chapter 11

Case No. 01-16034 (AJG)

Jointly Administered

## ORDER PURSUANT TO SECTION 363(b)(1) OF THE BANKRUPTCY CODE APPROVING AND AUTHORIZING KEY EMPLOYEE RETENTION PROGRAM AND AUTHORIZING ADMINISTRATIVE EXPENSE PRIORITY FOR INDEMNIFICATION CLAIMS ARISING FROM POSTPETITION SERVICES OF DIRECTORS AND OFFICERS PURSUANT TO SECTIONS 503(b) AND 507 OF THE BANKRUPTCY CODE

Upon the motion, dated March 29, 2002 (the "Motion"), of Enron Corp. and its affiliated debtor entities, as debtors and debtors in possession in the above-captioned chapter 11 cases (collectively, the "Debtors"), for an order pursuant to section 363(b)(1) of title 11 of the United States Code (the "Bankruptcy Code") approving and authorizing a Key Employee Retention Program (the "KERP") and authorizing administrative expense priority for indemnification claims arising from postpetition services of directors and officers pursuant to sections 503(b) and 507 of the Bankruptcy Code; and the Court having jurisdiction to consider and determine the Motion in accordance with 28 U.S.C. § 1334; and due notice of the Motion and the hearing thereon having been provided; and the Court having held a hearing on April 16, 2002 (the "Hearing") to consider the Motion and all objections thereto with the appearances of all parties in interest having been noted in the record; and the Court rendered its decision on the record at the Hearing; and after due deliberation and sufficient cause appearing therefor, it is

ORDERED that the KERP, as described in the Motion, is authorized and approved to the extent set forth below; and it is further

ORDERED that the retention and severance components of the KERP are approved; and it is further

ORDERED that the examiner for Enron North America (the "ENA Examiner") shall participate in the Debtors' Management Committee's determinations of amounts to be paid to KERP participants from the liquidation incentive pool (the "LIP") of the KERP, and the Liquidation Incentive Component of the KERP is approved on that basis; and it is further

ORDERED that the Debtors' Management Committee shall no* the ENA Examiner of the reallocation of any portion of a Retention Participant's Retention Payment (as such terms are defined in the KERP) forfeited under the terms of the KERP in the same manner provided for in Section VI(D) of the KERP with respect to the Creditors' Committee; and it is further

ORDERED that the scope of the ENA Examiner's duties is expanded to incorporate his duties under the preceding paragraphs; and it is further

ORDERED that the allocation of the cost of the KERP to each Debtor shall be included in the proposed overhead allocation that the Debtors shall propose to the Court after consultation with the ENA Examiner; and it is further

ORDERED that the releases of avoidance actions provided for in the KERP are not approved; provided, however, the Debtors may request their approval in a motion under Rule 9019 of the Federal Rules of Bankruptcy Procedure naming each releasee, the amount received, and identifying whether the person is an insider, and provided further that if the person is an insider the examiner to be appointed for Enron Corp. shall give priority to determining whether there is any reason not to release: the person; and it is further

ORDERED that, subject to the foregoing, the Debtors are authorized to take all action necessary to fully implement and carry out the KERP as described in the Motion, provided however, that: (i) no payments provided under the KERP shall be made to any KERP participant who does not execute an agreement representing that he or she has not sold the Debtors' shares in violation of the insider trading rules provided under Section 10(b) 5 of the Securities Exchange Act of 1934 and agreeing to disgorge any amounts paid under the KERP should such representation later be proved false; (ii) no person named as a defendant in the pending consolidated actions of Newby, et al. v. Enron Corp., et al. and The Regents of the University of California, et al. v. Lay, et al. Civil Action No. H –01-3624 (S.D. Tex.) has been made a participant of the KERP; (iii) no person identified as a wrongful actor in the "Report of Investigation by the Special Investigative Committee of the Board of Directors of Enron Corp." dated February 1, 2002, has been made a participant in the KERP; and (iv) KERP participants shall be required to disgorge all payments made under the KERP to the extent that any KERP participant is later adjudged by a court of competent jurisdiction to have engaged in acts of dishonesty or other willful misconduct detrimental to the interests of the Debtors, and it is further

ORDERED that any obligations of the Debtors under or in connection with the KERP shall be deemed allowed administrative expense claims under section 503(b)(1)(A) of the Bankruptcy Code; and it is further

ORDERED that the Debtors are authorized to extend to their current and future officers and directors their right to indemnification, provided for under the Articles of Incorporation of the Debtors, the Oregon Business Corporation Act and other applicable law, for claims and lawsuits based solely on their postpetition services; and it is further

ORDERED that such postpetition indemnification claims shall be entitled to administrative expense priority under sections 503(b) and 507 of the Bankruptcy Code; and it is further

ORDERED that the Debtors are authorized to advance to any current or future officer and director the costs of defending against any claim or lawsuit raised against such officer or director arising solely from postpetition services, to the extent that such advancement would be authorized under the Articles of

Incorporation of the Debtors, the Oregon Business Corporation Act and other applicable law, without further order of this Court, and it is further

ORDERED that nothing herein shall be deemed to provide indemnification to the Debtors' officers and directors beyond what is authorized under the Articles of Incorporation, Oregon law or other applicable law.

Dated: New York, New York
May 8, 2002

**s/Arthur J. Gonzalez**
UNITED    STATES    BANKRUPTCY
JUDGE

*Courtesy of Joseph J. Wielebinski, Munsch Hardt Kopf & Harr PC*

## Appendix P

## WRC AGREEMENT ORDER

The relief described hereinbelow is SO ORDERED.

Signed August 04, 2003.

Ronald B. King
United States Bankruptcy Judge

UNITED STATES BANKRUPTCY COURT
FOR THE WESTERN DISTRICT OF TEXAS
SAN ANTONIO DIVISION

| | | |
|---|---|---|
| IN RE: | § | |
| | § | |
| WRC INGRAM SQUARE, INC., | § | CASE No. 02-54230- |
| RBK 11 | | |
| | § | |
| Debtor. | § | |

## FOURTH INTERIM AGREED ORDER AUTHORIZING THE USE OF CASH COLLATERAL AND THE GRANTING OF ADDITIONAL OR REPLACEMENT LIENS AND ADMINISTRATIVE PRIORITY CLAIMS

On September 30, 2002, there came on for a preliminary hearing the motion (the "Motion") for an order prohibiting the use cash collateral pursuant to § 363(c)(2) and (3) of title 11 of the United States Code, §§ 101-1330, as amended (the "Bankruptcy Code") and Rule 4001(b) of the Federal Rules of Bankruptcy Procedure (the "Bankruptcy Rules") filed by ORIX Capital Markets, LLC, f/k/a ORIX Real Estate Capital Markets, LLC, the Successor Special Servicer to CRIIMI MAE Services Limited Partnership and the attorney-in-fact for State Street Bank & Trust Company as Trustee and REMIC Administrator, acting in its capacity as special servicer and attorney-in-fact for State Street Bank & Trust Company, the Trustee for the registered holders of Mortgage Capital Funding, Inc., Multifamily/Commercial Mortgage Pass-Through Certificates, Series 1998-MC2 (the "Trust"), a secured creditor and a party in interest in the bankruptcy case of WRC Ingram Square, Inc. (the "Debtor"). The Court was informed that the Trust and Helen Schwartz, the chapter 11 trustee (the "Chapter 11 Trustee") agree as follows:

### PROCEDURAL BACKGROUND

On September 3, 2002 (the "Petition Date"), the Debtor filed its voluntary petition for relief under chapter 11 of the Bankruptcy Code.

Under 11 U.S.C. § 301, the filing of the petition constituted an order for relief under chapter 11 and, since said filing, under 11 U.S.C. §§ 1107 and 1108, the Debtor continued in possession and control of its assets and property and has continued to operate its business and manage its affairs.

This Court has jurisdiction to hear this Motion under 28 U.S.C. § 1334. This is a core proceeding under 28 U.S.C. § 157(b)(2)(A), (M) and (O).

Venue of this bankruptcy case and this Motion is proper before this Court in this district under 28 U.S.C. §§ 1408 and 1409.

On October 1, 2002, this Court entered an order whereby the Debtor's Motion to Dismiss Chapter 11 Case was denied and the Office of the United States Trustee (the "UST") was ordered to appoint a disinterested person, subject to this Court's approval, as a chapter 11 trustee. On October 9, 2002, the Court appointed the chapter 11 trustee that the UST had nominated in conformance with this Court's prior order.

Notice and opportunity for a hearing have been given to the extent required for the entry of this Fourth Agreed Order pursuant to Bankruptcy Rule 2002, 4001(b) and 9006, and as required by 11 U.S.C. §§ 102, 361, 362 and 363, in order to prevent immediate and irreparable harm to the bankruptcy estate. No further notice of, or hearing on, the relief sought in the Motion or granted herein is necessary or required.

The terms and the conditions of this Fourth Agreed Order with regard to the use of cash collateral have been negotiated by the parties at arms' length and in good faith, are fair and reasonable under the circumstances, and enforceable pursuant to their terms.

## FACTUAL RECITALS

On or around March 5, 1998, the Debtor executed a promissory note (the "Note") in the original principal amount of $4.5 million in favor of Financial Federal Savings Bank ("Financial Federal").

The Note was secured by a Deed of Trust, Assignment of Rents and Security Agreement (the "Deed of Trust) which was executed by the Debtor on that date as well. Under the Deed of Trust, the Debtor granted Financial Federal, for the payment of the Note, a security interest in a 10,019 acre tract of land in San Antonio, Bexar County, Texas, as more particularly described on Exhibit "A" attached to the Note (the "Property"). The Deed of Trust was duly and properly recorded in Volume 7375, Page 1496, of the Deed Records of Bexar County, Texas on March 6, 1998.

Additional security granted under the Deed of Trust, for the repayment of the Note, included all of the Debtor's assets (the "Collateral"), such as: (a) all leases to the Property; (b) all rents, earnings, income, profits, benefits and advantages arising from the Property and the leases to the Property; and (c) all reserve, deposit and escrow accounts under the loan originated by the Note. See the Deed of Trust, p. 1.

The Note was also secured by an Assignment of Leases and Rents (the "Assignment"), which was executed by the Debtor in favor of Financial Federal on March 5, 1998. The Assignment was duly and properly recorded in Volume 7375, Page 1512, of the Deed Records of Bexar County, Texas, on March 3, 1998 (the Note, Deed of Trust and Assignment, collectively, the "Loan Documents").

Through a series of assignments, the Trust is now the current owner and holder of the Note and has valid, continuing, fully perfected, unavoidable, enforceable, first in priority, security interests in all of the assets of the Chapter 11 Trustee.

The Trust has valid, continuing, fully perfected, unavoidable, enforceable, first in priority, security interests in and to its pre-petition Collateral as set forth in the Loan Documents and has filed the necessary documentation with the appropriate local or state offices as required by applicable state law or by maintaining possession thereof, or otherwise as required by applicable state law. The indebtedness, as defined below, is absolute, unconditional, due, owing, unpaid, and not subject to any offset, cross-claim, demand, claim, suit, action, proceeding, counterclaim, or other dispute.

As of the Petition Date, the total principal indebtedness wing by the Debtor to the Trust was approximately $4,449,658.31 (such principal indebtedness, together with interest, costs and attorneys' fees as provided in the Loan Documents and as allowed by law, the "Indebtedness"). The Indebtedness continues to accrue interest and attorneys' fees.

The Indebtedness will be deemed without further order of the Court to be secured by valid, continuing, perfected, unavoidable, enforceable, first in priority, security interests in and to the pre-petition Collateral, and in and to all proceeds, products, offspring, rents or profits from the pre-petition Collateral, and all other cash, negotiable instruments, documents of title, securities, deposit accounts, or other cash equivalents in which the bankruptcy estate and the Trust have an interest, which constitute cash collateral, as that term is defined in 11 U.S.C. § 363(a) (collectively, the "Cash Collateral").

The Trust has agreed to allow the Chapter 11 Trustee to use certain of the Cash Collateral in the ordinary course of the estate's business under 11 U.S.C. § 363(c)(2)(A) in accordance with the terms and conditions of this Fourth Agreed Order. The terms and conditions of this Fourth Agreed Order are in the best interests of this estate, and its creditors.

The Chapter 11 Trustee believes that it is necessary to use the Cash Collateral in order to continue this estate's present business operations, and that the Trust is entitled to certain protections including those agreed to herein.

This estate requires funds in order to continue present operations as well as for its maintenance and preservation. Without authorization to use the Cash Collateral, this bankruptcy estate's continued business operations would be jeopardized to the detriment of itself, and the Debtor's creditors.

The only available adequate protection against the diminution of the interests of the Trust in the prepetition Collateral that may result from the Chapter 11 Trustee's and/or the bankruptcy estate's use of the Cash Collateral is to provide post-petition replacement liens and security interests in and to all property of the type comprising the prepetition Collateral, new liens and security interests in and to all post-petition Collateral, as hereinafter defined, and to the extent necessary, an administrative expense in accordance with 11 U.S.C. § 507(b).

The Trust has reached an agreement with the Chapter 11 Trustee regarding the use of the Cash Collateral. Pursuant to this agreement, the Chapter 11 Trustee has agreed to provide the Trust with, and by agreement set forth in this Fourth Agreed Order seeks to grant the Trust, post-petition replacement and additional liens and security interests in and to certain property of the bankruptcy estate, as more fully described below.

Entry of this Fourth Agreed Order is in the best interests of this estate, and its creditors.

All facts exist which are necessary to support the entry of this Fourth Agreed Order.

The Court is requested to enter this Fourth Agreed Order and to set a final hearing on the Motion.

Based upon the foregoing agreements it is therefore

ORDERED, ADJUDGED and DECREED that:

Incorporation of the Factual Recitals. All of the factual recitals set forth above are, true, correct, binding on the parties hereto and incorporated herein by reference as If fully set forth at length.

Acknowledgement of the Indebtedness. The Chapter 11 Trustee acknowledges and agrees to the calculation of the Indebtedness set forth above. The Chapter 11 Trustee acknowledges and agrees that the Indebtedness is absolute, unconditional, due, owing, unpaid, and not subject to any offset, cross-claim, demand, claim, suit, action, proceeding, counterclaim, or other dispute.

Objection Bar Data. The Debtor, the Chapter 11 Trustee and any creditor or party in interest had twenty (20) days from the date of the entry of this Agreed Order on November 18, 2002, to review and file with this Court any objection to the pre-petition liens and security interests of the Trust. Since no objections were timely filed, the Trust is hereby deemed to have valid, continuing, perfected, unavoidable, enforceable, first In priority, security interests in and to the prepetition Collateral and all proceeds, products, offspring, rents, or profits thereof, to secure the Indebtedness.

Cash Collateral. All income generated from the Property, including, without limitation, all rental income from leases to the Property, is and for all purposes shall be deemed to constitute Cash Collateral in which the Trust has an Interest under 11 U.S.C. §§ 363(a) and (c)(2), properly perfected under 11 U.S.C. § 546(b) and any other applicable law. The Trust has valid, properly perfected, unavoidable, enforceable, first In priority liens on all property of the Chapter 11 Trustee and the estate. To the extent, if any, not covered by the Trust's pre-petition liens on property of the estate, the Trust is granted a security interest in all proceeds, products, and profits of all of the leases and rents and any other Cash Collateral acquired by this estate after the Petition Date.

Authorization For the Limited Use of Cash Collateral. The Chapter 11 Trustee is hereby authorized to use the Cash Collateral, subject to and upon the terms and conditions and the interim period of this Fourth Agreed Order for the payment of certain operating expenses which are necessary to prevent the immediate and irreparable harm as contemplated by Bankruptcy Rule 4001, as set forth and in accordance with the operating budget (the "Budget") which is attached hereto as Exhibit "A" and incorporated herein by reference as if fully set forth at length. The Chapter 11 Trustee's actual expenditures on a cumulative basis, and per each line item, shall not exceed the projected expenditures set forth in the Budget by more than 5% without the prior written consent of the Trust. Subject to the strict compliance with the terms and conditions of this Fourth Agreed Order, and so long as no Termination Event, as defined below, occurs, the

Chapter 11 Trustee is permitted to use the Trust's Cash Collateral, during the periods, in the amounts, and for the purposes set forth herein.

Restraint Against the Unauthorized Use of Cash Collateral. The Chapter 11 Trustee is enjoined and restrained from using the Cash Collateral, except as specifically provided in this Fourth Agreed Order and the Budget.

Operating Budget. During the term of this Fourth Agreed Order, the Chapter 11 Trustee shall operate the Property within the parameters of the Budget. Within twenty (20) days of the date of the entry of this Fourth Agreed Order, the Chapter 11 Trustee shall provide to the Trust a full accounting of all Cash Collateral received by the Chapter 11 Trustee and/or this estate from the Petition Date to the time such Cash Collateral is deposited into the Cash Collateral Trust Account, as defined below, to the extent that the Debtor has provided such information to the Chapter 11 Trustee. In addition, within twenty (20) days of the date of the entry of this Fourth Agreed Order, the Chapter 11 Trustee will provide the Trust with a detailed accounting of the disposition of all rents generated by the Property from March 5, 1998 through the Petition Date, to the extent that the Debtor has provided such information to the Chapter 11 Trustee. The Chapter 11 Trustee shall not, in the aggregate, or for any line item, exceed the expenses set forth in the Budget by more than 5%. If the Chapter 11 Trustee does, in the aggregate, or for any line item, exceed the expenses set forth in the Budget by more than 5%, this shall constitute a Termination Event, as defined below.

Segregation. The Chapter 11 Trustee shall segregate and deposit all of the Cash Collateral in a segregated debtor In possession bank account (the "Cash Collateral Trust Account") in accordance with 11 U.S.C. § 363(c)(4). The Chapter 11 Trustee shall at all times during the pendency of this bankruptcy case keep all Cash Collateral, whether the Chapter 11 Trustee previously collected the Cash Collateral, received the Cash Collateral that had been previously collected by the Debtor, or hereafter collects the Cash Collateral, and all other Cash Collateral that comes into the possession, custody or control of this estate, together with all proceeds, profits or products thereof, separate and distinct from all other property of this estate and of the Chapter 11 Trustee.

Cash Collateral Trust Account. The Chapter 11 Trustee shall establish the Cash Collateral Trust Account with a financial institution which is on the approved list of depositories maintained by the Office of the United States Trustee for the Western District of Texas. The Chapter 11 Trustee shall immediately following the entry of this Fourth Agreed Order deposit into the Cash Collateral Trust Account (a) all Cash Collateral currently in the possession of the Chapter 11 Trustee and/or this estate, together with all proceeds, products, and profits thereof, and (b) all Cash Collateral, together with all proceeds, product and profits thereof, hereafter collected by or on behalf of this estate. It is acknowledged and agreed that all cash currently in the possession, custody or control of the Chapter 11 Trustee, and/or this estate, is Cash Collateral.

Deposits Into and Disbursements From the Cash Collateral Trust Account. No funds shall be deposited Into the Cash Collateral Trust Account other than those deposited therein in accordance with this Fourth Agreed Order. No funds shall be disbursed from the Cash Collateral Trust Account except for the payment of the actual and necessary expenses for the operation and maintenance of the Property in accordance with the limitations set forth in this Fourth Agreed Order and the Budget. All disbursements shall be made in strict compliance with the terms of this Fourth Agreed Order and the Budget. The funds deposited into the Cash Collateral trust Account, and all Cash Collateral generated by the Property, shall not be disbursed or otherwise used for the payment of any other expenses not specifically included in this Fourth Agreed Order and the Budget, incurred by or on behalf of this estate and /or the Chapter 11 Trustee without the prior written authorization of the Trust. Funds in the Cash Collateral Trust Account shall not be used for the payment of any expenses incurred by or on behalf of any party or entity other than as set forth in this Fourth Agreed Order and the Budget and shall not be commingled with funds used for the payment of any other expense.

Capital Improvements. The Chapter 11 Trustee shall not use the Cash Collateral for any capital improvements on the Property without the Trust's prior written authorization. The Trust's specific approval shall be required in advance, both with respect to the particular improvement or problem to be addressed and the amount of funds that may be expended. The Trust makes no commitment and is not required to grant any such approval. The Trust shall respond to a written request for a capital improvement to the Property, or a problem that the Chapter 11 Trustee reasonably believes needs to be addressed by the Trust, within ten (10) days of receipt of such written request.

No Payment To Partners, Insiders, Affiliates, or Professionals. The Chapter 11 Trustee shall not use the Cash Collateral to make any payments to partners, insiders, or affiliates of the Debtor, nor shall the Cash Collateral be used to pay the professionals employed or required to be employed by the Debtor pursuant to 11 U.S.C. § 327 seeking compensation under 11 U.S.C. §§ 330 or 331. The Chapter 11 Trustee shall not be entitled to and shall be prohibited from using the Cash Collateral to pay any management fee with respect to the Property, unless the Chapter 11 Trustee retains, pursuant to the prior written authorization of the Trust, an Independent property management company acceptable to the Trust. The Trust shall provide the Chapter 11 Trustee with the names of up to two (2) independent property management companies that are acceptable to the Trust, within ten (10) days of the date of the entry of this Fourth Agreed Order.

Collection and Receipt of Rents. During the term of this Fourth Agreed Order, for so long as the Chapter 11 Trustee complies with the provisions of this Fourth Agreed Order, the Chapter 11 Trustee shall be responsible for the collection and receipt of the rents on the Property, and all other Cash Collateral, and for the deposit of such rents and Cash Collateral into the Cash Collateral Trust Account in strict accordance with the provisions of his Fourth Agreed Order. Within two (2) days after the receipt of rent on the Property, or other Cash Collateral, the Chapter 11 Trustee shall be required to deposit the same into the Cash Collateral Trust Account. The Chapter 11 Trustee' shall at all times hold any and all of such rents, and other Cash Collateral in trust for the Trust In the event of any non-compliance on the part of the Chapter 11 Trustee with any of the provisions of this Fourth Agreed Order, the Chapter 11 Trustee's authority to collect, receive and use such rents, and other Cash Collateral, shall terminate three days after receiving written notice by the Trust of such non-compliance. Nothing in this Fourth Agreed Order shall be construed to limit the right of the Trust to seek a modification of this Fourth Agreed Order, even if the Chapter 11 Trustee remains €n compliance with its terms and conditions. Similarly, nothing in this Fourth Agreed Order shall be construed to limit the right of the Chapter 11 Trustee to seek a modification of this Fourth Agreed Order even if the Trust remains in compliance with its terms and conditions. The Chapter 11 Trustee warrants that it shall make every reasonable effort to collect all such rents, and other Cash Collateral generated by the Property during the term of this Fourth Agreed Order.

The Obligation to Account and Report. The Chapter 11 Trustee shall strictly account for all Cash Collateral, together with all proceeds, products, or profits thereon that come into the estate's possession, custody and control, and shall furnish to the Trust, and the Trust's counsel, such reports relative thereto as the Trust, in its sole discretion, shall reasonably request, including those reports specifically mentioned below. The Chapter 11 Trustee shall keep records which shall be of such character as will enable the Trust to determine at any time, the status of the Cash Collateral, together with all proceeds, products, or profits thereon. The Chapter 11 Trustee shall further permit the Trust, its agents, and employees, upon reasonable notice, to inspect, audit, and make copies of all records and other payments in the possession, custody or control of the Chapter 11 Trustee pertaining to the Cash Collateral, with all proceeds, products and profits thereof. The reports that the Chapter 11 Trustee shall be required to provide to the Trust, and the Trust's counsel, include, without limitation:

Accounting. A monthly accounting (the "Accounting") which shall be prepared on a cash basis and shall be in the form of a statement of income and expenses having a breakdown by line item, which Accounting shall account for all sources and uses of rents and any other revenues generated by the Property during the immediately preceding period and the balance of the Cash Collateral Trust Account at the beginning and end of such period. The Accounting shall be provided by the Chapter 11 Trustee no later than fifteen (15) days following the period covered by the Accounting.

Rent Roll. A monthly rent roll that identifies, in respect of the immediately preceding month, the name of each tenant and the monthly rent that each tenant pays. Each rent roll is to be provided by the Chapter 11 Trustee no later than fifteen (15) days following the month covered by the rent roll.

Interim Statements and Operating Reports. The Chapter 11 Trustee shall provide interim monthly statements and operating reports in accordance with the general requirements of the Office of the United States Trustee for the Western District of Texas. These interim statements shall be provided by the Chapter 11 Trustee no later than fifteen (15) days following the period covered by such statements and the operating reports shall be provided by the Chapter 11 Trustee no later than fifteen (15) days following the conclusion of the month covered by the operating report. The Chapter 11 Trustee shall timely file all reports generally required by the Office of the United States Trustee and shall contemporaneously serve same on the Trust, and its counsel.

Asset Disposition Documentation. Any and all documentation which in any way relates to a solicitation, offer, or proposed sale or disposition of any material amount of the Collateral, including, but not limited to, letters of enquiry, solicitations, letters of intent or asset purchase agreements.

Other Financial Information. Such financial and other Information concerning the business and financial affairs of the Chapter 11 Trustee as the Trust may reasonably request from time to time.

Termination. The occurrence of any of the following shall constitute an event of termination (a "Termination Event") under this Fourth Agreed Order: (a) the Chapter 11 Trustee defaults In the performance or observance of any of its covenants or agreements contained in this Fourth Agreed Order; (b) the Debtor dissolves or terminates its existence or discontinues its usual business, or the Chapter 11 Trustee is enjoined, restrained, or in any way prevented by court order or order of any governmental authority from conducting all or any material part of its business; (c) this bankruptcy case is dismissed or converted to a case under chapter 7 of the Bankruptcy Code; (d) an application is filed by any other party other than the Trust for the approval of any other superpriority administrative expense, (e) this Fourth Agreed Order is stayed, modified, or vacated in any respect whatsoever; (f) this Court enters an order or orders granting relief from the automatic stay applicable under 11 U.S.C. § 362 to the holder or holders of any security interest, other than the Trust's, to permit foreclosure, or other state law rights and remedies (or the granting of a deed in lieu of foreclosure or the like), in any assets of the Chapter 11 Trustee as to permit the exercise of any other rights or remedies with respect to secured assets, unless the Trust consents in writing; (g) the Chapter 1.1 Trustee uses any of the Cash Collateral for any purpose other than the payment of approved expenses as set forth in this Fourth Agreed Order and in the Budget; (h) any plan of reorganization is filed without the prior written authorization of the Trust and does not propose to pay the Indebtedness in full; (i) any representation or warranty made by the Chapter 11 Trustee In this Fourth Agreed Order proves to have been untrue in any material respect as of the date hereof or thereof; (j) any financial statement or other financial information submitted by the Chapter 11 Trustee to the Trust pursuant to this Fourth Agreed Order proves to have been knowingly and intentionally untrue in any material respect as of the date as of which the facts therein set forth were stated; (k) any loss or material damage or destruction of any of the Collateral occurs that is uninsured or insufficiently insured by the bankruptcy estate; or (1) the Chapter 11 Trustee exceeds in the aggregate, or for any line item, the expenses set forth in the Budget by more than 5%.

The Result of a Termination Event. Three (3) days after receiving written notice, by the Trust, of a Termination Event, and at all times thereafter, and without further act or action by the Trust, the Chapter 11 Trustee, the Debtor, or this Court, the Chapter 11 Trustee's authority to use the Cash Collateral and any and all obligations of the Trust under this Fourth Agreed Order shall immediately terminate and all obligations of the Chapter 11 Trustee and indebtedness of the Debtor to the Trust shall become immediately due and payable.

Pre-Petition Perfection. The security interests and liens of the Trust in and to the pre-petition Collateral referenced herein shall be deemed created and perfected without the necessity of the execution, filing or recording of any documents otherwise required under bankruptcy law for the creation or perfection of security interests and liens. Notwithstanding the foregoing, the Chapter 11 Trustee shall, upon request of the Trust, execute and deliver such documents as may be requested by the Trust to create and/or perfect the security interests and liens described herein under applicable non-bankruptcy law and the Trust shall be authorized to file and record such documents thereto and take such other actions as may be necessary to perfect such security interests and liens under all such laws and to correctly describe the Collateral subject thereto.

Post-Petition Perfection. The Trust's liens against and security interests in the pre-petition Collateral are valid and enforceable liens and security interests securing the Indebtedness, therefore all proceeds, products, offspring, rents or profits of such pre-petition Collateral acquired by the estate after the Petition Date (including, without limitation, all improvements, fixtures, and personal property constructed or placed upon the pre-petition Collateral on or after the Petition Date and all proceeds, products, offspring, rents or profits thereof) to the extent provided by the loan Documents and by applicable non-bankruptcy law, likewise secure the

Indebtedness, notwithstanding any authority of the Court to order otherwise pursuant to 11 U.S.C. § 552(b).

Post-Petition Liens. To secure the aggregate amount of all of the Cash Collateral used by the Chapter 11 Trustee, whether pursuant to this Fourth Agreed Order or otherwise, and to secure any diminution in the value of the Trusts interest in the pre-petition Collateral, the Trust is hereby granted, without the need of further act or documentation: (a) a replacement lien and security interest under 11 U.S.C. §§ 361(2) and 363(e), junior to no other parties, on all of the pre-petition Collateral and all proceeds, products, offspring, rents or profits thereof (including, without limitation, all improvements, fixtures, and personal property constructed or placed upon the pre-petition Collateral on or after the Petition Date and all proceeds, products, offspring, rents or profits thereof); and (b) an additional post-petition lien and security interest under 11 U.S.C. §§ 351(2) and 363(e), junior to no other party, in and to all other property (as defined by 11 U.S.C. § 541) of the bankruptcy estate, of any nature whatsoever, whether acquired before or after the Petition Date, which does not secure the Indebtedness, and all proceeds, products, offspring, rents or profits thereof. To the extent that any applicable non-bankruptcy law otherwise would restrict the granting, scope, enforceability, attachment, or perfection of the liens and security interests authorized or created by this paragraph, or otherwise would impose filing or registration requirements with respect to such replacement liens, such law is hereby preempted to the maximum extent permitted by the Bankruptcy Code, other applicable federal law, and the judicial power of the United States Bankruptcy Court.

Superpriority Administrative Expense. To adequately protect the Trust for the Chapter 11 Trustee's use of the Cash Collateral, the Trust is hereby granted a superpriority administrative expense under 11 U.S.C. §§ 503(b)(1)(A) and 507(b). Any such superpriority administrative expense of the Trust shall be junior to no other party, but shall be pari passu with the Chapter 11 Trustee's Court approved fees and expenses.

Prohibition Against the Payment of Junior Liens and Pre-Petition Unsecured Claims. The Chapter 11 Trustee shall not make any payments out of the Cash Collateral Trust Account to the holders of any junior secured claims which exist with respect to the Property or upon any pre-petition unsecured claims against the Chapter 11 Trustee.

Maintenance and Preservation of the Property. The Chapter 11 Trustee agrees to maintain, keep and preserve the Property in accordance with the terms and conditions of this Fourth Agreed Order and agrees further to use its best efforts is collecting all rents and maximizing the occupancy and profitability of the Property.

Utility Deposits. To the extent that the Chapter 11 Trustee makes any post petition deposits for the benefit of utility companies, such deposits will be made from the Cash Collateral subject to the liens of the Trust.

Purchase Offers. The Chapter 11 Trustee agrees to advise the Trust of all bona fide offers to purchase the Property within five (5) days of receipt of any such offer and to transmit to the Trust, and its counsel, copies of any such written offers within five (5) days of their receipt. In addition, the Chapter 11 Trustee shall provide the Trust within five (5) days following the entry of this Fourth Agreed Order with copies of all written offers to purchase the Property.

Bank Records Inspection. The Trust shall specifically have the right to make enquiries of the bank in which the Chapter 11 Trustee maintains the Cash Collateral Trust Account. The Trust may provide instructions to said bank so as to implement the Trust's right hereunder to inspect, audit, and examine the Cash Collateral Trust Account maintained by the Chapter 11 Trustee. The Chapter 11 Trustee, upon request by the Trust, shall execute such documents or take such further action as may be reasonably necessary to facilitate and ensure that such inspections, audits and examinations are permitted.

General Right of Inspection. The Chapter 11 Trustee shall make its books and records pertaining to this case and those of the Debtor, that are in the possession, custody or control of the Chapter 11 Trustee, available to the Trust and its representatives for the purposes of audit on a regular and routine basis during regular business hours or during such other time as conveniently arranged with the Chapter 11 Trustee. Any such review of these books and records shall not unreasonably interfere with the business operations of this estate. The Trust and its employees, representatives, attorneys and consultants shall be granted full access to the Collateral during all reasonable business hours (and all reasonable times with respect to unimproved land) for the purposes of inspection and appraisal, and the Chapter 11 Trustee will advise the Trust, upon request, of the location with particularity of all Collateral.

Insurance. The Chapter 11 Trustee shall furnish proof of insurance, listing the Trust as the first mortgagee loss-payee, to the Trust within five (5) days following the entry of this Fourth Agreed Order. Such insurance shall be in such amounts as are acceptable to the Trust, which acceptance shall not be unreasonably withheld, and shall include, without limitation, fire, personal liability and property damage coverage. The insurance carrier is subject to the Trust's approval and such approval shall not be unreasonably withheld. To the extent that the Budget permits, the Chapter 11 Trustee shall timely pay and maintain any and all insurance coverage for the Property, which is required under the Loan Documents. To the extent that the Budget permits, the Chapter 11 Trustee shall maintain such coverage in full force and effect at all times. The monthly operating reports to be supplied by the Chapter 11 Trustee pursuant to this Fourth Agreed Order shall include proof of payment of the insurance premium relating to the Property.

Tax Escrow Account. The Chapter 11 Trustee shall establish and maintain, with a banking institution which is on the approved list of depositories maintained by the Office of the United States Trustee for the Western District of Texas, a tax escrow account for the payment of real property taxes and assessments with respect to the Property. No later than the tenth ($10^{th}$) day of each month, the Chapter 11 Trustee shall transmit for deposit into this tax escrow account a pro rata payment to cover $1/12^{th}$ of the total sum of the annual real property taxes and assessments with respect to the Property, to the extent the budget permits.

Prohibition Against Seeking Surcharge of the Collateral. The Chapter 11 Trustee and/or any other representative of the bankruptcy estate shall be barred and prohibited from seeking to surcharge the Trust's Collateral under 11 U.S.C. § 506(c) or any other provision of applicable law.

Release By the Chapter 11 Trustee. Except with respect to the covenants of the Trust arising hereunder, for good and valuable consideration, the receipt of which is hereby acknowledged, the Chapter 11 Trustee does hereby release and forever discharge the Trust and the Trust's affiliates, heirs, successors, representatives, assigns, agents, employees, and attorneys (the "Trust Group") of and from any and all claims, debts, liabilities, demands, obligations, costs, expenses, actions and causes of action of every nature, character and description known and unknown, which the estate and/or the Chapter 11 Trustee now own or hold, or have at any time heretofore owned or held, or may at any time own or hold and the Chapter 11 Trustee waives and relinquishes all rights and benefits afforded by the laws of the State of Texas. The Chapter 11 Trustee understands that the facts with regard to which its release of the Trust

Group in this Fourth Agreed Order Is given may hereinafter turn out to be other than or different from the facts in that connection now known or believed by the Chapter 11 Trustee to be true and hereby accepts and assumes the risk of the facts turning out to be different and agrees that this Fourth Agreed Order shall be and remain in all respects effective and not subject to termination or rescission for any reason, including, but not limited to, any difference in facts. This release is for the time period beginning prior to October 9, 2002 and ending on that date.

No Violation of State Law. Application of payments received by the Trust to the indebtedness shall not violate, without limitation, any state law, including anti-deficiency, one form of action, or any other law requiring resort to security prior to enforcement and/or collection of indebtedness.

Representation by Counsel. Each of the parties acknowledges that it has been represented by independent legal counsel of its own choice throughout all of the negotiations which preceded the entry of this Fourth Agreed Order and that it has agreed to this Fourth. Agreed Order with the consent and on the advice of such independent legal counsel. Each of the parties further acknowledges that it and its counsel have had an adequate opportunity to make whatever investigation or enquiry they may deem necessary or desirable in connection with the subject matter of this Fourth Agreed Order prior to the entry hereof.

No Subordination or Adverse Affect Upon the Trustee's Liens. The Trust's liens on the Collateral and on any other property of the estate shall not be subordinated, altered or otherwise adversely affected in any manner, or for any purpose Including, without limitation, as a result of any financing approved under 11 U.S.C. § 364, any priority claims that are granted pursuant to 11 U.S.C. §§ 364, 503, or 507 or any other provision of federal or state law, or by any action of the Chapter 11 Trustee and/or the Chapter 11 Trustee, any other party, or this Court.

Other Documents. The parties to this Fourth Agreed Order shall execute any agreements or other documents that are reasonably required in order to effectuate the terms, conditions, purposes and objectives of this Fourth Agreed Order.

Integration. This Fourth Agreed Order constitutes and contains the entire agreement and understanding of the subject matter between the parties and supercedes and replaces all prior negotiations, proposed agreements, or agreements, written or oral. Each of the parties acknowledge that any party or any agent or attorney of any party has not made any promise, representation or warranty whatsoever, express or implied, written or oral, not contained herein concerning the subject matter hereof to Induce it to agree to this Fourth Agreed Order and each of the parties acknowledges that it has not agreed to this Fourth Agreed Order in reliance upon any promise, representation, or warranty not contained herein.

Interpretation. This Fourth Agreed Order and negotiations in connection therewith have been carried on by the joint efforts of the parties. This Fourth Agreed Order is to be construed simply and fairly and not strictly for or against any of the parties hereto.

Waiver. The failure to enforce at any time any of the provisions of this Fourth Agreed Order or to require at any time performance by the other party of any of the provisions hereof shall in no way be construed to be a waiver of said provision or to affect either the validity of this Fourth Agreed Order, or any part hereof, or the right of any party thereafter to enforce each and every provision in accordance with the terms of this Fourth Agreed Order. Except as expressly stated, this Fourth Agreed Order is without prejudice to any of the rights of the Trust under the Loan Documents, the Bankruptcy Code, the Bankruptcy Rules, or under any other applicable law, and shall not preclude the entry of other orders by the Court as may be appropriate and necessary to protect the interests of the Trust in this bankruptcy case. Specifically, this Fourth Agreed Order in no way constitutes a waiver by the Trust of its right to exercise its other remedies under the Loan Documents, the Bankruptcy Code, the Bankruptcy Rules, and any other applicable law, nor does the Trust waive its right to contest or object to the validity, necessity, or reasonableness of any actual expenditure of the Chapter 11 Trustee. Except as set forth herein, this Fourth Agreed Order does not impair or impede the Chapter 11 Trustee's duties as set forth In the Bankruptcy Code.

Trust Not Liable for Debts or Acts of Chapter 11 Trustee. Except as set forth in this Fourth Agreed Order and in the Budget, the Trust shall have no obligation to make any payments, and shall not have any liability for payment or nonpayment, of any expenses or other obligations of the Chapter 11 Trustee, including without limitation those relating to the Property, except as is set forth in this Fourth Agreed Order and in the Budget. Specifically, the Trust shall have no obligation or liability for payment of payroll or other taxes applicable to the Property, and the

Chapter 11 Trustee shall pay all such payroll and other taxes and charge when and as they become due. Except as set forth herein, the Trust shall have no liability to the Chapter 11 Trustee for any act or omission with regard to the subject matter hereof, nor shall any act or omission of the Trust taken in good faith under this Fourth Agreed Order give rise to any defense, counterclaim, or right of setoff under the Loan Documents or any other agreement. The Chapter 11 Trustee expressly waives any such defense, counterclaim, or right of setoff. This Fourth Agreed Order in no way constitutes a waiver or forgiveness by the Trust of existing defaults by the Debtor under the terms of the Loan Documents and does not constitute a waiver by the Trust of the remedies exercised by or available to the Trust under the Loan Documents against the Debtor and/or the Chapter 11 Trustee, or any other party, under applicable law.

Priority. Except as set forth herein, no costs or expenses of administration which have been or may be incurred in this case or in any other bankruptcy cases related hereto, and no priority or other claims are or will have priority over or be on parity with the obligations created by this Fourth Agreed Order, and no priority or other claims are or will be prior to or on a parity with the claims of the Trust against this estate, except for the Court approved fees and expenses of the Chapter 11 Trustee. No such costs or expenses of administration, including without limitation any costs or expenses pursuant to 11 U.S.C. §§ 330 or 506(c), shall be imposed upon or against the Trust, its claims against the Chapter 11 Trustee's estate or the pre-petition collateral or post-petition collateral securing such claims.

Amendments. This Fourth Agreed Order shall not be modified or amended except as may be mutually agreed upon by the parties hereto in writing.

Parties Bound. This Fourth Agreed Order will be binding on and inure to the benefit of the assigns, representatives, and successors of the parties hereto, and all creditors and parties in interest in this case.

No Pre-Payment. The Chapter 11 Trustee shall not pre-pay expenses in anticipation of the final hearing, except in the ordinary course of business, and except as necessary to prevent immediate and irreparable harm.

Delay. No delay or failure by the Trust in exercising any right, power or privilege under this Fourth Agreed Order and no single or partial exercise thereof or any abandonment or discontinuance of steps to enforce such right, power or privilege shall effect or Impair such right, power or privilege of the Trust.

    Notices. All notices, reports, or other correspondence or Information to be transmitted to the parties pursuant to this Fourth Agreed Order shall be transmitted by facsimile and deposited in the United States mail, postage prepaid, return receipt requested, addressed as follows, or to such other addresses as hereinafter be designated in writing by the respective parties hereto:

> If to the Chapter 11 Trustee: Helen Schwartz, Habbeshaw, Kalmans & Schwartz, P.C., The Colonnade, 9901 I.H. 10 West, Suite 770, San Antonio, Texas 78230, Telephone No. (210) 699-8086, Facsimile No. (210) 699-3409.

> If to the Trust: Joseph J. Wielebinski, Munsch Hardt Kopf & Harr, P.C., 4000 Fountain Place, 1445 Ross Avenue, Dallas, Texas 75202-2790, Telephone No. (214) 855-7500, Facsimile No. (214) 855-7584.

A party may, by prior written notice hereunder to the other parties, change the address to which such notices shall thereafter be sent.

    Jurisdiction. This Court shall retain exclusive jurisdiction over the subject matter of this Fourth Agreed Order in order to resolve any dispute in connection with the rights and duties specified hereunder.

    Governing Law. This Fourth Agreed Order Is made and entered in the state of Texas and shall be interpreted and enforced to the extent that Texas law is applicable under and pursuant to the laws of said jurisdiction.

    Counterparts. This Fourth Agreed Order may be executed in any number of counterparts, any and all of which shall be deemed to be the original.

    Capacity. Each person signing this Fourth Agreed Order as a representative of a named party hereby represents and warrants that he or she is authorized to so sign; and that the execution, formation, and performance of this stipulation by the parties is duly authorized, subject to court approval, if necessary.

    Captions. The captions and headings of the various paragraphs herein are for convenience only, and none of them is intended to be any part of the body or text of this Fourth Agreed Order, nor are such captions or headings intended to be referred to in construing the meaning or substance of any of the provisions hereof.

Survival of the Trust's Interests. The termination of this Fourth Agreed Order shall not affect or in any way impair any right, Interest, or lien granted to the Trust under this Fourth Agreed Order. The security interests granted hereunder shall survive any termination of this Fourth Agreed Order. Except as specifically set forth herein, neither the Chapter 11 Trustee nor the Trust waive any rights provided to them under the Bankruptcy Code or any other applicable law. Moreover, by executing this Fourth Agreed Order, the parties hereto have not waived any of their rights or remedies contained in any of the Loan Documents between them

Duration. This Fourth Agreed Order shall terminate at the earlier of: (a) a Termination Event; or (b) 60 days from the date of the entry of this Fourth Agreed Order.

### 

Agreed as to form and content:

MUNSCH HARDT KOPF & HARR, P.C.

By: _____

Joseph J. Wielebinski
Texas Bar No. 21432400
Seymour Roberts, Jr.
1445 Ross Avenue, Suite 4000
Dallas, TX 75202-2790
Telephone: (214) 855-7500
Facsimile: (214) 855-7584

ATTORNEYS FOR ORIX CAPITAL MARKETS, LLC,

F/K/A ORIX REAL ESTATE CAPITAL MARKETS, LLC, THE SUCCESSOR SPECIAL SERVICER TO CRIIMI MAE SERVICES LIMITED PARTNERSHIP AND THE ATTORNEY-IN-FACT FOR STATE STREET BANK & TRUST COMPANY AS TRUSTEE AND REMIC ADMINISTRATOR, ACTING IN ITS CAPACITY AS SPECIAL SERVICER AND ATTORNEY-IN-FACT FOR STATE STREET BANK & TRUST COMPANY, THE TRUSTEE FOR THE REGISTERED HOLDERS OF MORTGAGE CAPITAL FUNDING, INC., MULTIFAMILY/COMMERCIAL MORTGAGE PASS - THROUGH CERTIFICATES, SERIES 1998-MC2

**CHAPTER 11 TRUSTEE**

By: _____

Helen Schwartz
Habbeshaw, Kalmans & Schwartz, P.C.
The Colonnade
9901 I.H. 10 West
Suite 770
San Antonio, Texas 78230
Telephone No, (210) 699-8086
Facsimile No. (210) 699-3409

## <u>CERTIFICATE OF SERVICE</u>

This is to certify that the undersigned caused a true and correct copy of the foregoing document to be served on the parties listed on the attached service list by depositing same in the United States Mail, first class, postage prepaid, properly addressed, on the 29th day of July, 2003.

_____
Helen G.
Schwartz

## EXHIBIT A

*Courtesy of Joseph J. Wielebinski, Munsch Hardt Kopf & Harr PC*

## Appendix Q

# CHAPTER 11 PREPARATION DOCUMENT

WORKBOOK FOR THE PREPARATION OF DOCUMENTS TO
COMMENCE A CASE UNDER CHAPTER 11

Dated:
STUART M. BROWN
WILLIAM E. CHIPMAN
EDWARDS ANGELL PALMER & DODGE LLP
919 N. Market Street
15th Floor
Wilmington, DE 19801
(302) 777-7770
(302) 777-7263 Facsimile

## I. Required Information for Commencement of Chapter 11 Case

Note:   All financial information provided herein should be prepared on a consolidated basis if more than one entity will be filing a petition. Individual lists of creditors and summaries of liabilities and assets for each filing entity should be prepared and provided to Edwards Angell Palmer & Dodge LLP ("EAPD").

1.      Name of Debtor[1] _____
(Exactly as it appears on corporate seal)

2.      Address _____

3.      Employer Identification Number _____

4.      State of Incorporation _____

5.      Telephone No. _____

6.      Description of Business(es) _____

7.      Fiscal Year _____

8.      Officer executing papers: _____

9.      Provide an SEC Questionnaire, to be annexed as Exhibit "A" to the Petition. (See sample provided in Section II.B. herein).   Provide information in the form requested if the Debtor(s) have issued any outstanding securities registered under Section 12 of the Securities & Exchange Act of 1934. The information requested should be presented on a consolidated basis.

10.     Provide a corporate resolution of the Board of Directors, to be annexed as Exhibit "B" to the Petition. (See Section II.C herein).

11.     If the Debtor owns or has possession of any property that poses or is alleged to pose a threat if imminent and identifiable harm to public health or safety, then Exhibit "C" is required to be annexed to the Petition. (See Section II.D herein).

12.     We will be preparing a number of "First-Day" Motions. Please see Section III of this workbook and provide the information specified therein for inclusion in the motions.

13.     With the Company's assistance, we will be preparing a comprehensive officer's affidavit to accompany the First-Day Motions. (See Section III.A herein).

---

[1]   Also referred to herein as Debtors, Company or Companies. If more than one Debtor, please attach a separate sheet for each with the requested information.

14. Identify on a separate schedule (see schedule 1 annexed hereto) all directors, officers, their titles, and the annual compensation paid to each for the past three (3) years and the respective terms of service for each.

15. Prepare an alphabetized list of all of the Debtor's creditors. Set forth names and full mailing addresses in the format described on Schedule 2 (photocopy as necessary). It is not necessary to list the amounts owed to each creditor for this list.

16. Prepare a separate alphabetized list of all the Debtor's equity security holders, setting forth names and last known mailing address, in the format described in Schedule 2.

17. Prepare a list of the Debtor's thirty largest unsecured creditors in descending order by the amount of their claims, to be annexed as Exhibit "C" to the Petition (see sample provided in Section II.D. herein).

18. Prepare schedules of leases and contracts. Schedules 3, 4, and 5 are formats for the preparation of these Schedules.

19. Information with respect to each unexpired lease of nonresidential real property. Schedule 6 sets forth the required information.

20. Collective Bargaining Agreements.

(a) Provide copies of all collective bargaining agreements to which the Debtor is a party.

21. List all pending law suits. The information required is on Schedule 9.

22. Provide a schedule in the form of Schedule 10 describing all bank accounts maintained by the Debtor(s).

23. Provide a schedule in the form of Schedule 11 listing all utilities providing service to the Debtor(s) and the average monthly billing to the Debtor(s) for each utility.

24. Provide information required on Schedule 12 indicating anticipated expenses of ordinary course operations for a thirty day period after filing.

25. Provide a list of vendors that have provided goods to the Company in the ordinary course of business and trade terms.

26. Provide a short summary on Schedule 13 indicating the reasons for the Debtor's financial difficulties and projected future operations.

27. Provide a schedule in the form of Schedule 14 summarizing pension plans to which the Debtor(s) is required to make contributions and the current funding status of each plan.

28. Provide a schedule in the form of Schedule 15 summarizing ordinary course of business expenditures for such items as reimbursement

of employee expenses, corporate credit card charges, monthly insurance premiums for property and liability and health insurance which may not have been paid for the period of 180 days prior to filing.

**II.    Sample Forms of Chapter 11 Petition and Related Filing Documents – Voluntary Petition (Official Form 1)**

**A.  Annex "1" to Petition**

| Pending or Concurrent Bankruptcy Case Filed by Affiliate/Partner | | | |
|---|---|---|---|
| Name           of Affiliate | | | |
| Date Filed | | | |
| District | | | |
| Case Number | | | |
| Judge | | | |
| Relationship   to Debtor | | | |

**B.  Exhibit "A" to Voluntary Petition – SEC Questionnaire**

1.    The Debtor's securities are registered under Section 12 of the Securities Exchange Act of 1934. The SEC File number is _____.

2.    Unless expressly stated otherwise herein, the following financial data refers to the latest available information detailing the unaudited financial condition of the Company, on a consolidated basis, as of _____,200__.

     a.      Total Assets

$_____
_____

     b.      Total Liabilities (including debts listed in 2.c. below)

$_____
_____

     c.      Debt Securities held by more than 500 holders:

| Type of Security | Approximate Aggregate Principal Outstanding Amount | Approximate Number of Record Holders as of _____, 200__ |
|---|---|---|
| | $_____ | _____ |
| | $_____ | _____ |
| | $_____ | _____ |
| | $_____ | _____ |
| | $_____ | _____ |

| | Number of Shares Outstanding | Approximate Number of Record Holders as of _____, 200__ |
|---|---|---|
| d. Number of shares of preferred stock | _____ _____ | _____ _____ |
| e. Number of shares of common stock | _____ _____ | _____ _____ |

3.      Brief description of Debtor's business: _____.

4.      List the names of any person who directly or indirectly owns, controls, or holds, with power to vote, 5% or more of the voting securities of the Debtor:

### C.  Exhibit "B" to Petition – Authorizing Resolution

[Name of Debtor], a [state of incorporation] corporation (the "Company"), hereby certifies that the following is a true and correct copy of resolutions duly adopted at a meeting of the board of directors of the Company on [date], in accordance with the requirements of applicable [state of incorporation] law and that said resolutions have not been modified or rescinded, and are still in force and effect on the date hereof:

RESOLVED, that, in the judgment of the Board of Directors, it is desirable and in the best interests of the Company that the Company [and certain of its subsidiaries] [each] commence a chapter 11 case by filing a voluntary petition seeking reorganization under the provisions of chapter 11 of title 11, United States Code (the "Bankruptcy Code"); and

RESOLVED, that the appropriate officers of the Company be, and each hereby is, authorized and empowered on behalf of, and in the name of, the Company to execute and verify or certify a petition under chapter 11 of the Bankruptcy Code and to cause the same to be filed in the United States Bankruptcy Court for the District of [      ] at such time as such authorized officer executing the same shall determine; and

RESOLVED, that the appropriate officers of the Company be, and they hereby are, authorized and empowered on behalf of, and in the name of, the Company to execute and file all petitions, schedules, lists, and other papers and to take any and all action that any of the authorized officers may deem necessary, proper, or desirable in connection with the chapter 11 case, with a view to the successful prosecution of the case; and

RESOLVED, that the law firm of Edwards Angell Palmer & Dodge LLP be, and it hereby is, employed as attorneys for the Company under a general retainer; and

RESOLVED, that the appropriate officers be, and they hereby are, authorized and empowered on behalf of, and in the name of, the Company to retain and employ other attorneys, investment bankers, accountants, restructuring professionals, financial advisors, and other professionals to assist in the Company's chapter 11 case on such terms as are deemed necessary, proper, or desirable; and

RESOLVED, that in connection with the commencement of the chapter 11 case by the Company, the appropriate officers of the Company be and hereby are, authorized and empowered on behalf of, and in the name of, the Company to negotiate, execute, and deliver a debtor in possession loan facility and/or agreement for the use of cash collateral and adequate protection (including, in connection therewith, such notes, security agreements, and other agreements or instruments as such officers consider appropriate) on the terms and conditions presented to this meeting together with such other terms and conditions as such officer or officers executing the same may consider necessary, proper, or desirable, such determinate to be conclusively evidenced by such execution or the taking of such action, and to consummate the transactions contemplated by such agreements or instruments on behalf of the Company and any pertinent affiliates; and

RESOLVED, that the appropriate officers of the Company, and any employees or agents (including counsel) designated by or directed by such officers, be, and each hereby is, authorized and empowered to cause the Company and such of its affiliates as management deems appropriate to enter into, execute, deliver, certify, file, record, and perform such agreements, instruments, motions, affidavits, applications for approvals or rulings of governmental or regulatory authorities, certificates or other documents, and to take such other actions, as in the judgment of such officer shall be necessary, proper, and desirable to prosecute to a successful completion the Company's chapter 11 case, to effectuate the restructuring of the Company's debt, other obligations, organizational form and structure, and ownership of the Company and its subsidiaries consistent with the foregoing resolutions and to carry out and put into effect the purposes of the foregoing resolutions, and the transactions contemplated by these resolutions, their authority thereunto to be evidenced by the taking of such actions; and

RESOLVED, that any and all past actions heretofore taken by officers or directors of the Company in the name of and on behalf of the Company in furtherance of any or all of the preceding resolutions be, and the same hereby are ratified, approved, and adopted.

IN WITNESS WHEREOF, I have hereunto set my hand this [day] of [month], 200[ ].
[NAME OF DEBTOR]

BY:
[Name]
Corporate Secretary

**D.  Exhibit "C" to Petition – Description of Property that poses or may pose a threat of imminent and identifiable harm to the public health or safety**

**E.  Exhibit to Petition – Consolidated List of 30 Largest Unsecured Creditors**

Following is the list of the debtor's creditors holding the consolidated 30 largest unsecured claims. The list in prepared in accordance with Fed. R. Bankr. P. 1007(d) for filing in this Chapter 11 case. The list does not include (1) person who come within the definition of "insider" set forth in 11 U.S.C. §101, or (2) secured creditors unless the value of the collateral is such that the unsecured deficiency places the creditor among the holders of the consolidated 30 largest unsecured claims. The information contained herein shall not constitute an admission by, nor shall it be binding upon, the Debtor.

| (1) Name of creditor and complete mailing address including zip code | (2) Name, telephone number and complete mailing address, including zip code, of employee, agent or department of creditor familiar with claim who may be contacted | (3) Nature of claim (trade debt, bank loan, government contract, etc.) | (4) Indicated if claim is contingent, unliquidated, disputed or subject to setoff* | (5) Amount of claim [if secured also state value of security]** |
|---|---|---|---|---|
|  |  |  |  |  |
|  |  |  |  |  |
|  |  |  |  |  |
|  |  |  |  |  |
|  |  |  |  |  |
|  |  |  |  |  |
|  |  |  |  |  |
|  |  |  |  |  |
|  |  |  |  |  |
|  |  |  |  |  |
|  |  |  |  |  |
|  |  |  |  |  |
|  |  |  |  |  |

| (1) Name of creditor and complete mailing address including zip code | (2) Name, telephone number and complete mailing address, including zip code, of employee, agent or department of creditor familiar with claim who may be contacted | (3) Nature of claim (trade debt, bank loan, government contract, etc.) | (4) Indicated if claim is contingent, unliquidated, disputed or subject to setoff* | (5) Amount of claim [if secured also state value of security]** |
|---|---|---|---|---|
| | | | | |
| | | | | |
| | | | | |
| | | | | |
| | | | | |

\* If contingent, enter C; if unliquidated, enter U; if disputed enter D, if subject to setoff, enter S.

\*\* Amounts shown are consolidated amounts for all of the Debtors whose estates are being jointly administered in these cases.

I, the undersigned officer of [Name of Debtor], the debtor in this case (the "Debtor"), declare under penalty of perjury that I have read the foregoing list of 30 largest unsecured creditors of the Debtor and that it is true and correct to the best of my knowledge.

Dated: [Date] _____
[Name]
[Title]

## III. Required Information for Preparation of First-Day Motions and Orders

A. First-Day Affidavit

IN THE UNITED STATES BANKRUPTCY COURT
FOR THE [DISTRICT OF _____]

| | | |
|---|---|---|
| In re: | ) | Chapter 11 |
| | ) | |
| [name of debtors], | ) | Case Nos. _____ |
| | ) | |
| Debtors. | ) | |

## AFFIDAVIT OF [NAME OF OFFICER]

STATE OF _____ )

                                                    ) ss.:

COUNTY OF _____ )

[Name of Affiant], being duly sworn, deposes and says:

1.     I am the [title] of [Name of Debtor], the above-named debtor (the "Debtor"). I am familiar with the Debtor's business and financial condition.

2.     Substantially simultaneously with the filing of the Debtor's petition, [number] affiliates of the Debtor, [names] (collectively with the Debtor, the "Debtors"), are each filing a voluntary petition for relief under chapter 11 of title 11, United States Code (the "Bankruptcy Code").

3.     I am authorized to submit this affidavit in support of the Debtors' petitions for relief under chapter 11 of the Bankruptcy Code.

4.     Unless otherwise indicated, the financial information contained herein is unaudited.

# DEBTORS' BUSINESS OPERATIONS AND CIRCUMSTANCES LEADING TO COMMENCEMENT OF THESE CASES

<u>Debtors' Business Operations</u>

5.    [Describe Debtor's business operations]

<u>Debtors' Prepetition Debt and Capital Structure</u>

6.    [Describe Debtor's pre-petition debt/capital structure]

<u>Circumstances Leading to the Commencement of These Cases</u>

7.    [Describe circumstances leading to the Debtors' filing under chapter 11]

8.    To the best of my knowledge, information, and belief, no committee has been organized prior to the order for relief in these chapter 11 cases. [If an unofficial committee has been formed, describe the circumstances surrounding its formation and the date of its formation]

## OTHER INFORMATION CONCERNING THE DEBTORS

9.    The information concerning the holders of each of the Debtors' 30 largest unsecured claims is annexed to the Debtors' petitions for relief, and is incorporated herein by reference.

10.    The Debtors intend to continue to operate their businesses and manage their properties in accordance with sections 1107(a) and 1108 of the Bankruptcy Code, and intend to propose a plan or plans of reorganization pursuant to chapter 11 of the Bankruptcy Code.

[Name of Affiant]

Sworn to before me this

_____ day of _____, 200__

_____

Notary Public

B. Joint Administration of Debtor(s)' Case(s)

| List Full Legal Name of Each Proposed Debtor |
|---|
|  |
|  |
|  |
|  |
|  |
|  |
|  |
|  |
|  |
|  |

C. Retention of EAPD as General Counsel – Required information to permit the firm to perform a comprehensive conflicts check

| "Connection" to Debtor | Description of Information Sought |
|---|---|
| Thirty Largest Unsecured Creditors | Provide names of holders of claims for borrowed money or similar indebtedness (actual, contingent, or unliquidated), including claims on account of guarantees or legal judgments. |
| Other Significant Creditors | Provide names of significant lessors, lessees, licensors, licensees, other contract counterparties, and principal taxing authorities. |
| Remaining Unsecured Creditors | Provide remaining Unsecured Creditors, to the extent known on the Petition Date. |
| Secured Creditors | Provide names of all creditors with a security interest in the Debtor's property, to the extent known at the Petition Date. |
| Attorneys and Accountants for Creditors | Provide names of creditors' attorneys and accountants, to the extent known on the Petition Date. |
| Other Significant Relationships of the Debtor | Provide names of those persons with other connections to property of the Debtor, including copyrights, patents, distribution, franchise, or similar agreements, as well as the attorneys and accountants for such parties, to the extent known on the Petition Date. |
| Members of Ad Hoc or | Provide names of the members of creditor or |

| "Connection" to Debtor | Description of Information Sought |
|---|---|
| Unofficial Committees | equityholder committees formed prior to the Petition Date, as well as their attorneys and accountants. |
| Holders of Partnership Interests | If the Debtor is a partnership, provide the names of its general and limited partners, as well as their attorneys and accountants, to the extent known on the Petition Date. |
| Significant Stockholders | If the Debtor is a corporation, provide the names of its significant stockholders, including all entities holding in excess of 5% of such stock. |
| Officers, Directors, and Other Insiders | Provide names of current and former (up to three years) senior officers, directors, and other insiders. Provide the names of any third parties with which such officers, directors, and insiders are/were affiliated. Provide names of each person or entity's attorneys and accountants, to the extent known on the Petition Date. |
| Affiliates | Provide names of all significant affiliates, including entities that control the Debtor, are controlled by the Debtor, other affiliates that have a continuing business relationship with the Debtor, or represent an asset or liability that is significant to the Debtor. |
| Debtor's Prepetition Attorneys and Accountants | Provide names of all firms employed by the Debtor in the three years prior to the Petition Date, or longer, if relevant. |
| Underwriting Investment Bankers | Provide names of all entities that served as underwriter for the issuance of the Debtor's securities outstanding on the Petition Date or issued during the three years prior to the Petition Date. Provide names of such entities' attorneys and accountants, to the extent known on the Petition Date. *Changes as a result of the Bankruptcy Abuse Prevention and Consumer Protection Act of 2005: Section 101(14) of the Bankruptcy Code will be modified to remove the per se disqualification for investment bankers (effective as of 10/17/05).* |

| "Connection" to Debtor | Description of Information Sought |
|---|---|
| Indenture Trustees | Provide names of all entities that served as indenture trustee on the Debtor's securities outstanding on the Petition Date or outstanding during the three years prior to the Petition Date. Provide names of such entities' attorneys and accountants, to the extent known on the Petition Date. |
| Former Employees of the Debtor Now Employed by EAPD | Provide names of all former employees of the Debtor now employed by EAPD. |
| Former Employees of the Debtor's Underwriters Now Employed by EAPD | Provide names of all former employees of firms that served as underwriter for the issuance of the Debtor's securities outstanding on the Petition Date or issued during the three years prior to the Petition Date, who are now employed by EAPD. |

D. Retention of Special Counsel

| Name, Address, and Contact at Law Firm to Be Retained | Description of Past Relationship and Services to be Provided in Chapter 11 Case |
|---|---|
|  |  |
|  |  |
|  |  |
|  |  |
|  |  |

E. Retention of Other Professional Advisors

| Name, Address, and Contact at Accounting, Advisory, or Other Firm to Be Retained | Description of Past Relationship and Services to be Provided in Chapter 11 Case |
|---|---|
|  |  |
|  |  |
|  |  |
|  |  |
|  |  |

F. Retention of Ordinary Course Professionals

| Name, Address, and Contact at Professional Firm to Be Retained | | Description of Services to be Provided During Chapter 11 Case | |
|---|---|---|---|
| | | | |
| | | | |
| | | | |
| | | | |

| Estimated Maximum Monthly Fees Payable to Any One Ordinary Course Professional | Estimated Maximum Monthly Fees Payable to All Ordinary Course Professionals | Estimated Maximum Annual Fees Payable to Any One Ordinary Course Professional | Estimated Maximum Annual Fees Payable to All Ordinary Course Professionals |
|---|---|---|---|
| | | | |

G. Extension of Time to File Schedules and Statements

| Information Required | Response |
|---|---|
| Number of All Debtors | |
| Estimated Number of Creditors for All Debtors | |
| Anticipated Difficulties in Preparing Information Required by Schedules and Statements | |
| Estimated Length of Extension Required | |

H.  Maintenance of Bank Accounts and Business Forms, Maintenance of Existing Cash Management Systems, and Waiver of Section 345 Requirements for Investments

| Information Required | Response |
|---|---|
| Total Number of Bank Accounts Maintained by Debtor(s) | |
| Provide List of Banks (with addresses) and related Accounts Maintained by Debtor(s) | |
| Describe the Debtor(s)' Current Cash Management System, Including Daily Deposits, Sweeps, Lock Boxes, Automated Debits, etc. | |
| How Long Has Existing Cash Management System Been in Place? | |
| Does Cash Management System Involve the Co-Mingling of Funds of Non-Debtor Affiliates? | |
| Can All Cash Management Transactions Between Affiliates Be Traced and Documented? | |
| How Are Excess Funds Invested? Provide Descriptions of Financial Instruments, Including Obligor | |
| Describe Any Special Types of and Preprinted Business Forms Used by the Debtor(s) | |

I. Payment of Pre-petition Employee Wages and Benefits

| Information Required | Response |
|---|---|
| Total Number of Debtor(s)' Employees | |
| Basis of Periodic Employee Payroll (Weekly, Monthly, etc.) | |
| How Many Employees Are Paid in Excess of $10,000 in Salary and Benefits Per Pay Period? | |
| Estimated Accrued But Unpaid Wages, Salaries, and Commissions as of the Petition Date – Provide Both the Aggregate Amount and the Average Amount Per Employee | |
| Estimated Federal, State, and Local Payroll Withholding Taxes Due With Respect to Accrued But Unpaid Wages, Salaries, and Commissions as of the Petition Date, as Well as any Other Prepetition Amounts Owed. | |
| What Date Is Expected to be the Last Pay Day Prior to the Petition Date? | |
| Estimate the Dollar Amount of Payroll Checks Issued Prepetition Which Will Not Have Been Cashed Prior to the Petition Date. | |
| List All Payroll Banks and Provide Account Numbers | |
| Do the Debtors Use a Substantial Numbers of Contract Workers (*i.e.*, Non-Employees)? If so, Estimate Number and Percentage of Total Workforce. Describe Means of Paying Such Workers. | |

| Information Required | Response |
|---|---|
| Describe the Employee Benefits Provided to the Debtor(s)' Employees. Include Names of Insurance Companies Providing Such Benefits and Describe the Nature of the Debtor(s)' Obligations to Such Insurers. | |
| Estimate the Amounts Owed on the Petition Date to Employees in Respect of Prepetition Reimbursable Business Expenses, Both in the Aggregate and the Average Amount Owed to Any Individual Employee. Describe any Significant Amounts Owed to Senior Officers. | |
| Describe and Estimate Aggregate Amounts Held on the Petition Date by the Debtor(s) in Respect of Monies Withheld from Employee Pay Checks for the Payment of Union Dues, Support Payments, Credit Union Obligations, Charity Donations, and Other Purposes. | |

J. Payment of Pre-petition Amounts Due Under Insurance Policies

| Required Information | Response |
|---|---|
| List All Insurance Policies Currently Held by the Debtors (including Workers' Compensation, General Liability, Officer/Director Liability, etc.) and Estimate Unpaid Amounts Accrued as of the Petition Date for Each Policy. | |
| Describe Any Unusual Problem or Issue Pertaining to Insurance Policies Held by the Debtors. | |

K.  Payment of Pre-petition "Trust Fund" Taxes

| Required Information | Response |
| --- | --- |
| Does the Debtor Collect or Hold Monies In Respect of Sales Taxes or Other Similar "Trust Fund" Taxes, Not Including Payroll Taxes Provided Above? If So, Describe and Estimate Amounts Held/Owed on the Petition Date, and the Approximate Number of Entities to Which Such Funds Are Owed. | |

L.  Payment of Pre-petition Customs-Related Obligations (if relevant)

| Required Information | Response |
| --- | --- |
| Describe the Debtor(s)' Activities Involving the Import of Goods and the Payment of Customs Duties. | |
| List the Names and Addresses of Customs Brokers Employed by the Debtors on the Petition Date, and Estimated Amounts Owed to Each Such Broker on the Petition Date. | |
| Estimate the Amounts of Unpaid Customs Duties Owed on the Petition Date. | |

M.  Payment of Pre-petition Customer-Related Obligations (if relevant)

| Required Information | Response |
|---|---|
| Describe the Debtor(s)' Activities Involving Customer Practices including Return Programs, Refund Programs, Exchange Programs, Warranty Programs, Rebates, Incentive Programs, Advance Payment Programs, Customer Credit Policies and any other customer programs. | |
| List the Names and Addresses of Major Customers of the Debtors on the Petition Date, and Estimated Amounts Owed to Each Such Customer as of the Petition Date. | |
| Estimate the Amounts of Unpaid Customer Obligations Owed on the Petition Date. | |

N.  Provision for Adequate Assurances to Utilities

| Required Information | Response |
|---|---|
| Describe the Nature of Utility Services[2] Used by the Debtor(s). | |
| Provide a Complete List of All Utilities Offering Service to the Debtors, Including Name, Mailing Address, Contact Person at the Utility (if Available), the amount of any deposit that may be held by the utility and the Debtor(s)' Account Number With Such Utility. | |
| Have the Debtor(s) Been Current With Payments Owed to Utility Companies in the Year Preceding the Petition Date?  Are There Any Defaults or Arrearages With Respect to Such Utility Service as of the Petition Date? | |

---

[2] Utilities includes, without limitation, providers of electricity, natural gas, water, sewer, telephone and cell phone services.

| Estimate Aggregate Amounts Owed to Utilities on the Petition Date. | |
|---|---|

O. Post-Petition Financing Arrangements

| Information Required | Response |
|---|---|
| Describe the Debtor(s)' Prepetition Financing Arrangements, Including Amounts Expected to Be Outstanding on the Petition Date. | |
| Have the Debtor(s)' Received a Commitment to Provide Post-Petition Financing? If So, Provide A List of All Proposed Lenders Under Such Facility. | |
| Provide a Copy of a Draft Post-Petition Financing Agreement or Outline of Terms. | |
| Do the Debtors Plan to Use a Secured Creditor's Cash Collateral During the Chapter 11 Case? If So, Describe Collateral and Provide Name(s) of Secured Creditor(s). | |
| Does the Debtor have a Cash Flow Budget? If So, Please Provide. | |
| Does the Debtor Require Funding Beyond Which is Generated from Cash Flow in the Ordinary Course of Business? | |

## IV. Schedules of Information to be Provided

A. Schedule 1: Directors and Officers

| Name of Director | Annual Compensation |
|---|---|
| | |
| | |
| | |
| | |

| Name of Director | Annual Compensation |
|---|---|
|  |  |
|  |  |
|  |  |
|  |  |
|  |  |
|  |  |
|  |  |

| Name of Officer | Title | Annual Compensation |
|---|---|---|
|  |  |  |
|  |  |  |
|  |  |  |
|  |  |  |
|  |  |  |
|  |  |  |
|  |  |  |
|  |  |  |
|  |  |  |
|  |  |  |

B. Schedule 2: Matrix Instructions

The creditor matrix must be saved in ASCII format. All information should be left justified. The first line of the file must be the name on the creditor matrix. The second line should be either the company name or the first line of the address. The third and any additional lines should be the complete address. The last line of the address must be the city, state and zip code. All of this information should not exceed six lines. Leave one blank line between each creditor. DO NOT put any other information on the matrix. It must contain creditors only.

C. Schedule 3: Nonresidential Real Property Leases

| Name and Address of Landlord | Location of Premises | Monthly Rental & Other Charges | Lease Expiration Date |
|---|---|---|---|
| | | | |
| | | | |
| | | | |
| | | | |
| | | | |
| | | | |
| | | | |
| | | | |
| | | | |
| | | | |
| | | | |

D. Schedule 4: Employment Contracts

| Name of Employee | Position | Term of Agreement | Annual Compensation |
|---|---|---|---|
| | | | |
| | | | |
| | | | |
| | | | |
| | | | |
| | | | |
| | | | |
| | | | |
| | | | |
| | | | |
| | | | |
| | | | |

E. Schedule 5: Other Contracts (including equipment leases, service contracts, etc.)

| Name and Address of Other Contracting Party | Term of Contract | Termination Date | Monthly or Annual Payments |
|---|---|---|---|
| | | | |
| | | | |
| | | | |
| | | | |
| | | | |
| | | | |
| | | | |
| | | | |
| | | | |
| | | | |
| | | | |
| | | | |
| | | | |
| | | | |
| | | | |
| | | | |
| | | | |
| | | | |
| | | | |
| | | | |
| | | | |
| | | | |
| | | | |
| | | | |
| | | | |
| | | | |
| | | | |
| | | | |
| | | | |

F. Schedule 6: Questionnaire for Unexpired Leases of Nonresidential Real Property – Attach a separate Schedule F for each location/lease.

1.    Location of Leased Premises:

2.    Name and address of Landlord (and landlord's mortgagee, if known):

3.    Name and address of tenant as set forth on the lease:

4.    Commencement date of lease:

5.    Expiration date of term of lease (specifying all options to renew and dates by which options must be exercised):

6.    Monthly rental (including all additional rent and other charges i.e., taxes, utilities, common area maintenance) for which you, as tenant, are responsible under the lease:

7.    Amount due to landlord under the lease prior to filing the chapter 11 petition (specifying the period of time for which such debt is due):

8.    Describe the current use of the premises by you, as tenant:

9.    Are the Premises Necessary to Continued Operation of the Business and Why?

10. Is the lease above or below market? Do you intend to assume, assign or reject your interest in the lease and why? (If you cannot answer these questions, state why and how long it will be before you expect to be able to decide whether you wish to keep the lease, assign the lease to a third party or reject the lease and terminate your interest.)

11. The premises subject to the lease are (Check the appropriate box):

☐1 - Located in a free-standing single building

☐2 - Located in a shopping center

☐3 - Located in a strip center (containing other stores/premises attached to your premises)

12. Attach a complete copy of the lease (including all amendments, if any).

G. Schedule 7: Collective Bargaining Agreements

| | | |
|---|---|---|
| | | |
| | | |
| | | |
| | | |
| | | |
| | | |
| | | |
| | | |

H. Schedule 8: Narrative Concerning Amendments Made to Collective Bargaining Agreements in Preceding Twelve Months

| Collective Bargaining Agent | Describe Amendments and/or Status of Negotiations and Reasons Therefor | Employee of Debtor Responsible For Negotiations |
|---|---|---|
| | | |
| | | |
| | | |
| | | |
| | | |
| | | |
| | | |
| | | |
| | | |

I. Schedule 9: Pending Law Suits Against Debtor(s)

| Court Where Action Pending | Name of Plaintiff | Nature of Action which Debtor (s) | Amount Sought | Name and Address of Plaintiff's Attorney |
|---|---|---|---|---|
| | | | | |
| | | | | |
| | | | | |
| | | | | |
| | | | | |
| | | | | |
| | | | | |
| | | | | |
| | | | | |
| | | | | |
| | | | | |
| | | | | |

J. Schedule 10: Bank Accounts

| Name and Address of Bank and Branch Number | Account Number | Type of Account |
|---|---|---|
| | | |
| | | |
| | | |
| | | |
| | | |
| | | |
| | | |
| | | |
| | | |
| | | |
| | | |

K. Schedule 11: Utilities

| Name and Address of Utility | Account Number | Type of Service | Average Monthly Bill | Projected Estimated Monthly Bills |
|---|---|---|---|---|
| | | | | |
| | | | | |
| | | | | |
| | | | | |
| | | | | |
| | | | | |
| | | | | |
| | | | | |
| | | | | |
| | | | | |
| | | | | |

L.  Schedule 12:  Projected Operations for Thirty-Day Period After Filing

1.      Estimated total payroll to employees, including all                    $_____
federal, state and local withholding taxes

2.      Estimated ordinary course operating expenses (other           $_____
than payroll and officers' salaries).  Including rents, utilities,
insurance, anticipated security deposits, inventories and supplies
and other ordinary course of business expenditures

3.      Annual volume of business for last fiscal year.                    $_____

4.      Total number of employees.                                             _____

5.      How long has the Debtor(s) been in business?                  _____

6.      The amount paid and proposed to be paid for services        _____
        for the 30 day period following the filing of the chapter
        11 petition to officers, stockholders, and directors

M.  Schedule 13:  Reasons for the Debtor's Financial Difficulties and How
Projected Future Operations will Address and Resolve these Difficulties

1.      Reasons for Debtor's financial difficulties:

_____

_____

_____

2.      How projected future operations will address and resolve
these difficulties (interim and exit strategies).

_____

_____

_____

N. Schedule 14: Pension Plans

| Plan, Title and Trustee | Type of Plan | Current Funding Status |
|---|---|---|
| | | |
| | | |
| | | |
| | | |
| | | |
| | | |
| | | |
| | | |
| | | |
| | | |
| | | |

O. Schedule 15: Ordinary Course of Business Expenditures

| Type of Expenditure | Estimated Amount |
|---|---|
| | |
| | |
| | |
| | |
| | |
| | |
| | |

Estimated Total:

$_____

## V. Additional Due Diligence Documents

The following is a preliminary list of additional documents and information which we would like to review in connection with our due diligence review of the Companies. Please note that this is a preliminary list and not exhaustive.

A. Corporate Documents

a.      Certificate of Incorporation/Formation of the Companies and their affiliates (as amended, with all amendments to date).

b.      Certificates of Change of Name (if any)or any other charter documents of the Company and their affiliates.

c.      Bylaws of the Companies (or operating agreement if an LLC, partnership agreement if a partnership) and their affiliates (as amended, with all amendments to date including any shareholder agreements).

d.      A list of all the respective subsidiaries of the Companies indicating the state of   incorporation/formation of each subsidiary.

e.      To the extent any subsidiary is not wholly-owned, a list indicating the percentage ownership of each Company and the names and percentage ownership interest of each other stockholder of such subsidiary.

f.      Minute Books of Stockholders of the Companies and their affiliates for the past five years.

g.      Minute Books of the Board of Directors of the Companies and their affiliates for the past five years.

h.      Disclosure documents and related memoranda or proposals used by the Companies or any of their affiliates in private placements, bond financings, institutional and bank loan applications, or attempted sales of securities of the  Companies or their affiliates.

i.      Any and all agreements relating to the ownership of, or voting rights pertaining to, the stock of the Companies or their affiliates.

j.     All forms of contracts, if any, covering a material portion of the sales of the Company.

k.     Terms for purchase orders and invoices.

l.     A list of key creditors of the Companies and their affiliates.

B.  Organization

a.     A list of names and positions of all officers, directors, and key employees of the  Company and their affiliates, and a brief biography of each.

b.     A list of all corporations, partnerships, associates, joint ventures and other business entities in which the Company owns, directly or indirectly, an interest or  any shares of capital stock. Such list shall include the nature of the interest, number of shares (if applicable), the percentage ownership of each Company in each such entity, the jurisdiction where each such entity is qualified to do business and the business presently conducted and, if different, proposed to be conducted by each such entity.

c.     To the extent any subsidiary is not wholly-owned, a list indicating the percentage ownership of each Company and the names and percentage ownership interests of each       other stockholder of such subsidiary.

C.  Management

a.     A copy of the most current organizational chart for the Companies and their affiliates.

b.     Names of current officers and directors and other key employees of the Companies' subsidiaries.

c.     Information concerning previous and current year's schedule of compensation for the Companies' top 20 officers.

d.     Copies   of   management   bonus   plans   or   arrangements, compensation arrangements, medical reimbursement plans, death benefit plans, etc.

e.     Loans to officers, directors and key employees.

f.      Copies of existing or proposed employment agreements with management, including severance agreements.

D.  Capital Stock of the Companies

a.      All agreements with the stockholders, including voting trusts, continuing proxies, subscription agreements, registration rights, preemptive rights, restrictions on transfer and ownership or similar matters.

b.      All agreements relating to outstanding options.

c.      A schedule of dividend declarations, record dates, and payments.

d.      Securities authorized and outstanding (including share ledgers and records).

e.      All agreements relating to the purchase, sale or issuance of securities.

f.      A schedule setting forth the precise holding of the Company's major shareholders, including option and warrant holders, whether or not vested (including a description of how the shares are held, *e.g.* street name or trust).

g.      Form(s) of the Company's capital stock certificates.

h.      All share transfer deeds executed, reports of share transfers filed and the per-share price of each block of shares transferred in respect of the share capital of the Company from the date of its inception.

i.      All agreements relating to payments of dividends by the Company.

E.  Financial Information

a.      Financial Statements, including accompanying schedules (for the last five years and the current fiscal year).

b.      Most recent activity and income statements for the company.

c.      Auditors' letters and opinions (for the last five years).

d.      Budget for the current year.

e.      Auditors' annual management letters (for the last five years).

f.      Summary of the debtor's assets and liabilities - this should be a balance sheet for the Company (and separately for any other entity we file) for the period ending closest to the filing.

g.      Schedules of all assets (including real property, personal property, bank accounts, etc.) and all liabilities.

h.      A detailed statement of financial affairs including income from employment or operation of business for the two years preceding this calendar year:

(i.)     income other than from employment of operation of business;

(ii.)    payments to creditors within the 90 days before filing;

(iii.)   payments to creditors who are insiders within 2 year of filing;

(iv.)    Law suits to which debtor was a party within 1 year of filing;

(v.)     attachments of the debtor's property within 1 year of the filing;

(vi.)    repossessions or foreclosures within 1 year;

(vii.)   assignments and receiverships within one year of filing;

(viii.)  gifts to charity within 1 year;

(ix.)    losses from fire or theft within 1 year of filing; other transfers;

(x.)     closed financial accounts;

(xi.)    setoffs;

(xii.)   list of all bookkeepers and accountants who supervised the keeping of the books within 6 years of filing;

(xiii.)    list of all firms that audited the company's books within 2 years of filing;

(xiv.)    all persons who were in possession of books and records at the time of filing;

(xv.)    all financial institutions or creditors to whom financial statements were issued in the last two years;

(xvi.)    list the dates of last two inventories of property and who supervised them;

(xvii.)    list current officers, directors, and shareholders and all former officers, directors, and shareholders for the last 2 years; and

(xviii.)    all distributions to insiders within 2 years of filing.

i.    Schedule, for the 30 day period following the filing of the chapter 11 petition, of estimated cash receipts and disbursements, net cash gain or loss, obligations and receivables expected to accrue but remain unpaid, other than professional fees, and any other information relevant to an understanding of the foregoing.

F.  Material Contracts and Agreements

a.    All material franchise, joint venture and partnership agreements to which the Companies or any of their affiliates are a party.

b.    Directors and officers' insurance policies of the Companies or any of their affiliates or heir respective employees (showing names of insurers, risks covered, amount of coverage, etc.). To the extent insurance carriers and coverages have changed during the last five years, please so indicate. Also, please summarize any major claims filed during the last year.

c.    All material leases pursuant to which the Companies or any of their affiliates has leased equipment or other personal property from or to others, including information as to the lease term, the lessee or lessor, the periodic payments and the amount of equipment leased.

d.      Any material contracts, agreements or other documentation relating to transactions entered into during the past 10 years by the Companies or any of their affiliates with any officer, director or 5% stockholder or any company or other entity in which such person has an interest.

e.      All agreements of the Companies and their affiliates with their 10 largest suppliers, including any service contracts, future contracts, supply contracts or requirements contracts.

f.      All material intercompany agreements between the Companies and their affiliates.

g.      A schedule of all material confidentiality agreements, license and royalty
        agreements, patents, trademarks, service marks, trade names and trade secrets, or applications or agreements pertaining thereto, including any correspondence or  documents relating to the use by a third party thereof.

h.      All material marketing, sales, dealer and distributor agreements, product development, consignment and pricing agreements, exhibition and distribution agreements of, and a list of any independent sales persons or distributors for, the Companies or any of their affiliates.

i.      Any and all loan agreements, revolving line of credit agreements, loan commitments, indentures, other debt instruments or capitalized leases, together with all amendments to date and any related security documents (including any  guaranties of such loans to another person) involving the Companies or their subsidiaries.

j.      All correspondence concerning the above, including all compliance certificates, officers certificates and opinions of counsel provided thereunder.

k.      Any loans, stockholder or repurchase agreements made for the benefit of any officer, director, stockholder or employee of the Companies or its subsidiaries.

l.      All insurance coverage of the Companies or any of their subsidiaries or their respective  employees, including director and officer liability insurance.

m.      All agreements of the Companies and their subsidiaries with suppliers.

n.      Information regarding the Companies' merchandising programs and promotions.

o.      All other material contracts and agreements involving the Companies or any of their subsidiaries not otherwise covered by the foregoing or following items.

G.  Operational Matters and Other Material Agreements

a.      Schedule of insurance policies (showing names of insurers, risks covered, amount of coverage, etc.), including casualty, property, liability, errors and omissions, officer and director, etc. To the extent insurance carriers and coverages have changed during the last five years, please so indicate. Also, please summarize any major claims filed during the last five years.

b.      Documentation relating to material acquisitions or divestitures (last three years).

c.      Secrecy, confidentiality and nondisclosure agreements with employees or third parties.

d.      Security agreements, liens and/or financing statements affecting any of the Company's assets or properties.

e.      Contracts outside the ordinary course of business.

f.      Letters of credit, performance guarantees and bonds.

g.      Indemnification contracts and similar arrangements for officers and directors.

h.      Agreements with management or key personnel other than employment or consulting agreements.

i.      Schedule describing all material transactions involving the Company and (i) any officer or director or (ii) any other affiliate (including

**417**

5% shareholders) of the Company, and any agreements pertaining to the foregoing, which are not reflected in the   items heretofore listed.

H.   Acquisitions and Dispositions

a.      All agreements or plans for the acquisition or disposition of assets involving the Companies or any of their affiliates (last three years).

b.      Schedule of all dispositions or joint ventures under review.

c.      All agreements made outside the ordinary course of business.

I.   Material Real Estate Agreements

a.      A schedule showing all real property owned or occupied by the Companies or any of their affiliates, showing, in the case of leased properties, dates of lease expiration.

b.      Schedule and description of all real property and other material assets owned or leased by the Company (denoting whether the property is owned or leased).

c.      Copies of all deeds, mortgages, title reports and policies and all other agreements related to the Companies' owned properties.
d.      Copies of abstracts of title and other title papers (including all deeds) and title insurance or title searches relating to real property and equipment to be acquired or owned by the Company.

e.      All insurance coverage of the real property owned or occupied by the Companies or any of their affiliates.

f.      Leases and subleases and related agreements for a property and equipment used or owned or to be acquired by the Company.

g.      All plans for present and pending real estate development.

h.      List of all liens or encumbrances against real property.

i.      Current appraisals of property owned or to be acquired by the Company prepared by independent appraisers and furnished to the Companies by lessees or future lessees of the Companies.

j.      Evidence of compliance for each parcel of real property with relevant real estate laws, including building and zoning laws.

## J.  Employee and Labor Matters

a.      All collective bargaining agreements, side letters and other agreements with any labor organization or union binding upon or to which the Companies or any of their affiliates is a party, including any analysis by labor counsel or consultants regarding the foregoing and the Company's relationship with any of these entities.

b.      Health and Safety Materials.

c.      All documents relating to pending or concluded unfair labor practice charges, complaints or NLRB or state proceedings, and union representation petitions or demands for recognition.

d.      All documents relating to pending or concluded grievances, arbitration proceedings and outstanding arbitration awards.

e.      All employment contracts, confidentiality agreements, and non-competition agreements, including a written description of any oral contract or agreement, to which the Companies or any of their subsidiaries is a party or pursuant to which any of the parties is liable.

f.      All employee manuals, handbooks and other personnel policies.

g.      A list of all U.S. government contracts (if any) valued at over $10,000, indicating the period of performance of each contract, the facilities involved in such performance and the number of employees at each such facility.

h.      Documents relating to employee application and hiring procedures and termination and retirement policies.

i.      All documents relating to any pending or concluded union or internal employee complaints, grievances, arbitration, court or administrative proceedings, and outstanding judgments or orders relating to equal employment opportunity, discrimination or wage and hour matters.

K.  Employee Benefit and Compensation Matters

a.  Copies of all pension plans and amendments thereto covering employees of the Companies or any of their subsidiaries, including information regarding the number of employees and other participants covered by such plans.

b.  Copies of all employee welfare benefit plans and amendments thereto covering employees of the Companies or any of their subsidiaries, including information regarding the number of employees and other participants covered by such plans.

c.  Copies of all incentive compensation plans or policies and amendments thereto covering employees of the Companies or any of their subsidiaries, including information regarding the number of employees and other participants covered by such plans or policies.

d.  Copies of all employee stock option plans and amendments thereto covering employees of the Companies or any of their subsidiaries, including information regarding the number of employees and other participants covered by such plans.

e.  Copies of all bonus plans or policies and amendments thereto covering employees of the Companies or any of their subsidiaries, including information regarding the number of employees and other participants covered by such plans or policies.

f.  Any employees benefit plans and amendments thereto not covered by the foregoing requests, including, but not limited to, any plans for top management personnel, whether or not funded.

g.  Other benefits materials.

L.  Personnel

a.  Union/collective bargaining agreements, labor contracts and employee management pacts.

b.  Employment and compensation agreements and non-competition agreements (including a list of employees and consultants party thereto, and including any   change of control arrangements and "golden parachute" agreements), and a schedule of compensation for officers, directors and key employees of the Company.

c.      Consulting contracts.

d.      Employee benefit, pension, health, deferred compensation, bonus, share option, incentive, deferred compensation, retirement severance or retention and profit-sharing plans or programs in which any director or executive officer of the Company participates (including summary plan descriptions) (other than plans available to all employees on the same basis) for each of the last two plan years.

If any plan is not set forth in a formal document, please provide a reasonably detailed description of the plan.

e.      Share ownership plans, share option and share appreciation rights plans, incentive share option plans, bonus plans or similar arrangements in which any director or executive officer of the Company participates, and a schedule of the salaries of executive officers of the Company.

f.      Loans and guarantees to or from directors, officers or employees of the Company.

g.      Completed officers' and directors' questionnaires relating to management disclosures.

h.      Copies of personnel policies, personnel manuals and employee handbooks.

i.      Affirmative action plans.

j.      Describe any employ retention policy the Debtor would like to implement post-petition. Further, describe your rationale for such a policy – *i.e.* why the need to keep these peopleemployed by the debtor.

M.   Pending or Threatened Litigation

a.      A schedule of all material pending or threatened litigation, disputes, grievances, arbitrations, claims or settlements (either pending, threatened or contemplated) involving the Companies or any of their affiliates, whether as plaintiff or defendant, including those relating to employee terminations.

b.     Materials relating to any litigation involving an executive officer or director concerning bankruptcy, crimes, securities law or business practices (last five years).

c.     Materials relating to any material disputes (either pending, threatened or contemplated) with governmental agencies (federal, local or foreign) relating to tax, environmental and antitrust matters.

d.     Materials relating to any disputes with suppliers, competitors or customers regarding any claim in excess of $100,000 or which may otherwise have a material impact on the Company.

e.     A list of all attorneys representing the Companies, indicating each case or matter or area of law to which such representation relates.

f.     All management representation letters to, and reports and management letters from, the independent public accountants of the Companies or any of their subsidiaries concerning the Companies or any of their subsidiaries covering the three most recent fiscal years and the current fiscal year.

g.     Copies of all counsel's letters to the independent public accountants of the Companies or any of their subsidiaries with respect to litigation, contingent liabilities and other matters  covering the three most recent fiscal years and the current fiscal year.

N.  Tax Matters

a.     Copies of tax returns and filings for the last three years, including income, sales, use, property and franchise tax.

b.     A list of open tax years with respect to any federal, state, local and foreign tax for the Company.

c.     Copies of any notices and communications from federal, state, local and foreign taxing authorities regarding any tax disputes, tax deficiency, proposed adjustment, audit, pending or threatened litigation or appeal involving the Company for any open tax year.

d.     A list of all statute of limitations waivers or extensions with respect to any federal, state, local and foreign tax agreed to by the Company and explain the duration thereof and the reasons therefor.

e.     All management, service and tax-sharing agreements.

f.     All federal and state income tax deficiency notices, audit and settlement proposals.

O.  Audit Reports and Related Information

a.     Internal memoranda (particularly internal audit memoranda) concerning problem areas.

b.     Auditors' letters (including annual management letters) and opinions for the last two years.

c.     Auditors' reports to management and management's response for the last three years.

d.     Name and phone number of audit manager responsible for most recent audit.

P.  Environmental Documents

a.     Notices to and from environmental regulatory authorities, including notices of violation, regarding activities of the Companies or any of their subsidiaries.

b.     Audit and inspection reports of the Companies or any of their subsidiaries, whether performed by the Companies or any of their subsidiaries or by third parties.

c.     Insurance policies and related analyses or memoranda of the Companies or any of their subsidiaries.

d.     All material consent decrees, judgments, other decrees or orders, settlement agreements or similar matters (for the last five years).

e.     Reports and studies relating to material environmental exposures.

f.     Any environmental assessment reports, environmental audit reports, inspection reports or similar documents prepared during the past five years regarding any property owned or leased by the Company.

g.       Any notices, notices of violation or information requests from any state, local or foreign governmental agency regarding environmental matters relating to the Company, and any correspondence to or from such agencies and any enforcement-related documents, pending or closed, such as consent decrees, etc. regarding environmental or health and safety matters within the past five years.

h.       Any documents, including any spill reports or notifications, from the Company relating to any spills or other unpermitted releases of hazardous substances, whether or not such spill or release was reported to any governmental agency.

i.       Any documents relating to expenditures or anticipated expenditures by the Company, including establishment of reserves, in connection with environmental liabilities (whether present or contingent) or compliance with environmental regulations.

j.       Any information with respect to any potential liability or consent orders or known or suspected problems under any federal, state, local or foreign environmental laws and   regulations.

k.       Previous environmental assessments, including any Phase I audits.

l.       All environmental permits, licenses or other governmental approvals (including
        pending applications relating thereto).

m.      Any agreements, including provisions relating to environmental conditions (including   representations, warranties, indemnities, escrow provisions).

n.       Documents relating to the existence and monitoring of underground storage tanks.

Q.  Government Regulation of Business Activities

a.       Reports resulting from inspections, audits or studies of operations of the Companies or their subsidiaries conducted during the past three years by the following:

        (1)      Federal Trade Commission;

        (2)      Federal Communications Commission;

(3)     Environmental Protection Agency;

(4)     Department of Labor;

(5)     Internal Revenue Service; or

(6)     Any other federal or state regulatory authorities.

b.     Correspondence during the past three years between the Companies or any of their subsidiaries and any of the regulatory authorities listed in items a(1)-(6) above.

c.     List of all licenses and permits issued to the Companies or any of their subsidiaries by any of the regulatory agencies listed in items a(1)-(6) above.

d.     All other regulatory information involving the Companies or any of their subsidiaries not otherwise covered by the foregoing or following items.

e.     A summary of documentation relating to all grants, funding or research awards issued to the Company, and all applications therefor.

f.     Any correspondence, memoranda or notes concerning any material disputes or settlements with government officials (*e.g.* environmental, tax, health and safety, antitrust or contract violations.

g.     Any attorney's opinion letters to the Company received within the past two years concerning the potential effects of any proposed change in law which may have a material impact on the Company.

h.     List of all material administrative and governmental proceedings or investigations threatened, pending, settled or concluded.


R.   Governmental Regulations and Filings

a.     All communications to directors and shareholders (including annual and other         periodic reports to shareholders).

b.     All memoranda, prospectuses, offering circulars, private placement memoranda and other disclosure documents relating to the offering of securities of the Company, copies of correspondence with investors and written proposals for the acquisition of any securities (for the last five years).

c.　A list of any governmental permits, consents, licenses and approvals (excluding those listed elsewhere herein) held by or involving the Company.

d.　A summary of documentation relating to all grants, funding or research awards issued to the Company, and all applications therefor.

e.　A summary of all documents filed for the past three years with respect to the　Company, as　filed with all government authorities and regulatory bodies.

f.　Copies of any correspondence, memoranda or notes concerning any disputes or settlements with governmental officials (e.g., environmental, tax, health and safety, antitrust or contract violations).


S.　Compliance with Laws

a.　A schedule setting forth all governmental (local, state, federal and foreign) agencies to which the Company reports.

b.　Governmental permits, licenses and consents.

c.　All communications to and other filings with local, state, federal and foreign governmental agencies during the last five years in jurisdiction(s) where assets are located or operations are conducted by the Company.

d.　Any reports, notices, citations or correspondence relating to any purported violation or infringement by the Company and any suspended or revoked governmental permits or licenses and copies of all other material correspondence with federal, state, local and foreign governmental agencies.

T. Intellectual Property

a.     All licenses, royalty, research and development and other agreements related to the technology, inventions and technological projects of the Company.

b.     List of all patents, trademarks, trade names, copyrights and applications and license agreements therefor, owned or used (or applied for) in the business of the Companies, giving a brief description of use, registration number and date of filing, date of expiration, name and address of any person to or from whom such item is licensed, and a brief description of any such arrangement.

ç.     All patent and invention disclosures made by employees of the Company.

d.     All correspondence regarding the Companies' or third parties' patent rights, trademarks or copyrights, as well as letters received by the Companies, or other  possible indications of which it has knowledge, regarding material intellectual property infringement or related problems regarding patents owned by or licensed to it.

U. Financing

a.     Any and all loan agreements, credit agreements, revolving line of credit agreements, letters of credit (including reimbursement agreement with respect thereto), performance guarantees and bonds, loan commitments, promissory notes, indentures, other debt instruments or capitalized leases, together with all amendments to date and any related documents (including any guaranties of such loans to another person, liens and/or financing statements, sale-lease-back transactions  and  installment purchases) involving the Companies or their affiliates or their respective assets or property.

b.     Any material correspondence between lenders (including entities committed to lend) and the Company (including compliance reports, waivers, consents and default notices, if any).

c.     Presentations, if any, given to creditors in connection with obtaining credit or prepared for potential lenders in connection with proposed financings since the beginning of the Companies' last full fiscal year.

d.　　Any presentations to rating agencies or security analysts since the beginning of the Company's last full fiscal year.

e.　　An indication of where financing statements or other documents evidencing encumbrances are filed.

f.　　Statements from governmental authorities listing the liens on the assets of the Company.

g.　　Summary of usages under any revolving credit agreement.

h.　　Reports to creditors, waivers, default notices and correspondence regarding possible defaults.

i.　　Any loans, stockholder or repurchase agreements made for the benefit of any officer, director, stockholder or employee of the Companies or its affiliates, including any　　entity directly or indirectly associated with any such officer, director, stockholder or　employee.

j.　　Documents pending or still in effect relating to agreements with finders, brokers　or underwriters.

k.　　Documents relating to banking accounts and services.

l.　　Credit agreements, debt instruments, promissory notes, security agreements, mortgages, guarantees and reimbursement agreements for letters of credit and documents relating to any other financing arrangements, including sale-lease-back transactions and installment purchases, and all correspondence with lenders.

m.　　All other material agreements with creditors.

V.　Media Materials

a.　　Any and all recent (within the past 6 months) press releases, articles or brochures issued by the Companies or any of their affiliates relating to the Companies or any of their affiliates or any of their products, services, or material events involving any of them.

b.　　Copies of all speeches delivered by any officer or director of the Companies or　their subsidiaries.

c.        Copies of all articles or press clippings from financial or other publications concerning the Companies and their subsidiaries.

W.  Critical Vendors

a.        To determine whether a supplier should be considered a "Critical Supplier" the company should look at:

      i.        whether the product supplied is essential to the continued operation of the company's business;

      ii.       whether the supplier holds a unique relationship with the Company;

      iii.      whether the supplier will refuse to supply services or material essential to the conduct of the business until their prepetition claims have been paid;

      iv.      whether there is a possibility that the supplier will employ an immediate sanction failing payment;

      v.       whether there is a compelling business justification for payment of prepetition amounts other than appeasement of a major creditor; and

      vi.      whether payment is necessary to permit the greatest likelihood of survival of the company.

b.        For each supplier you deem "critical" please provide the following information:

      i.        the name of the supplier;

      ii.       the type of product supplied;

      iii.      a description of why the product is essential to the Company's operations;

      iv.      a description of why the product/supplier is unique or difficult to replace;

v.         a summary of why you believe the supplier will not ship without being paid prepetition amounts;

vi.        an approximate amount that would be past due at filing (if available); and any other information you deem relevant to this analysis.

*Courtesy of Stuart M. Brown, Edwards Angell Palmer & Dodge LLP*

ASPATORE